Critical Essays on
Bertolt Brecht

Critical Essays on World Literature

Robert Lecker, General Editor
McGill University

Critical Essays on Bertolt Brecht

Siegfried Mews

G. K. Hall & Co. • Boston, Massachusetts

Copyright © 1989 by Siegfried Mews

Library of Congress Cataloging-in-Publication Data

Critical essays on Bertolt Brecht / [compiled by] Siegfried Mews.
    p. cm. — (Critical essays on world literature)
  Bibliography: p.
  Includes index.
  ISBN 0-8161-8844-0 (alk. paper)
  1. Brecht, Bertolt, 1898–1956—Criticism and interpretation.
I. Mews, Siegfried. II. Series.
PT2603.R397Z5838 1989   89-30571
832'.912—dc19   CIP

This publication is printed on permanent/durable acid-free paper
MANUFACTURED IN THE UNITED STATES OF AMERICA

CONTENTS

INTRODUCTION

In his best-seller, *The Closing of the American Mind*, Allan Bloom cites as a conspicuous example of the "astonishing Americanization" of German value relativism — a consequence of the Nietzschean revaluation of values — "the smiling face of Louis Armstrong as he belts out the words of his great hit 'Mack the Knife.' As most American intellectuals know, it is a translation of the song 'Mackie Messer' from *The Threepenny Opera*, a monument of Weimar popular culture, written by two heroes of the artistic Left, Bertolt Brecht and Kurt Weill. . . . Lotte Lenya's rendition of this song has long stood with Marlene Dietrich's singing *'Ich bin von Kopf bis Fuss auf Liebe eingestellt'* in *The Blue Angel*" as "the symbol of a charming, neurotic, sexy, decadent longing for some hazy fulfillment not quite present to the consciousness." After all, Bloom asserts, in "that ambiguous Weimar atmosphere . . . anything was possible for people who sang of the joy of the knife in cabarets."[1]

Bloom's sweeping statement acknowledges the singular position in terms of wide appeal of *The Threepenny Opera* that, in the Marc Blitzstein version and with Lotte Lenya as Jenny, opened on 10 March 1954 in the Theatre de Lys in New York City for a seven-year run with a total of 2,611 performances. At the same time, Bloom's view of the play as a symptomatic expression of, rather than an artistic manifestation against, prevailing Weimar cultural and political norms will be found objectionable by "true" Brechtians — if only on the grounds that *The Threepenny Opera* is not Brecht's most characteristic work. Bloom's implicit condemnation of Brecht offers but one example for the continuing controversy about the playwright more than thirty years after his death.

On 10 February 1988 Bertolt Brecht would have turned ninety, an occasion that was duly noticed and commemorated in both German states. Particularly in the German Democratic Republic (GDR), where Brecht has obtained the status of quasi-official writer, his significance was acknowledged by the dedication of a Brecht statue in front of the East Berlin Theater am Schiffbauerdamm, home of Brecht's famous troupe, the Berliner Ensemble. Such official recognition tends to obscure the ambiguities and complexities of Brecht's position in East Berlin during the last years of his life. On the one hand, after his return from the United States in 1947, Brecht in 1949 ultimately opted for permanent residence in East Berlin; on the other, his decision to settle in the GDR "because he wanted 'another Germany,' one based on the principles of peace and socialism"[2] was facilitated, as Martin Esslin points out, by the "possibility of obtaining what he had wanted all his life, a theatre of his own and lavish means to experiment to his heart's content," as well as by the acquisition of an Austrian passport that enabled him to travel freely in the West.[3]

Further contradictions exist. Brecht biographer Klaus Völker claims that in the GDR Brecht "was able to preserve his independence and artistic integrity." But he also points out that Brecht "welcomed the politicization of art while vigorously defending his work against any state ideology. His theatre . . . was opposed to the official GDR doctrine on art (Socialist Realism). . . . On principle, he rejected the use of art and theatre to conform to state requirements of taste." In short, "Defiance, contradiction, and doubt were among the most important elements of [Brecht's] artistic production"[4] — elements that were not and are not in high demand in the GDR and mark Brecht's privileged distance from conformist writers assiduously propagating the official party line.

In contrast to Thomas Mann and other writers who left Germany after the Nazis came to power, Brecht's return to Germany after World War II was a foregone conclusion; the German language was his medium of expression, in the German-speaking countries he hoped to find his audience, and, last but not least, he considered Germany his home. In fact, he insisted on being recognized as an "exile" who was forced to leave Germany rather than as an "emigrant" who left voluntarily; in the poignant poem "Concerning the Label Emigrant" from the *Svendborg* collection (ca. 1936) the poet states unambiguously: "Not a home, but an exile, shall the land be that took us in."[5]

Brecht's appearance before the House Committee on Un-American Activities on 30 October 1947 (documented in this volume) was then merely a potentially dangerous interlude that Brecht escaped from unharmed on account of both his cunning and a set of fortunate circumstances; it did not significantly affect his decision to return to Europe the very next day — first to Switzerland and, eventually, to war-ravaged Berlin. In Berlin, the political and cultural capital of the Weimar Republic, Brecht had experienced his greatest theatrical triumph, the phenomenal popular, almost legendary success of *The Threepenny Opera* that premiered on 31 August 1928 and greatly contributed to that "strange nostalgia among many of the American intelligentsia for this moment just prior to Hitler's coming to power" that Bloom deplores.[6] Ironically, the successful post-World War II revival of *The Threepenny Opera* that opened in July 1945 in the Hebbel Theater in Berlin confronted Brecht with the problem of unintended and undesirable audience reaction — a problem that Brecht encountered frequently and that was not, by any means, limited to the unfocused indictment of the capitalist order in *The Threepenny Opera*. In 1945, hungry Berliners who had to subsist on exceedingly small rations found, for example, in the play's perhaps best-known line, "Erst kommt das Fressen, dann kommt die Moral" ("Food is the first thing. Morals follow on"[7]) "a welcome form of protest against the occupying powers who wanted to de-Nazify them without feeding them properly."[8] Brecht, unable to exert any influence on the production, in September 1945 commented in his diary: "In the absence of a revolutionary movement the 'message' [of *The Threepenny Opera*] is pure anarchy."[9]

Even before he achieved a hit with *The Threepenny Opera* in 1928 — a success to which composer Kurt Weill's catchy tunes contributed considerably — Brecht had determinedly pursued his goal of transforming the German theater via his dramatic theory and practice. In his stylized autobiographical poem "Of Poor B. B." in *Manual of Piety* (1927) the poet claims: "I, Bertolt Brecht, came out of the black forests" (*Poems*, 107); actually, he was born on 10 February 1898 in Augsburg, a city located about forty miles northwest of Munich, where he grew up in comfortably middle-class circumstances — owing to his father's rise from clerk to manager of a paper mill. He began writing at an early age; at the outbreak of World War I young Brecht temporarily got caught up in the rampant patriotism that bordered on chauvinism and gave it literary expression. Conversely, in 1916 he was almost expelled from school for writing a "defeatist" essay. His first drama, the one-act play *The Bible* (1913), attests to the lasting influence that Luther's German Bible made upon him. In 1928, when Brecht had begun studying Marx, he was asked by a magazine to name the strongest literary influence in his life. He responded in deliberately unexpected fashion: "You will laugh: the Bible!"[10]

Both for their own enjoyment and with the aim of provoking the comfortable and content burghers Brecht and his circle of friends and followers sang songs that Brecht had composed and that he accompanied on the guitar in the manner of the balladeer Frank Wedekind; Brecht and his clique lived a comparatively carefree existence in Augsburg and its bucolic environs. Yet the radically satirical "Ballad [Legend] of the Dead Soldier" (*Plays*, 1:369–71), which was written in 1918 and is supposed to have caused the Nazis to put Brecht's name on their blacklist in the early twenties, is unequivocal in its rejection of war.

Brecht's first major play, *Baal*, was written in 1918 and repeatedly revised thereafter — a mode of production that was to become the hallmark of a playwright who subscribed to the notion of change in all realms of human endeavor. The protagonist, a highly unconventional, crassly materialistic, and voraciously promiscuous poet, is the antithesis of the idealistic artist figures favored by some expressionist dramatists before, during, and immediately after World War I. A self-portrait only in a very remote sense, *Baal* nevertheless conveys the strong antibourgeois sentiments of its young author—sentiments that are also evident in his first short stories. *Baal* has served some critics as psychobiographical evidence for Brecht's anarchic tendencies that were later harnessed by his embrace of Marxism.[11]

Since 1917 Brecht had been studying literature and medicine at the University of Munich; although he never obtained a degree, Munich afforded him the opportunity of exchanging ideas with established writers—notably Lion Feuchtwanger (1884–1958), who became his mentor, friend, and collaborator. In 1919 Brecht completed *Drums in the Night,* the drama that was awarded the prestigious Kleist Prize in 1922 and had successful runs in Munich and Berlin in the same year—despite then Munich resident Thomas Mann's reservations. Mann informed his American readers that *Drums in the Night* was "the bitter story of a soldier returning from the war, [the play] has two good acts but then falls flat." Brecht's third play, *In the Jungle,* produced in the Munich Residenztheater in 1923, Mann found even worse than *Drums in the Night,* and with dubious taste he approved the "popular conservatism" of the audience that reacted against "Bolshevist art"—a term used without specific political connotations—by throwing gas bombs in the theater.[12]

Unlike Mann, the influential Berlin critic Herbert Ihering praised *Drums in the Night* effusively and drew attention to a young writer who was to become one of the most innovative and successful playwrights of the twenties: "The poet Bert Brecht, twenty-four years old, has changed Germany's poetic face overnight. With Bert Brecht a new tone, a new melody, a new vision has arisen."[13] Ihering's emphasis on the poetic quality of Brecht's play(s) resurfaces in the arguments of some post–World War II critics. Esslin states unequivocally: "Brecht was a poet, first and foremost a poet," whose chief distinction is to have created " 'memorable speech,' " and whose plays would not be noteworthy because of the ideas they express, the new structures they display, or the new staging techniques they require. Rather, the "new dramatic convention they represent lives above all through the grace of their language and the poetic vision of the world it conveys."[14] Similarly, editor and translator John Willett, who is intimately familiar with the difficulties of rendering Brecht's idiom into English, considers Brecht a "poet beneath the skin."[15] While other critics also rank Brecht very highly as a poet, not all of them are inclined to subsume his entire literary output under the category of poetry. Jan Knopf, for example, compares Brecht favorably to the two foremost twentieth-century German poets, Rainer Maria Rilke and Gottfried Benn, on account of his substantial poetic oeuvre that quantitatively surpasses that of both Rilke and Benn but forms only part of Brecht's total work. More importantly, Knopf attributes Brecht's pioneering role to his departure from the bourgeois tradition of the lyric as an expression of innermost feelings and subjective states of mind.[16] To be sure, poetic diction is evident in all of Brecht's plays; yet overemphasizing the omnipresent manifestations of his poetic gifts ignores the fact that Brecht considered himself primarily a playwright and very deliberately used the stage as a means to promote his concept of a new theater and his own fortunes.

Despite some initial success in Munich, the young writer considered the Bavarian capital merely a stepping stone on his way to Berlin, the cosmopolitan literary and theatrical metropolis that attracted talented people from everywhere. Brecht settled permanently in Berlin in the fall of 1924 and remained there until 1933, the beginning of his exile. Brecht adapted easily to anonymous existence in the "asphalt city," as he called Berlin in "Of Poor B. B."; in "A Reader for Those Who Live in Cities" (*Poems*, 131–50) he provided instructions about how to survive in the big city, that is, by not succumbing to illusions about man's autonomy. Berlin life sharpened Brecht's perception of the social processes and problems in a mass society; in the comedy *A Man's a Man* (1927), for example, Brecht posits the social conditioning of human nature — although in a curious, geographically remote setting that was inspired by Rudyard Kipling. From Kipling Brecht "derived his central image of an exotic-military-imperial world somewhere between Suez, Hong Kong and the South Pacific (which he knew from Gauguin's *Noa-Noa*), peopled by Malays, Chinese and elephants and dominated by brutal and licentious British soldiers."[17]

In Berlin Brecht fully developed his characteristic mode of production that relied on the teamwork of friends and collaborators — among them several women with whom he had liaisons. Brecht's "polygamous" nature has been the subject of much comment; at the age of twenty-six he had fathered three children with three different women: son Frank with Paula Banholzer, daughter Hanne with Marianne Zoff, and son Stefan with Helene Weigel (whom he married in 1929; daughter Barbara was born in 1930). Although Brecht's collaboration with women is often presented by critics as an indication of a new concept of the writer and his function in society, Brecht's dominant position in the collective resulted to some degree in the exploitation of the ideas and the work of its other members, treatment that was resented, for instance, by Marieluise Fleißer.[18]

A turning point in Brecht's life occurred in 1926, the year in which he began to read Karl Marx in order to comprehend the transactions at the Chicago Wheat Exchange that was to figure prominently in his projected play *Joe Fleischhacker*. In a sense, Brecht's study of Marx was the outgrowth of his endeavors to find an adequate form of representation of a complex social reality; at any rate, Brecht's turning to Marxism has been the subject of considerable attention by critics and biographers. Esslin's psychological thesis about Brecht's "divided nature" that was constantly confronted with a "choice of evils" — that is, anarchy and hedonism in the manner of *Baal* on the one hand, and stern, authoritarian party discipline on the other — has been both adapted and challenged by other critics.[19] Völker, for instance, devotes an entire section to Brecht's "Marxist Studies" and argues that Brecht turned to Marxism-Leninism as a means of imparting a new quality to his writing that would enable him to render social processes more effectively on the stage.[20]

Brecht's study of Marxism coincided with his more clearly focused criticism of contemporaneous drama and staging practices that eventually evolved into his theory of epic theater. The term *Verfremdungseffekt*, often ambiguously translated as "alienation effect" and a commonplace in drama theory of the twentieth century, does not appear in Brecht's writings until 1935 (in the essay "Alienation Effects in Chinese Acting"[21]). There is no unanimity among critics as to whether the *Verfremdungseffekt*, which on its simplest level entails "gaining new insights into the world around us by glimpsing it in a different and previously unfamiliar light,"[22] should be seen in the philosophical-historical context of the Hegelian-Marxist concept of *Entfremdung*, correctly translated as "alienation," or simply as a staging device, a formal technique in the service of the author's personal message. Yet, apart from the origin of the term and from the pre-Marxist Brecht's tendency to use estrangement devices, divorcing the *Verfremdungseffekt* entirely from Brecht's Marxist convictions seem problematic inasmuch as aesthetics and philosophical method combine to raise the spectator's level of consciousness to the point of new and liberating insights[23] that were also the aim of director Erwin Piscator's political theater.

Brecht's Marxism asserts itself vigorously in his *Lehrstücke* (written 1928–1931), "plays for learning" attempting a new form of participatory communication by spectator involvement rather than doctrinaire "didactic plays." In *The Exception and the Rule* the audience is exhorted: "Observe the conduct of these people closely: / Find it estranging [*befremdend*] even if not very strange [*fremd*] / Hard to explain even if it is not the custom / Hard to understand even if it is not the rule. . . ."[24] Curiously, the *Lehrstück The Measures Taken* in particular did not find favor with the self-ordained representatives of the masses, the functionaries of the Communist party. Alfred Kurella, whose review of the 1930 Berlin premiere is reprinted in this volume, castigated the "petty-bourgeois writer" Brecht for deviating from the party line and espousing the ideas of "right-wing opportunism"; he found the play to be revolutionary in style rather than substance. Conversely, in 1947 the House Committee on Un-American Activities was more interested in Brecht's presumed advocacy of human sacrifice for the sake of political expediency and his pro-Communist sympathies — although the committee members did not pursue this line of questioning very forcefully, as the record of the hearings (reprinted in this volume) shows.

Communist tendencies were only one among the numerous sins that Brecht had committed in the eyes of his contemporaries. In 1931 the critic Julius Bab, who like Brecht was to become an exile, informed American readers about the ways in which the playwright — then virtually unknown in America — had offended persons "of taste and culture": "The manner in which the man takes advantage of the slogans of communism as though they were his own, plunders foreign authors, opens great law suits to defend his alleged film rights, and employs in his intellectual polemics a jargon which has otherwise been confined solely and always to tap-rooms, all these things are calculated to call forth anything rather than admiration or liking."

But Bab was fair enough to admit that the production of *The Measures Taken* "was a highly important theatrical event" and that Brecht was "without a shadow of a doubt an uncommonly gifted writer."[25] Brecht's transgressions with regard to the alleged "plundering" of foreign authors had been noted before, particularly by the prestigious Berlin critic Alfred Kerr, who charged Brecht with plagiarism in the case of *The Threepenny Opera*. It was not the fact that *The Threepenny Opera* was a free adaptation of John Gay's *The Beggar's Opera* (1728) that incensed Kerr; rather, he objected to Brecht's unacknowledged use of verses from a German translation of François Villon. Brecht countered the charge — without really refuting it — by stating his disdain for all bourgeois notions of property rights and provocatively professing his "laxity in matters of intellectual property"[26] — a stance that he did not adhere to in the case of his own works.

When Brecht was asked to produce a film treatment of *The Threepenny Opera*, he sharpened its social and political message but was rebuffed by the film producers who had expected a treatment along the lines of the original play. Without doubt, the "culinary" aspects of *The Threepenny Opera* — that is, those aspects that produced pleasurable sensations rather than a critical attitude in the spectator — contributed greatly to its successful runs all over Europe. The European success story was not matched in America, however; in 1933 *The Threepenny Opera* closed after only twelve performances in New York City. The film company then produced a film that was not based on Brecht's script — although elements of it were used. Brecht insisted on his individual and artistic rights and sued the producers for breach of contract; he settled out of court for a considerable sum in December 1931.

Although Brecht formulated around 1936 that there was no fundamental contrast between "theatre for pleasure [and] theatre for instruction,"[27] and although his turning to Marxism did not entail abandoning the "theatre for pleasure" in his dramatic production of the late twenties and early thirties, the pleasurable and the instructional do not always appear in perfect balance. For instance, whereas bourgeois audiences hugely enjoyed *The Threepenny Opera* as pure entertainment, the powerful and complex *Saint Joan of the Stockyards*, a play about a modern-day Joan of Arc in the stockyards of Chicago that, among other sources, is indebted to Upton Sinclair's novel *The Jungle* (1906), is unequivocal in its indictment of the capitalist order. Written in 1930–31, the play could not be produced on stage during the waning years of the Weimar Republic; it premiered in Hamburg after Brecht's death, in 1959.

After Hitler's coming to power on 30 January 1933 and the burning of the Reichstag on 27 February 1933 — blamed by the Nazis on the Communists as a pretext for the wholesale arrest of leftist opponents, among them writers and intellectuals — Brecht, his wife Helene Weigel, and their son, Stefan, left for Prague to begin life in exile that was, contrary to Brecht's initial "Thoughts on the Duration of Exile" (*Poems*, 301–302), to last until 1947.

"Changing countries oftener than our shoes," as Brecht stated with but little exaggeration (*Poems*, 320), he and his family — often accompanied by female collaborators such as Margarete Steffin and, later, Ruth Berlau — went from Prague to Vienna and then to Paris. They lived in Svendborg, Denmark, from December 1933 to April 1939, moved to Lidingö in Sweden (1939-40), and, after the occupation of Denmark by Nazi troops in April 1940, spent the last months before their departure to the United States via the Soviet Union in Finland (April 1940–May 1941).

In the poem "To Those Born Later" Brecht characterizes the exile years as "truly . . . dark times" (*Poems*, 318) on account of the horrors perpetrated by Hitler. As a consequence, these years were also a "Bad Time for Poetry," as Brecht put it in a poem of that title written in 1939 (*Poems*, 330–31). Yet he continued to write; after leaving Berlin his first major project was a novel, a genre that did not require the medium of the stage to reach its public outside of Nazi Germany and was thus more appropriate for the severely curtailed publishing and staging opportunities of exile. *Dreigroschenroman*, the only novel that Brecht ever completed, was published in 1934 in Amsterdam and translated into English as *A Penny for the Poor* (1937). In the novel Brecht returned one more time to the materials of *The Threepenny Opera*. After his abortive attempt to have his film treatment produced, the novel resolves to some extent the dilemma that was created by the play's lack of an anticapitalist thrust. The novel dispenses with traditional individual conflicts and the probing of states of mind; instead it substitutes economics and business deals as the main ingredient. The epilogue in particular exposes the Bible as an ideological prop of a society divided into classes and a justification for the prevailing system of injustice.

In Denmark Brecht sought to influence events within Germany by means of his pen and to strengthen the opposition to Hitler abroad. His anti-Nazi play *The Private Life of the Master Race* that was used by Brecht's American promoter, Eric Bentley, to acquaint Americans with the Brechtian theater is a notable case in point.[28] But in addition to completing his major collection of poetry, *Svendborg Poems*, in 1939, beginning in 1937 and through the end of Brecht's European exile, those plays that are generally regarded as his best were written in fairly quick succession: *The*

Good Person of Szechwan, the first version of *Life of Galileo*, *Puntila and Matti, His Hired Man*, and *Mother Courage and Her Children*. *Galileo* (September 1943), *The Good Person* (February 1942), and *Mother Courage* (April 1941) premiered in Zurich during World War II; it was particularly the latter play that contributed to Brecht's eventual world fame. In part, at least, the acclaim *Mother Courage* received was based on a misunderstanding of Brecht's intentions; rather than the "hyena" of the battlefields that Brecht wished to present, the spectators saw a tragic mother figure. Hence it is dubious whether the play convincingly conveyed its intended message: "That in wartime the big profits are not made by little people. . . . That no sacrifice is too great for the struggle against war" (*Plays*, 5:339).

The Resistible Rise of Arturo Ui, written in 1941, was intended to demonstrate to audiences in Brecht's new host country, the United States, the connections between capitalism, gangsterism, and the rise of Nazism by using Chicago — a city that had also served as a setting for *In the Jungle* and *Saint Joan* — and Al Capone as models to which Americans could relate.[29] The play was not staged at all until after Brecht's death; but the playwright's preoccupation with the American market while in Finland as well as his efforts to obtain U.S. visas raises the question why he did not follow his convictions and settle in the Soviet Union. Brecht, who is credited with "uncanny shrewdness"[30] in matters of survival, realized full well that under Stalin the Soviet Union would not provide a hospitable artistic and intellectual climate; his stylized and complex theater ran counter to the brand of realism propagated in Moscow by the literary historian Georg Lukács and others. Presumed dissidents were dealt with harshly; Brecht's friend Carola Neher, who had played Polly Peachum in *The Threepenny Opera*, was among those who perished during the purges.

On their way from Helsinki to Vladivostok in Siberia, the embarkation point for the West Coast of the United States, the Brecht party had to leave his collaborator Margarete Steffin behind in Moscow; she died of consumption shortly afterwards.

Brecht's arrival in California — he settled in Santa Monica — on 21 January 1941 began his American sojourn, a period that was, by no means, unproductive but yielded little in terms of new publications and stage productions of his plays. A brief interlude, Brecht's New York visit from October to November 1935 on the occasion of the Theatre Union's staging of *The Mother*, adapted from Maxim Gorky's novel, had preceded his extended stay in the forties. Brecht's difficulties with the play's producers and director — sympathetic to the revolutionary message — concerning the proper staging on the one hand and the *New York Times* critic's review of the play as "an interesting experiment in stagecraft" on the other[31] did not augur well for the playwright's prospects in the United States.

The necessity of making a living motivated Brecht to attempt selling his film stories to the Hollywood studios. Despite his genuine interest in film as a new medium, he despised the unadulterated commercialism of the film industry in which the writer accounted for little. He expressed his ambivalent feelings in the wistful poem "Hollywood": ". . . to earn my daily bread / I go to the market where lies are bought / Hopefully / I take my place among the sellers" (*Poems*, 382). The behavior of some of his fellow exiles in California, among them the Frankfurt School scholars Theodor W. Adorno, Max Horkheimer, and Herbert Marcuse, gave him cause for reflection on the role of intellectuals or—in Brechtian terminology—"Tuis" at a time when everything, including intellect, has become a salable commodity.

In 1944 Brecht completed *The Caucasian Chalk Circle*, the play that premiered in Northfield, Minnesota—in Eric Bentley's translation—after Brecht's departure from the United States (May 1948). The second version of *Life of Galileo*, which originated in a collaboration with Charles Laughton and had assumed new relevance in view of the dropping of the atom bomb on Hiroshima, premiered in Los Angeles in July 1947 and was produced in New York City after Brecht had left the country. He had failed to make a significant impact but—unlike the hero of his play—he had escaped the charge of (political) heresy.[32]

Thus Brecht's ascendancy to the position of "modern classic" in the West was not at all a foregone conclusion once he had left the United States. In fact, the appropriateness of Brecht's "discovery or rediscovery . . . in the countries of the West"[33] was seriously questioned for political reasons. Internationally renowned political philosopher Hannah Arendt, for example, stated erroneously that Brecht had written an "ode to Stalin" and praised "Stalin's crimes."[34] Brecht's plays were virtually boycotted in theaters of the Federal Republic as a consequence of such events as the workers' strike and revolt in the GDR on 17 June 1953, the Hungarian uprising in 1956, and the construction of the Berlin Wall on 13 August 1961. Although Brecht could hardly be blamed for the latter two events—he had died on 14 August 1956—his well-known Marxist/Communist views were widely construed by parts of the West German press as an explicit—and, paradoxically, posthumous—endorsement of any repressive measures perpetrated by the Soviet Union or the GDR. In the intolerant cold war climate of the early fifties opinions polarized concerning Brecht: he was acceptable to those who considered him primarily a poet whose politics were subordinate to his craft; he was anathema to those who regarded him chiefly as a propagator of Communist ideas in poetic guise.[35] Curiously, as Willett observes, "Brecht's politics were, and still are, resented with a virulence quite spared to more orthodox communist writers like Aragon or Neruda or Aimé Césaire, earning him a leading place in the cold war propagandists' Pandaemonium."[36]

An important touchstone in any discussion of Brecht's politics is his attitude toward the June 1953 workers' uprising in East Berlin. On 17 June 1953 Brecht had dictated a brief note, addressed to Walter Ulbricht, General Secretary of the Socialist Unity Party (SED), in which he intimated that an open discussion about the "speed of socialist construction" was in order. But only the last sentence of the note was published by the party organ, *Neues Deutschland*, on 21 June 1953; taken out of context, the sentence was widely construed in the West as an expression of abject servitude to the regime that provided Brecht with a theater and other amenities of life while the workers suffered.[37]

More than ten years later Günter Grass took a more differentiated — if ultimately negative — view of Brecht's noninvolvement in the workers' uprising by pointing out that "Brecht emerged without visible harm from the workers' revolt: he retired to Buckow and wrote such poems as 'Der Radwechsel' ['Changing the Wheel'], 'Eisen' ['Iron'], and 'Böser Morgen' ['Nasty Morning']. His Ensemble continued to play, he continued to be the cultural property and advertisement of a state to which, according to his passport, he did not belong."[38] Grass's *The Plebeians Rehearse the Uprising* (1966) hovers uneasily between documentary theater and illusionary drama; in his play Grass uses a Brecht-like figure, the "Boss," to advance his thesis that Brecht remained aloof for aesthetic reasons when he was approached by workers who asked for his moral support as well as his help in formulating a call for a general strike. Although he does not refuse outright to lend his support to the workers' cause, the Boss does nothing to advance it. Rather, he uses the workers as extras in his rehearsal of Shakespeare's *Coriolanus* until Soviet tanks have crushed the uprising — thereby violating his artistic creed that demands the application of the insights gained in the theater to social practice. Thus the revolution remains confined to the theater, Grass suggests; for Brecht "everything becomes . . . an aesthetic question: a man of the theater, serene and untroubled."[39]

Grass's criticism of Brecht and of leftist intellectuals in general is based on his conviction that the artist and writer must engage in political action at the grass-roots level rather than cling to abstract theoretical models for social progress. Granted that Grass's emphasis on the discrepancy between the postulates of Brecht's theater and his personal conduct cannot be dismissed lightly, there is good reason to doubt Brecht's unperturbed serenity, as such poems as "Nasty Morning" — quoted by Grass himself — and "The Solution" (*Poems*, 440) indicate.

At any rate, in the 1960s Brecht's fortunes in terms of the reception of his plays took a turn for the better; the sixties became almost "a golden age for Brecht."[40] A new generation of directors, among them Brecht's disciples Peter Palitzsch and Carl Weber, who had remained in the West after the building of the Berlin Wall, began staging his plays in Brechtian fashion along the lines suggested by the "model" productions of the Berliner Ensemble that performed Brecht's plays in London, Moscow, and Paris. At the same time, the proliferation of productions that in the 1971–72 season propelled Brecht into the position of most-performed author in the Federal Republic tended to result in the predominance of entertainment at the expense of social analysis and political message. The frequent stagings of "culinary" works such as *The Threepenny Opera* and the comparative neglect of plays with a forceful political thrust such as *Saint Joan of the Stockyards* contributed to productions of Brecht's plays as theatrical spectacles and artistic events that could be enjoyed by audiences without recourse to the playwright's underlying socio-critical intent.

Less than ten years after Brecht's death, in 1964, the Swiss novelist and playwright Max Frisch coined a poignant phrase concerning Brecht's "penetrating ineffectiveness of a classic." The widely quoted phrase alludes to the curious phenomenon that Brecht, the once maligned political propagandist, had now been elevated to artist and even genius status — albeit an artist in an apolitical vein whose effect on the political thinking of the audience remained negligible.[41]

Whereas Brecht's presumed political "ineffectiveness" may be attributed to particular staging strategies — for example, productions of *The Caucasian Chalk Circle* in the West commonly omitted the prologue that takes place in the Soviet Union — gradually a more fundamental criticism emerged that challenges the very premises of Brecht's theater. Critics began questioning the allegedly simplistic, fairy-tale–like Brechtian models that presented clearcut patterns of good and evil without complexity and found them ill-suited for stimulating critical or activist thought regarding social ills.[42] In 1968 Austrian writer Peter Handke published an essay, provocatively entitled "Horváth Is Better Than Brecht,"[43] in which he castigated Brecht for offering solutions that inadequately reflect complex states of consciousness; instead of Brecht — overrated in his opinion — he implicitly proposed playwright Ödön von Horváth as a model worthy of emulation.

Handke's arguments were adapted by others, including British playwright Christopher Hampton. In his play, *Tales from Hollywood* (1983), Hampton imaginatively pits his spokesman Horváth against Brecht and has the former categorically reject the latter's notion of theater as a potential vehicle for an eventual change of society that is to be initiated by a process of reflection on the spectators' part.[44] Such criticism that shifts its focus from the content and nature of Brecht's ideas on politics to the mode of their presentation on stage and the underlying assumptions of his theater is but an extreme expression of the *Brechtmüdigkeit* (being tired of Brecht) that became the battle cry of directors and critics, but not of spectators, in the sixties and seventies.

Although there have been experimental productions, among them those of the newly appreciated early plays, and "actualizations" that endeavored to relate Brecht's plays to such contemporary issues as ecological concerns, unemployment, and rampant technological progress, the tendency to offer Brecht plays as pure entertainment continues to persist in the eighties. Entertainment in the Federal Republic and other Western countries, quasi-official authority, invoked as a deterrent to change, in the GDR — Brecht's fortunes in terms of a vital, challenging, and inspiring theater seem to be at a low point.

But such an assessment requires elucidation. Brecht's significance as a dramatist is by no means limited to Europe and the United States; actually, in third-world countries in general and in Asia in particular Brecht is recognized as a modern classic whose dichotomous pattern of poor and rich, good and evil, servant and master that no longer accurately reflects the complex social reality in Western countries corresponds fairly closely to less developed, predominantly agrarian conditions and may thus be taken as shrewd insight and cogent analysis.[45]

As the foregoing remarks have shown, Brecht is chiefly and justly renowned as an immensely successful playwright. Yet there are other dimensions of his literary output that cannot entirely be encompassed by exclusively focusing attention on the production of his plays and their reception. Brecht, both the man and his work, has not escaped scholarly attention — with the result that there exists a thriving international Brecht "industry" whose productivity shows no sign of abating and is positively unaffected by "Brecht fatigue." Commemorative events serve as stimuli for scholars' and publishers' initiatives; one notable result of the planning for Brecht's aforementioned ninetieth birthday is the virtually unprecedented cooperation between Brecht's West German and East German publishers — Suhrkamp and Aufbau, respectively — as well as East German and West German scholars on the project of a comprehensive and annotated thirty-volume edition of Brecht's works. At the time of this writing several volumes have appeared in both parts of Germany — with identical texts.[46]

A further significant contribution that, in a sense, complements the edition of Brecht's works is the voluminous biography by East German scholar Werner Mittenzwei that in its subtitle accords Brecht the position of a sage whose life's work was devoted to finding the right answer to mankind's fundamental problems (*Welträtsel*), that is, poverty, exploitation, and injustice.[47] Although Mittenzwei's work offers a wealth of information, it does not provide a major reappraisal of Brecht; rather, it essentially confines itself to cautious revisions in politically sensitive areas. Hence it is unlikely that it will entirely replace such predecessors as the biographies by Marianne Kesting (1959; rev. ed., 1982), Martin Esslin (1959; 4th rev. ed., 1984), Frederic Ewen (1967), Klaus Völker (1976; English translation, 1978), James K. Lyon (1980), and Ronald Hayman (1983).[48]

Biographies are but one facet of the scholarly Brecht industry. While biographies attest to Brecht's status as a major literary figure and contribute to cementing this status, they generally lack the detailed readings of individual works or encompassing analyses of the total oeuvre that is to be found in other scholarly and critical works. As indicated earlier, the literature on Brecht is vast; given the restriction of producing a manageable (in terms of total pages) yet informative volume, the present collection of essays is based on several assumptions.

First of all, the great majority of essays selected for this volume were first published in English during the last ten years or so. These essays do not necessarily offer more definitive or more cogently argued readings than those by critics writing in other languages — especially in German — but in conjunction with reviews of American Brecht productions reprinted here they do provide an indication of approaches to and assessments of the playwright in the English-speaking world. Such documentation, albeit highly selective, is an indispensable prerequisite in a volume that seeks to convey a sense of Brecht's reception in a broadly defined Anglo-American context without completely neglecting either Brecht's specific German roots or his present-day international significance. At any rate, as several of the essays in this volume attest, the English-speaking world in general and America in particular (or, strictly speaking, Chicago)[49] fascinated Brecht long before he became known in this country — an additional reason to explore the playwright's American reception.

Second, this volume adheres to the unexceptional notion that Brecht is known primarily as a playwright both by virtue of the fact that plays form the bulk of his literary output — seven volumes in the widely used twenty-volume edition of his works (GW) — and that the impact of his plays has been immeasurably greater than that of his other writings, including his poetry. Hence a number of essays have been assembled that engage in readings of specific facets of individual plays from all phases of the playwright's creative endeavor but concentrate on those that may be legitimately considered central to the Brecht canon.

Third, despite the overriding significance of Brecht's plays, the current state of Brecht scholarship does not permit an exclusive concentration on Brecht, the playwright. Thus a second section is devoted to such topics as Brecht's poetry, his theory of the epic theater, and his politics, that is, his attitude toward Stalin. Even more so than in the preceding section the wide range of opinions concerning Brecht is evident; far from pretending to be an authoritative pronouncement on or summary of the current state of scholarship this critical anthology deliberately presents divergent points of view — including those with which the editor does not completely agree. The Brecht discourse features many discordant voices; hence the reader is invited to inform him- or herself about ideologically and methodologically differing contributions to the current debate that range from both sophisticated and somewhat undifferentiated Marxist readings to revisionist claims of Brecht's Stalinism, from psychobiographical interpretations of texts to the elucidation of Brecht's use of Freudian insights. In a sense, a procedure that places the onus of finding (correct) answers to the problems posed by contradictory readings on the reader is eminently Brechtian. In the epilogue to *The Good Person of Szechwan* a player exhorts the audience faced with open, unresolved questions: "There's only one solution comes to mind: / That you yourselves should ponder till you find / The ways and means and measures tending / To help good people to a happy ending" (*Plays*, 6:104). Ultimately, of course, the reader eager to find answers will use this anthology as a means of gaining access to Brecht's texts—as reader and/or spectator. In spite of the enormous strides that Brecht scholarship has taken during the last three decades or so, in the final analysis it has not been able to resolve the question that was posed almost thirty years ago in a similar collection, that is, the question of "our attitude toward Brecht's total achievement—so rich in grace and irritation, fruitful insight and terrible simplifications, vitality and wit. To close our eyes for political reasons to the charm of his theater would be as foolish as the blind admiration of his orthodox devotees, who are willing to devour all of Brecht, lock, stock, and trash."[50]

Several of the articles reprinted here originally included quotations in German from Brecht's and other authors' works. In general, these quotes, apart from those deemed necessary for clarification, have been omitted— but these omissions have been indicated in the notes to the respective articles and, in most instances, reference has been made to the original text in Bertolt Brecht, *Gesammelte Werke in 20 Bänden* (1967). The source of English translations and/or the translator have also been indicated; owing to authors' and translators' lack of consistency in rendering titles of Brecht's works into English, some titles appear in several variants; however, appropriate references have been made.

I wish to gratefully acknowledge the contribution of the College of Arts and Sciences toward permission costs.

SIEGFRIED MEWS

University of North Carolina at Chapel Hill

Notes

1. Allan Bloom, *The Closing of the American Mind* (New York: Simon & Schuster, 1987), 151, 154.

2. Klaus Völker, "Brecht Today: Classic or Challenge," *Theatre Journal* 39 (1987):425–26.

3. Martin Esslin, *Brecht: A Choice of Evils. A Critical Study of the Man, His Work and His Opinions.* 4th, rev. ed. (London: Methuen, 1984), 78, 79–81.

4. Völker, "Brecht Today," 426.

5. Bertolt Brecht, *Poems 1913–1956*, ed. John Willett and Ralph Manheim with the co-operation of Erich Fried (New York: Methuen, 1976), 301. Subsequently cited as *Poems*.

6. Bloom, *Closing*, 155.

7. Bertolt Brecht, *Collected Plays*, ed. Ralph Manheim and John Willett (New York: Vintage Books, 1971–), 2:202. Hereafter cited as *Plays*.

8. James K. Lyon, *Bertolt Brecht in America* (Princeton, N. J.: Princeton University Press, 1980), 311.

9. Bertolt Brecht, *Arbeitsjournal*, 2 vols., ed. Werner Hecht (Frankfurt am Main: Suhrkamp, 1973), 2:756.

10. Bertolt Brecht, *Gesammelte Werke* (Frankfurt am Main: Suhrkamp, 1967), 18:12*. Subsequently cited as *GW*. See also Esslin, *Brecht*, 98.

11. See Ronald Speirs, *"Baal,"* and Antony Tatlow, "Mastery or Slavery?," in this volume.

12. Thomas Mann, "German Letter (September 1923)," *Dial* (October 1923):375.

13. Herbert Ihering, review of *Drums in the Night*, *Berliner Börsen-Courier*, 5 October 1922, in *Brecht in der Kritik*, ed. Monika Wyss, 5 (Munich: Kindler, 1977).

14. Esslin, *Brecht*, 95.

15. John Willett, "The Poet Beneath the Skin," *Brecht Heute – Brecht Today* 2 (1972):88. See also Claude Hill, "The Poet Beneath the Skin," in this volume.

16. Jan Knopf, *Brecht Handbuch: Lyrik, Prosa, Schriften. Eine Ästhetik der Widersprüche. Mit einem Anhang: Film* (Stuttgart: Metzler, 1984), 10–11.

17. John Willett, "The Case of Kipling," *Brecht in Context: Comparative Approaches* (London: Methuen, 1984), 47.

18. See, for example, Siegfried Mews, "Portraits of the Artist as Committed Writer: Brecht in the Context of Literature," in *Exile and Enlightenment: Studies in Honor of Guy Stern on his 65th Birthday*, ed. Uwe Faulhaber et al., 247–55 (Detroit, Mich.: Wayne State University Press, 1987).

19. Esslin, *Brecht*, 137–83.

20. Klaus Völker, *Brecht: A Biography*, trans. John Nowell (New York: Seabury Press, 1978), 87–169.

21. *GW*, 16:619–31. See also Arrigo Subiotto, "Epic Theatre: A Theatre for the Scientific Age," in this volume.

22. John Willett, "Brecht, Alienation and Karl Marx," *Brecht in Context*, 218.

23. See Reinhold Grimm, "Der katholische Einstein: Brechts Dramen- und Theatertheorie," in *Brechts Dramen: Neue Interpretationen*, ed. Walter Hinderer, 23–24 (Stuttgart: Reclam, 1984).

24. Bertolt Brecht, *The Exception and the Rule, The Jewish Wife and Other Short Plays*, trans. Eric Bentley (New York: Grove Press, 1965), 111, 143 (with minor variations).

25. Julius Bab, "Germany," *Drama Magazine* (April 1931):17.

26. Brecht, "[Eine Erklärung]," [May 1929], *GW*, 18:100.

27. *Brecht on Theatre. The Development of an Aesthetic*, ed. and trans. John Willett (New York: Hill and Wang, 1964), 69-77.

28. See Eric Bentley, *"The Private Life of the Master Race,"* in this volume.

29. See Ernst Schürer, "Revolution from the Right: Bertolt Brecht's American Gangster Play *The Resistible Rise of Arturo Ui*," in this volume.

30. Esslin, *Brecht*, 147.

31. See Brooks Atkinson, " 'Mother' Learns and Teaches the Facts of Life," in this volume.

32. See Irwin Shaw, "The Earth Stands Still," in this volume.

33. Herbert Luthy [*sic*], "Of Poor Bert Brecht," *Encounter* 7, no. 2 (July 1956):33.

34. Hannah Arendt, "What is Permitted to Jove," *New Yorker*, 5 November 1966, 68.

Rpt. Hannah Arendt, "Bertolt Brecht: 1898–1956," in *Men in Dark Times*, 207–50 (New York: Harcourt, 1968). See also John Willett, "Brecht, Stalin, and Hannah Arendt," *Brecht in Context*, 211–18.

35. See, for example, Siegfried Mews, *Bertolt Brecht: Der Kaukasische Kreidekreis*, 3d, rev. ed. (Frankfurt am Main: Diesterweg, 1988), 85–87.

36. Willett, "The Changing Role of Politics," *Brecht in Context*, 178.

37. Esslin, *Brecht*, 169; Völker, *Brecht*, 354–58.

38. Günter Grass, "The Prehistory and Posthistory of the Tragedy of *Coriolanus* from Livy and Plutarch via Shakespeare Down to Brecht and Myself," *The Plebeians Rehearse the Uprising: A German Tragedy*, trans. Ralph Manheim (New York: Harcourt, Brace & World, 1966), xxxv.

39. Grass, "Prehistory," xxxvi.

40. Völker, "Brecht Today," 426.

41. See Völker, "Brecht Today," 427.

42. See, for example, Hans-Dieter Zimmermann, "Die Last der Lehre. Fünf Thesen zu den späten Stücken Bertolt Brechts," *Beyond Brecht — Über Brecht hinaus: Brecht Yearbook* 11 (1982):105–6.

43. Peter Handke, "Horváth ist besser als Brecht," *Theater heute*, 9, no. 3 (1968):28.

44. See Siegfried Mews, "Von der Ohnmacht der Intellektuellen: Christopher Hamptons *Tales from Hollywood*," *Exilforschung: Ein internationales Jahrbuch* 3 (1985):270–85.

45. See Peter von Becker, "Brecht in Asien: Beobachtungen zwischen Kalkutta und Peking," *Theater heute* 28, no. 2 (1987):15–19.

46. Bertolt Brecht, *Werke: Große kommentierte Berliner und Frankfurter Ausgabe*, 30 vols., ed. Werner Hecht, Jan Knopf, Werner Mittenzwei, and Klaus-Detlef Müller (Frankfurt am Main: Suhrkamp, 1988–1991).

47. Werner Mittenzwei, *Das Leben des Bertolt Brecht oder Der Umgang mit Welträtseln*, 2 vols. (Frankfurt am Main: Suhrkamp, 1987).

48. Marianne Kesting, *Bertolt Brecht in Selbstzeugnissen und Bilddokumenten*, rev. ed. (Reinbek: Rowohlt, 1982). For other bibliographical details, see note 3 (Esslin), note 8 (Lyon), note 20 (Völker), and "Bibliography," (Ewen, Hayman) in this volume.

49. See Reinhold Grimm, "Bertolt Brecht's Chicago — A German Myth?," in this volume.

50. Peter Demetz, "Introduction," *Brecht: A Collection of Critical Essays* (Englewood Cliffs, N. J.: Prentice-Hall, 1962), 15.

ON THE PLAYS

Baal

Ronald Speirs*

Brecht's first full-length play, *Baal*, was written in the closing months of the First World War. The destruction in the war of countless lives and of a whole way of life elicited a great variety of responses. For some it was a cause of utter despair, for others a chance for civilisation to make a brave new beginning. As a civilian for most of the war Brecht had direct experience only of the privations it caused, but the deaths of so many of his contemporaries at school kept him constantly alive to the terrible waste of young lives "out there." For him the central question arising from this experience was: how should the individual respond to a world that will eventually, inevitably destroy him? After his disillusionment with nationalist ideals at the beginning of the war he had come to distrust all idealism as a guide to life. He now insisted that ideals were merely ridiculous attempts to erect defences against the harsh realities of life; in the hands of the strong ideals were a means of exploiting the weak, a task which was ironically made easier by the need felt by the weak for ideals to prop up their crumbling lives:

> If one only had the courage, it would be as easy as pie to ascribe nearly every ideal and institution . . . to the human race's desperate need to conceal its true situation. Respect for the family, glorification of work, the lure of fame, likewise religion, philosophy, art, smoking, intoxication, aren't just isolated, clearly calculated and generally recognized means (moyens) of combating mankind's sense of isolation, abandonment and moral outlawry; but visible guarantees of an immense stockpile of values and securities. It is from this seductive cosiness that man's enslavement springs. (*Diaries*, 158)[1]

Baal, the dramatic biography of an anarchic poet modelled on François Villon, attempts to envisage a life lived positively although without the prop of faith in an ideal. The play is a fantasy of mastery achieved over a destructive world by accepting that life is a matter of strength or weakness

---

*From *Brecht's Early Plays* by Ronald Speirs (London & Basingstoke: Macmillan, 1982), 17–29, 190–92. Reprinted by permission of Macmillan, London & Basingstoke, and Humanities Press International, Inc., Atlantic Highlands, N. J.

(as opposed to good or evil) and by extracting the maximum intensity of pleasure from each passing moment.

The immediate stimulus for the drama was Brecht's dislike of a play entitled *Der Einsame* (*The Lonely One*) by the minor Expressionist dramatist Hanns Johst. Johst's play took as its subject the life of the late (or post-) Romantic playwright Christian Dietrich Grabbe; its theme was the clichéd one of the poet as a misunderstood genius. When Grabbe's wife dies in childbirth his idealism is diverted into self-punishing immorality, by means of which he hides his injured sensitivity behind a façade of cynicism, brutality and debauchery. Essentially his life is full of pain, remorse and self-pity which issues in repeated comparisons of his situation with that of the suffering Christ. In the end Johst has him die — in verse — with his hands folded in childlike humility, well rid of a world in which there is no room for souls like his. Brecht countered this tear-jerking display of self-hating, perverted idealism with a vision of a life of self-indulgent amoralism. Johst's play was, however, not the most important object of Brecht's scorn in *Baal*. By giving his hero the name of an ancient god of fertility who was abominated and defeated by Jehovah, Brecht was aligning himself with a tradition of modern paganism which included amongst its deities Nietzsche's Dionysos and Wedekind's Lulu.[2] This cult of vitality was intended by these writers as a challenge to their contemporaries to overcome the decadent fear of life evident in their attachment to convention and in the other-worldliness of their religion and philosophy. It was characteristic of Brecht's aggressive will to master life that he should turn to this particular tradition for help in confronting the physical, social, moral and emotional devastation wreaked by the First World War.

The most direct approach to Baal's mind is through his poetry. The "Ballad of the Adventurers," the last song Baal sings before his death, contains a protest against the limits of human existence. The adventurer of the poem searches restlessly for "the land where it is better to live," but is bound to fail in his search because what he is looking for is a state of existence in which there are no reminders of transience: "he dreams from time to time of a little meadow with blue sky above it and nothing else" (*B*, 85). Having on the one hand abandoned the security of unconscious life in his mother's womb, while on the other having no access to any transcendental world ("driven from Heaven and Hell"), the adventurer cherishes the dream of a form of existence that would be physical yet timeless. Because he knows that his dream cannot be realised his wanderings take the form of self-exposure to the fiercest ravages of transient experience so that its intensity may compensate him for the tranquillity he cannot have.

The angry awareness of the limits of human existence is only one element in Baal's consciousness. It is balanced by more relaxed moods when he calmly enjoys the richness of the world. The permanence of the sky which in the "Ballad of the Adventurers" was a goading reminder of human transience is seen in the "Chorale of the Great Baal" as a reassuring symbol, a guarantee that the individual's life partakes for a while of eternity:

> only the sky, but *always* the sky
> covered his nakedness with its might. (B, 7)

> As in the earth's dark womb lay rotting Baal
> the sky was still as great and calm and pale. (B, 9)

Baal is able in this mood to savour his taste of eternity by refusing to be distressed by the thought of his own transitoriness. Viewed with such equanimity transience can even appear to be a blessing. Not only does the death of others mean less competition for the favours of *Frau Welt* ("Dame World")[3] but transience also prevents pleasure becoming stale. Thus the Baal of the "Chorale" simply abandons any woman when he has had enough of her and thinks of death simply as the "full stop" at the end of a satisfied life: "what is the world to Baal now? Baal has had his fill." A life of such undisturbed, bovine tranquillity as is conjured up in this poem is, of course, as one-sided a fantasy of wish-fulfilment as the "Ballad of the Adventurers" was one of raging intensity. Taken together, however, the poems reveal the tension between opposing attitudes to which Baal's consciousness is subject. In other poems the opposing pulls in the poet's mind between calm enjoyment of the world as it is and angry awareness of life's inadequacy express [themselves] in a variety of tones, ranging from the metaphysical lavatory humour of "Orge's Favourite Place" ("A place that humbles, where you ascertain / that you're a man who nothing may retain" — B, 22) to the mixture of sensuous lyricism and harshness in the elegiac "Ballad of the Drowned Girl" (B, 74). Baal's poetry does not always succeed in controlling the conflict between his perception of life's harshness and his dreams of transcending the limits of existence. Thus, in the poem "Death in the Forest" there is an awkward change of focus from a close-up cf a man's desperate death-agonies to a distant, sentimental vision of the early sun lighting the crown of the tree under which the man is buried. This lapse into false pathos was originally Brecht's, but it is put to good dramatic use in the context of the play, since the loss of poetic control is presented ironically as a symptom of the hero's apprehensions about the approach of death; his companion Ekart comments drily, "Well. Well. So that's how far things have gone" (B, 80).

Baal's poems show him as having both a reflective and a determined cast of mind. He is constantly aware of his own transience, yet always bent on mastering the problem. With this degree of self-consciousness he cannot simply be regarded as an "animal" or as a mythical figure, since gods and animals are presumably spared either the fore-knowledge or the experience of personal death. On the other hand, Baal is larger than life in so many respects, particularly in his ruthless ability to live with the contradictions in his own nature, that the play cannot be read as a consistently realistic character-study. Baal is an embodiment of vitality which is of such enormous proportions that it often exercises a strange, almost magical fascination over men and women alike, but which also, very occasionally, has to struggle to assert itself against his own human weaknesses. He is a symbolic hero whose imaginative function is to exorcise the existential fears in the mind from which he sprang. The wish-fulfilling fantasy of *Baal* lies in its offering as an answer to the problems of conflict and transience, not a flight into a conflict-free existence, but a dream of transience accepted, of conflict enjoyed and of contradiction sustained with equanimity.

At first sight *Baal* can give the impression of being a formless, loose play in which the protagonist just seems to drift in and out of a number of more or less unconnected situations and meet a variety of unrelated characters. While it is certainly true that it does not have anything like the economy and inner necessity of sequence characteristic of classical drama, it does have a unifying pattern of action which holds together the variety of his experience. As Eric Bentley puts it, the play presents a variant of "the archetypal battle of life and death, Eros and Thanatos."[4] To perceive this underlying unity we need to consider the imagery of the play, the music accompanying Baal's "Dance with Death."[5]

The play opens with a party given in Baal's honour by Mech, a capitalist who would like to publish Baal's poetry. The party ends in disarray after Baal has insulted his would-be patron and blatantly attempted to seduce his wife. There is more to Baal's treatment of Mech than the Bohemian's dislike of bourgeois convention or the anarchist's revolt against capitalist exploitation. The clash of two social types is also a clash between a figure of life and a figure of death. Mech has made his fortune in the timber business: "Whole forests of cinnamon-wood swim down Brazilian rivers for me" (*B*, 11). Throughout the play trees figure as life-symbols, while rivers, by an ancient tradition, represent transience, the force of death. Thus from the moment Mech introduces himself to Baal he is presenting himself in the role of an embodiment of death. His party therefore has macabre implications which are hinted at by the words with which he offers Baal food: "That is the corpse of an eel" (*B*, 11). The celebration which is to lead to Baal's commercial exploitation is thus revealed as a threat to kill him spiritually by making his poetry an object of use (like the trees felled for Mech's profit) and consumption (like that other delicacy, the eel), and foreshadows his eventual literal submission to the power of death. Baal's response to this challenge, his seduction of Mech's wife Emily, also has symbolic overtones: faced with the advance of his enemy, death, Baal wrests from his hands an object of beauty and pleasure which he might otherwise have allowed to pass him by. From this first encounter it can be seen that death is both enemy and ally to Baal, since every confrontation with it stimulates him to extend his vital energies and appetites to the full before death claims its eventual victory. Although he will cling to life to the very last Baal is not concerned with mere survival. Not only does he accept the fact of his transience, he even accelerates his own destruction by his pursuit of the utmost intensity of experience.[6] Knowing that he can do nothing to increase the quantity of life ceded to him, Baal is willing to side with his enemy in the task of attrition in exchange for the heightened quality of life thereby achieved. Baal is strong enough to face up to the paradox that the "blossoming" country of life is also the "hostile territory" of death.[7] Whereas many are dismayed by the knowledge that in living they are dying, Baal is able to rejoice in the fact that in dying he is living, that death, as Hofmannsthal put it, is a "great God of the soul."[8]

Baal's need to experience constantly the transitoriness of his life is the impulse that governs all his behaviour. All Baal's encounters with other individuals or with nature form part of a symbolic confrontation between the protagonist and his constant but hidden antagonist, death. It is this underlying symbolic action which links such public scenes as "In the all-night café Cloud of the Night" (B, 42–6) or "Village pub. Evening" (B, 47–51) with scenes of a more intimate kind. In the scene in the all-night café Baal, who is employed to sing to the guests, breaks his contract with the owner of the establishment, ostensibly because he is not given enough schnapps, but the backdrop of the scene ("When the door is open the blue night can be seen" — B, 42) suggests that the deeper reason for his behaviour is his need to be free of any ties with a routine way of life in order to be able to hold at the centre of his consciousness the conflict between eternity (represented by the sky) and the brevity of his own life. There are similar symbolic overtones in the scene in the village pub where Baal persuades some greedy peasants to bring all the bulls from the surrounding district into the village that evening by promising to buy the bull with the most powerful loins. The bull is a traditional symbol of the fertility-god whose name Baal bears. Besides the superficial "Till Eulenspiegel" pleasure of duping the peasants, Baal's motive in making this arrangement is his desire to stage a celebration of vitality against the background of the evening sky:

> BAAL: [*leans back in his chair*] At twilight, in the evening — It has to be evening, of course, and of course the sky must be cloudy, when the air is mild and a slight breeze is blowing, then the bulls will arrive. They will trot in from all sides, it will be a powerful sight. (B, 50)

The pleasure aroused by the sight of the bulls' vitality is inseparable in Baal's mind from the fact that they will be seen in a setting of wind, clouds and evening sky, the beauty of which heightens and is heightened by the mood of transience it expresses. Baal's overriding preoccupation with death informs all his behaviour, even where this is not clearly indicated by scenic or verbal symbolism. His brutality towards his lovers of both sexes, for example, is rooted in his determination to allow nothing to set premature limits to his pursuit of pleasure. For his will to accept any form of inhibition would mean the impairment of his vitality. When he murders Ekart for flirting with a barmaid, Baal's motive is not simply sexual jealousy, but stems from long-seething anger at Ekart's resistance to his domination. He is prompted to violence because Ekart's refusal to submit to his will at a time when Baal's vital energies are beginning to ebb is a painful reminder of the final limit which the world will set to his self-assertion.

Baal's ambivalent experience of transience, as a threat and as a source of intensified pleasure, pervades the imagery of the play. Both the river and the wind are traditional symbols of transience. In Baal's experience, however, both become sources of sensuous pleasure and vital renewal. As Baal walks through the fields at the height of summer he revels in the sensations it gives him:

> BAAL: [*walking slowly through the fields*] Since the sky is greener and pregnant, July air, no shirt in my trousers! [*Calls back to Ekart*] They whet my bare thighs. My skull is filled by the breeze, in the hair of my armpits hangs the smell of the fields. The air is trembling as if it were drunk on brandy. (*B*, 46)

Baal's love of the wind becomes identification with it at certain moments:

> BAAL: And now you belong to the wind, white cloud! [*Goes to her quickly, flings the door shut, takes Sophie Barger in his arms*] (*B*, 37)

The suicide by drowning of Johanna, a girl whom Baal seduces, establishes early in the play the sombre aspect of the river symbolism. Its sensuous aspect, on the other hand, is brought out in scenes where Baal lies in the sun after soaking in the warm water of a stream or when he advises the young Johannes to revel in life instead of wasting it writing poetry:

> BAAL: What do you have to write poems for anyway? When life's so decent: like when you lie on your back on a tearing current, shooting downstream, naked under an orange-coloured sky and you see nothing except the sky as it turns violet and then becomes black as a hole. (*B*, 26)

In the "Ballad of the Drowned Girl," a poem inspired by Johanna's suicide, Baal's imagination manages to hold together the beautiful and the deadly aspects of this symbol in its sensuous evocation of a corpse's slow drift down a stream. On two occasions Baal goes off to bathe in the river after particularly repulsive encounters with death — at a Corpus Christi procession and in the paupers' hospital. His immersion in the stream, by virtue of the ambiguity of the river symbol, is both a ritual surrender to death and at the same time a renewal and purification of his will to go on living.

Colours are much used in the play to convey the fullness of experience

Baal derives from his confrontation with transience. His favourite colours — white, black, red — all acquire the same ambiguity, as they are
variously applied to images of life at one moment and of death at the next.
White is the colour of appetising young flesh *and* of corpses, while black is
associated both with growth in the womb and with rotting in the grave.
These are not simply contrary associations, but mutually enriching ones.
The whiteness of young skin is made the more appetising rather than less
by the fact that its pallor conveys a message of *memento mori* which
intensifies Baal's pleasure in the passing moment.[9] While Baal enjoys the
sheer fact of the sky's permanence, he also enjoys it as a constantly
changing showplace of colour and movement: were it not for the passing
of time Baal would not be able to relish the sight of the sky sometimes
filled with clouds, sometimes with stars, sometimes empty, or variously
pale, dark, green, orange, purple, yellow, violet, apricot. These striking,
but truly observed colours convey the intensity of Baal's perception of his
world. The simple sentence-structures in which they occur give full weight
to each individual image, just as, on a larger scale, the "balladesque"
composition of the play as a sequence of short scenes also helps to suggest
the repleteness of Baal's life, because it picks out only moments of
particular intensity which, taken together, give an impression of kaleido-
scopic variety. As well as giving his hero a sensuousness of language (what
one of his victims describes as "his bloody wonderful chat" — B, 20) to
convey the vividness of Baal's perception of the world, Brecht also creates
a richly textured environment for him to respond to. Most of the people he
meets are what one would call "colourful" characters — the indignant but
understanding landlady with her earthy, comical mixture of metaphor,
slang and dialect, the particularly vulgar and cynical exploiters, Mech and
Mjurk, the tough lumberjacks in whose hut he dies. The play operates
with stark contrasts: in one scene Baal is shown composing a poem in
celebration of summer as the zenith of life ("Red. Scarlet. Voracious" — B,
34) while in the background there can be heard a beggar's hurdy-gurdy,
symbol of life's monotony and exiguousness. The contrasts in Baal's
consciousness acquire an almost Baroque grotesqueness and antithetical
sharpness in the poor-house scene, where a baby cries in the background as
a group of cancerous, mad or syphilitic adults carouse, squabble and
attempt to fornicate in the foreground. By these various means Baal is
given a heightened, at times melodramatic, world to live in, in order to
suggest the intensity of experience which Brecht imagines could be
achieved by a man who never for one moment forgets that in living he is
dying.[10]

Baal challenges the traditional emphases of *Vanitas* poetry. Whereas
the sinful, ugly or impermanent features of temporal existence were once
cited to persuade men to turn their minds away from the delusions of this
world and towards the glory of the next, *Baal* urges positive acceptance of
the transitoriness, ugliness and so-called evil of life as sources of pleasure,

amusement and heightened awareness. Brecht's presentation of Baal's life aims to unhinge our normal moral judgements. The various ways in which he suggests the exciting texture of Baal's experiences are part of this strategy. The constant focus on the fact of his transience also contributes to the task of moral subversion, as does the lack of morality in many of Baal's competitors, since this makes him appear to be simply more successful at playing life's dirty games than others. Where his victims are not seen to merit rough treatment because of their moral faults, the characters' own weakness or stupidity make it seem that they share at least some of the blame for Baal's exploitation of them. This applies to Johannes and Johanna, Emilie, Sophie and Ekart who are all willing victims in the sense that they all feel a degree of erotic attraction to Baal's animal vitality. Ekart's fate is that of a Pied Piper who is killed by a rat, since it is he who first challenges Baal to shake off the last vestiges of attachment to life in the city in order to confront fully the oneness of life and death in nature. In the event he proves not to be strong enough to live with the ruthless vision of life which he himself conjures up at the beginning. Yet it is not the case that no strong objections are raised in the play to Baal's conduct. The scene where he leaves the pregnant Sophie completely alone in the dark forest, for example, ends with her screams of terror. Baal's later desertion in *his* extremity by the woodcutters, however, does not so much suggest that some kind of natural moral order is punishing Baal for his deviancy from its laws, as confirm that he was right in believing that no individual *really* cares for another. The callousness of the woodcutters towards the dying Baal seems only to be a particularly clear instance of existential isolation and mutual indifference. Yet Baal is himself not completely immune from remorse. The drowning Johanna stays in his memory for a long time, so that he is compelled to write the "Ballad of the Drowned Girl" to exorcise this particular "Gespenst" ("ghost" — *B*, 74). His murder of Ekart both produces an immediate sense of shock in him and returns to haunt him in his dying minutes. Yet these "scruples" are only introduced into the play in order to be trampled down. Taken as a whole the play argues that moral considerations are simply a means of evading the imperative of the appetites, a form of weakness which must be overcome if the human animal is not to be prevented from living life to the full by the spurious illusions of communal bonds conjured up by his fear of existential isolation.[11] This movement "beyond" morality is very clearly the effect achieved through the presentation of Baal's dying moments:

> [*Silence*]
> BAAL: Mamma! Tell Ekart to go away, the sky's so damned near, close
>   enough to touch, everything's dripping wet again. Try sleeping.
>   One. Two. Three. Four. You can't breathe in here. It must be bright
>   outside. I want to go out. [*Raises himself*] I shall go out. Dear Baal.
>   [*Sharply*] I am *not* a rat. It must be bright outside. Dear Baal. One

can still reach the door. One still has knees, it's better at the door. Damnation! Dear Baal! [*He crawls on all fours to the threshold*] Stars . . . hmmm. [*He crawls outside*] (*B*, 92)

Although Baal experiences familiar human conflicts he does not allow them to destroy him. At the last he is given heroic stature by his ability to push aside his fears and remorse and to devote his last strength to crawling out of the hut for a last glimpse of the stars. His dying grunt of satisfaction is the reward for the brutal consistency of his life.[12]

Baal has strengths and weaknesses which are connected with its nature as a fantasy of mastery over life. The task of imagining a life which would succeed in transforming what are usually the causes of pain into sources of pleasure produced a play of varied, nuanced moods and richness of texture. The underlying symbolic action of a duel or dance with death meant that the biography had thematic unity. Whether this unity, which is conveyed through the ambiguities of the imagery, can be successfully rendered in theatrical performance is, however, questionable. The adoption of Baal's perspective on life, which is the source of the play's colour and intensity, unfortunately resulted in too little attention being paid to the development of the other characters. All too often the dialogue lacks any true dramatic tension because Baal's *Größe*, his strength, vitality and capacity for intense experience are not matched by equal qualities in those around him or sufficiently challenged by opposing forces. Dramatic balance is best achieved in those scenes where Baal's powers are clearly confronted by those of his true antagonist, Death, as in "Trees in the Evening" (*B*, 51), where Baal's confidence is shaken by the sight of the felled trees (the mighty who are fallen), or in the poor-house scene where the ravages of death and decay leer at Baal from all sides, eventually putting him to flight. Although the size of the problems Baal confronts calls for a figure of superhuman stature to master them, and although the oppressive experience of transience makes it attractive to suspend disbelief in his ability to get the better of the problem, the fantasy is ultimately unsatisfying. Caspar Neher commented aptly to Brecht, "Your *Baal* is as good as ten litres of gin" (*dbB*, 99); it is a play which offers temporary intoxication but leaves behind a nasty hangover. Precisely because it would take a character as implausible as Baal to achieve the imagined mastery over life, the play only serves to magnify the lack of such mastery attainable by normal men. Despite its celebration of human vitality, an important thing to do in the dark months of the war and its aftermath,[13] the play does not in the end leave one any better equipped to cope with the complicated muddle of egotism and altruism, desire and apathy, strength and weakness which is what constitutes real experience for most of us, as it did for Brecht himself.

Despite its faults the emotional vigour of Brecht's first play has lasted well, and it continues to enjoy successful productions. It is also indispensable reading for anyone who would understand Brecht's development. It is interesting, for example, that the fascination with *Größe* ("grandeur") evident in his earlier nationalist enthusiasm was capable of detaching itself from an abstract and general object and attaching itself to a particular individual. If this was possible, the process could presumably be reversed, as indeed happened some ten years later. It is also worth knowing that Brecht began, not as a realist first and foremost, but as a subjective rebel both against the limitations of an imperfect world and against the constraints, compromises and complexities of psychological reality. The emotional energy apparent in *Baal* enabled him later to create effective characters and situations which manage to live theatrically despite the intellectual burden they have to bear as agents of the historical dialectic. Brecht's early sympathy with the transient individual, and his understanding that men may be ruthless in the pursuit of happiness simply because they are "only here once"[14] provided a counterpoise to the tendency of ideology to encourage a person to take an abstract, oversimplified view of behaviour. It is also important to appreciate the independence and irreverence of Brecht's early attitudes to prevailing literary trends and tastes, since it is these qualities of spirit which later enabled him to resist pressures to conform to the formulae of "socialist realism." On the other hand, the powerful will to master reality which worked *with* Baal in this play was equally capable of turning against him and his like when a different kind of mastery became the goal.

Notes

1. [Ed. note: The following abbreviations for works by Brecht have been used by the author in this article: B, *Baal* (Potsdam: Kiepenheuer, 1922); *dbB, Baal. Der böse Baal der asoziale*, ed. Dieter Schmidt (Frankfurt am Main: Suhrkamp, 1968); *D, Im Dickicht der Städte*, ed. Gisela Bahr (Frankfurt am Main: Suhrkamp, 1968); *Diaries, Diaries 1920-1922*, ed. Herta Ramthun, trans. John Willett (London: Eyre Methuen, 1979); *GW, Gesammelte Werke in 20 Bänden* (Frankfurt am Main: Suhrkamp, 1967); *T, Tagebücher 1920-1922: Autobiographische Aufzeichnungen 1920–1954*, ed. Herta Ramthun (Frankfurt am Main: Suhrkamp, 1975). Quotations in the original German have been omitted here; translations from the German are by the author.]

2. The influence of Frank Wedekind's *Erdgeist (Earth-Spirit)* on *Baal* was very evident in the first version of the play, where Baal's repeated shouts of "Hoppla!" were reminiscent of the ringmaster who speaks the prologue to Wedekind's play — see *Baal: Drei Fassungen* (Frankfurt a.M., 1966) pp. 16, 30, 32. In his admiration for Wedekind Brecht went so far as to describe him as one of the "greatest educators of the new Europe" (*GW*, 15, 4).

3. The figure of "Frau Welt" (called "das große Weib Welt" in the Chorale) was a popular subject of medieval literature and illustration. She is depicted as alluring when seen from the front, but disgusting from behind, and thus serves as an allegory of the world's deceitfulness. Brecht's early diaries contain a poem which appears to have been influenced by this tradition: "She turned her back toward me / A great fat worm appeared / (He wanted to reward me / And stood up to applaud me) / but I was simply scared." (*Diaries*, 17) [free translation].

4. *Theatre of War* (London, 1972) p. 126.

5. *Baal* was not Brecht's only play to be modelled on the medieval "Dance of death." The production notes for the *Songspiel Mahagonny* (1927) contain the following statement: "If the work is performed in some hall other than a theatre or concert-hall this has the advantage of making evident a certain affinity with the travelling theatres of the medieval period. MAHAGONNY IS A DANCE OF DEATH." *Songspiel Mahagonny*, ed. David Drew (Vienna, 1963) p. 7.

6. Brecht once noted "Life as a passion! That is how I conduct it. It is self-evident that it will destroy me" (*T*, 198). Brecht always lived intensely. In particular he had an extraordinary — and very bourgeois! — appetite for work. Had he not also been so unswervingly devoted to large, strong cigars, he might possibly have been spared a heart-attack at the age of 57. However, like Baal he chose quality rather than quantity of life.

7. In the first version of the play Baal says to a prison chaplain: "I withdraw into enemy territory. Into blossoming country . . . I flee from death into life," *Baal: Drei Fassungen* (Frankfurt a.M., 1966) p. 54. This territory is both blossoming and hostile because it is the domain of both life and death.

8. When Death visits the fool Claudio in Hofmannsthal's *Der Tor und der Tod (Death and the Fool)* he says to him: "A great god of the soul stands before you," *Gedichte und kleine Dramen* (Frankfurt a.M., 1966) p. 83. Although one tends to think of the coarse-grained Brecht and the finely-veneered Hofmannsthal as belonging to quite different worlds, Hofmannsthal was sufficiently interested by *Baal* to write a prologue for a performance of the play in Vienna in 1926.

9. One of Brecht's early sonnets takes as its theme the renewed stimulus to love and desire created by a sudden awareness of the first signs of grey in a woman's hair (*GW*, 8, 160–1).

10. Kenneth Tynan aptly remarked in his review of a London production of *Baal:* "The ideal audience for *Baal* would be entirely composed of people who remember, more than once or twice a day, that they are going to die. Firstnighters, as a group, do not like their noses rubbed in the fact of mortality; they prefer it to keep its distance and speak blank verse," *Observer Weekend Review*, 10 February 1963.

11. In his more cynical or despairing moments, which were not infrequent, the young Brecht would take the (Nietzschean) view that morality is an illusion created by men for their own comfort: "The purpose of morality is to make you believe you have something in common! But in reality there is no-one keeping an eye on you" (*D*, 136); "Almost all bourgeois institutions, almost the whole of morality, virtually the whole Christian legend are founded on man's fear of being alone, they distract his attention from his unutterable desolation on this planet, from his minute significance and his hardly perceptible roots" (*GW*, 15, 59–60). It must be remembered, however, that Brecht did not hold this view consistently. The liveliness of his early plays stems largely from the clash of competing perspectives in them.

12. In 1922 Brecht expressed the hope that he had succeeded in *Baal* and in *In the Jungle* in avoiding a great mistake of much art, namely the "attempt to whip up the spectator's emotions" ("ihre Bemühung mitzureißen" — *GW*, 15, 62). He then added, "It is usual for writers of tragedies to take the part of the hero towards the end, or in fact throughout. This is an abomination. They should take sides with nature" (*GW*, 15, 62). By the time he made these observations Brecht's writing had begun to incorporate an element of critical distance, but he neither had this intention, nor did he create this effect in the composition of *Baal*.

13. Hermann Hesse's "Novelle" *Klingsors letzter Sommer (Klingsor's Last Summer)* (Zurich, n.d.) which was written in 1919, when Brecht was working on the second draft of *Baal*, is remarkably similar to *Baal* in a number of respects. The story responds to the mood of anger and loss produced by the war with a sympathetic portrayal of an artist who throws his whole reserve of vitality into the struggle with his melancholy sense of transience. With

symbolic deliberation Klingsor chooses to paint in water colours which will rapidly fade; a much coarser version of the same attitude is to be seen in Baal's decision to hang up his latest poems for use in the lavatory (B, 40).

14. Cf. the remark made by Brecht in 1920: "I wish all things to be handed over to me, including power over all animals, and give as the reason for my demand the fact that I am only present *once*" (T, 197).

Mastery or Slavery? [On Brecht's Early Plays]

Antony Tatlow*

In the course of a celebrated essay Roland Barthes took issue with traditional Racine criticism which proceeded discreetly from play to play, evaluating their internal dynamics from a view of history or belief read through posited authorial biography. He reflected that it might well be time to "psychoanalyse the University."[1] When the critic's sympathies and those of the author coincide, such symbiosis can elicit wonders of recreative interpretation whose limits will lie where the interpretive frame can no longer satisfy the reader's perception of wider dynamics. Hugh Kenner's account of Pound in *The Pound Era* (London, 1972) derives from such sympathetic capacity and is likewise tested by the boundaries of its frame. But when the critic chooses to locate the structural properties of works of art in terms of psychobiography, interpretation may well be grounded in the "subconscious impulse" (3)[2] of that critic who has projected them onto the object of investigation.

Ronald Speirs seeks to disengage Brecht's early plays from their position in orthodox Marxist criticism, represented for him by Ernst Schumacher's work,[3] which stands for all readings of the early work as an anticipatory and superceded stage, at most the product of anarchic energy, before the transition to objectivity and partisanship. The early plays are read through later authorial exculpation, a smokescreen of rectifying commentary, and the text, where possible, is the sanitised 1950ies version. In the last thirty years, however, the elaborations of Brecht's manuscripts have been more or less clarified. Although the first versions of his plays have not all been coherently published, it is possible to reconstruct them, hence to argue from material evidence unavailable to Schumacher in 1955, no matter what use he might have made of it.

Although Speirs is aware of problems concerning Brecht's Marxism, it does not suit his purpose to investigate, even if only to argue with, more complex Marxist or "materialist" readings of these early plays or of their relation to the later work. His book contains an extensive bibliography but

*From *Colloquia Germanica: Internationale Zeitschrift für germanische Sprach- und Literaturwissenschaft* 17, no. 3/4 (1984):289–304. Reprinted and revised by permission of the author.

little evidence either of any engagement with arguments in studies uncongenial to his own position, or that he has taken much account of methodological debates during the last twenty years. Marxist criticism is restricted to a one-dimensional "theory of reflection" which he, like many Marxist critics, finds tedious. His study therefore stands outside and against contrary positions adequate to his own reading, hence it must rest on its internal consistency and on the inherent claim to represent the most persuasive account of the structure and value structure of Brecht's work. Speirs does not completely ignore the problems in such a procedure. In writing for "a wider readership than a purely academic one" (4) — good luck to him — he is conscious of presenting one side of an "*implicit* debate" (4), obviated in the interest of this readership. By and large we get the readers we deserve — though not always the reviewers — and some of those readers may feel underestimated. I wish to make part of that debate explicit by describing his judgments and examining the assumptions on which they rest. Since he claims his stance explains the early work but can also be extended as a means of evaluating the later plays, the subject of the last chapter, this implicit debate ranges over all Brecht's dramatic work. The claim of his method is larger than the title of his book.

How is this claim grounded? He wishes to understand Brecht's early plays "in their own terms" (2f.). The "imaginative structure" (4) as object of analysis is not therefore projected onto the plays from an extraneous, prevalidated theoretical frame, but in some as yet unspecified manner derived from those plays themselves. Given this methodological claim, it is surprising that he does not investigate the structural properties of these plays as texts or compare the considerable variations between manuscript stages. Perhaps this is thought unnecessary since the "imaginative structure," common to all the early plays, offers the key to their understanding.

Given the considerable structural differences among the early plays, ranging from *Die Bibel* (*The Bible*) to *Mahagonny*, this imaginative structure, with its implications for the later work, may only be discernible at the cost of a high level of abstraction which might well conflict with the initial and empirical supposition that they could indeed be read "in their own terms." Speirs squares this hermeneutic circle by thus qualifying his methodological perspective: "in their own terms and in relation to the views he held at the time of writing them" (3). Claiming Brecht's "views" between *Baal* and *Mahagonny* hardly changed, and seeing the "imaginative structure" as shaping the juvenile war poetry and his first play, *The Bible*, as well as extending to the later work, Speirs argues that the products of these distinct ideological phases rest upon a common base, upon an "interpretive construct" (4), the concept of "mastery." With its synonym, "control," this latter term occurs more than ninety times in a text of 188 pages. It is the book's obsession. What does it imply?

It implies that the "views" Brecht held derive, not from any theoretically clarified political, psychoanalytical or linguistic structure, but from an apparently empirical psycho-biographical construct, called Brecht. The evidence is largely selected from the plays themselves and we enter, at such a juncture, into a familiar circle; with some assistance from the *Diaries*,[4] though almost none from the poetry, an author is constructed whose predilections then justify the "imaginative structure" of those plays. In addition, the work offers an imaginative solution for a psychothera-peutic problem, held constitutive for the constructed psycho-biography, underlying all superficial dramatic objectifications. This solution is also imaginary for the problem is essentially insoluble. How is this problem located, and to what extent do the plays attempt to offer respite from its pressure?

This study's dominant analytical method consists in observing a series of opposite terms ranging from the biographical to the abstract — dominance/softness, hysteria/control, nature/civilisation, mastery/life are some examples. These oppositions are constantly juxtaposed. One recurrent stylistic device is therefore the phrase: "on the one hand . . . on the other hand." The basis for this procedure lies in the psycho-biographical assumption that Brecht's was a "divided mind" (8) and that the character-istics of such a "divided personality" (3), and the energy of the work, consist in an attempt to bring these opposing terms, or what they stand for, into relation, in order to establish "artistic unity" (30), "emotional balance and control" (50).

But a fundamental dilemma underpins these oppositions: the desire, and ultimate failure, of the "existential self" (59) to acquire "mastery" (passim) over "the harsh realities of life" (17). Though the content of these particular terms might be thought to shift, with consequences for the consistency of the argument, this dilemma, as fundamental opposition, appears to find its explanation in psycho-biography, but is ultimately contained by a theological frame of explanation. Every attempt of the existential self to achieve mastery over "life's problems" (13) is doomed to fail, because the only true solution, access to a "transcendental world" (18), is denied almost from the start. Such suppositions provide the deep structure of this study.

If the ultimate fundament is theological, finally justified by critical predilection, though it goes without saying that this structure is not quite gratuitously imposed upon the work, for then we would dismiss rather than engage with the critic's evaluations, the other consequence from the division of Brecht's mind apparently affords less satisfaction, since it entails potentially disastrous consequences, as it enabled the work. The predicament of the sympathetically observed "existential self" calls forth in Brecht the urge to mastery, to find a "grand design for life" (172), an enterprise that appears inherently inimical to the spirit of empiricism. The purpose of this grand design, apart from promising "comprehensive mastery" (172) lies in its capacity for sanctioning aggressive impulses and hence satisfying, while combining private and public, an intrinsic and clearly proto-Nietzschean will to power. The characters in the early plays therefore exhibit various degrees of sado-masochism. Brecht's teenage enthusiasm for Germany's spiritual mission in war stems from the same impulse to totalisation, promising "complete mastery of life" (15), that later offered, in Communism, a necessary "outlet for his pugnacity" (172), for "Brecht saw no sense in backing a loser" (172). In another characteristic disjunction, after abandoning nationalism Brecht's "critical intelligence" (172) was brought into conflict with his "other impulses" (172).

The attempts to overcome this opposition between the emotions and the intellect constitute the basis of Speirs's whole argument. Brecht should have recognised this contradiction because its spurious resolution later led him into error and resulted in inferior work, though it may have brought emotional contentment. Through Marxism "Brecht was able to re-integrate to a considerable extent moral, emotional and intellectual impulses" (172) in conflict since his early nationalism. Such integration, in his nationalist phase, enabled him to hero-worship the Emperor and, in the later manifestation, to embrace the butcher. The trouble, in other words, always begins at that point where Brecht — or his work, but they are treated synonymously — moves from depicting a tragic existential predicament towards the search for a means of overcoming it. There are no such means, the existential predicament is absolute. The endemic quest for mastery therefore constitutes the whole problem, one which is then read into the work, emerging out of it as judgments that can only appeal, to recycle one of his own revealing phrases, to "the ignorant or the already converted" (181).

It is therefore apparent, and Speirs does not conceal it, that this book returns, in a more sophisticated form, to Esslin's argument of the late Fifties. As such it partakes of a new vogue in Brecht criticism.[5] The model schizophrenic rides again, combatting "subconscious impulse" with "conscious control" (3). These neglected "subjective factors" (3) have, in reality, shaped the work. The attempt to extend the scope of such factors beyond psycho-biography rests on how they are ultimately explained by that phenomenological abstraction: the "existential self." As product of the "human condition" (96), resulting from "individual isolation" (92), subject to the "fierce truths at the heart of life" (157), conscious of the "transcendental void" (89), and in view of the "destructive forces . . . ranged against Man" (96), the existential self moves, during the course of this analysis, from a convenient objectification, and simplification, of a biographical subject to a dominant position as theoretical concept in the study's deep structure.

The isolated existential self can only be judged in terms of moral absolutes, since it is, by definition, independent of all relativities. The absence of social contact, its apparent impossibility, is merely proof of the value of the phenomenological construct. Given the logic of such a position, it is unsurprising that, for example, the soldiers in *The Life of*

Edward II of England are not just seen as helpless victims, as pawns of fortune, slaughtered in the struggles of the great, but as such existential selves with the capacity and responsibility of moral analysis and choice: "On the other hand, the contradiction between the soldiers' willingness to fight senseless battles and their awareness, expressed through their songs, of this very senselessness must also raise the question of their responsibility for their fate" (112). This passage also illustrates a trait of critical thinking that consistently risks violating the structure of Brecht's plays, in supposing that the words spoken by characters represent conscious and clarified analysis of that character's position which is available to, because spoken by, that character him- or herself. It implies, furthermore, a standard of psychological realism that, in my view, plays havoc with interpretation.

Since the psycho-biography is firmly linked to, is indeed practically synonymous with the dilemma of the phenomenological existential self, Speirs looks to the works, as trace of the former, for solutions or at least response to the latter's problems. Since the construct is categorical, everything is adduced as evidence of its persuasiveness. Since only the consolations of religion might lighten its burden, the critic welcomes appropriate symbolic suggestion from the work. The allusions may appear farfetched to those who do not share these predilections, the interpreta-tions overwrought. Brecht's first play, *The Bible*, written at the age of sixteen, offering the choice of sacrificing a daughter to the desires of an enemy general or the destruction of her town, pits religious and moral principle against human survival. Speirs finds the play paradigmatic. The grandfather insists that principles are sacrosanct, the girl's virginity will be protected, honour will be undamaged but the town, the girl and all inhabitants, in consequence, destroyed. To many he will appear a disas-trous bigot, but to Speirs "the play comes over as a drama of conflicting wills, which leaves as the strongest impression on the mind and feelings of the reader not an awareness of the insolubility of the moral dilemma, but admiration for the old man's integrity, strength and . . . 'greatness' " (13). His behaviour illustrates Brecht's "attraction to an ideal of personal strength as a way of achieving mastery over life's problems" (13). Here mastery takes the form of symbolic suicide, and there is far more than a casual connection between such symbolically suicidal imposition of the will and fascist proclivities.

That such ambivalence is present in Brecht has recently become a familiar theme. It is easy to see how the concept of mastery, exercised for its own sake, though doomed to failure by the inviolable conditions imposed on the existential self, can be aligned with a notion of a triumph of the will. By this process, Brecht's early interest in Nietzsche eventually turns him into a Nietzschean Marxist. Speirs argues, for example, that Brecht may well have misrepresented fascist anti-Semitism in *Round Heads and Pointed Heads* because he himself had felt "the insidious perennial attractions of all socially approved opportunities for the exercise of irrational aggression" (182). Though convinced that Brecht "genuinely felt scorn for the anti-Semitism of the Nazis" (182), he does speculate that Brecht, in 1918, denigrated the "supposed 'Jewish spirit' in the literature of German Expressionism" (182). Brecht does not refer to any "Jewish spirit"; the quoted passage sets expressionist ecstaticism against his own "material- ist" position, Brecht's own term in the 1918 letter to Neher which Speirs quotes, as drastically excerpted by Feilchenfeldt.[6] It is one thing to find the treatment of anti-Semitism in that play wanting, but quite another to attribute this inadequacy to an unconscious predilection for aspects of what is attacked, especially when so little evidence is adduced. Such a supposition would need powerful corroboration. Speirs's gloss stands on the edge of smear and insinuation.

Brecht's later work oversimplifies, though occasionally affording evidence of the religious paradigms that offer the only hope of combatting the fears of a transcendental void. Thus "Marian overtones in the maid Grusha's love for the 'high-born child' . . . cannot be ignored" [in *The Caucasian Chalk Circle*] (165 f.). But the plays are more likely to deny their characters consolation. *Life of Galileo* does not sufficiently consider that the new cosmology "will threaten the spiritual peace of faithful and simple Christians everywhere" (183), and such historical-materialist hard- headedness "precludes any serious consideration of the existential desola- tion and revulsion at the thought of . . . 'the terrifying starcovered sky' (*Diaries*, 39) which the young Brecht was honest enough to admit to feeling" (183).

Such passages make it abundantly clear that the critic thinks within a traditional Christian and Western perceptual frame, challenged and abandoned by Brecht himself, and that this forms the real standard for measuring the work. Mother Courage, for example, is thought to prove that "all man's misery" is attributable to "the imposition of a false 'order' on to the rich anarchy of the natural world" (183); this comment proves utter incomprehension of the dynamics of that play. In *Schweyk in the Second World War* "man's physical appetites are hymned as the source of all human goodness, whereas all evil is seen as issuing from the lack of suppression of appetite" (183). Again, this is a travesty of that play's stratagem and does not even, for example, take into account the damage done by Baloun's irrepressible appetite, whose celebration is anyway a carnival theme. Speirs "suspects that, underlying the propagandist reasons for glorifying nature and the appetites, there was a continuous personal reaction against his own lack of powerful appetites and against his awareness of the world's hostility to man" (183). Yet we are earlier told that Brecht's "various mistresses" (11), not to speak of his young playmates, all suffered from his "desire to dominate others" (11), though this may of course imply his sexuality was entirely sadistic, though that would scarcely make it any less an appetite, merely a nastier one.

The "problems of evil are too insistently reduced to the status of mere by-products of economic circumstance" (181) and although Shen Te and Shui Ta [in *The Good Person of Szechwan*] are "not intended to be understood psychologically" (182), they appear "arbitrary, constructed, even escapist" (182) when compared with "Brecht's neurotic, alcoholic, but above all jealous mistress" (182) Ruth Berlau. Instead of searching for social themes and a voice to express the social unconscious, Brecht should evidently have been portraying the tribulations of his jealous mistress in a style of psychological naturalism. These plays are, therefore, by no means judged "in their own terms," which is, of course, a methodological impossibility. This evident bias for psychological realism encourages Speirs to think of plots and characters as the naturalistic embodiment of real people, leading to literalist readings which inevitably flatten the ironies of interpretation. Hence, in the final chorale of *The Threepenny Opera*, "the audience is exhorted to be more charitable in the future" (149). The existentialist deep structure underlies all phenomenological realism. He sees Peachum's "belief in brutality as the obvious and proper response to the brutality of life" (150), which in turn explains "the despair of the transient individual as he contemplates his world, itself transitory, and his inability to satisfy his hunger for eternity" (150).

Mahagonny is read in terms of such existentially grounded psychological realism. Jim Mahoney "evokes compassion and respect for a man's efforts to meet suffering with dignity" (166) and because Brecht "did not, exceptionally, distort his poetic vision by forcibly imposing simplistic solutions on painful and difficult problems but sustained the conflicts and ambiguities in his vision to the bitter end" (169), this "tragically ambivalent" (156) figure, bereft of "metaphysical comfort" (157), subject to "the malevolence of an unreliable world" (167) and echoing Christ's Passion, sustains a "work of unusual force and integrity" (169). I do not wish to dispute these ecclesiastical parallels so much as the tone that accompanies their evaluation. Speirs concedes the ironic and parodistic use of biblical parallels but, given the nature of his deep structure, then recuperates the Christian existentialist problematic minus the ironies; then similarities turn out to be more persuasive than the differences, even when this whole play shows a "need for" not a "belief in" (167) transcendence. There is a Last Supper, a Gethsemane, Mahoney is tied to a Cross—though this was apparently a cage in the first version and is a lantern in my piano score, not a tree; why these changes if it was so significant?—a parallel to the release of Barabas and to Christ's commendation of his mother to his discipline (all on p. 166). The play thus becomes a via negativa. The beautiful crane duet expresses a "dream of transcendence" (167), constituting "the fullest articulation of a feeling that runs through the whole opera" (159), "melancholy" (160), where there is "no possibility of transcendence" (161), and proving "that Brecht's early reading in Eastern philosophy was rooted in something deeper than mere intellectual curiosity" (159).

The Mahoney/Christ parallel is taken as absolutely constitutive for the work, both as deliberate parody and as surrogate Imitatio, struggling to come to terms with the post-Nietzschean world. However one judges this use of biblical allusion, the underlying obsession, according to this view, cannot be denied. The analysis draws on Gaede's and Sehm's work.[7] Though Brecht clearly made extensive use of the Bible, in my view they all overestimate the importance of these echoes — is Galy Gay (in *Man is Man*) really the Apostle Peter? — which on occasion seem farfetched. Yet pressing the particularity of these parallels is less necessary to Speirs because the argument from existential isolation does not require, and in the case of the other plays does not receive, any such biblical gloss. This allusion to Eastern philosophy must appear marginal to many but is in fact central to the issues raised in this whole study. Representing a "dream of transcendence," the duet between Jim and Jenny, separately printed in *Hundert Gedichte* under the title "Die Liebenden" (The Lovers),[8] relates both to the narrower but elaborate parallel with the Bible and to the deep structure in all the early plays, yet [is] most satisfyingly expressed in *Mahagonny*.

Unlike W. H. Auden and Chester Kallman, Speirs understands the poem's imagery. The partners in flight across the sky are not, as in their Methuen translation, two cranes but crane(s) and cloud(s). Envisaging the lovers as two cranes, Auden's and Kallman's version upsets the poem's metaphorical texture.[9] But partly because of his penchant for psychological realism, for reading the text as if it expressed the dramatic situation directly, Speirs misses the point of that metaphorical structure. Conforming to his realist reading, this song illustrates "post-coital mood" (159) while Jenny makes ready for the next customer in the brothel. But though she will betray him when the money runs out, Jenny is still Mahoney's girl, ever since shedding her underwear to satisfy her "Christ." Speirs then refers "on the one hand" to his bugaboo, a Marxist reading, which should in fact suit his gloss that the scene illustrates "the destruction of human relations by the capitalist cash-nexus" (159), adding that Adorno, in this context, "comments weightily" (i.e., with teutonic heaviness, 203, n.),[10] only to suggest "on the other hand, and more plausibly" that it is "concerned with the brevity of sexual relations and with their failure to satisfy spiritual needs" (159). The song is then analysed in support of this supposition.

Leaving aside the false dichotomy, as an example of the simple antithetical binary form that sustains this whole study, we need to ask if, or to what extent, the poem supports such a reading as a post-coital dream of transcendence, suggestive of Eastern philosophy. [Speirs's] reading of the images shows the lovers as inviolably separate, as substantially incompatible in their existential isolation as are crane and cloud. Their "absorbing relationship . . . encloses them in a private sphere of seeming timelessness," as the whole poem "expresses a desire to transcend the material, instinctual sphere of mutual use and possession" (159). Given his presuppositions, this is a good reading, for he is sensitive to the poem's contradictions. The Marxist criticism, apparently rejected, is in fact absorbed into a critique of "materialism," but from a transcendental perspective — an approach characteristic of the whole study.

In my view, however, this poem should not be read, no more than most of the songs in Brecht's plays, as a direct equivalent for or articulation of dramatic representation. In some sense, of course, it arises, as they all do, from the dynamics of the play, though in fact the song was moved around, presumably because it does not grow organically out of this scene, in any realist sense. It is, in reality, grossly misconnected to the manic activity in the brothel, though on a deeper level the contradictory juxtaposition is entirely appropriate. On this deeper level, the poem has more to do with the expression of a collective or social unconscious than with any naturalistically grounded, masculine, post-coital gloom. It is a lyrical abstraction from, rather than a dramatic representation of the characters' plight. What, therefore, are the metaphorical implications of the imagery?

In East Asia the crane has always been revered as a symbol both of longevity and of faithfulness; it became one of the most popular icons in East Asian art. Apart from a deep admiration for their beauty, for their elaborate courtship dance and for the marvel of their flight, the "material" basis for such symbolisation lay in the observation that cranes mate for life and, after their migrations, often return to the same nests, year after year. Thus they stood for continuance, fortitude, dignity and the gracefulness of nature. In the Buddhist context of opposition to the dust of the world, clouds signify purity, but they also associate irrevocable transience in East Asian poetry, just as they do for Brecht.

In this poem there are two sets of apparent oppositions: between the crane(s) and the cloud(s), and between them both and the wind. In the first set they stand to each other as longevity to transience, fidelity to fickleness, substantiality to the ephemeral. In the second set of oppositions these seemingly contrary terms are related and unified in the difference that is established between what they have in common, as beautiful, natural phenomena, and the invisible wind which, nevertheless, stands to them not just antithetically as agent of "das Nichts" [the void] but relationally as the sustaining and limiting condition of their existence. Beyond these oppositions, therefore, lies another which appears, but only appears, absolute: between all that which is and nothing.

The fascination of the poem depends on how the metaphors, in their relationships, merge and disperse, both as images, objective correlatives of that which they evoke, and as symbolised perception. Although this song most assuredly transcends the values of the brothel, and although we may read it as lyrical speech from the unconscious, the force and lightness of its desire, so finely realised in its interlacing terza rima, do not suggest that it can be most satisfactorily read as an absolute, as a "dream of transcendence" tout court. As finely wrought poetic thought, the song envisages the conditions of life, testing the limits of the ascertainable, not in the hope that they might be transcended, for that is impossible, but as an expression of desire that the attainable might be attained, though here it can only be actualised lyrically in the unconscious. In the metaphorical language of the poem, the wind cannot dispel the lovers who hold with each other, even though they will eventually be separated; on the contrary, the wind has brought them together, it has created them. The poem is, therefore, not a dream of transcendence but rather a denial of the possibility of transcendence and here, precisely, lie the most stimulating connections with East Asian thought. It must be said that these are not the associations many anticipate. These expectations usually involve some form of philosophical quietism and a denial of meaning in the material world, of material substantiality in the name of some metaphysical value. But East Asian philosophy can be differently categorised. Of course, Buddhism has its ascetic practices and there are also metaphysical and symbolic systems which recall Western analogies, in terms of which they are usually viewed, but the most stimulating thought is differently aligned. Even the Buddhist nirvana had an affirmatory character quite alien to any avowedly Buddhist-influenced Schopenhauerian pessimism. To what extent Brecht perceived this is a secondary question. What matters is that these other analogies exist, and they point beyond Brecht's perspectives to future possibilities.

We can see that this poem presents a view of reality strikingly akin to the process-orientated, relational mode of thinking in Taoism, philosophical Buddhism, pragmatic Zen, which all realise human values as relationally constrained by the natural world. Such refusal to think in absolutist and idealist categories which have so dominated Western thought, this reluctance to indulge in dreams of transcendence, because the pursuit is vain and irrelevant since process constantly transcends fixed form in real spirit-matter and abstractions deny time as well as experiential human values, this acceptance of nothing as a condition within existence, leads to an ultimately unregretting, though naturally saddened, acknowledgment of personal transience because that self has never been predicated on any form of transcendental validation. Just as the self is socially interwoven with all other selves, its own materiality is in constant process, and this passage, this flight through time, must be savoured in its fullness for what it is. Validation is the realisation of the self's natural potential as a relational, not absolute, being. There is no cause to fear the wind, and the cloud's transience is merely another form of the crane's longevity. Cultures which can only think in terms of transcendent absolutes, which are reified absences, show signs of philosophical psychosis.

Mahagonny's lovers' duet links themes of the early and late work. Speirs reads it back into, and only in terms of, the early work, as an expression of his fundamental category: the existential self. But Brecht's understanding of East Asian culture changed and since he was beginning to study East Asian philosophy by 1929, the way he "studied" anything, picking out what was of use, there may well be a connection between this poem and his growing appreciation of relational thought. In a world subject to process, there is no "Halt"; it is precluded by the conditions of existence. Such thinking, like philosophical and social Taoism, is much closer to a Marxist relational philosophy of process and its call to realise human potential, also as a function of this process, than to any abnegating, isolationist or quietist pessimism that so often stands for the whole of East Asian philosophy. Brecht's early reading shows plainly enough that East Asian philosophy then functioned as abjuration, in the name of unflinching realism, of his mother's Christianity and its promise of transcendence as well as of his father's optimistic, bourgeois positivism. As several critics have indicated, there is a distinctly Nietzschean ring in his acceptance of man's absolute impotence in the face of nature: "A Chinese sentence: When the grains of sand turn against people, people must go away" (*Diaries*, 49). He read Lao Tse in similar terms. But such a view must itself be situated, as I have indicated elsewhere.[11] It does not represent the range and force of Taoist thought, no more than Lao Tse, as Speirs tells us, taught a "denial of the will" (8). This is a particularist, ascetic distortion of Taoist thought. At most it can stand for denial of the self-centered will in favour of realising the self's relational nature, whether with a partner in love, or by rejecting social dominance which others seek to impose in disregard of their own relational obligations. Brecht's affinity with Taoist relationalism, evident in a poem like "Vergnügungen" (*GW*, 10:1022; "Pleasures")[12] came later and via his appreciation of the inalienable social component in Taoist thought which suited his own form of Marxism so well. But in his early Nietzschean phase, and here Speirs is absolutely right, the main hope of response to such an apparently indifferent nature lay, not in quietism, let alone relationalism, but in an assertion of the will.

Mahagonny constitutes for Speirs the culmination of Brecht's achievement because it shows, without "forcibly imposing simplistic solutions" (169), the harsh realities of man's existential predicament. In this study's terminology, the play does not pretend to offer mastery of life's problems for they, in truth, cannot be mastered. What follows *Mahagonny* is a vain attempt to achieve such mastery in the social world. The fundamental categorical confusion is never completely eradicated and surfaces again at the end of his life, when it qualifies all efforts by the "pragmatic will" (188) to overcome the deficiencies of the "asocial vision" (188). Brecht's later work is vitiated by its inability to deal with, due in part to Brecht's unwillingness to engage with, the fundamental socio-anthropological contradiction between "the 'asocial' tendency of the transient individual to take self-satisfaction as his absolute in life, and the opposite tendency of society to regard each individual only as a function of the social whole"

(186). There is indeed a problematic, which Brecht later addresses, in the relationship between the individual and society, but this study's existentialist vocabulary proves inadequate as a method of analysing, let alone solving, these problems, for it reduces them all to the one insoluble existential dilemma. This attempt to press Brecht into the desired mould, and the condemnation of what cannot be so accommodated, results in a presentation that would normally be thought incompatible with the concept of critical objectivity, quite apart from its adequacy to the methodological claim on which it is based. But the analysis might not prove so damaging to this study's main topic, the early plays, provided that they prove more amenable to the categories of his analysis.

Writing in early 1922 of the need for "powerful new plays," Brecht supposes that they call "not so much for a heroic religion, as in the case of the great Greek tragedies, as for a powerful and consistent philosophy" (*Diaries*, 160). Though I have surmised that Speirs prefers a religious solution to the existential problem, and that this influences his analysis, in spite of the claim that it is located in Brecht's work and his personal thought, it is obvious, given such language in Brecht's biographical writing, that the interpretive construct, and the analysis it sustains, has its use. Yet the study argues, in effect, that such a philosophy is not forthcoming and that Marxism cannot later substitute for it, though it may function as surrogate. In the absence of such a philosophy, the characters' attempts at achieving mastery will mostly end in masochistic self-destruction. I would interpret this as the covert counterpart to, and indeed the only possible consequence of, the Nietzschean triumph of the will. Another possible course of action, however, is to forego the attempt at imposing one's will directly on circumstance, even though this leads to self-annihilation, but to change the self instead. By so changing, it is sometimes possible both to retain control and to survive. In the first category we find Baal, Shlink, Edward II and Fairchild; in the second, Kragler, Garga and Galy Gay.

In Speirs's analysis the behaviour of all of these characters is judged a function of the one interpretive construct, mastery, itself determined by the existentially-grounded psycho-biographical need of the author, as posited by the critic. That he does not always implement the stated intention of evaluating the plays "in their own terms," no matter how methodologically problematic that might be, is suggested by the surprising discovery that one play in each category meets with the same criticism, subsequently extended to the whole of Brecht's later Marxist work, that in them Brecht avoids facing up to the "harsh aspects of life" (58) or the opportunity to "render experience in its full harshness and complexity" (117). This failing vitiates the conclusions of these plays. Here the criteria of judgment clearly derive from existential suppositions extraneous both to the plays and their author. Edward II, for example, should have been despatched, as he was in Marlowe, in a savage parody of his homosexuality, by having a red-hot poker rammed up his arse. He is not, Speirs argues, because this would have detracted from the sense of mastery Brecht wished to project, though one could equally suppose such a death could be considered the ultimate "heroic-masochistic triumph" (117), an incomparably finer challenge than merely submitting to being smothered by a pillow. In fact, the manner of Edward's death had been altered in Brecht's source, Heymel's translation.[13]

Likewise, the ending of *Drums in the Night* displays more of a desire to "master problems than an attempt to explore and define them honestly" (57). The criteria here employed suggest a fundamental flaw in Speirs's reading of the play. Let us therefore now look at details in his arguments concerning these early plays.

The reading of *Baal* is based, without justification, on the Potsdam first edition, instead of on earlier stages available in the *edition suhrkamp*.[14] Speirs foregoes all discussion of the considerable variations between the various stages of this play. The analysis is predicated on the assumption that the play shows "the conflict between [Brecht's] perception of life's harshness and his dreams of transcending the limits of existence" (20). *Baal* is a "wishfulfilling fantasy" (20) and Baal, the character, "a symbolic hero whose imaginative function is to exorcise the existential fears in the mind from which he sprang" (20). As evidence for Baal's dream of transcendence, he cites the poem "Der Tod im Wald" (*GW*, 1:55–57; "Death in the Woods"),[15] which Brecht had written in 1917, thus establishing the imaginative identity between author and character. The sunlight in the top of the tree under which the man has just been buried is interpreted as a "sentimental vision" (20), and as such put to good dramatic use since it demonstrates Baal's "loss of poetic control" (20). But there is surely no need to read the image in such terms, as if it stood for hope of transcendence, or even the light of the soul. The young men ride off in the sunlight. They ride away; his body enters the natural cycle. Surely *Baal* is not so much about any dream of transcendence as the necessity of descendence, though the vigour with which this end is pursued suggests it stems from consciousness of the irrevocable loss of transcendence, and hence belongs to the same categorical sphere. The path affirmation takes in *Baal* suggests that the negation of transcendence is a painful experiential truth. This tension, and the choice of direction, is well expressed in one of the play's remarkable metaphorical passages: "Shall we soak up the tepid water of a blue pool? Otherwise the white country roads will draw us like angels' ropes into heaven" (*GW*, 1:33).

The play is a "fantasy of mastery over life" (27) but since it is continuously located in the necessary identification between author and character, too little attention is paid to its actual dynamics. Since imagined mastery is not real mastery, *Baal* remains an unsatisfactory play. But the play itself contains a refutation of the supposition that even imaginative mastery can ever be achieved, when the Beggar tells Baal that stories which can be understood have been badly told (*CP*, 1:43). At the same time, Speirs objects to the play because it is too far removed from "real experience" (28). This criterion, psychological realism, is clearly an important factor in his psycho-biographical interpretation of Brecht's work. Hence there is no discussion of the play's actual language, because its metaphorical intensity cannot really be accommodated to such criteria.

This constant penchant for psychological plausibility, which Brecht sacrifices in favour of establishing an imagined mastery over experience through his characters, makes *Drums in the Night* also a finally unsatisfactory play. It shows "Kragler's struggle to gain control over the hysterical tendencies in those around him and within himself" (31). Speirs rejects Bathrick's view that "Kragler is the revolution" (193),[16] because Kragler is in search of "the benefit of such protection as the ordered world of civilisation can afford" (193). In this context, it is interesting to observe how often he uses New Critical terms like irony, order, balance, control, suggesting a penchant for their implied staticism, which he projects onto the plays and their author. But Bathrick, whose argument was accompanied by a sophisticated analysis of the play's metaphorical language, contended that the early, and better, version employed Kragler as a metaphor of the revolution and showed, therefore, why that revolution failed. In overcoming a German "tendency to emotionalism" (56), Kragler wins our sympathy by his "calm, pipe-smoking manner" (54) which bolsters "our idea of what is natural and dignified in man" (54). This begins to sound a little like the Senior Common Room, where that breast surrogate is much in evidence. Compared with Bathrick's subtle discussion of the interrelationship between metaphorical language and existential-social predicament, Speirs's analysis appears rather too crudely ideological.

The most useful section of the book is the account of *In the Jungle* and Shlink's struggle with Garga. Otto Best's stimulating discussion of Brecht's early work, *Bertolt Brecht: Weisheit und Überleben* (Frankfurt 1982), aligns it with Spinozan thought and the Western tradition of adaptation, survival and resistance. Best argues from the 1927 version which marks for him the bridging point between present self-preservation, a characteristic of the early work, and future oriented change, symbolised by Garga's departure for New York. Speirs argues from the 1922 version, in which Garga remains in Chicago and the play ends with the word "Ostwind" [East wind], implying Garga's survival is bought at the price of turning into another Shlink. Speirs gives the most coherent account of the plot of the play's first version that I have read, and conveys a lively sense of the play's dynamics, as a clash between the existential self and an inhospitable civilisation. Evolution into the cities leads to inescapable loneliness. The most that Shlink can do is to attempt to determine the cause of his own death. His passivity is therefore an extreme act of will. Garga, meanwhile, must resist the older man's challenge in the name of freedom. The conflict ends when Garga loses interest in it. Both have won and both have lost. Brecht said he was on the scent of a mythology.

The account of *Man is Man* [*A Man's a Man*] is also good, based of course on the first version and from the by now familiar perspective. [Speirs] reads it in terms of Farce, when we laugh so as not to weep, and as a portrayal of the "uncertainty of human identity" (141), as a traditional comic theme, its "instability" (137) deriving from "the general unreliability of life" (137).

The motto which prefaces the book is taken from Brecht's notes to *Puntila:* "We need an art which masters nature" (*GW,* 17:1165). Yet its context in those notes has nothing to do with any Nietzschean assertion of the will in the face of inimical nature or the transcendental void, but with aesthetic perception: it amounts to a call for aesthetically sophisticated comic forms. Mastery is to be achieved, not by subjugation of the plot, or of nature in any fallacious elaboration of Bacon, for the only way to "conquer" nature is to obey it first, which is what Bacon actually said, but by imaginative invention in the portrayal of contradictory social and natural reality. This does not involve, on either plane, the reduction of contradictions, but their representation. Anything less than this is a betrayal of Brecht's legacy.

The "existential self" is a non-relational category and irrelevant for Brecht's later work. The early work sometimes portrays the dilemma of such a self, yet also represents the beginnings of a method whereby that categorical construct can be relativised. That this is impossible, constitutes the main assumption in Speirs's book and to this extent it is flawed. But it also offers a useful account of that early work when Brecht's perspectives, as they sometimes did, coincide with those of the critic.

Notes

1. Roland Barthes, *On Racine,* trans. Richard Howard (1964; reprint, New York: Octagon Books, 1977), 165.

2. Ronald Speirs, *Brecht's Early Plays* (Atlantic Highlands, N.J.: Humanities Press, 1982). Page references will be given in the text.

3. Ernst Schumacher, *Die dramatischen Versuche Bertolt Brechts 1918–1933* (1955; reprint, [West] Berlin: Verlag des europäischen Buches, 1977).

4. Bertolt Brecht, *Diaries 1920–1922,* ed. Herta Ramthun, trans. John Willett (London: Eyre Methuen, 1979). Subsequently cited as *Diaries.*

5. Martin Esslin, *Brecht: A Choice of Evils. A Critical Study of the Man, His Work and His Opinions* (1959; 4th rev. ed., London: Methuen, 1984).

6. Letter of June 1918, in Konrad Feilchenfeldt, *Trommeln in der Nacht: Materialien, Abbildungen, Kommentar* (Munich: Hanser, 1976), 158, n. 34. [Ed. note: see also Bertolt Brecht, *Briefe 1913–1956,* ed. Günter Glaeser (Frankfurt am Main: Suhrkamp, 1981), 45–46.]

7. Friedrich Wolfgang Gaede, "Figur und Wirklichkeit im Drama Brechts" (Ph.D. diss., University of Freiburg im Breisgau, 1963); Gunter G. Sehm, "Moses, Christus und Paul Ackermann: Brechts *Aufstieg und Fall der Stadt Mahagonny,*" *Brecht-Jahrbuch 1976:*83–100.

8. Bertolt Brecht, *Hundert Gedichte 1918–1950* (Berlin: Aufbau Verlag, 1951), 38.

9. See Bertolt Brecht, *Aufstieg und Fall der Stadt Mahagonny, Gesammelte Werke in 20 Bänden* (Frankfurt am Main: Suhrkamp, 1967), 2:535 (subsequently cited as *GW*), and the British translation of *Rise and Fall of the City of Mahagonny*, by W. H. Auden and Chester Kallman, *Collected Plays*, ed. Ralph Manheim and John Willett (London: Eyre Methuen, 1979), 2.3:36–37.

10. Theodor W. Adorno comments in *Der Scheinwerfer* 3, no. 14 (Essen, 1930):12: "The reification of human relationships is rendered by the image of prostitution" in *Mahagonny*.

11. Antony Tatlow, *The Mask of Evil* (Berne: Peter Lang, 1977), 363.

12. Bertolt Brecht, *Poems 1913–1956*, ed. John Willett and Ralph Manheim with the co-operation of Erich Fried (New York: Methuen, 1976), 448.

13. Christopher Marlowe, *Eduard II. Tragödie*, trans. Alfred Walter von Heymel (Leipzig: Insel Verlag, 1914).

14. [Ed. note: see Ronald Speirs, "*Baal*," in this volume.]

15. Bertolt Brecht, *Collected Plays*, ed. Ralph Manheim and John Willett (New York: Vintage Books, 1971–), 1:48–49. Subsequently cited as *CP*.

16. David Bathrick, *The Dialectic and the Early Brecht* (Stuttgart: Akademischer Verlag H.–D. Heinz, 1975), 40.

Brecht's Victorian Version of Gay: Imitation and Originality in the *Dreigroschenoper* [*The Threepenny Opera*]

Ulrich Weisstein*

The *Dreigroschenoper*, Brecht's first major play written after his conversion to Marxism, is undoubtedly the author's most popular creation, although hardly his most widely performed stage work. Its popularity must, in fact, be credited to the worldwide dissemination of the recorded songs rather than to the experience of live performances. Paradoxically, the drama is also one of Brecht's least thoroughly studied and least exhaustively analyzed from a scholarly point of view; and in spite of a handful of more or less detailed investigations (to which reference will be made in due course), the standard reference invariably cited in the secondary literature is a German dissertation written in the early thirties.[1] One suspects that this conspicuous neglect is partly due to the fear of wasting time on a work that appears, at first glance, to be primarily designed as entertainment, with some didactic elements tacked on to it. Without settling the issue at this point, I should like to stress that literary entertainment — especially if it involves parody and other forms of humorous imitation — fully deserves our professional attention.[2] For as literary

*From *Comparative Literature Studies* 7 (1970):314–35. Reprinted by permission of The Pennsylvania State University Press, University Park.

critics and historians, we should concern ourselves not only with aristocratic forms but also with those genres or subgenres couched in a lighter
vein. Like the commedia dell'arte and the farcical operettas of Offenbach
or Gilbert and Sullivan, the *Dreigroschenoper* occupies a uniquely important place in modern theatrical history, without seeking, in any way, to
compete with works belonging to the grand tradition of drama.

As I have shown in an essay dealing with Brecht's reception in the
Anglo-Saxon world, the *Dreigroschenoper* (which owes its enticing name
to Lion Feuchtwanger rather than Bertolt Brecht)[3] had rough going when
it was first introduced to English and American audiences.[4] With the
single exception of Joseph Wood Krutch, who was greatly touched by the
play's "morbid and mordant humor," most New York critics, for example,
were either bored or annoyed when, in the spring of 1933—more than
four years after the German premiere—they witnessed the performance of
an unpublished version by Gifford Cochran and Jerrold Krimsky. On John
Bull's island, E. W. White, writing two years later in the periodical
English Life and Letters, voiced the opinion that, in his view, neither
Aufstieg und Fall der Stadt Mahagonny (Mahagonny) nor *Mann ist Mann
(Man is Man)* could ever prove successful in America or the *Dreigroschenoper* (the *Threepenny Opera*) in England. White boldly suggested a
change of setting from the London of the 1880s to Saint Petersburg or even
Berlin, so as to create what he considered to be the requisite exotic
environment for the latter work. Judging by a subsequent conversation
with Giorgio Strehler, the famous director of the Piccolo Teatro in Milan,
Brecht would probably have welcomed such a shift.[5]

The "Weavers of Expressionism,"[6] as one critic pithily though rather
inappropriately called the *Dreigroschenoper*, also failed to catch on in any
of the versions made, from 1937 on, by Desmond Vesey—at times in
collaboration with Eric Bentley—although it is such a version which was
ultimately chosen for inclusion in the standard Grove Press edition of
Brecht's works.[7] The form in which the play most commonly appears on
American stages, however, is the sensationally successful adaptation by
Marc Blitzstein, which is marred by a Victorian tendency toward bowd-
lerization.[8]

"As we live by the Muses, it is but gratitude in us to encourage
poetical merit wherever we find it. The Muses, contrary to all other ladies,
pay no distinction to dress, and never partially mistake the pertness of
embroidery for wit, nor the modesty of want for dullness." With these
words, the player in the Introduction to John Gay's *Beggar's Opera* of 1728
expresses the willingness of his company to perform a piece "originally
writ for the celebrating of the marriage of James Chanter and Moll Lay,
two most excellent ballad singers," and previously performed "in the great
room at St. Giles, where the Company of Beggars is wont to stage its
weekly festivals."[9] By means of this ingenious and convenient fiction, the

friend of Jonathan Swift and Alexander Pope, and the secretary of the famous Scriblerus Club, prepared his audience for a work in which the style of grand opera (meaning, in those days, primarily opera written in the Italianate style of George Frederic Handel) is most effectively ridiculed. Indeed, so great was the force of his attack that in the decade following the unprecedented sixty-two performances of the *Beggar's Opera*, Italian opera lost its appeal and Handel gradually turned to the oratorio as his principal means of musico-dramatic expression.

From its beginning in the late Renaissance in the circle of the Florentine *camerata*, opera had been an aristocratic pastime suited to the courtly atmosphere, although in Italy it soon gained widespread popularity with the founding of public opera houses in Venice and other cities. In the England of Handel's day, it remained inaccessible to the general public insofar as it was sung either entirely in Italian or in a mixture of two vernaculars. In a pair of essays published in the *Spectator*, Joseph Addison condemned this practice, which, he insinuated with tongue in cheek, might cause a future historian, unfamiliar with the peculiar taste of his "wise forefathers," to assume that "in the beginning of the eighteenth century, the Italian tongue was so well understood in England that operas were acted on the public stage in that language."[10] Gay's *Beggar's Opera* is a creative answer to that critique; for it employs the native tongue throughout and undermines the social foundations of the music drama by substituting beggars, robbers, whores, and stooges for the customary mythological or heroic dramatis personae.

In the true spirit of parody, Gay, while discarding some of the familiar operatic features — such as the recitative, the prologue and the epilogue — yet retained certain of its formal characteristics, most notably "the similes that are in all your celebrated operas: The Swallow, the Moth, the Bee, the Ship, the Flower, etc." (Introduction). To top off his parody, he also copied the common practice of contemporary librettists to show a "nice impartiality" toward the prima donnas and castrati engaged for a given season by assigning approximately the same number of set musical pieces to each of the leading singers. He even went so far as to transplant the notorious quarrel between the two female stars Faustina and Cuzzoni into the plot of his ballad opera, where it is reflected in the rivalry between Polly Peachum and Lucy Lockit, which culminates in the duet of Air 38:

> Why, how now, Madam Flirt?
> If you thus must chatter,
> And are for flinging dirt,
> Let's try who best can spatter . . .
> Why, how now, saucy jade?
> Sure, the wench is tipsy!
> How can you see me made
> The scoff of such a gypsy?

Although the German Handelian revival of the 1920s — ushered in by Professor Oscar Hagen of Göttingen[11] — did not entail a similar dictatorship of the prima donna, Brecht retained this interesting feature of the *Beggar's Opera* by confronting his Polly and his Lucy in a duet in which Brown's daughter challenges Peachum's offspring to display her pretty legs:

> Come right out, Old Soho's beauty queen!
> Let me see those legs they call so pretty!
> I should like to recite the praises
> Of the fairest figure in our city![12]

An age in which librettists were instructed to write equal parts for the leading sopranos, to create a heroic role for the chief male character, to arrange the other male parts proportionately, song for song, in the three acts, and to place the duet at the end of the second act[13] was not exactly conducive to the creation of well-made plays for the lyric theater. Accordingly, in most of Handel's operas the countless arias and sparse ensembles are strung up like so many beads in a necklace, the plot being little more than a string holding them together, without giving them any kind of unity. It is, thus, no exaggeration to state that, traditionally, the operatic plot was important only to the extent to which it furnished situations demanding vocal outbursts. Not infrequently, the operas then produced in England and on the Continent contained musical numbers culled from different works by one or several composers; and occasionally, each act of a work commissioned for the musical stage was composed by a different musician.

The *Beggar's Opera* imitates contemporary practice by offering sixty-nine different airs — more than any drama intended for the legitimate stage could possibly include without losing its generic identity. Especially in the final act, these pieces sometimes follow so closely upon each other that they turn into veritable medleys. Thus, in one page of printed text, Macheath, placed in the Condemned Hold, runs through a total of ten numbers (Airs 58–67). Setting the pace for ballad operas to come, Gay went one step beyond the usual practice by using the melodies of popular airs (mostly of the "broadside" variety) to accompany texts that were of his own making and typically in stark contrast with the lyrics they replaced. By employing Kurt Weill to compose original music for his show, Brecht voluntarily renounced this parodistic technique;[14] for while parody invariably harks back to specific, clearly identifiable models, Brecht's censure of the prevailing taste is so general as to deserve, at best, the label "burlesque," even though, in the literary domain, the German playwright made frequent use of the Bible, just as his English predecessor placed poetic quotations from *Othello* and *Twelfth Night* in the mouths of his questionable characters.[15]

Although the *Beggar's Opera* outwardly emulates the Handelian prototype by oversaturating plot with music — some of it borrowed directly from that composer[16] — Gay retains rather tight dramaturgical control over his material. He does so, in part, by consistent use of satire, wavering between the universal (as in Gulliver's voyage to the Houyhnhnms) and the particular (as mirrored in Lilliput); whereas Brecht's satire never quite descends into the realm of the topical. Thus, Gay's public rightly understood the piece to entail a critique of contemporary political mores, and Walpole, the leading politician of the day, is said to have risen and exclaimed "That was levelled at me" in echoing response to the following air sung by the connivers Peachum and Lockit:

> When you censure the age,
> Be cautious and sage,
> Lest the courtiers offended should be:
> If you mention vice or bribe,
> 'T is so pat to all the tribe;
> Each cries: That was levelled at me.
>
> (Air 30)

In the *Beggar's Opera*, this sally is combined with a satirical thrust at city life, which Gay (whom Swift had originally urged to write a Newgate pastoral) regarded as thoroughly corrupt — thereby in some ways anticipating Rousseau's call for a return to nature.

Especially in the communist camp, but by no means only there, the author of the *Dreigroschenoper* stands accused of having abdicated his political responsibility by failing to use the play as his mouthpiece or, at least, as a faithful mirror of the troubled times in which he created it.[17] One of the first to broach this view, and thereby suggest an unfavorable comparison with Gay, was Alfred Kerr, then one of Germany's most formidable and outspoken critics, who wrote: "Swift influenced Gay politically. If I am properly informed, his opera for beggars was full of political allusions. Didn't Brecht pull this tooth? Didn't he renounce any references to contemporary life? Didn't he merely deal in generalities of a vaguely ethical nature? . . . I almost think so."[18] Kerr's view has been echoed ever since, most recently by George Salomon, who, writing in the *Kenyon Review*, complained that "the play had no positive message, least of all an orthodox political one."[19]

Indeed, it is impossible to deny that the thirty-year-old author of the *Dreigroschenoper* made more concessions to the spirit of sheer entertainment than his material would seem to warrant. Just as the hero of Brecht's *Trommeln in der Nacht* (*Drums in the Night*), written a decade earlier, abandons the cause of the revolution and creeps into bed with his long-lost fiancée, so in the *Dreigroschenoper* the social protest is romanticized in the stereotyped and sentimentalized Pirate Song which is Polly's contribution to the wedding festivities.[20] Sung in a halo, or haze, of "golden light," this musical number is not exactly fit to rouse the rabble or start a social-reform movement. But critics like Kerr and Salomon forget that although Brecht had begun to study the gospel according to "Saint Marx" as early as 1926, the *Dreigroschenoper* and *Mahagonny* were, by his own confession, primarily designed as formal experiments.[21] After the abortive experiment with *Joe Fleischhacker* — a play intended to deal with economic processes connected with the production and distribution of wheat — form and content were merged only at the conclusion of the decade, in the didactic plays [or: plays for learning] (*Lehrstücke*), in the adaptation of Gorky's novel, *Die Mutter* (*The Mother*), and most triumphantly, in the magnificent full-length drama *Die heilige Johanna der Schlachthöfe* (*Saint Joan of the Stockyards.*)

Even if one regrets Brecht's political immaturity at the time of writing the *Dreigroschenoper*, one has to admit that this work sheds new light on a psychological problem very close to the playwright's heart: the breakdown of personality and the dissolution of the ego. This problem governs the action of *Mann ist Mann*, although it is treated somewhat flippantly there. One of the most striking features of the play about Mackie Messer, Peachum, and their retinue is the fact that the songs interspersed throughout the action are psychologically ambivalent, since more often than not, they seem to be totally "out of character." In other words, Brecht seems to have chosen the wrong medium for his message by "uncomfortably putting his favorite clichés into the mouths of unsavory characters."[22] Thus, while the theme of sexual bondage is obviously pertinent to the philandering protagonist both in the Solomon Song and the Ballad of Sexual Submissiveness, Mr. Peachum's apologetic reference to the conditions (*Verhältnisse*) in the first finale blatantly contradicts his own behavior; for he himself exploits these conditions and thus carries some of the blame for the state of affairs he so eloquently deplores.

Similarly, in the second finale, Mackie plays the devil's advocate for those paupers whom the *Verhältnisse* keep from cutting their slice out of the big loaf. Following Brecht's suggestion ("In a love scene with Macheath, Polly is not only Macheath's mistress but also Peachum's daughter; and, throughout, not only daughter but also her father's employee"),[23] we take this patent discrepancy to mean that in the *Dreigroschenoper* the characters are split into social and personal selves, and that this dichotomy precludes any consistency in their thoughts, feelings, and actions. Their constant invocation of high moral principles is, therefore, not necessarily to be regarded as showing a lack of sincerity, although we realize that, on the whole, many of them thrive — to use Brecht's own words — not so much by living morally as by living off morality.[24] This is the onus of modern life, and as the events on stage reveal, it can only be lifted in the make-believe world of opera and fairy tale.

Although on the level of moral censure Gay and Brecht have much in common, they differ at least insofar as Gay's message is much simpler. For as the Beggar asserts just before the happy ending of the ballad opera, its moral — which is ineffectual because the performers decide fo bow to the pleasure principle — would have demonstrated "that the lower sort of people have their vices in a degree, as well as the rich; and that they are punished for them" (p. 82). But even without this tag, the audience would go home with the knowledge that the two walks of life run amazingly parallel. Indeed, "through the entire piece you may observe such a similitude of manners in high and low life that it is difficult to determine whether (in the fashionable vices) the fine gentlemen imitate the gentlemen of the road, or the gentlemen of the road the fine gentlemen" (p. 82).

The English playwright sought to demonstrate that in reality it is the outlaw who copies the manners of the courtier and that the likes of Peachum, Macheath, and Lockit merely ape the example of high society. Following her natural inclinations and emulating the sentimental stories she has read, Polly alone rejects these base conventions, which decree that a woman should marry coolly and deliberately for honor or money and that she should immediately undertake to get rid of her newly wedded husband. Her father, who is a rogue's rogue if ever there was one, calmly condones the act of murder (on p. 11, "No gentleman is ever looked upon the worse for killing a man in his own defense; and if business cannot be carried on without it, what would you have a gentleman do?") and base treachery (on p. 24, "Where is the woman who would scruple to be a wife, if she had it in her power to be a widow whenever she pleased?"). But at the same time, he incessantly refers to his honor. In his world, where absolute moral standards are obviously lacking, honesty and knavery have become virtually interchangeable; and even though in Peachum's eyes "all professions berogue one another," they are, nevertheless, all respectable. In his opinion, "a lawyer is an honest employment, and so is mine. Like me, too, he acts in a double capacity, both against rogues and for them; for 't is but fitting that we should protect and encourage cheats, since we live by them" (pp. 6–7). The pivot around which this world revolves is the highly pragmatic concept of economic profit, the end to which all means (even the affection of a father for his daughter) must be subordinate.

Like his English forerunner, Brecht seems to think that "of all animals of prey, man is the only sociable one"[25] — that man is a veritable "zoon politicon." For as he tells us in the opening *Moritat*,

And the shark he has his teeth and
There they are for all to see.
And Macheath he has his knife but
No one knows where it may be.

Whereas the shark proudly displays the tools of his murderous trade, Mackie hides his true intentions by dressing immaculately in the latest fashion and pretending he was not there. But why is it that he is, after all, trapped by the law, which his rival Peachum has set in motion? Foisting his own, modern, interpretation on Gay's story, Brecht announces that Mackie's undoing must be blamed on the fact that—unlike most of his illustrious predecessors (a Rinaldo Rinaldini or Schinderhannes)—he is at heart a hopeless bourgeois who, violating the hardened criminal's ironclad code of ethics, longs for the lazy, comfortable life and is convinced that "none but the well-to-do can live at ease."

Degenerating into a *Bürger*, Mackie has become a creature of habit whom nothing will deter, for instance, from visiting the whores of Tu[r]nbridge regularly every Thursday afternoon, and who unctuously admonishes his beloved Polly—whom he has just put in the command of the gang—to rise punctually at seven o'clock in the morning and not to forget her weekly bath. In fact, Brecht's underworld is so thoroughly bourgeois that weddings (even those celebrated in stables) have to come off in style and that the brothel where Mackie is apprehended after Jenny's betrayal offers the perfect setting for a scene of Victorian respectability. Perhaps the ladies who live there can afford to be respectable because they are fortunate enough to be in undisputed possession of their means of production,[26] while the beggars under Peachum's sway have to pay for these.

As for the proper way of conducting business, both Peachum and Mackie know that the glorious age of chivalry is over and that modern life, shunning the rhetorical style, requires smooth professional techniques. Unlike Gay's recklessly brave Macheath, Brecht's elegant and squeamish hero is perturbed by any show of violence. When his men report the accidents that occurred while they gathered the equipment needed for the wedding, he reproaches them: "My directive was to avoid bloodshed. I get sick when I think of what you've done. You'll never be real business men. Cannibals, yes, but not businessmen."

Seeking to adjust to a rapidly changing world of commerce, Mackie is about to turn himself from a shark into a loan shark and plans to get rid of his henchmen by calmly handing them over to the police. Once his hands are free, he will open a bank—a venture which succeeds not in the *Dreigroschenoper* itself but in its narrative sequel, the much more frankly satirical *Dreigroschenroman* (*Threepenny Novel*). Somewhat romantically, the play's protagonist indulges in the role of burglar-craftsman and bitterly complains about being put out of business by the trusts and corporations. "What is a picklock compared with a share? What is a bank robbery compared with the founding of a bank? What is the killing of a man compared with the hiring of a man?," he asks shortly before his scheduled execution, thereby implying that big business is a legalized and highly lucrative form of expropriation.

Unlike Mackie, who is desperately and unsuccessfully trying to catch up with modern "accounting" techniques, Peachum runs his business with the precision of an industrial manager. It is this machinelike perfectionism that gives him the edge over his rivals, who live in an anachronistic world and embrace outmoded or sentimental values. For Peachum himself, sentimentality is a tool he handles with consummate skill — as when he notes that the four or five sayings from the Bible which tend to soften people's hearts lose their appeal so quickly that beggars will soon be out of work: "Take that one here: 'Give and it shall be given unto you.' How threadbare it has become in the three weeks we've had it. Always something new must be offered. We can fall back on the Bible again, but how often can that be done?"

Sentimentality, Peachum's pet peeve in the socioeconomic sphere, is Brecht's principal target in the aesthetic realm. His attack, however, is aimed not so much at Handel — as one would suspect after what I have said so far — as at the Wagnerian *Gesamtkunstwerk*, that apogee of romanticism in the arts. As early as the final decades of the nineteenth century, many composers (most of them French) had begun to rebel against this all-encompassing scheme and especially against Wagner's call for an unconditional surrender of the audience. Wagner's mature operas (most notably *Tristan und Isolde*) are so designed as to compel the listener and viewer, seated in the darkened auditorium of the Bayreuth Fest-spielhaus, to share the heightened feelings of the characters on stage rather than allowing him to judge the events with some degree of objectivity. The former attitude has since come to be known as empathy, the latter as estrangement (*Entfremdung*) or, if a shock is administered, as alienation [or: estrangement] (*Verfremdung*). The French were perhaps predisposed for their role as anti-Wagnerians, because with the exception of Hector Berlioz and certain followers of Brahms, such as Gabriel Fauré and César Franck, they tend to be classicists at heart and generally prefer a graceful melodic line to the heavy orchestral harmonies to which Wagner so insistently treats us.

The first, though hardly decisive, step toward a break with Wagner was taken by Claude Debussy, who had twice witnessed the spectacle of Bayreuth and had come away with the impression that this music represented, historically speaking, a cul-de-sac and that a new point of departure must be found.[27] Without repudiating the German master, he wished to redefine his art by suffusing it with the spirit of clarity, subtlety and nuance. The result of these reflections was the richly textured music of *Pelléas et Mélisande* (1902), an opera which, in spite of its filigree, has earned the nickname "*Tristan* of Impressionism" because it is still decid-edly Wagnerian.

One generation later, the French poet Jean Cocteau became the spokesman of a group of composers known as "Les Six," who, partly out of resentment against Germany, slapped Debussy for having been too timid in his reforms. Their manifesto was Cocteau's *Le Coq et l'arlequin* (*The Cock and the Harlequin*), a treatise composed of pithy and witty aperçus, and thus even in its external form, a gesture of defiance toward the ponderous, overly systematic Germans. Emulating Nietzsche's attack on his former idol in *Der Fall Wagner* (*The Case of Wagner*), Cocteau, praising his eccentric and capricious composer-friend Erik Satie (just as Nietzsche had lauded Bizet), fulminates against musical impressionism: "The dense fog pierced by the lightning of Bayreuth turns into a light snowy mist flecked by the impressionistic sun. Satie speaks of Ingres; Debussy prepares a Russian version of Claude Monet."[28] *Pelléas*, Cocteau declared emphatically, "is still music to be listened to with one's face in one's hands. All music listened to with face in hands is suspect."

Oddly enough, Cocteau's attack on the Teutonic and Slavic — as opposed to the Gallic — spirit in music initially extended to Igor Stravinsky, the very man who was shortly to become the founding father of epic opera. To be sure, the Russian composer's sumptuous and superabundant scores for *L'Oiseau de feu* (*The Firebird*) and *Le Sacre du printemps* (*The Rite of Spring*) essentially constitute music that "affects our nerves." Cocteau exclaimed, "This is music of the bowels; octopuses one must flee if one doesn't want to get entangled. That's the fault of the theater. There is theatrical mysticism in the *Rite*." What the French poet prescribed as a cure against the Teutonic ill was a form of theatrical entertainment derived from the circus, the music hall, and the performance of American jazz bands. Although he personally concocted such a show — the famous ballet *Parade*, for which Satie wrote the music and Picasso designed the sets — the decisive step was taken by the very composer he had previously maligned. In collaboration with the Swiss novelist Ramuz, Stravinsky conceived and executed a work for the musical stage which must have appealed to Brecht: *L'Histoire du soldat* (*The Story of the Soldier*), which is based on a Russian fairy tale. It was first performed at Lausanne in 1918 and was shown in Berlin in 1927 or 1928. Brecht is certain to have been acquainted with the piece, in the production then mounted at the Staatsoper and conducted by Otto Klemperer.

In his highly informative autobiography, Stravinsky relates the circumstances which, in the final year of World War I, forced him to abandon any large-scale plans and, out of economic necessity, suggested to him and his Swiss writer-friend the creation of "a sort of little travelling theater, easy to transport from place to place and to show even in small localities."[29] As the two artists went about their business, they constantly reminded each other of the modest means at their disposal. Stravinsky, for example, realized that he would have to make do with a very small orchestra and, accordingly, settled on a group "which would include the most representative types, in treble and bass, of the instrumental families: for the strings, the violin and the double bass, for the wood, the clarinet . . . and the bassoon; for brass, trumpet and trombone; and, finally, the percussion manipulated by only one musician."

To these practical, because purely economic, reasons, aesthetic considerations were soon added, however. The following observations, also culled from the composer's account of his life, underscore Stravinsky's affinity with Brecht, the experimentalist: "Another consideration which made this idea particularly attractive to me was the interest afforded to the spectator by being able to see these instrumentalists, each playing his own part in the ensemble. I have always had a horror of listening to music with my eyes shut, with nothing for them to do. The sight of the gestures and movements of the various parts of the body producing the music is fundamentally necessary if it is to be grasped in all its fullness. All music created or composed demands some exteriorization for the perception of the listener. . . . As a matter of fact, those who maintain that they only enjoy music to the full with their eyes shut do not hear better than when they have them open, but the absence of visual distractions enables them to abandon themselves to the reveries induced by the lullaby of its sounds, and that is really what they prefer to the music itself."

What a slap in the face of the proponents of the theater of empathy, and how forceful a rejection of the hypnotic effect intended by Wagner, who wanted to dissolve reality by making the orchestra invisible to the Festspielhaus audience! Stravinsky's kinship with Brecht is clearly demonstrated by their stress on the material aspects of the theatrical production. It was Brecht, after all, who proposed that in order to counterbalance the magnetism of the stage, the spectators in his theater of the future should be allowed, and even urged, to smoke — which would automatically keep them from melting away with sympathy.

As for the action on stage, both artists call for the dissection of the *Gesamtkunstwerk* and a separation of its ingredients. Once again, Stravinsky led the way: "These ideas induced me to have my little orchestra well in evidence when planning *Histoire du Soldat*. It was to be on one side of the stage, and a small dais for the reader on the other. This arrangement established the connection between the three elements of the piece which, by their close cooperation, were to form a unity: in the center, the stage and the actors, on one side of them the music, on the other the reader. Our idea was that the three elements should sometimes take turns as soloists and sometimes combine as an ensemble."

Destroying the semblance of intermittent unity still envisaged by the composer, Brecht advocates an even more radical break among the constituent parts of his anti-*Gesamtkunstwerk*, to the point that song and dialogue are manifestly shown to occupy two qualitatively different levels of stage reality. Epic opera is, naturally, the culmination of epic theater because it has more ingredients than legitimate drama and because the spectacle of their visible or audible separation is even more stunning than it would be in a regular play. Hence the paradigmatic value of that section of the notes to the *Dreigroschenoper* which carries the title "Über das Singen der Songs" ("Concerning the Singing of the Songs"). Here the playwright outlines a technique for divorcing the basic modes of vocal projection: "By singing, the actor takes on a different function altogether.

Nothing is more detestable than for an actor to pretend that he doesn't notice his having left the firm ground of sober speech and his already having begun to sing. The three levels — sober speech, exalted speech, and singing — must always be separated, in such a way that the exalted speech never seems to be a mere intensification of ordinary speech, and the song an intensification of exalted speech. Thus singing effectively ceases to function as the natural mode of expression when language fails in moments of overwhelming emotion" (my translation).

In line with this theoretical position, Brecht urged his actors to avoid "blindly following the melody" of a song and to speak, wherever feasible, "against the music," thereby asserting a decisive measure of self-control at moments when they should have been swept off their feet. Thus, while the songs in the *Dreigroschenoper* are sung in an atmosphere wrapped in a golden haze, the romantic aura is destroyed by the manner of delivery.

What then, are we to make of the passage at the end of the wedding scene, where Mackie and Polly, left alone to indulge in the appropriate mood, intone a *Liebeslied* (*molto tranquillo*, followed by a Boston)? Does it constitute a lapse from the new aesthetic back into the old? Decidedly not; for Brecht forewarns us of the stereotyped nature of this effusion by having Mackie observe: "And now sentiment must come into its own, for otherwise man becomes a mere slave to his work. Sit down, Polly, do you see the moon over Soho?" The ironic effect of this scene is enhanced by the cloying sweetness of the tune; for as Brecht himself states explicitly: "Thus, by behaving altogether emotionally and renouncing some of the usual narcotic stimuli, music aided in the unmasking of bourgeois ideologies."[30] By being either dissonant or romantic, the music of the *Dreigroschenoper* confirms Weill's observation: "I was faced with a realistic action; accordingly, I had to make the music contrast with it, since I do not believe that it can have any kind of realistic effect."[31]

Within the fictional world of the *Dreigroschenoper*, the glaring discrepancy between genuine feelings and their outward expression is carefully studied by Mr. Peachum, who propounds his own theory of acting, which — unbeknown to him — harks back to views broached by Denis Diderot. Rejecting Stanislavsky's method, the beggar king dissuades his charges from identifying with their roles and urges them to project a type of misery other than their own. Bitter experience has taught him that nobody can tell his own story of woe persuasively. Hence his mocking reply to Filch's autobiographical litany:

FILCH: Well, you see, Mr. Peachum, I've had bad luck ever since I was a boy. My mother was a drunkard, my father was a gambler. . . . And without the loving hand of a mother to guide me, I sank deeper and deeper into the morass of the great city. I never knew a father's care or the blessings of a happy home. So now you see me . . .

PEACHUM: So now I see you . . .

FILCH: . . . see me . . . completely destitute, a prey to my own desires.

PEACHUM: Like a wreck on the high seas, and so on. Tell me, wreck, in which district do you recite this nursery rhyme?

In rounding out my critical analysis, I ought to touch briefly on the circumstances surrounding the creation of the *Dreigroschenoper* insofar as we are able to reconstruct them. It was in 1927 that Brecht's trusted friend and collaborator Elisabeth Hauptmann was alerted to the popular success of the recently revived *Beggar's Opera*. She got hold of the English text and immediately set to work on a literal translation. Piece by piece, this version was submitted to Brecht, who caught fire and undertook an adaptation. As for the turbulent history of the stage rehearsals, Lotte Lenya Weill has given us a graphic account, which, by way of a preface, appears in the Grove Press edition of the play.[32]

Unfortunately, the manuscript of Miss Hauptmann's translation seems to have disappeared without leaving a trace, whereas the director's promptbook is in the possession of the Bertolt Brecht Archiv. Although we are thus deprived of the pleasure of following the process of adaptation in its early stages, we have clear indications that Brecht's version was originally much closer to its model than is now the case, and even that the text spoken and sung at the premiere had a little more in common with Gay than did the printed text.[33] But even in its familiar guise, the *Dreigroschenoper* sticks rather closely to its prototype, though the author has wrought a number of significant changes.

For example, the wedding scene—which occupies so much space in the second act and can be very boring when performed without the necessary mimetic skills—is entirely Brecht's own invention, although it may well owe its existence to the already quoted passage from the Introduction to the *Beggar's Opera*. In the German play, it nicely balances the "charmingly pathetic" prison scene borrowed from Gay's ballad drama. Among the other symptomatic changes, I mention only the heightened parallel between Mackie and Christ (which may have been suggested by Gay's Air 25, "At the tree I shall suffer with pleasure") and the substitution of the business partnership between Mackie and Tiger Brown for the alliance between Peachum and Lockit.

The most radical pruning of the English text occurred, naturally enough, in the songs; for Brecht could only use a tiny fraction of the airs which fill the *Beggar's Opera* to the brim. Although no detailed study of Brecht's borrowings has as yet been made, it can be shown that, in some instances, he has fused the content of several tunes or transferred certain lines from an air to the prose dialogue of his play. A good case in point is Air 7 ("Oh, Polly is a sad slut"), which Gay concludes with the punchline "As men should serve a cucumber, she throws herself away."[34] This phrase sufficiently impressed Brecht for him to have Mrs. Peachum utter: "First one loads her fore and aft with dresses, hats, gloves, and parasols, and when she's cost as much as it costs to rig out a sailing ship, she flings herself in the gutter like a rotten cucumber." Air 6 from the *Beggar's Opera* ("Virgins are like a fair flower in its lustre"), on the other hand, is still found in the promptbook but was dropped before the first performance.[35] A brief prologue after Gay was also cut — or better, reduced to the status of a projected title. In substitution, the opening *Moritat* was inserted at the request of one of the actors.[36]

To call the *Dreigroschenoper* a mere imitation of Gay (as was done by most American critics) is altogether a gross oversimplification. For Brecht actually reached beyond the eighteenth century in both chronological directions. It is common knowledge that he borrowed a sizable number of songs from the lyrical oeuvre of the fifteenth-century French vagabond poet François Villon; and the dexterity with which he — facing the charge of plagiarism — adapted the standard German versions of these ballads by K. L. Ammer (pseudonym for Karl Klammer)[37] has been repeatedly demonstrated, most tellingly by Joel Hunt.[38] Much less thoroughly understood, however, is the German playwright's use of material from Kipling's ballads. Yet this debt was openly proclaimed on the bill issued for the premiere of the *Dreigroschenoper*.[39]

If asked to identify Kipling's ballads, or more precisely, the ballads modeled on Kipling's style, Brecht experts are bound to name the Cannon Song. Echoing the British poet's imperialism and enhancing it with cannibalistic traits —

> And should they chance to sight
> Pallid or swarthy faces
> Of uncongenial races
> They maybe'll chop them up to make some beefsteak tartare —

this song, too, is apparently out of context, since Mackie and Brown, who are here reminiscing about their military past, are elsewhere shown to be such perfect gentlemen. What is more, their hearts are united in such tender friendship that if the one goes "somewhere," the other goes "somewhere" too.[40]

Brecht is known to have esteemed Kipling's style while at the same time detesting his chauvinistic weltanschauung. That the two authors shared certain views (see their skeptical attitudes toward organized religion) is demonstrated by Brecht's quoting from Kipling's poem, "Mary, Pity Women!" — a parody of prayer which, in a literal translation, appears at the end of the farewell scene between Mackie and Polly. A tentative survey of the German author's debt to the English author has recently been made by Sara Zimmerman, who also seeks to show that several songs in the *Dreigroschenoper* were jointly influenced by Villon and Kipling.[41]

Regarding the overall perspective embraced by the chief dramatis personae of our epic opera, I would not hesitate to say that while the Peachums generally cling to the lifeline thrown out by Gay, Mackie Messer gradually drifts from Gay to Villon; whereas Kipling's spirit is not restricted to a single character but seems to have been homogenized in certain scenes. As it is, the principal figures of the *Dreigroschenoper* form a dramaturgical constellation that is unique precisely because it is eclectic. As J. T. Shaw puts it in an essay concerned with the problem of literary indebtedness, "the original author is not necessarily the innovator or the most inventive, but rather the one who succeeds in making all his own, in subordinating what he takes from others to the new complex of his own artistic work."[42] Far from being a mere translation or transposition, the work which forms the subject of this essay is, in the words of Judith Sherwin, "a different interpretation of the same story, like Cocteau's [*La Machine infernale*] *Infernal Machine*, which reinterprets the Oedipus legend."[43]

Notes

1. Cäcilie Tolksdorf, *John Gays "Beggar's Opera" und Bert Brechts "Dreigroschenoper"* (dissertation, University of Bonn, 1932; Rheinberg, 1934). [Ed. note: quotations from the German and French have been omitted.]

2. For a historically oriented attempt to define parody in relation to similar techniques, see my essay "Parody, Travesty, and Burlesque: Imitations with a Vengeance," *Proceedings of the Fourth Congress of the International Comparative Literature Association*, ed. François Jost (The Hague, 1966), pp. 802–811.

3. See Lotte Lenya Weill, "Das waren Zeiten," in *Bertolt Brechts Dreigroschenbuch*, ed. Siegfried Unseld (Frankfurt, 1960), p. 224. Originally, the play was to be called *Gesindel* (*Rabble*). In his autobiography, Ernst Robert Aufricht, the manager of the Theater am Schiffbauerdamm, reports Brecht as stating during their first encounter: "I also have a minor work. Tomorrow you can read six of its seven scenes. It is an adaptation of John Gay's *Beggar's Opera*. I have entitled it 'Gesindel.' The *Beggar's Opera* was premiered in 1728 — not in London but in a suburban barn. It deals, in coded form, with a corruption scandal: the notorious gangster is on intimate terms with the chief of police and engages in business transactions with him. The gangster steals the daughter of a very powerful man and marries her. That man is the chief of the beggars, whom he fits out and stations according to their qualities. The rest is found in the seventh scene, which I have only sketched"; Ernst Robert Aufricht, *Erzähle, damit du dein Recht erweist* (Berlin, 1966), p. 64. It is to be noted that Brecht designated the *Dreigroschenoper* a "Nebenwerk" ("a minor product") and that he described it as having seven (rather than nine) scenes, of which one was still unfinished. In recalling the conversation, Aufricht obviously failed to realize that Brecht's plot summary referred to his own work rather than to the *Beggar's Opera*.

4. Ulrich Weisstein, "Brecht in America: A Preliminary Survey," *MLN* LXXVIII (1963), 373–396. The following quotations from J. W. Krutch and E. W. White are documented in this essay.

5. See "Gespräch zwischen Brecht und Giorgio Strehler über die bevorstehende Mailänder Inszenierung der *Dreigroschenoper* am 25. lo. 1955," in Unseld, ed. *Bertolt Brechts Dreigroschenbuch* (n. 3 above), p. 131.

6. See Weisstein, "Brecht in America," p. 381. [Ed. note: the reference is to Gerhart Hauptmann's naturalistic drama *The Weavers*.]

7. For bibliographical details concerning the various versions, see Weisstein, "Brecht in

America," p. 382, n. 22. [Ed. note: a more recent translation of *The Threepenny Opera* is that by Ralph Manheim and John Willett, *Collected Plays*, ed. Ralph Manheim and John Willett (New York: Vintage, 1971–) 2:145–226.]

8. The Blitzstein version was first performed at the Theatre de Lys in New York on 10 March 1954.

9. Quotations from the *Beggar's Opera* are from the edition prepared by E. V. Roberts for the Regents Restoration Drama series (Lincoln: University of Nebraska Press, 1969). Hereafter, the references are given parenthetically in the text.

10. Joseph Addison, *Spectator*, No. 18 (21 March 1710).

11. Ernst Schumacher gives a succinct account of the circumstances surrounding this revival in his book *Die dramatischen Versuche Bertolt Brechts, 1918–1933* (Berlin, 1955), pp. 218–219.

12. The translations quoted in the text are (unless otherwise noted) from the Vesey-Bentley version published by the Grove Press. The German quotations [omitted here] come from Bertolt Brecht, *Stücke*, Vol. III (Berlin, 1955). [Ed. note: also in Bertolt Brecht, *Gesammelte Werke in 20 Bänden* (Frankfurt am Main: Suhrkamp, 1967), 2:395–497.]

13. This is an almost literal quotation from a letter written by Giuseppe Riva in 1725; see R. A. Streatfeild, "Handel, Rolli, and Italian Opera," *Musical Quarterly*, III (1917), 428–445.

14. The producer of the *Dreigroschenoper*, Ernst Robert Aufricht, had originally intended to use orchestral accompaniments prepared by Gay's contemporary Pepusch. According to Lotte Lenya's account, it was only after hearing the Ballad of the Fancy Man ("Zuhälterballade") that he decided in favor of Weill's score (Unseld, ed. *Bertolt Brechts Dreigroschenbuch*, p. 223). See also Aufricht, *Erzähle* (n. 3 above), pp. 65, 68.

15. For instance, Gay had Polly say "One kiss and then – one kiss – begone – farewell" (p. 29) and had Macheath quote "If music be the food of love, play on" (p. 37).

16. Air 20, "Let us take the road," is labelled "March in *Rinaldo*, with drums and trumpets."

17. See, for example, Schumacher, *Die dramatischen Versuche* (n. 11 above), p. 232.

18. Alfred Kerr in *Berliner Tageblatt*, 1 September 1928; the review is reproduced in Unseld, ed. *Bertolt Brechts Dreigroschenbuch*, pp. 199–201.

19. George Salomon, "Happy Ending, Nice and Tidy," *Kenyon Review*, XXIV (1962), 542–551.

20. The "Lied der Seeräuber-Jenny" was brilliantly analyzed by Ernst Bloch; see Unseld, ed. *Bertolt Brechts Dreigroschenbuch*, pp. 195–197.

21. A number of relevant statements are to be found in the *Anmerkungen* (1931); see Unseld, ed. *Bertolt Brechts Dreigroschenbuch*, pp. 141 ff., 259 ff.

22. Salomon, "Happy Ending," p. 547.

23. Bertolt Brecht, "Winke für Schauspieler," in Unseld, ed. *Bertolt Brechts Dreigroschenbuch*, p. 150.

24. See Brecht, "Über die Dreigroschenoper" [1929], in *Gesammelte Werke* (Frankfurt, 1968), XVII, 990.

25. The statement is made by Lockit in *Beggar's Opera* (n. 9 above), p. 61.

26. See Brecht, "Winke für Schauspieler," in Unseld, ed., *Bertolt Brechts Dreigroschenbuch*, p. 152.

27. I have dealt with the evolution of epic opera in an essay entitled "Cocteau, Stravinsky, Brecht, and the Birth of Epic Opera" (*Modern Drama*, V [1962], 142–153), from which some of the following arguments are drawn.

28. Jean Cocteau, *Le Coq et l'arlequin: Notes autour de la musique*, in *Oeuvres*

complètes, (Paris, 1950), IX, 24. The quotations that follow in this and the next paragraph are from IX, 39.

29. Igor Stravinsky, *An Autobiography* (New York, 1962), p. 70. The quotations that follow in this and the next two paragraphs are from pp. 72, 72, and 73 respectively.

30. Bertolt Brecht, "Über die Verwendung von Musik für ein episches Theater," *Gesammelte Werke* n. 24 above), V, 474.

31. Kurt Weill, "Zur Komposition der *Dreigroschenoper*" (1929), in Unseld, ed. *Bertolt Brechts Dreigroschenbuch,* p. 219.

32. See also Unseld, ed. *Bertolt Brechts Dreigroschenbuch,* pp. 220–221.

33. The first printed text—apart from the *Klavierauszug* published in 1928 in Vienna—appeared in 1931 as part of the third issue of Brecht's *Versuche* (Berlin). It is nearly identical with the standard text found in all subsequent editions. [Ed. note: *The Beggar's Opera. Die Ludenoper. Von John Gray* (sic). *Übersetzt von Elisabeth Hauptmann. Bearbeitung: Bert Brecht. Musik: Kurt Weill,* was published as "Bühnenmanuskript" (typescript to be used for stagings) by Felix Bloch Erben in Berlin (1928). See Bertolt Brecht, *Werke. Große kommentierte Berliner und Frankfurter Ausgabe.* 30 vols., ed. Werner Hecht, Jan Knopf, Werner Mittenzwei, and Klaus-Detlef Müller (Frankfurt am Main: Suhrkamp, 1988–), 2:429–33.

34. In his edition of *Beggar's Opera* (n. 9 above), E. V. Roberts quotes R. S. Hunting as stating that "cucumbers were often thought to be poisonous, and thus should be served by being thrown away" (p. 18). This may explain why in his translation, Vesey substitutes "tomato" for "cucumber."

35. In the *Regiebuch* (BBA Mappe 2106), a German version of Air 11 from Gay's ballad opera ("A fox may steal your hens, sir") is also to be found.

36. See Lotte Lenya Weill, in Unseld, ed. *Bertolt Brechts Dreigroschenbuch,* p. 223.

37. See Reinhold Grimm's essay "Werk und Wirkung des Übersetzers Karl Klammer," *Neophilologus,* XLIV (1960), 20–36.

38. Joel Hunt, "Bert Brecht's *Dreigroschenoper* and Villon's *Testament,*" *Monatshefte,* XLIX (1957), 273–278. See also A. J. Harper's "Brecht and Villon: Further Notes on some *Dreigroschenoper* Songs," *Forum for Modern Language Studies,* I (1965), 191–194.

39. As reproduced on p. 472 of Unseld, ed. *Bertolt Brechts Dreigroschenbuch,* the notice reads: "*Die Dreigroschenoper* (The Beggars Opera): Ein Stück mit Musik in einem Vorspiel und 8 Bildern nach dem Englischen des John Gay (Eingelegte Balladen von François Villon and Rudyard Kipling)."

40. I.e., to the bathroom.

41. Sara Zimmerman, "The Influence of John Gay, François Villon, and Rudyard Kipling on the Songs in Bertolt Brecht's *Dreigroschenoper*" (master's thesis, Indiana University, 1968). The *Regiebuch* previously referred to contains—in addition to a complete translation of "Mary, Pity Women!"—a faithful rendition of Kipling's poem "The Ladies," to be sung by Mackie under the title "Die Ballade von den Ladies." [Ed. note: See also James K. Lyon, *Bertolt Brecht and Rudyard Kipling. A Marxist's Imperialist Mentor* (The Hague: Mouton, 1975).]

42. J. T. Shaw, "Literary Indebtedness and Comparative Literature Studies," in *Comparative Literature: Method and Perspective,* ed. N. P. Stallknecht and H. Frenz (Carbondale: Southern Illinois University Press, 1961), p. 60.

43. Judith Sherwin, "The World is Mean and Man Uncouth," *Virginia Quarterly Review,* XXXV (1959), 258–270.

S[ain]t Joan of the Stockyards   Patty Lee Parmalee*

Here finally Brecht's years of study [of economics] take clear dramatic form; here finally he finishes a play incorporating his old interest in the stock market and the results of his reading on political economy. *St. Joan of the Stockyards*, the first major play since *A Man's a Man*, is in every sense the culmination of Brecht's early work. The plays following *St. Joan* take up new themes and new styles; many are directed against fascism, and none are as purely socialist as *St. Joan* and *The Mother* (written in 1931, the year *St. Joan* was finished). Those two plays represent the zenith of Brecht's early creativity; not only because they are the last before exile, and not only because of their literary and ideological excellence, but also because *St. Joan* gathers up all the motifs Brecht had worked on and left in fragmentary form since 1924 and fits them into a coherent whole — while *The Mother* accepts those hard-won insights as given and goes on to show the next step: how to organize the struggle at which Joan (and the unemployed in *The Bread Store*) failed.

Concerning the quality of *St. Joan*, many of the critics who are not obliged to reject it for being "doctrinaire" consider it one of Brecht's major accomplishments. Theodor Adorno calls it "the central conception of his dialectical theater."[1] Frederic Ewen praises it at length, beginning with: "*St. Joan of the Stockyards* constitutes not only an intrepid *tour de force*, but it is probably one of Brecht's most brilliant and successful dramatic efforts."[2] André Müller describes the play's success at its premiere in Hamburg in 1959: "Half an hour after the end of the performance the room was still filled with an enthusiastically applauding audience. . . . In recent years there has hardly been a theater event in the Federal Republic that came close to this."[3]

Ernst Bornemann . . . calls it "the noblest and most beautifully balanced play that Brecht ever wrote."[4] And although he still regarded it as a fragment, Brecht himself counted *St. Joan* among his three favorite plays.[5]

There are few plays in the history of drama that are more derivative and eclectic than *St. Joan of the Stockyards*, yet every line is unmistakably Brecht. He has succeeded in this work in exposing the major stylistic and ideological traditions of modern bourgeois Germany, by measuring them against his new Marxist insights. Rülicke-Weiler describes the effect of the clash between form and content (parody) as a technique of *Verfremdung*: "The verse forms of Shakespeare, Schiller and Goethe come to contradict the content; the inhumanity of a society is exposed through confrontation with a form that was created to express human content. It becomes evident that the vestments of the classic-humanist ideal do not fit the

*Reprinted by permission from chapter 5 (pp. 244–64, 287–88) of *Brecht's America*, by Patty Lee Parmalee (Columbus: Ohio State University Press [for Miami University], 1981). © 1981 by Miami University. All rights reserved.

affairs of monopoly capitalism."[6] Besides the classic poets, she could have mentioned the Bible, which permeates the style of the entire play. It was in 1928 that Brecht was asked what book influenced him most, and answered, "You will laugh: the Bible" (*GW* 18:12*).[7]

In 1929 Brecht asked whether a playwright could write about money in iambic forms (*GW* 15:197); in *St. Joan* he gives the answer: yes, but only in parody. In parodying the style of the classics, Brecht by no means meant to ridicule them—he had the strongest respect for them, especially Shakespeare—but rather to demonstrate the Marxist principle that the bourgeoisie was a progressive and creative force when it was the revolutionary class, but that its early ideology and art are hypocrisy when used by today's bourgeoisie to restrain progress and creativity (revolution). Faust's ambivalence was honest a century earlier; but when mouthed by Mauler, Brecht's twentieth-century Faustian man, it is duplicity. In the age of individualism, acts of charity were virtuous; in the age of mass struggle, Brecht's Salvation Army objectively serves the enemies of the individuals it feeds. Even martyrdom is perverted: the true martyrs in Brecht's scheme are not canonized by the ruling class; they are the Saccos, Vanzettis, Luxemburgs and Liebknechts, whose deaths anger and instruct the people. Joan's tragedy is that she is unable to pass on what she learned to anyone who should hear it; her sacrifice is futile because its meaning is perverted by her enemies, and that is possible because she always acts as an individual.

In short, *St. Joan* is a play about how ideology is used to obscure reality. Simultaneously, its effect on the audience is to teach them how to see through the ideology to the reality; as such it is a *Lehrstück par excellence*. The ideology is: Mauler's "humane nature" and philanthropy, the Salvation Army's promise of reward and punishment in heaven for those who accept the status quo on earth, Joan's individualism and reformism and her disapproval of violence, and of course the pact between the capitalists and the church. The reality is: Mauler's "letters from New York," the need for revolutionary violence and solidarity, and the workings of the capitalist system.

The last theme is brilliantly demonstrated by the very structure of the play. The audience can see that each one of Mauler's apparent concessions to the poor is actually motivated by advice from the inner workings of the system (Wall Street). Each phase of the action is introduced by a letter predicting and advising on the coming stage of capitalist development. The play is divided into five sections representing five stages: (1) the end of prosperity; (2) overproduction; (3) crisis; (4) stagnation; and finally (5) the tendency toward monopoly as a (temporary) solution. Joan merely provides Mauler with the ideological excuses he needs so he will look as though he is not acting only in his own interest. But his every apparent good and spontaneous act is premeditated on the basis of better knowledge of the system. If there is any doubt on that point, a passage in a draft that

Brecht did not publish (probably because he thought it unnecessarily obvious) should clear it up:

> SLIFT: helping people mauler you must be ill
>
> MAULER: don't say that   i have a letter here from my dear friends in newyork (BBA 118, 74)[8]

A detailed and excellent description of the economic plot (i.e., the Marxist analysis of the phases of capitalism), and of the ideological superstructure that Mauler imposes to mislead Joan and that Brecht tears away to teach his audience, is contained in an article by Käthe Rülicke.[9] It would be redundant to repeat her definitive analysis here, except to point out the genius of the play's structure and the audacity of the attempt to dramatize [Marx's] *Capital*.

It is an attempt that necessarily requires simplification, as well as stylization, of reality into what Brecht would call realism (which shows how to change reality) as opposed to naturalism (which portrays reality as inevitable). The simplification and stylization are aided by the use of the American setting. Rülicke-Weiler again: "Dramatic alienation [*Verfremdung*] by means of a milieu largely unknown in Germany, in which details could be treated on a large scale or left out, made it easier for Brecht to bring out the economic processes clearly and to make evident the fact that these processes (which, erupting inexplicably and seemingly overnight, determined the events in Germany as well) follow certain laws."[10] That is not so very different from Brecht's early rationale for using America as the setting for *In the Jungle*. . . .

The theory of *Verfremdung* by means of setting remained remarkably the same, and continued to do so through Brecht's late works, which are set in Sichuan [Szechwan], the Caucasus, ancient Rome, Renaissance Italy, the Thirty Years' War—only once in contemporary Germany and once ([*The Resistible Rise of Arturo*] *Ui*) in America. [Brecht's] purpose is to be able to concentrate on the paradigmatic aspects (*Modellcharakter*) of the plot and not be distracted by incidental exceptions and variations with which the audience would be familiar in its own country. (Perhaps [*Arturo*] *Ui* failed to arouse interest in the United States because Americans expected to see themselves mirrored in a play set in America.)[11]

But although the dramaturgical reason for using America stayed the same, the image of America changed. And yet it did not change: it retained all the same outward characteristics. Only the focus was sharpened, so that a formerly illegible background appeared, creating a qualitatively different picture. The new focus, of course, was the result of Brecht's own clearer vision, sharpened by reading *Capital* as well as . . . books on America, . . . attending classes and provoking countless discussions on Marxism, experiencing and understanding the depression, and committing himself to active struggle on the side of the working class, socialism, and the Communist Party.

Thus, in *St. Joan* Brecht is still using a background that corresponds to the character types in his play, in order that the audience not think them romantic or exceptional; but it is no longer "freedom" ("Freiheit") and "offensiveness" ("Anstößigkeit") that characterize the types and he would not call them "great human types" ("große Menschentypen") without some qualification. There are now moral judgments attached to the characters; in fact, they are no longer interesting as individuals but as the embodiment of moral categories and representatives of specific forces in society. The scheme for the setting of *In the Jungle* no longer fits for *St. Joan* because the latter is not a play about the characters, who are just given a fitting background; to return to the analogy, the background is now in such clear focus that it has become the foreground, and the focus on individual figures is less clear. (Thus Western critics find Mauler too simplified, and [the Marxist critic Ernst] Schumacher finds the workers too undifferentiated.)

The background that has become foreground is simultaneously the capitalist system and America. More than any of Brecht's other plays, *St. Joan* is a play *about* America — not just set in America. The setting has none of the mythical qualities and geographical absurdities of *Mahagonny* or *In the Jungle*; it is very concrete and very real, adopted carefully and as accurately as necessary from the many sources Brecht read on the United States, Chicago, and finance. Chicago does still correspond to Berlin, but not as a metaphor or allegory: now Chicago is the *cause* of Berlin. For not only was the capitalist-democratic Weimar Republic a direct product of American postwar investment and influence, the entire capitalist world suffered an economic crisis as a result of the American stock market crash. The German depression was worse than the American because of the German economy's extreme dependence on American capital.

Thus *The Bread Store*, which demonstrates the *effects* of the depression, is set in Berlin,[12] but often mentions New York as the origin of the crisis. In that play Falladah Heep of the Salvation Army asks Washington Myers the *Gretchenfrage* (the question Gretchen puts to Faust), how he feels about God, and he answers: "yes, miss heep, positive, completely positive. but, he naturally has very little influence in new york. it's always said that he has a crowd of rich friends, mr. ford and mr. rockefeller, but unfortunately his friends very often seem to leave him in the lurch" (BBA 1353, 24). The song "Hosanna Rockefeller," written in 1924[13] but included among the materials to *The Bread Store*, repeats [the] names [of Rockefeller and Henry Ford] as business partners with God (BBA 1353, 78). . . .

Brecht comments on the plot of *The Bread Store:* "Mrs. Q. has bad luck because of New York" and "He [Myers] rebels against New York, the law, and the army."[14] Finally, Herr Flamm, the richest man the unemployed have ever seen, explains to his tenant the baker that he must pay his rent or be evicted, because Flamm is at the mercy of the small banks, which are in the hands of the great banks, which are in crisis because the state is actually thinking of demanding taxes from industry, which has never happened in the memory of mankind, "because America, to which Europe is in debt up to its neck, is writhing in a horrible crisis, the reasons for which are a complete mystery to the greatest scholars of political economy" (GW 7:2923).

Whereas *The Bread Store* leaves everyone wallowing in futile actions or resignation because of ignorance of causes, *St. Joan* exposes those same causes. Since it intends to teach the cause as well as the effect of the crisis, it is set in the country that is itself the cause. Insofar as the mechanisms revealed in the play apply universally to capitalist countries and will be applied by the audience to Germany, and insofar as Brecht uses the American setting as a vehicle for simplification, it is, as usual, a means of *Verfremdung*. But insofar as the background has become foreground so that statements and value judgments are made about America itself, and the relation between America and Germany is one of cause and effect rather than analogy, the American setting is *not* a means of *Verfremdung* but is necessary and natural. Distance in this play is achieved primarily through the style (verse, parody, and unnatural diction and syntax) and the elaborate, "scientific" structure, rather than through the setting.

If America is then in part the subject of *St. Joan*, what is Brecht saying about his subject?

That religion there is hypocritical. That a few men can ruin the lives of millions. That violence is used to keep those men in power. That this situation can be changed if it is understood, but that the ruling class propagates ideologies that prevent understanding. In short, that the United States is capitalist (and how that capitalism works). The two concepts are fused: every detail is both a characterization of America and a characterization of capitalism (at first competitive capitalism, then monopoly capitalism).

Brecht has come a long way since *In the Jungle*. There he intuited that the degradation caused by poverty and the isolation between people were somehow native to America, the land of plenty, but he was not certain that that was bad; it was the cost of progress, the new age required strong men. Now, in *St. Joan*, he knows *why* people fight each other as in a jungle, why they live in poverty in the land of unlimited opportunity; and he knows that it is bad, that it was in fact the cost of progress but that American capitalism itself was only a stage in the progression. *America no longer represents the new age:* it is now the dying culture, and the socialist countries are The New that always fascinated Brecht so much. The classes of people who seemed to him in *Jungle* and *Fleischhacker* to be dying as a sacrifice to the cruel new age become and remain for Brecht the carriers of life and progress into the just new age.

As in [the poem "Late Lamented Fame of the Giant City of New York"; GW 9:475–83],[15] the details are the same, but the context and the evaluation are utterly different.

The details about America even come from many of the same sources as [in] Brecht's earlier plays, or they are further developments of those plays (and fragments) themselves. Virtually every source . . . is reflected in *St. Joan*, and virtually every theme from the earlier works that are set in America (particularly the unfinished ones) is incorporated into this rich play. We will look first at the sources, then at Brecht's adaptation of his own work.

In *St. Joan* we have the fruits of the first work we know Brecht read on America, [Upton Sinclair's] *The Jungle*. . . . [T]he general atmosphere of *The Jungle* must have informed Brecht's emphasis on poverty and his treatment of Chicago, prostitution, and coldness, as well as the concept of the city as Darwinian jungle. The influences on *St. Joan* are much more specific, so much so that we must assume Brecht reread the novel before or while working on *St. Joan*. Nowhere but from Sinclair could Brecht have got his information about the human ingredient in leaf lard; and that accident is explained to the widow in both works with the packers' lie that the man has gone off on a trip. We have here a clear example of Brecht's reaction to, and use of, his reading. The description of that accident caused more sensation than any other passage in the very influential novel. (Sinclair: "I aimed at the public's heart and by accident I hit it in the stomach."[16]) But Brecht, with his command of the technique of dramatic alienation that eludes Sinclair, is able to prevent excessive interest in the gory detail and focus instead on the reaction to which poverty and bribery force the dead worker's widow.

There are other details that Brecht clearly adopted from *The Jungle*. One is the fascinating gravity method of slaughtering hogs, in which the hog's own weight is his undoing. Another is the presence of vast numbers of unemployed, which means that jobs are only available through other workers' misfortune. More general common themes are the evaluation of charity organizations, the strike, the cold, and of course the entire structure of the meat industry.

By now Brecht had also come to agree with Sinclair's conclusion, that socialism is the solution to the horrors of the meat industry. But that conclusion is not very convincing in Sinclair's book, partly because it is an afterthought and partly because the worst horrors described are excesses, which can easily be remedied (and were, partly as a result of Sinclair's book and with the blessing of the government and the larger industries) without altering the structure of the system at all. On his first reading of *The Jungle*, Brecht was moved by the lot of the poor but uninterested in socialism; but in *St. Joan* he is far more revolutionary and more astute in his analysis than Sinclair. In *St. Joan* the need for a socialist revolution is an integral part of the conception of the whole play. It is not a *protest* play, i.e., an appeal to those in power; Brecht never wrote protest literature. It is a *revolutionary* play, an appeal to those not in power to take power.

None of the American works Brecht read are revolutionary: Gustavus

Myers['s *History of the Great American Fortunes*, 1910] comes the closest, with his exposé of the immorality of every last link in the system, but his book is only the king of muckraking books: it suggests no alternative and no means of attacking the wrongs he lists, either individually or collectively. George Lorimer, Bouck White, Ida Tarbell, Frank Norris, Theodore Dreiser, all provide fascinating studies of the minds of capitalists and the workings of capitalism, but there are no conclusions even implicit in their studies. Johannes V. Jensen affirms the order of the system over chaos, and Sherwood Anderson mourns what is past more than he envisions a way to a better future.[17] The principal themes of the novels by the last two authors are themes that Brecht no longer takes up in writing *St. Joan:* destructive personal fascination (and homosexuality) and the "Human Migration to the Big Cities." The absence of the second theme is particularly significant because it was the rubric under which he united all his previous American plays, from *Jungle* to *Mahagonny*. But in *St. Joan* there is never a mention of nostalgia for the plains, the savannahs, the countryside, Alaska, Tahiti—there is no comparison of industrial capitalism with feudalism or the early agrarian-frontier ethic. That concern is finished for Brecht. To repeat: newness is represented no longer by capitalism but by socialism; the important conflict is not between the old values and structures and those of the present, but between those of the present and the forces that are struggling to change them in the future.

Thus, ironically, although almost all the American literature Brecht read was social protest, in the play that reflects the sources most he only used them for their inside information on capitalism. He could as well have used the financial journals—and in fact he did. We know about his studies for *Fleischhacker*, including newspaper clippings, and the interview with the Viennese stockbroker. With the materials to *St. Joan* in the Brecht Archive, there is also a floor plan of the Chicago Board of Trade, printed in 1931 (BBA 894, 103–5). The floor areas for the different kinds of grain are indicated, and the accompanying text, underlined by Brecht, explains the techniques of trading, such as hand signals. The scenes of *St. Joan* set in the cattle exchange take account of the buying and selling techniques, at the same time rendering them grotesque with biblical language. In production of course the hand signals can be used, as Brecht undoubtedly intended.[18]

That plan of the Board of Trade also indicates that even in 1931 Brecht still thought of *St. Joan* as an adaptation of the relations of the wheat exchange to the beef trust; we have assumed that the reasons for the change were a rereading of *The Jungle* and the rich possibilities in the symbol of slaughtering [cattle and hogs] (for instance, the Black Straw Hats compare today's world to a slaughterhouse).

But although the setting in the stockyards is taken from *The Jungle*, the financial dealings are still basically those described by Norris in *The Pit*, assimilated into *St. Joan* by way of *Fleischhacker*. The most significant

difference between Curtis Jadwin's story and Brecht's version in both
Fleischhacker and *St. Joan* is that Jadwin loses and that is the end of it; he
goes off with his wife a happy man, relieved of the burden of wealth, and
the reader forgets the market in this conciliatory happy ending. Brecht
allows no such escape, and he does not exonerate his capitalists because
they are loving husbands. Both Fleischhacker and Mauler rise up to the
top again after apparent bankruptcy, Fleischhacker because war breaks
out and his wheat becomes a gold mine (BBA 524, 90), Mauler through the
conscious use of monopoly capitalism's tactics for pulling out of a crisis:
mergers and destruction of the excess product, plus cutbacks in production
to raise prices, and cutbacks in wages and employment. In both cases the
capitalist system is saved by becoming more brutal. In *The Pit* the future
course of the system is not indicated at all; in *Fleischhacker* too there is no
indication what will happen after the war. But in *St. Joan* Mauler's
solution clearly can only be temporary, because capitalist economics have
been shown to be cyclical. The seeds of the next, larger crisis are already
apparent in the larger numbers of unemployed and the lower salaries paid
to the workers: these two groups are supposed to be the market for the
meat that now has a higher price. Brecht is not just registering moral
outrage that the workers suffer most from the solution to a crisis; he is also
showing that the solution cannot work permanently.

Although Mauler's financial dealings are adopted mainly from *The
Pit*, his character has several other sources as well. There are two non-
American sources, Faust (Brecht: *St. Joan* "is supposed to show the current
stage of development of the Faustian person" [*GW* 2:4*] and Shaw's
Underhill in *Major Barbara*. The Faust theme, parodied especially at the
end of the play ("Human, there are two souls living / In your breast!") may
have occurred to Brecht when he read *Capital*. In volume 1, chapter 24,
shortly before his famous "Accumulate, accumulate! That is Moses and the
prophets!" Marx uses the Faust theme to describe the capitalist: "Two souls
alas do dwell within his breast; / The one is ever parting from the other."[19]
He is referring not to an earthly and a heavenly, or selfish and generous,
soul, but to the contradiction between consumption (avarice) and accumulation (abstinence). *Major Barbara* was mainly a negative influence on
the story of Johanna, since Brecht is protesting Shaw's extremely un-
Marxist conclusion that only the rich can help the poor. (I suspect that *St.
Joan* also embodies a similar reaction by Brecht against the class reconcili-
ation in Fritz Lang's great 1926 film *Metropolis:* the capitalist, the strike,
the saintly woman are all there, but with a very different, naïve message.)
Brecht's attitude toward Shaw fluctuated; at the end of the twenties it was
ambivalent.[20] From both internal and external evidence, Shaw's Saint Joan
seems not to have been a model;[21] Schiller's, on the other hand, was.

But Mauler as capitalist is more directly a conglomerate of the
capitalists in all the American books Brecht read. In him we find elements
of Dan Drew, the ruthless spectator and swindler, and naïve and hypocriti-

cal churchman and philanthropist; of Lorimer's John Graham, the kindly meat-packing king who gives homespun advice to his son Pierrepont; of Tarbell's Gary — the "good" capitalist who cooperated with government and originated mergers — and J. P. Morgan, who contributes Pierpont Mauler's name; of all the great merciless financiers in Myers's compendium; and of Dreiser's Cowperwood, who is essentially the same type as Norris's Jadwin. Brecht's first version of *St. Joan* is set at the turn of the century, in the period of old-style tycoons described by most of the American books we know Brecht read. Angered by the pieties expressed by so many of these powerful exploiters, Brecht has Joan learn that goodness of character in the class enemy is irrelevant, that it even helps make him more powerful.

We also see the influence of many of Brecht's readings about Chicago in his use of the cold and snow. We have already noted that Chicago's cold is extraordinarily emphasized in books like *The Jungle*, *The Wheel*, and *The Pit*, and that Brecht reflected that emphasis in *Jungle* and in talk of "cold Chicago," meaning Berlin. In *The Bread Store* and *St. Joan* he learns how to make cold and snow socially relevant, not just part of the American "aroma." Brecht himself noted in 1942: " 'Nature' is reflected curiously in my works. . . . In *Drums* and *Jungle* the battlefield is the city. . . . In *St. Joan* [the landscape] is battlefield again (the snowfall is a social phenomenon). *Mother* has no landscape . . . *Courage* renders landscape like *St. Joan*. . . . Human relationships of a direct sort are depicted only in the *Mother*."[22] This important statement says in effect that all the "landscapes" or settings Brecht has used have been creators of alienation; their role has been to show that capitalist society prevents meaningful relations between men. He probably realized that with hindsight when looking at the earliest plays, but in *St. Joan* (and *The Bread Store*) it is deliberate. There even the weather becomes a social phenomenon. Nature no longer has the symbolic *deus ex machina* character it had in *Mahagonny;* rather it is a day-to-day danger the workers have to cope with. And responsibility for the weather (i.e., for the suffering it causes) lies with the rich.

Herr Flamm, the richest man in *The Bread Store*, enjoys the winter crispness that is killing the homeless and unemployed: "At last, a real, lovely winter again! With snow and ice! You actually never feel fresher than in winter, at noon you bring a real appetite home with you" (*GW* 7:2922). If they could choose whether to be in a heated house or in the fresh air, winter would be something completely different to the unemployed. The winter as they know it is created by the capitalists.

In a discussion of the poem "Places to Sleep," Erck and Gräf explore the snow metaphor and point out that for Brecht the cold of winter is synonymous with the depression: "What determines whether the influence of natural forces on the life of working people is harmful or useful is the social situation. That is why the winter snow is identified with the elementary force of the crisis."[23] They note that snow is mentioned twenty

times in *St. Joan*, and that in this as well as other works by Brecht snow
has a meaning completely different from its traditional poetic associations.
The key to the significance of snow for Brecht, they say, is in an
autobiographical poem from 1935 called "The Playwright's Song": "I see
snowfalls appear there / I see earthquakes coming forward there / . . . But
the snowfalls have hats on / The earthquakes have money in their breast
pockets / . . . / This I expose" (*GW* 9:790; *Poems* 258).

This poem explains the development of Brecht's treatment of natural
catastrophe; first it was a symbol of divine punishment, but the depression
made him see it as individual responsibility. The snowstorms wearing hats
are his own metaphor for what he has learned. (Compare, however, the
poem ["Solely Because of the Increasing Disorder" (*GW* 9:519; *Poems*
225): "Some of us have now decided / . . . / To speak . . . / . . . / Of
snowfalls (they're not merely cold, we know) /. . . ."]).

What Brecht has learned is also what Joan learns: that whoever says
"Misfortune comes like the rain, that no one maketh but that comes
anyway" is lying; that there are persons who deliberately inflict misfortune; that it is not just "fate." Brecht emphasizes that this is the most
elementary lesson the oppressed must learn, so that they know they can
change their situation by fighting their enemies. The necessity of naming
the enemy is a lesson he repeated often, starting from the time of *St. Joan*.
The song "In Praise of the Revolutionary," from *The Mother*, is an
example: "And where oppression rules and the talk is of fate / He will
name names" (*GW* 2:859).

In *Refugee Conversations* (1940–41) Ziffel observes how the workers
are misled by reading the social-democratic papers: "They keep hearing
that they're ruled by capital, so they overlook the capitalists. They hear
conditions are bad, that distracts from bad people" (*GW* 14:1502). And by
a picture of a Berlin woman standing next to her bombed-out house,
Brecht writes in the *War Primer* (published 1955):

> Look no longer, woman: you'll not find them now!
> But providence, woman, shouldn't get the blame!
> The dark powers, woman, that oppress you there
> They have a face and address and a name.
> (*GW* 10:1038)

In *St. Joan* this theme takes the particular form of criticizing
capitalism's use of religion to distract from the guilty individuals and
guilty class. Because of its focus on the poor, the Salvation Army is an
excellent vehicle for that criticism, which is probably why it so fascinated
Brecht. The Salvation Army makes a brief appearance in *The Bread Store*,
too, where it plays the same role as in *St. Joan*: it aids the rich and confuses
the poor. In notes to *The Bread Store* Brecht complains about the
uselessness of the Salvation Army's idealism (only in *St. Joan* does he have
the "Army" *consciously* collaborate with the capitalists): "Salvation Army:

its function: it drags everyone into the swamp with its idealism" (BBA 1353, 21). Another note on the same subject shows that the story of Joan was probably originally conceived for *The Bread Store*:

> Act 1
> Show the uselessness of religion. Not attack on the Salvation Army!
> Salvation Army has an interest only in itself, its own advancement, it is not interested in people. Wants donors, big earners, not unemployed.
> Girl is thrown out because she cares too much about people.
>
> (BBA 1353, 2)

Also in notes to *The Bread Store*, Brecht compares schematically the characteristics of the Salvation Army ["helps the individual / separates him from the mass / combats force / thinking ideally / . . . "] and the Communist party ["at first helps no one / leads the individual to the mass / considers force a resource / thinking materially / . . . "]. This list demonstrating the Salvation Army's reformism (BBA 1353, 87) is especially applicable to *St. Joan*, where the Communists are actually present on stage to show the alternative to reformism. . . . The first two points [about the relationship of the individual to the masses] are also a major concern of the *Lehrstücke* [plays for learning], especially *The Measure[s] Taken*.

The reasons why capitalism needs the ideological figleaf provided by the Salvation Army, and the exact techniques used, are clear only in *St. Joan*. But both *St. Joan* and *The Bread Store* represent a strong qualitative difference from [Elisabeth Hauptmann's] *Happy End*, although *Happy End* is the only source Brecht names for *St. Joan* in his introductory note (*GW* 2:4*). . . . [But] the context and ideology of Brecht's play are completely different from Hauptmann's. [Brecht apparently accepted] Bernhard Reich's advice . . . on how to make the Salvation Army theme more relevant: by allowing the "Army" to convert capitalists instead of petty gangsters[24] [and wedded] *Happy End* and *Joe Fleischhacker*, two very different plays.

St. Joan is, of course, a great deal more than the marriage of those two plays, especially stylistically, but they provide the primary themes and two of the three interwoven plots: the plot concerning Joan and her relations with the Salvation Army, and the plot concerning Mauler and his machinations on the commodity exchange. The third plot, which is partly new and partly a development of themes from *The Bread Store*, concerns the actions of the workers. They present the real opposition to Mauler, which Joan only thinks she presents, and they replace the equally non-antagonistic Mitchel family in *Fleischhacker*. Like the comparison of Joan with Hallelujah-Lilian [in *Happy End*], a comparison of the workers in *St. Joan* with the Mitchel family shows how far Brecht had come. The Mitchels are basically like the Gargas in *Jungle*: poor, ambitious, and full of dreams of individual escape, they are trapped by the American urban system and by their very dreams; and they simply go down, without fighting back, except for the sons — George Garga and Calvin Mitchel — who retain the illusion that they have somehow escaped. The overwhelming mood of *In the Jungle* is isolation, and that carries over into *Fleischhacker*. The Mitchel family succumbs because of false consciousness — it does not realize that it belongs to the victims rather than the beneficiaries of capitalism (or Chicago) — and because it is completely isolated, believing it can escape poverty alone, through sheer force of individual, American will.

Something of that isolation or individualism remains in Joan. But the workers in *St. Joan* understand — up to a point — that their strength lies in acting together; they are hardly portrayed as individuals. They are, dramatically, real antagonists to Mauler, not just victims.

The story of a speculator who corners the commodity market, then fails, from *Joe Fleischhacker;* the story of a Salvation Army girl who is expelled for taking the job too seriously, from *Happy End;* and the story of an attempted general strike, from Brecht's new experience and conviction — these are the three concurrent plots of the play and their sources. But *St. Joan* also incorporates themes from Brecht's other earlier works. It is the only play he was able to finish on all the economic themes that interested him from 1924, and it represents both his mastery of the theory of capitalism and, apparently, his liberation from the need to write about it. But concerns of the less directly economic plays are also incorporated into *St. Joan*. The possibility of "rebuilding" people is shown by the bribery of Frau Luckerniddle, wife of the man who fell in the vat of lard, as well as in *A Man's a Man*. The problem of reformism, from the *Lehrstücke* and many other works of this period (such as "Places to Sleep"), is a central theme of *St. Joan*. *St. Joan* and *The Mother* are certainly also didactic plays, but Brecht does not call them *Lehrstücke* because their form is completely different, and they are meant to teach the audience, not only the actors.

The conscious adoption of *Lehrstück* themes in *St. Joan* is indicated by the use of some lines in both it and *The Exception and the Rule* (1929–30), such as, "Something like that won't raise itself any higher than the edge of a bowl" (*GW* 2:807; 2:677), and the prologue to the latter play, which uses words of the Black Straw Hats' song: "In such an age of bloody confusion / Organized disorder, well planned arbitrariness / Dehumanized humanity" (*GW* 2:793; 2:671).

Also treated in the *Lehrstücke*, and closely related to the problem of reformism, is the problem of individualism. For Joan and for Brecht, that problem arises because they both want to take on the cause of the working class without having been brought up with its oppression or, therefore, its solidarity. With Joan, Brecht shows how middle-class reformers tend to get involved in doubts — most often about the question of violence — and follow the dictates of their (irrational) conscience at precisely the crucial moment when they are being depended upon. But that conscience itself has been formed by their middle-class upbringing. If they really want to work with the working class, they must learn to have more trust in collective decisions than in individual ones. That is what Joan's failure to deliver the letter is about: first, she is afraid there is something about violence in it; second, since she does not have the same background as the workers and does not know what it is like to have nothing to lose, she cannot stand the cold.

These are likely the hesitations that Brecht too had to overcome and against which he struggled. Since *St. Joan of the Stockyards* is a revolutionary play, it is more involved with the author's view of his own life than social criticism, or protest literature, which merely records the faults of society without demanding a course of action from the readers, audience, or author himself. It is the play that represents Brecht's final break with the familiar bourgeois world.

That break begins for Joan when she cannot understand why the unemployed workers leave her sermon for a possible job. She tells the Black Straw Hats, "But then I want to know who is to blame for all this." They try to dissuade her, but she is determined to investigate although it jeopardizes her job, and she declares, "I want to know it" (*GW* 2:679). The break begins for Brecht when he cannot understand how the wheat exchange works. He sends a letter to Elisabeth Hauptmann announcing that he is reading *Capital* (even though his need to know will jeopardize his writing for three years), and declaring, "I've got to know that now exactly."[25] The break is completed for Joan in her final speech of the play, and symbolically for Brecht in the writing of that speech.

That Brecht did successfully learn to feel at home in the working class is clear from the complete identification with the workers in *The Mother* and subsequent plays. It is partly because he tailored his language to workers that his style achieved its profound simplicity.

Future themes are also prefigured in *St. Joan*. The most important one is the concept of the impossibility of doing good instinctively in an evil society, which finds expression not only in the Salvation Army but also in the dramatic device of the split character. Mauler's two Faustian souls become the two Annas in *The Seven Deadly Sins of the Petty Bourgeoisie* and Shen Te and Shui Ta in *The Good Person of Sichuan*, as well as Puntila [in *Puntila and Matti, His Hired Man*] and other morally if not physically split characters.

St. Joan is not only the culmination of Brecht's early work but also the kernel of much of his future development. In particular, it expresses the political position that he retained firmly through the rest of his life: he deepened his emphasis on humanism later, but he never wavered in his commitment to communism.

We can see from Brecht's poems that the commitment became all-pervasive. By 1931 the majority were political, a change from his statement of 1926 that his poetry had "a more private character."[26]

His theoretical writings on drama from the thirties are also full of political concepts; or, more correctly, Brecht now fit his dramaturgy into a political and economic framework. This is the time when he started speaking of "dialectical" drama instead of "epic" drama. The important fragment "Dialectical Dramatics," written in 1931, is only one example of the totality of Brecht's Marxism. It is subtitled "Basic Idea: Application of the Dialectic Leads to Revolutionary Marxism" (GW 15:211); and in speaking of the theater, it uses Marxist concepts like "commodity," "means of production," "the viewer as mass," "class character" and, of course, the broader categories of dialectics and economics. In attempting to explain the social role of theater in this essay, Brecht gets so involved in Marxist terminology that he has to explain parenthetically, "an understanding of revolutionary economics is indispensable here" (GW 15:223).

But the piece written in 1931 is not a brief outburst. Precisely the same terminology fills Brecht's writings on the theater from his last years; his emphasis shifts only from unmasking and destroying capitalism to building socialism.

Notes

1. Theodor W. Adorno, *Noten zur Literatur II* (Frankfurt am Main, 1965), 118.

2. Frederic Ewen, *Bertolt Brecht: His Life, His Art and His Times* (New York: Citadel Press, 1967), 260. [Ed. note: quotations in the original German have been omitted; translations are by the author. See also Bertolt Brecht, *Saint Joan of the Stockyards*, trans. Frank Jones, introd. Frederic Grab (Bloomington: Indiana University Press, 1969).]

3. André Müller, "Mit einer Verspätung von 27 Jahren. *Die heilige Johanna der Schlachthöfe* im Deutschen Schauspielhaus," *Theater der Zeit* 14, no. 6 (1959):58–61.

4. Ernst Bornemann, "Epitaph für Bertolt Brecht," *Sinn und Form. Zweites Sonderheft Bertolt Brecht* (1957):151.

5. Lion Feuchtwanger, "Bertolt Brecht," *Sinn und Form. Zweites Sonderheft Bertolt Brecht*, 103.

6. Käthe Rülicke–Weiler, *Die Dramaturgie Brechts: Theater als Mittel der Veränderung* (Berlin, 1968), 145.

7. [Ed. note: Bertolt Brecht, *Gesammelte Werke in 20 Bänden* (Frankfurt am Main: Suhrkamp, 1967). Hereafter cited as *GW*.]

8. [Ed. note: Bertolt-Brecht-Archiv, Berlin. Hereafter cited as BBA plus folder and page(s) number(s).]

9. Käthe Rülicke, "Zu Brechts *Die heilige Johanna der Schlachthöfe*," *Theater der Zeit* 16, no. 1 (1961):22–39. Shorter versions [of this article] can be found in Rülicke-Weiler, *Dramaturgie*, 137–46, and Rülicke, "*Die heilige Johanna der Schlachthöfe*: Notizen zum Bau der Fabel," *Sinn und Form* 11 (1959):429–44. All three treatments are excellent. (The five-part structure described here is [Rülicke(-Weiler)'s] formulation.)

10. Rülicke-Weiler, *Dramaturgie*, 137.

11. [Ed. note: see Ernst Schürer, "Revolution from the Right: Bertolt Brecht's American Gangster Play *The Resistible Rise of Arturo Ui*," in this volume.]

12. See *GW* 7:2949.

13. Dated by Herta Ramthun of the Brecht Archive, in an interview [with Patty Lee Parmalee].

14. Bertolt Brecht, *Gedichte* (Frankfurt am Main, 1960), 2:247.

15. [Ed. note: see Bertolt Brecht, *Poems 1913–1956*, ed. John Willett and Ralph Manheim with the co-operation of Erich Fried (New York: Methuen, 1976), 168–74. Subsequently cited as *Poems*.]

16. Upton Sinclair, *The Jungle*. 1906 (New York, 1960), 349.

17. [Ed. note: see Reinhold Grimm, "Bertolt Brecht's Chicago — A German Myth?," in this volume.]

18. In the 1968 Berliner Ensemble version, the scene on the floor of the exchange was the high point of an otherwise fairly uninspired production. The scene was highly stylized and even choreographed, with the groups of growers, buyers, and packers changing their hand signals simultaneously as though in involuntary reaction to some sensed command by the invisible System; the pre-taped choruses were spoken over loudspeakers, and the traders had only to go through the steps of their compulsive dance like marionettes. The printed program showed pictures of the hand signals.

19. Karl Marx, *Capital* (New York, 1960), 1:349.

20. In 1928 Brecht spoke of "the great mediocre G. B. S." (*GW* 18:67).

21. See Ewen, *Brecht*, 261, and n.

22. BBA 279, 21. Printed in Bertolt Brecht, *Baal, der böse Baal der asoziale. Texte, Varianten und Materialien*, ed. Dieter Schmidt (Frankfurt am Main, 1968), 110. [Ed. note: see also Bertolt Brecht, *Arbeitsjournal*, 2 vols., ed. Werner Hecht (Frankfurt am Main: Suhrkamp, 1973), 1:390.]

23. A[lfred] Erck and K. Gräf, "Bertolt Brechts Gedicht 'Die Nachtlager': Versuch einer Interpretation," *Weimarer Beiträge* 13, no. 2 (1967):244. [Ed. note: the poem "Die Nachtlager" (*GW* 8:373–74) has been translated as "A Bed for the Night," in *Poems* 181.]

24. Bernhard Reich, "Erinnerungen an Brecht," *Theater der Zeit. Beilage* 21, no. 14 (1966):14. [Ed. note: see also Bernhard Reich, *Im Wettlauf mit der Zeit* (Berlin: Henschelverlag, 1970), 308–9.]

25. *Erinnerungen an Brecht*, ed. Hubert Witt (Leipzig, 1966), 52. [Ed. note: see also Elisabeth Hauptmann, "Notes on Brecht's Work. 1926," *Brecht as They Knew Him*, ed. Hubert Witt, trans. John Peet ([East] Berlin: Seven Seas, 1974), 53.]

26. *Erinnerungen*, 44. [Ed. note: see also Bernard Guillemin, "On What Are You Working? A Talk with Bert Brecht. 1926," *Brecht as They Knew Him*, 46.]

What Was He Killed For?
Criticism of the Play *Strong Measures* [*The Measures Taken*] by Brecht, Dudov and Eisler

A[lfred] Kurella*

Brecht's new play, which he produced in Germany [in 1930] in co-operation with Dudov and Eisler,[1] has given rise to a lively discussion both in the bourgeois and the workers' press. This fact alone shows that it is a work of very much more than average importance. For this reason it is particularly necessary to give a true and searching criticism of this dramatic experiment. The play combines in a very original way the workers' choir, the talking choir, modern orchestral effects and epic drama.

The subject of the play is quite simple. Four agitators come before a Party tribunal, which is represented by a choir, to give an account of their illegal work in support of the Chinese Communist Party. Their work has been successful, but the agitators do not wish to accept the approval of the Party meeting before relating a certain incident. They themselves have had to shoot a fifth communist in order to carry out their task successfully. In order to bring out clearly the circumstances leading up to the shooting of their comrade the agitators reproduce before the Party meeting the main outlines of the events, each acting one of the parts. This acting is divided into different episodes and between each comments are made by the choir and there is argument and singing in which the specific principles that are involved are brought out.

The following episodes are reproduced: (1) How the young comrade who is afterwards shot comes to join the four agitators. (2) The preparation for illegal work; the putting on of a disguise, symbolizing the sinking of their personality. (3) The first false move on the part of the young comrade, who, out of pity, takes a step which betrays individualism and compromises the work. (4) The second false move on the part of the young comrade, who, from an idealist idea of justice does something which leads to an immature partial strike which is harmful to the mass movement. (5) The third false move on the part of the young comrade, who, from a feeling of decency breaks off his connections with the idealist of anti-imperialist convictions who is to supply him with arms for the uprising. (6) The fourth false move on the part of the young comrade, who under the pressure of the radical elements among the workers, who are impatient for an immediate uprising, infringes the discipline of the organization and disobeys the decisions of the Party, breaking out on his own into open fight; as in doing this he comes out into the open the four agitators shoot at

---

*Reprinted from *Literature of the World Revolution*, no. 5 (Moscow: State Publishing House, 1931), 156–60.

him and make their way out of the town. (7 and 8) Just as the four agitators arrive at the frontier with the young wounded comrade, intending to send him across and thus reduce the risk of their being discovered, the situation in the town comes to such a head that the agitators have to go back again. They are followed. If they merely abandon the young comrade he will be searched by the police and in this way the secret of his participation in the work of the Bolshevist agitators will be discovered. The young comrade recognizes the difficulty of the situation and agrees to their shooting him and covering up all traces by throwing him into a pit. In the 9th and last episode the choir expresses its approval of this action, since through it the desired aim was attained, namely the success of the revolution.

The authors call their production a didactic play [*Lehrstück*]. This sub-heading agrees with Brecht's view that art is only a branch of pedagogy. As the program promises, the play aims at showing the wrong way of doing things in order to teach the spectator the right way. Thus the word "didactic" which is applied to the play should be taken in a literal sense.

One has to assume that the young comrade is a personification of the wrong course of action and that the agitators give an example of the true bolshevism which everyone should learn. This aim, which the authors have set themselves in presenting the play, demands a criticism which shall examine very carefully the kind of ideology that is concealed by them in this "didactic performance."

The first and most simple question that arises is: was the young comrade wrong in the course he took and were the agitators right? And it is just here that the difficulty arises which the authors try to hide. The setting which the authors took for their play (the Chinese revolution, the rising up of the masses, the Union of Coolies, the anti-imperialist movement, the Chinese capitalists, the Chinese Communist Party, the Bolshevist Party of the Soviet Union etc.) is an actual historical setting. But in spite of this the authors assert that the setting is imaginary and that they have only selected here and there certain details from the actual historical events. We cannot agree with the authors, however, that their setting is imaginary. We cannot look upon it as merely a convenient site for an ideological field-day which can be altered at will so as to serve the purpose of demonstrating certain definite ideas. Such an artificial limitation of the field is quite inadmissable for the simple reason that the authors wrote their play not merely for the sake of writing but for a definite public, a definite section of the worker's movement to whom the circumstances of the Chinese revolution and other events made use of in the play are, in main outline, familiar, and amongst whom these circumstances give rise to a very definite set of associations.

In thus giving our opinion as to whose action can be looked upon as right and whose wrong and as to what our attitude should be to the didactic function of the play, we shall start from the assumption that the events take place against the perfectly real background of the Chinese revolution. If then we examine the behavior of the young comrade and the three agitators from this point of view we shall find that it is just the young comrade who represents the point of view of the consistent revolutionary and Bolshevik, while the course taken by the agitators serves as an excellent example of the policy which, in the language of the Third International, is called the right opportunist tendency, for advocating which more than one communist has been excluded from the Party. . . .

[T]he German worker for whom the play was written knows very well from his own experience that to advocate a point of view such as that of the three agitators means virtually to support right-wing opportunism. This opportunism consists in an underestimation of the readiness of the masses for the revolutionary fight. Opportunism is also shown in the subordination of the Party to the organization that it ought to be leading (For Coolie Union, read congress of workers). Finally, it is quite a false view to hold that arms must be obtained before the fight can be started instead of that they should be fought for and won in the course of the struggle, as also that no move should be made until an agreement has been entered into with the other districts. It was just this opportunist attitude which led to the revolutionary movement being smothered.

We could give many instances of the Bolsheviks and Lenin having acted, in corresponding circumstances, in exactly the same way as the young comrade. It is impossible from any reasonable point of view to detach oneself from the great spontaneous revolutionary movement of the masses, one must start guiding this movement even when there is no certainty of its leading to victory. A classic example of this was the "July days" in Leningrad in 1917 and the rising in Moscow in 1905. Menshevist right-wing opportunism was against the rising. Plekhanov pronounced his now famous formula "It is no good fighting for your weapons!" against which Lenin brought the full weight of his revolutionary theory. So as not to be accused of wandering from the subject of the Chinese revolution we may cite the instance of the rising in Canton, which was discountenanced by the right-wingers but approved of by the Third International, in spite of the fact that it had criticisms to make about certain false steps taken by the Party leaders.

A right opportunist point of view can be traced like a colored thread through Brecht's presentation of the young comrade's mistakes. Right-wing opportunism is also betrayed by setting the propaganda of the agitators, which one might call abstract, theoretical propaganda, over against those personal urges which the young comrade follows instinctively and perhaps in certain individual circumstances erroneously. Right-wing opportunism is also seen in the condemnation of the partial strike in the textile factory, a strike that the young comrade calls in the course of his open activities against the police. The inability of the agitators to lead the strikers is also a result of their opportunist tendencies. Instead of guiding it along revolutionary lines they allow it to be suppressed by the Coolie Union. The only mistake of the young comrade which one can really condemn is his attitude to the rice merchant who apparently represents the position of the Kuomintang. However, in order to settle this point one would have to know at what period of the Chinese revolution this event took place and whether or no[t] the young comrade's class instincts told him that a break with the Kuomintang, which had gone over to the camp of the imperialists, had now become a historical necessity.

Now what is the explanation of the fact that the authors have started out along one path but found themselves on another; that with the intention of writing an instructive Bolshevist play they have succeeded in producing an opportunist one? In order to answer this question we shall follow the whole chain of mistakes made by the authors, tracing them to their philosophico-ideological origins.

In order to make their ideas concrete the authors have created an artificial setting. They have not taken, as Lenin demands that they should, all the varied genuinely revolutionary situations from the dialectic-materialists in order to show them in all their aspects with all their affinities and causal connections. They have taken odd pieces of reality in order to make from them a bounderied field for carrying out manoeuvres with the ideas which they wish to demonstrate. They have acted to a certain extent like the amateur gods who try to create worlds starting from ideas. In other words they have approached reality and their material, idealistically (in the philosophical use of the word). This too is not merely by chance, for the idealist standpoint is apparent throughout the whole play. It is particularly noticeable in the way communism and the Communist Party are depicted. Communism is for the authors an idea which is to be found in the "doctrine of the classics." It is this that for them gives it its strength. The doctrine of the classics is the basis of the Party. When Brecht's *Strong Measures* praises the Party (such passages have genuine beauty from the poetical and musical point of view) and demands a sinking of personal aims in those of the Party, this is only because the Party incarnates a doctrine. The following statement is to be found in the text: — "Individuality may be annihilated but the Party can never be annihilated because it rests on the doctrine of the classics."

From the point of view of the authors the indestructability of the Party rests on the doctrine of the classics, and not on the fact that it represents the proletariat, the rising class, destined to come to power, which cannot be destroyed, since, if it was, the whole of society would return to barbarism.

We can now determine what are the class roots of this idealistic standpoint of the authors. Certain old survivals are evident in this way of thinking which is characteristic of the radical petty-bourgeois whom the chances of life have turned from the bourgeois camp into that of the proletariat. The petty-bourgeois, breaking away from the class in which he has been brought up defies its designation of communism as a senseless harlequinade of a crowd of bawling rowdies with the words "no, communism provides the only true banner representing the highest knowledge of reality attained in our days." The petty-bourgeois revolutionary thinks that he has thus completely understood communism. He does not see that here it is impossible to separate theory from practice, that communism is a concrete, historically founded, militant class movement, that it is impossible to understand the communist doctrine and not throw in one's lot with the revolutionary movement.

This one sided understanding of communism is so ingrained in Brecht that it colors his whole literary work. Brecht, the revolutionary dramatist who in his plays exhorts people to take up the communist ideas and even seeks to associate himself closely with the movement, has not yet succeeded in acquainting himself with the mass movement of the agitational-propagandist groups. These groups, however, give the true political setting for the creation of a revolutionary proletarian drama. Unless their experience is sufficiently assimilated the attempts of individual artists to create such a drama will prove futile. Brecht, on the other hand, supposes that it is quite sufficient to know the communist doctrine in order to create, like a scientist in his laboratory, revolutionary art.

As the ideological analysis which we have given of this play has shown, we are confronted with some obvious contradictions.

The play created a strong impression (and strong from the revolutionary point of view) amongst a considerable section of the actors and the audience, whereas it was criticised (in some cases quite severely) by the bourgeois press. From this it follows that under certain, concrete historical conditions the play must be adjudged revolutionary. The bourgeois press took up the same attitude to it as to a Bolshevist play. How can this be accounted for?

Strong Measures forms a contrast to bourgeois art in that it represents an entirely new style. Its style distinguishes it from a bourgeois play and so it is looked upon as revolutionary. We emphasize this question of style rather than form. In passing from bourgeois to proletarian art we always notice this difference in style. Proletarian culture, which is the culture of a new class based on the activity of the great masses of the people, diverts art into new channels. But not only are new channels found; the function of art in social life itself is changed, as also the relations the different arts bear to one another and the kind of methods of which they make use.

It was also a wish to write something that would be a contribution to the young proletarian culture that moved the authors of *Strong Measures* purposely to break with the traditions of the bourgeois theater. Such an attempt, in itself, however wrongly it may have been carried out, deserves particular notice. *Strong Measures* will have a very important place in the future history of proletarian art, and even when the play is no longer produced (which will probably very soon be the case) its influence will be felt in the programs of propaganda theater troops.

The immediate revolutionary effect of *Strong Measures* is, however, not confined to this. In those parts where right ideas from the proletarian ideological arsenal are clearly formulated, the play passes very considerable artistic merit. Such songs as that in praise of illegal work, the Song of Supply and Demand (which would be better named the Song of Merchandise), and that in praise of the Party (omitting the ideological mistakes referred to above) must be ranked with some of the most important revolutionary works of the age, and they will long outlive the play as a whole.

Finally we must not forget that this work of a petty-bourgeois writer appears at a time when the campaign of calumny against the communists is assuming the most violent forms, at a time when many intellectuals who recently sympathized with communism are going over to the other side and when on the other hand new sections of the intelligentsia are joining its ranks. Such a play as *Strong Measures*, even in its present form, helps the latter forward. Thus from this point of view *Strong Measures* is in the long run a revolutionary gesture, and one which the proletariat must defend against its bourgeois detractors.

Note

1. [Ed. note: The verso of the title page lists S[latan] Dudow and composer H[anns] Eisler as collaborators (*Mitarbeiter*). See Bertolt Brecht, *Die Maßnahme, Gesammelte Werke in 20 Bänden* (Frankfurt am Main: Suhrkamp, 1967), 2:632. See also *The Measures Taken, The Jewish Wife & Other Short Plays*, trans. Eric Bentley (New York: Grove Press, 1965), 75–108. Bentley also reprints "What Was He Killed For?," 163–72.]

[Bertolt Brecht on *The Measures Taken, Hangmen Also Die*, and *The Mother*]*

Mr. Stripling: Mr. Brecht, will you please state your full name and present address for the record, please? Speak into the microphone.

Mr. Brecht: My name is Berthold Brecht. I am living at 34 West Seventy-third Street, New York. I was born in Augsburg, Germany, February 10, 1898. . . . [1]

*Reprinted from *United States Congress House on Un-American Activities Committee. Hearings Regarding the Communist Infiltration of the Motion Picture Industry. Devoted to the Hearings of October 20, 21, 22, 23, 24, 27, 28, 29 and 30, 1947.* Washington, D.C.: U.S. Government Printing Office, 1947, 491-504.

Mr. Stripling: Now, Mr. Brecht, will you state to the committee whether or not you are a citizen of the United States?

Mr. Brecht: I am not a citizen of the United States; I have only my first papers.

Mr. Stripling: When did you acquire your first papers?

Mr. Brecht: In 1941 when I came to the country.

Mr. Stripling: When did you arrive in the United States?

Mr. Brecht: May I find out exactly? I arrived July 21 at San Pedro.

Mr. Stripling: July 21, 1941?

Mr. Brecht: That is right. . . .

Mr. Stripling: Were you issued a quota immigration visa by the American vice consul on May 3, 1941, at Helsinki, Finland?

Mr. Brecht: That is correct.

Mr. Stripling: And you entered this country on that visa?

Mr. Brecht: Yes.

Mr. Stripling: Where had you resided prior to going to Helsinki, Finland?

Mr. Brecht: May I read my statement?[2] In that statement —

The Chairman: First, Mr. Brecht, we are trying to identify you. The identification won't be very long.

Mr. Brecht: I had to leave Germany in 1933, in February, when Hitler took power. Then I went to Denmark but when war seemed imminent in '39 I had to leave for Sweden, Stockholm. I remained there for 1 year and then Hitler invaded Norway and Denmark and I had to leave Sweden and I went to Finland, there to wait for my visa for the United States.

Mr. Stripling: Now, Mr. Brecht, what is your occupation?

Mr. Brecht: I am a playwright and a poet.

Mr. Stripling: A playwright and a poet?

Mr. Brecht: Yes.

Mr. Stripling: Where are you presently employed?

Mr. Brecht: I am not employed.

Mr. Stripling: Were you ever employed in the motion-picture industry?

Mr. Brecht: Yes; I — yes. I sold a story to a Hollywood firm, *Hangmen Also Die*,[3] but I did not write the screen play myself. I am not a professional screen-play writer. I wrote another story for a Hollywood firm but that story was not produced. . . .

Mr. Stripling: Are you familiar with Hanns Eisler? Do you know Johannes Eisler?

Mr. Brecht: Yes.

Mr. Stripling: How long have you known Johannes Eisler?

Mr. Brecht: I think since the middle of the twenties, 20 years or so.

Mr. Stripling: Have you collaborated with him on a number of works?

Mr. Brecht: Yes.

Mr. Stripling: Mr. Brecht, are you a member of the Communist Party or have you ever been a member of the Communist Party?

Mr. Brecht: May I read my statement? I will answer this question but may I read my statement?

Mr. Stripling: Would you submit your statement to the chairman?

Mr. Brecht: Yes. . . .

Mr. Stripling: Now, I will repeat the original question. Are you now or have you ever been a member of the Communist Party of any country?

Mr. Brecht: Mr. Chairman, I have heard my colleagues when they considered this question not as proper, but I am a guest in this country and do not want to enter into any legal arguments, so I will answer your question fully as well I can.

I was not a member or am not a member of any Communist Party.

The Chairman: Your answer is, then, that you have never been a member of the Communist Party?

Mr. Brecht: That is correct.

Mr. Stripling: You were not a member of the Communist Party in Germany?

Mr. Brecht: No; I was not.

Mr. Stripling: Mr. Brecht, is it true that you have written a number of very revolutionary poems, plays, and other writings?

Mr. Brecht: I have written a number of poems and songs and plays in the fight against Hitler and, of course, they can be considered, therefore, as revolutionary because I, of course, was for the overthrow of that government.

The Chairman: Mr. Stripling, we are not interested in any works that he might have written advocating the overthrow of Germany or the government there.

Mr. Stripling: Yes; I understand.

Well, from an examination of the works which Mr. Brecht has written, particularly in collaboration with Mr. Hanns Eisler, he seems to be a person of international importance to the Communist revolutionary movement.

Now, Mr. Brecht, is it true or do you know whether or not you have written articles which have appeared in publications in the Soviet zone of Germany within the past few months?

Mr. Brecht: No; I do not remember to have written such articles. I have not seen any of them printed. I have not written any such articles just now. I write very few articles, if any.

Mr. Stripling: I have here, Mr. Chairman, a document which I will hand to the translator and ask him to identify it for the committee and to refer to an article which refers on page 72.

Mr. Brecht: May I speak to that publication?

Mr. Stripling: I beg your pardon?

Mr. Brecht: May I explain this publication?

Mr. Stripling: Yes. Will you identify the publication?

Mr. Brecht: Oh, yes. That is not an article, that is a scene out of a play I wrote in, I think, 1937 or 1938 in Denmark. The play is called *Private Life of the Master Race*, and this scene is one of the scenes out of this play about a Jewish woman in Berlin in the year of '36 or '37.[4] It was, I see, printed in this magazine *Ost und West*, July 1946 [1947].

Mr. Stripling: Mr. Translator, would you translate the frontispiece of the magazine, please?

Mr. Baumgardt: "*East and West, Contributions to Cultural and Political Questions of the Time*, edited by Alfred Kantorowicz, Berlin, July 1947, first year of publication enterprise."

Mr. Stripling: Mr. Brecht, do you know the gentleman who is the editor of the publication whose name was just read?

Mr. Brecht: Yes; I know him from Berlin and I met him in New York again.

Mr. Stripling: Do you know him to be a member of the Communist Party of Germany?

Mr. Brecht: When I met him in Germany I think he was a journalist on the Ullstein Press. That is not a Communist — was not a Communist — there were no Communist Party papers so I do not know exactly whether he was a member of the Communist Party of Germany.

Mr. Stripling: You don't know whether he was a member of the Communist Party or not?

Mr. Brecht: I don't know, no; I don't know.

Mr. Stripling: In 1930 did you, with Hanns Eisler, write a play entitled, *Die Massnahme* [*The Measures Taken*]?

Mr. Brecht: *Die Massnahme*.

Mr. Stripling: Did you write such a play?

Mr. Brecht: Yes; yes.

Mr. Stripling: Would you explain to the committee the theme of that play — what it dealt with?

Mr. Brecht: Yes; I will try to.

Mr. Stripling: First, explain what the title means.

Mr. Brecht: *Die Massnahme* means [speaking in German].

Mr. Baumgardt: Measures to be taken, or steps to be taken — measures.

Mr. Stripling: Could it mean disciplinary measures?

Mr. Baumgardt: No; not disciplinary measures; no. It means measures to be taken.

Mr. McDowell: Speak into the microphone.

Mr. Baumgardt: It means only measures or steps to be taken.

Mr. Stripling: All right.

You tell the committee now, Mr. Brecht —

Mr. Brecht: Yes.

Mr. Stripling (continuing): What this play dealt with.

Mr. Brecht: Yes. This play is the adaptation of an old religious Japanese play and is called No Play, and follows quite closely this old story which shows the devotion for an ideal until death.

Mr. Stripling: What was that ideal, Mr. Brecht?

Mr. Brecht: The idea in the old play was a religious idea. This young people—

Mr. Stripling: Didn't it have to do with the Communist Party?

Mr. Brecht: Yes.

Mr. Stripling: And discipline within the Communist Party?

Mr. Brecht: Yes, yes; it is a new play, an adaptation. It had as a background the Russia-China of the years 1918 or 1919, or so. There some Communist agitators went to a sort of no man's land between the Russia which then was not a state and had no real—

Mr. Stripling: Mr. Brecht, may I interrupt you? Would you consider the play to be pro-Communist or anti-Communist, or would it take a neutral position regarding Communists?

Mr. Brecht: No; I would say — you see, literature has the right and the duty to give to the public the ideas of the time. Now, in this play — of course, I wrote about 20 plays, but in this play I tried to express the feelings and the ideas of the German workers who then fought against Hitler. I also formulated in an artistic—

Mr. Stripling: Fighting against Hitler, did you say?

Mr. Brecht: Yes.

Mr. Stripling: Written in 1930?[5]

Mr. Brecht: Yes, yes; oh, yes. That fight started in 1923.

Mr. Stripling: You say it is about China, though; it has nothing to do with Germany?

Mr. Brecht: No, it had nothing to do about it.

Mr. Stripling: Let me read this to you.

Mr. Brecht: Yes.

Mr. Stripling: Throughout the play reference is made to the theories and teachings of Lenin, the A, B, C of communism and other Communist classics, and the activities of the Chinese Communist Party in general. The following are excerpts from the play:

> "The Four Agitators: We came from Moscow as agitators; we were to travel to the city of Mukden to start propaganda and to create, in the factories, the Chinese Party. We were to report to party headquarters closest to the border and to requisition a guide. There, in the anteroom, a young comrade came toward us and spoke of the nature of our mission. We are repeating the conversation.
>
> "The Young Comrade: I am the secretary of the party headquarters which is the last toward the border. My heart is beating for the revolution. The witnessing of wrongdoing drove me into the lines of the fighters. Man must help man. I am for freedom. I believe in mankind. And I am for the rules of the Communist Party which fights for the classless society against exploitation and ignorance.

"The Three Agitators: We come from Moscow.

"The Young Comrade: The two of us have to defend a revolution here. Surely you have a letter to us from the central committee which tells us what to do?

"The Three Agitators: So it is. We bring you nothing. But across the border, to Mukden, we bring to the Chinese workers the teachings of the classics and of the propagandists: The ABC of communism; to the ignorant, the truth about their situation; to the oppressed, class consciousness; and to the class conscious, the experience of the revolution. From you we shall requisition an automobile and a guide.

"The Four Agitators: We went as Chinese to Mukden — 4 men and a woman — to spread propaganda and to create the Chinese Party through the teachings of the classics and of the propagandists — the ABC of communism; to bring truth to the ignorant about their situation; the oppressed class conscious, and class conscious, the experience of the revolution.

"The Young Comrade: The individual has two, the party has a thousand eyes. The party sees seven states. The party has many hours. The party cannot be destroyed, for it fights with the methods of the classics which are drawn from the knowledge of reality and are destined to be changed in that the teachings spread through the masses. Who, however, is the party? Is it sitting in a house with telephones? Are its thoughts secret, its revolutions unknown? Who is it? It is all of us. We are the party. You and I and all of you — all of us. In your suit it is, Comrade, and in your head it thinks; wherever I live there is its home and where you are attacked there it fights."[6]

Now, Mr. Brecht, will you tell the committee whether or not one of the characters in this play was murdered by his comrade because it was in the best interest of the party, of the Communist Party; is that true?

Mr. Brecht: No, it is not quite according to the story.

Mr. Stripling: Because he would not bow to discipline he was murdered by his comrades, isn't that true?

Mr. Brecht: No; it is not really in it. You will find when you read it carefully, like in the old Japanese play where other ideas were at stake, this young man who died was convinced that he had done damage to the mission he believed in and he agreed to that and he was about ready to die in order not to make greater such damage. So, he asks his comrades to help him, and all of them together help him to die. He jumps into an abyss and they lead him tenderly to that abyss, and that is the story.

The Chairman: I gather from your remarks, from your answer, that he was just killed, he was not murdered?

Mr. Brecht: He wanted to die.

The Chairman: So they kill him?

Mr. Brecht: No; they did not kill him — not in this story. He killed himself. They supported him, but of course they had told him it were better when he disappeared, for him and them and the cause he also believed in.

Mr. Stripling: Mr. Brecht, could you tell the committee how many times you have been to Moscow?

Mr. Brecht: Yes. I was invited to Moscow two times.

Mr. Stripling: Who invited you?

Mr. Brecht: The first time I was invited by the Volks Organization for Cultural Exchange. I was invited to show a picture, a documentary picture I had helped to make in Berlin.

Mr. Stripling: What was the name of that picture?

Mr. Brecht: The name—it is the name of a suburb of Berlin, *Kuhle Wampe*.

Mr. Stripling: While you were in Moscow, did you meet Sergi Tretyakov—S-e-r-g-i T-r-e-t-y-a-k-o-v; Tretyakov?

Mr. Brecht: Tretyakov; yes. That is a Russian playwright.

Mr. Stripling: A writer?

Mr. Brecht: Yes. He translated some of my poems and, I think one play.

Mr. Stripling: Mr. Chairman, the *International Literature* No. 5, 1937, published by the State Literary Art Publishing House in Moscow had an article by Sergi Tretyakov, leading Soviet writer, on an interview he had with Mr. Brecht. On page 60, it states:

He is quoting Mr. Brecht—

"I was a member of the Augsburg Revolutionary Committee," Brecht continued. "Nearby, in Munich, Levine raised the banner of Soviet power. Augsburg lived in the reflected glow of Munich. The hospital was the only military unit in the town. It elected me to the revolutionary committee. I still remember Georg Brem and the Polish Bolshevik Olshevsky. We did not boast a single Red guardsman. We didn't have time to issue a single decree or nationalize a single bank or close a church. In 2 days General Epp's troops came to town on their way to Munich. One of the members of the revolutionary committee hid at my house until he managed to escape."

He wrote *Drum at Night* [*Drums in the Night*]. This work contained echoes of the revolution. The drums of revolt persistently summon the man who has gone home. But the man prefers quiet peace of his hearthside.

The work was a scathing satire on those who had deserted the revolution and toasted themselves at their fireplaces. One should recall that Kapp launched his drive on Christmas Eve, calculating that many Red guardsmen would have left their detachments for the family Christmas trees.

His play, *Die Massnahme*, the first of Brecht's plays on a Communist theme, is arranged like a court where the characters try to justify themselves for having killed a comrade, and judges, who at the same time represent the audience, summarize the events and reach a verdict.

When he visited in Moscow in 1932, Brecht told me his plan to organize a theater in Berlin which would reenact the most interesting court trials in the history of mankind.

Brecht conceived the idea of writing a play about the terrorist tricks resorted to by the landowners in order to peg the price of grain. But this requires a knowledge of economics. The study of economics brought Brecht to Marx and Lenin, whose works became an invaluable part of his library.

Brecht studies and quotes Lenin as a great thinker and as a great master of prose.

The traditional drama portrays the struggle of class instincts. Brecht demands that the struggle of class instincts be replaced by the struggle of social consciousness, of social convictions. He maintains that the situation must not only be felt, but explained — crystallized into the idea which will overturn the world.

Do you recall that interview, Mr. Brecht?

Mr. Brecht: No. [Laughter.] It must have been written 20 years ago or so.

Mr. Stripling: I will show you the magazine, Mr. Brecht.

Mr. Brecht: Yes. I do not recall there was an interview. [Book handed to the witness.] I do not recall — Mr. Stripling, I do not recall the interview in exact. I think it is a more or less journalistic summary of talks or discussions about many things.

Mr. Stripling: Yes. Have many of your writings been based upon the philosophy of Lenin and Marx?

Mr. Brecht: No; I don't think that is quite correct but, of course, I studied, had to study as a playwright who wrote historical plays. I, of course, had to study Marx's ideas about history. I do not think intelligent plays today can be written without such study. Also, history now written now is vitally influenced by the studies of Marx about history.

Mr. Stripling: Mr. Brecht, since you have been in the United States, have you attended any Communist Party meetings?

Mr. Brecht: No; I don't think so.

Mr. Stripling: You don't think so?

Mr. Brecht: No.

The Chairman: Well, aren't you certain?

Mr. Brecht: No — I am certain; yes.

The Chairman: You are certain you have never been to Communist Party meetings?

Mr. Brecht: Yes; I think so. I am here 6 years — I am here those — I do not think so. I do not think that I attended political meetings.

The Chairman: No; never mind the political meetings, but have you attended any Communist meetings in the United States?

Mr. Brecht: I do not think so; no.

The Chairman: You are certain?

Mr. Brecht: I think I am certain.

The Chairman: You think you are certain?

Mr. Brecht: Yes; I have not attended such meetings, in my opinion.

Mr. Stripling: Mr. Brecht, have you since you have been in the United

States, have you met with any officials of the Soviet Government?

Mr. Brecht: Yes, yes. In Hollywood I was invited, sometimes three or four times, to the Soviet consulate with, of course, many other writers. . . .

Mr. Stripling: Mr. Brecht, can you tell the committee when you entered this country, did you make a statement to the Immigration Service concerning your past affiliations?

Mr. Brecht: I don't remember to have made such a statement, but I think I made the usual statements that I did not want to or did not intend to overthrow the American Government. I might have been asked whether I belonged to the Communist Party, I don't remember to have been asked, but I would have answered what I have told you, that I was not. That is what I remember.

Mr. Stripling: Did they ask you whether or not you had ever been a member of the Communist Party?

Mr. Brecht: I don't remember.

Mr. Stripling: Did they ask you whether or not you had ever been to the Soviet?

Mr. Brecht: I think they asked me, yes; and I told them.

Mr. Stripling: Did they question you about your writings?

Mr. Brecht: No; not as I remember, no; they did not. I don't remember any discussion about literature.

Mr. Stripling: Now, you stated you sold the book, the story, *Hangmen Also Die,* to United Artists; is that correct?

Mr. Brecht: Yes; to an independent firm; yes.

Mr. Stripling: Did Hanns Eisler do the background music for *Hangmen Also Die?*

Mr. Brecht: Yes; he did.

Mr. Stripling: Do you recall who starred in that picture?

Mr. Brecht: No; I do not.

Mr. Stripling: You don't even remember who played the leading role in the picture?

Mr. Brecht: I think Brian Donlevy played it.

Mr. Stripling: Do you remember any of the other actors or actresses who were in it?

Mr. Brecht: No; I do not. You see, I had not very much to do with the filmization itself. I wrote the story and then to the script writers some advice about the background of Nazis, nazism in Czechoslovakia, so I had nothing to do with the actors. . . .

Mr. Stripling: Did you collaborate with Hanns Eisler on the song "In Praise of Learning"?

Mr. Brecht: Yes; I collaborated. I wrote that song and he only wrote the music.

Mr. Stripling: You wrote the song?

Mr. Brecht: I wrote the song.

Mr. Stripling: Would you recite to the committee the words of that song?

Mr. Brecht: Yes; I would. May I point out that song comes from another adaptation I made of Gorky's play, *Mother*.[7] In this song a Russian worker woman addresses all the poor people.

Mr. Stripling: It was produced in this country, wasn't it?

Mr. Brecht: Yes, 35, New York.[8]

Mr. Stripling: Now, I will read the words and ask you if this is the one.

Mr. Brecht: Please.

Mr. Stripling: (reading):

> Learn now the simple truth, you for whom the time has come at last; it is not too late.
> Learn now the ABC. It is not enough but learn it still.
> Fear not, be not downhearted. Again you must learn the lesson, you must be ready to take over —

Mr. Brecht: No, excuse me, that is the wrong translation. That is not right. [Laughter.] Just one second, and I will give you the correct text.

Mr. Stripling: That is not a correct translation?

Mr. Brecht: That is not correct, no; that is not the meaning. It is not very beautiful, but I am not speaking about that.

Mr. Stripling: What does it mean? I have here a portion of *The People*, which was issued by the Communist Party of the United States, published by the Workers' Library Publishers. Page 24 says: "*In praise of learning*, by Bert Brecht; music by Hanns Eisler."

It says here:

> You must be ready to take over; learn it.
> Men on the dole, learn it; men in the prisons, learn it; women in the kitchen, learn it; men of 65, learn it. You must be ready to take over —

and goes right on through. That is the core of it —

> You must be ready to take over.

Mr. Brecht: Mr. Stripling, maybe his translation —

Mr. Baumgardt: The correct translation would be, "You must take the lead."

The Chairman: "You must take the lead"?

Mr. Baumgardt: "The lead." It definitely says, "The lead." It is not "You must take over." The translation is not a literal translation of the German.

Mr. Stripling: Well, Mr. Brecht, as it has been published in these publications of the Communist Party, then, if that is incorrect, what did you mean?

Mr. Brecht: I don't remember never — I never got that book myself. I must not have been in the country when it was published. I think it was published as a song, one of the songs Eisler had written the music to. I did not give any permission to publish it. I don't see — I think I have never saw the translation.

Mr. Stripling: Do you have the words there before you?

Mr. Brecht: In German, yes.

Mr. Stripling: Of the song?

Mr. Brecht: Oh, yes; in the book.

Mr. Stripling: Not in the original.

Mr. Brecht: In the German book.[9]

Mr. Stripling: It goes on:

> You must be ready to take over; you must be ready to take over. Don't hesitate to ask questions, stay in there. Don't hesitate to ask questions, comrade —

Mr. Brecht: Why not let him translate from the German, word for word?

Mr. Baumgardt: I think you are mainly interested in this translation which comes from —

The Chairman: I cannot understand the interpreter any more than I can the witness.

Mr. Baumgardt: Mr. Chairman, I apologize. I shall make use of this.

The Chairman: Just speak in that microphone and maybe we can make out.

Mr. Baumgardt: The last line of all three verses is correctly to be translated:

"You must take over the lead," and not "You must take over." "You must take the lead," would be the best, most correct, most accurate translation.

Mr. Stripling: Mr. Brecht, did you ever make application to join the Communist Party?

Mr. Brecht: I do not understand the question. Did I make —

Mr. Stripling: Have you ever made application to join the Communist Party?

Mr. Brecht: No, no, no, no, no, never.

Mr. Stripling: Mr. Chairman, we have here —

Mr. Brecht: I was an independent writer and wanted to be an independent writer and I point that out and also theoretically, I think, it was the best for me not to join any party whatever. And all these things you read here were not only written for the German communists, but they were also written for workers of any other kind; Social Democrat workers were in these performances; so were Catholic workers from Catholic unions; so were workers which never had been in a party or didn't want to go into a party.

The Chairman: Mr. Brecht, did Gerhart Eisler [brother of composer Hanns Eisler] ever ask you to join the Communist Party?

Mr. Brecht: No, no.

The Chairman: Did Hanns Eisler ever ask you to join the Communist Party?

Mr. Brecht: No; he did not. I think they considered me just as a writer who wanted to write and do as he saw it, but not as a political figure.

The Chairman: Do you recall anyone ever having asked you to join the Communist Party?

Mr. Brecht: Some people might have suggested it to me, but then I found out that it was not my business. . . .

Mr. Stripling: I would like to ask Mr. Brecht whether or not he wrote a poem, a song, rather, entitled, "Forward, We've Not Forgotten."[10]

Mr. McDowell: "Forward," what?

Mr. Stripling: "Forward, We've Not Forgotten."

Mr. Brecht: I can't think of that. The English title may be the reason.

Mr. Stripling: Would you translate it for him into German?

(Mr. Baumgardt translates into German.)

Mr. Brecht: Oh, now I know; yes.

Mr. Stripling: You are familiar with the words to that?

Mr. Brecht: Yes.

Mr. Stripling: Would the committee like me to read that?

The Chairman: Yes; without objection, go ahead.

Mr. Stripling: (reading):

> Forward, we've not forgotten our strength in the fights we've won;
> No matter what may threaten, forward, not forgotten how strong we are as one;
> Only these our hands now acting, build the road, the walls, the towers. All the world is of our making.
> What of it can we call ours?

The refrain:

> Forward. March on to the tower, through the city, by land the world;
> Forward. Advance it on. Just whose city is the city? Just whose world is the world?
> Forward, we've not forgotten our union in hunger and pain, no matter what may threaten, forward, we've not forgotten.
> We have a world to gain. We shall free the world of shadow; every shop and every room, every road and every meadow.
> All the world will be our own.

Did you write that, Mr. Brecht?

Mr. Brecht: No. I wrote a German poem, but that is very different from this. [Laughter.]

Mr. Stripling: That is all the questions I have, Mr. Chairman.

The Chairman: Thank you very much, Mr. Brecht. You are a good example to the witnesses of Mr. Kenny and Mr. Crum.

We will recess until 2 o'clock this afternoon.

(Whereupon, at 12:15 p.m., a recess was taken until 2 p.m. of the same day [30 October 1947].)

Notes

1. [Ed. note: for an account of Brecht's appearance before the House Un-American Activities Committee, see James K. Lyon, "Brecht Before 'HUAC,'" in *Brecht in America* (Princeton, N. J.: Princeton University Press, 1980), 273–81.]

2. [Ed. note: Brecht's unread statement is printed in *Thirty Years of Treason*, ed. Eric Bentley (New York: Viking Press, 1971), 220–23.]

3. [Ed. note: see Lyon, "A Qualified Winner—The Film *Hangmen Also Die*," in *Brecht in America*, 58–71.]

4. [Ed. note: Brecht is referring to the scene "Die jüdische Frau" ("The Jewish Wife") that was published in *Ost und West* 1, no. 1 (July 1947):72–76. See also Eric Bentley, "*The Private Life of the Master Race*," in this volume.]

5. [Ed. note: *Die Maßnahme. Lehrstück* was first published in *Versuche*, Heft 4 (Berlin: Kiepenheuer, 1930), and repeatedly revised thereafter. Eric Bentley translated several versions; his translation of the 1930 text appears in Bertolt Brecht, *The Jewish Wife and Other Short Plays*, trans. Eric Bentley (New York: Grove Press, 1965), 75–108.]

6. [Ed. note: the translation by Elizabeth Hanunian is reprinted in *Thirty Years of Treason*, ed. Bentley, 959–76.]

7. [Ed. note: see Petermichael von Bawey, "Dramatic Structure of Revolutionary Language—Tragicomedy in Brecht's *The Mother*," in this volume.]

8. [Ed. note: for an account of the staging of *The Mother*, see Lyon, "New York, 1935," in *Brecht in America*, 6–20.]

9. [Ed. note: *Die Mutter* was first published in *Versuche*, Heft 7 (Berlin: Kiepenheuer, 1933).]

10. [Ed. note: the reference is to an early version of "Solidaritätslied" ("Solidarity Song"). See Bertolt Brecht, *Gesammelte Werke in 20 Bänden* (Frankfurt am Main: Suhrkamp, 1967), 8:369–70; and Bertolt Brecht, *Poems 1913–1956*, ed. John Willett and Ralph Manheim with the co-operation of Erich Fried (New York: Methuen, 1976), 185–86.]

"Mother" Learns and Teaches the Facts of Life [Review of *The Mother*]

Brooks Atkinson*

After a considerable interval the Theatre Union has resumed activity with a play entitled *Mother*, which was acted in Fourteenth Street last evening. The German playwright who signs himself plain Brecht has adapted and improvised it out of Gorky's novel of the same title. Hanns

*From the *New York Times*, 20 November 1935, 26. Copyright 1935/©1980 by The New York Times Company. Reprinted by permission.

Eisler has equipped it with chorus chants to a double-piano score, and Paul Peters has translated the text from the German. As presented in the old Civic Repertory playhouse, it is a technically interesting, though emotionally tepid, exercise in stage craft that combines acting, stereopticon slides and singing. Since Brecht at one time worked with Piscator, this column assumes that the oversimplified and austere pattern of the production echoes some of Piscator's stage ideas.

Gorky's novel was published in Russia in 1907. Brecht's primer in revolutionary doctrine carries the idea ten years further. It is the simple narrative of an aging mother who enters the revolutionary movement only to protect her son from the police who suspect him, but soon comes to share the idea of the party and carries the red flag through many party crises. The story describes in words of almost one syllable the economic basis for political revolution and then shows how party insurgence is carried on in the face of police opposition by secret meetings, the distribution of leaflets, common school education and personal valor.

The style of the production is considerably more interesting than the drama. *Mother* is divided into eighteen episodes. The scenery is hardly more than a skeletonized background lighted by batteries of lamps that are quite visible. Above the background is a screen where movie titles are shown to clarify the story, to announce the title of the chant or to show photographs that symbolize the significance of the scene. In the shadows of the wings are two pianos. Eleven revolutionary chants are sung generally at the close of an episode as a sort of concluding emotional emphasis.

Although the style of the production may sound eccentric in this description, it seems thoroughly logical in the theatre, and in its free confession of stage mechanics it has a refreshing frankness. All the bars are down between the actors and the audience. If the actors are earnest, as they are in this instance, nothing is lost in their contact with the people out front. The performance, which has been directed by Victor Wolfson, is as simple as the drama and the staging and is packed with conviction.

What *Mother* lacks in the theatre is cumulative power. After the novelty of the staging has worn off, the conscious simplicity of the dramatic method turns *Mother* into an animated lecture on the theme of revolution, which may have an educational value but which is desultory theatre. It is a healthy thing to rid the theatre of trickery. But only uncommonly dramatic stories or characters have power enough to live in the theatre without benefit of stage artifice. To revolutionists *Mother* may be a sacred story that has to be told in the form of a religious masque. To this column it is an interesting experiment in stagecraft without much emotional vitality.

Dramatic Structure of Revolutionary Language — Tragicomedy in Brecht's *The Mother*

Petermichael von Bawey*

Bertolt Brecht's *The Mother* (1932), an adaptation of Maxim Gorky's novel with the same title (1906), expresses a central view of the German poet and playwright: that man "appears to be above all a creature used by and useful to human beings" (p. 149).[1] In this drama, Brecht analyzes how society's labor process perverts man's use and how this misuse can be eliminated only by changing society. His Marxian perspective in dealing with this idea creates a twofold time-sense: past time and future time.[2] While the first exposes history's strong impact on the play's characters, the second reveals that another world than the present is possible. Time gone by and time to come are juxtaposed, creating a dialectic of temporal tensions in the dramatic action.

In order to understand how this dual time-sense functions, we must look closely at the plot structure of *The Mother*, which also operates on two levels. One level gives us the story of a poverty-ridden, working-class mother and her son, whose struggle for survival is full of suffering. The drama's chronology of their personal lives provides a biographical account of a working-class family. What we have here is a tragedy, rooted in the historical past which has created oppressive conditions for the proletariat in a bourgeois world. But on another level, Brecht gives us a different perspective on these events by showing how personal despair is transcended through a gradual deepening of the mother's consciousness. With increased awareness of society's economic system, she seeks to free herself from the baneful confines of this "Lower World" of capitalism. Her struggle with the bourgeoisie reveals the progression of her class's ascent toward a freer "Higher World" of a communistic society. We now have a comedy, as Brecht develops this theme of future emancipation and thereby offers an historical logic with which to understand the dramatized events.[3] In this way, the playwright weaves a dual time-sense with a dual plot structure throughout *The Mother*.

If these two plot structures were understood separately, we would have either a mere biography of a worker's mother or a schematic history of her class. But by analyzing them together, we see the continuous dialectical interplay between mother and class, individual and society, as subjective and objective story components are united in the drama.[4] This interaction of *personal chronology* with a *logic of history* also combines the drama's two genres to produce a tragi-comedy, with its typical

*Reprinted by permission from *Clio: An Interdisciplinary Journal of Literature, History, and the Philosophy of History* 10 (1980):21-33.

antithetical tensions.[5] However, on careful examination of the play's tragic and comic elements, we become aware that comedy prevails over tragedy in this story, with the ultimate quest for proletarian liberation surpassing individual suffering. As we will see, the dramatic action moves toward what Northrop Frye calls comedy's "recognition of a new-born society rising in triumph."[6]

The historical development toward a more genuine community can be analyzed in two stages: 1) Ascent from a Lower World (Episodes 1-6); and 2) Ascent to a Higher World (Episodes 7-15). These two stages are respectively associated with discovery and recovery of identity, a theme common not only to comedy, but also to Marxism. Discovery of identity can be seen as the proletariat's knowledge of its exploited position within the socio-economic structure, or its "class consciousness." The recovery of identity goes a step further with the workers' active opposition to the ruling class. This takes the form of class conflict, including agitation against bourgeois ideology and, more explicitly, revolution. With this, the creation of a more liberated society, no longer distorting man's use value, allows all of humanity's identity to be recovered.[7] Through these two stages, Marxist theory is realized and put into practice.

In analyzing *The Mother*, we must look at the relationship between the historical presentation of Marxism and the aesthetic elements in the drama. Brecht combines the two in such a way that examining one without the other would result in an incomplete and even incorrect interpretation. The schema below, therefore, is helpful in organizing the following discussion:

I.   Ascent from a Lower World
      Episodes 1–5   *The Lexicon: Class Definition*
      Episode 6   *The Grammar: Class Consciousness*

II.   Ascent to a Higher World
      Episodes 7–11   *The Syntax: Social Function of Theory
                          and Practice*
      Episodes 12–15   *The Semantics: Historical Significance
                          of Theory and Practice*

The use of this outline permits us to see how Brecht integrates two traditionally separate forms of discourse — social theory and drama — in his artistic construction of revolutionary language.[8]

Ascent from a Lower World

The Lexicon: Class Definition.   The drama opens as Pelagea Vlassova (the mother) expresses the helpless realization that her son's hard work provides little money on which to live. Although talking to herself, the mother is simultaneously addressing the spectator, inviting him to face his own daily economic difficulties. Resignedly, she states that she sees no solution to her poor financial condition. Yet her problem begs for an answer, and as such, beckons the spectator to participate by searching for one. A revolutionary workers' chorus suddenly interjected into the drama facilitates this participation, as its song universalizes Vlassova's particular situation for the working class as a whole.

By poetically drawing a relationship between a part (Vlassova) and the whole (the working class), Brecht creates a synecdochic shift which elevates an individual problem to a higher social sphere. This kind of abrupt movement from the dramatic presentation of a specific scene (with all its personal denotations) to the cognitive signification of it (expressed through the lyrics with all of their social implications) repeatedly occurs in *The Mother*, enabling Brecht to provide an overall historical sense for his drama. As the last refrain of the chorus's song refers to the mother's situation by asking, "but what can you do?" (p. 39), the spectator is given a clue that the play may also deal with his own economic condition.

Brecht suggests a solution to the mother's situation in the next episode. In "The Song of What To Do?" a revolutionary worker informs Vlassova that if she is to better her living conditions, she will have to change the entire organization of society. What began on a personal level has now nearly reached epic proportions; and what started with a mother's despair will eventually lead to the overthrow of the state.

The didactic purpose of these lyrical passages is evident: they offer a theoretical perspective which stimulates us to think historically about the dramatized action. Brecht attempts to distance us from our commonly recognized and familiar reality by impelling us to imagine a world other than the one in which we live. Thus, he lets our imagination take flight through his lyrical pieces; but at the same time, he guides our fantasy in the direction of Marxism's historical vision.

To justify its taking over the state, Marxism must show us more than the workers' social misery. It must also supply us with a precise vocabulary to explain how this suffering originated. Brecht furnishes such a "lexicon" as Vlassova is given a lesson in Marxian economics by her son and his friends. He juxtaposes the theoretical knowledge of the young men with the political naiveté of the mother to illustrate a crucial aspect of communism: private property must be abolished. The mother (along with the spectator) learns it is human labor (Marx's means of production) that makes a factory useful, and without it the factory (Marx's mode of production) is worthless. On the other hand, the workers cannot survive economically without employment in the factory. The interdependency between the two shows Vlassova that, while the workers produce society's wealth, they lack control of its distribution.

By providing this Marxian definition of labor value, Brecht enables the mother to link her personal condition to that of the entire working class. In following the logic of this explanation, she learns that a strike is necessary to redress society's economic inequities. It is a way for the worker to obtain a political voice in a society which seeks to curtail his participation in it. The mother, however, wants a peaceful strike; she rejects outright force. We have come to one of Brecht's central issues: how and when is force justified in society?

Brecht gives us an answer to this in episode five, where we see Vlassova joining her son for a May Day demonstration of workers supporting the strike. In notes to the play, Brecht suggested that this episode be presented as if the workers stood before a court of law, reporting their participation in the demonstration. In the midst of their factual account, they recite an ardent lyric proclaiming future victory for the proletariat. Thus, when we hear that a worker is killed by the police, our sense of loss is quickly overcome through the poem's projection of hope in the future. As the documentary-like reportage of the protagonists gives a sense of historical authenticity to the tragedy of the workers' oppression, the lyric interjects comedy through its utopian vision of social liberation. This sort of staging brings tragic and comic aspects into close proximity of one another. And although the police disperse the workers, ensuring control by the upper class, a comic mood dominates this otherwise tragic situation by claiming the future for the oppressed.

The demonstration taught the mother the necessity of force. For Brecht, force is inherent in the class struggle; it is dictated by the bourgeoisie's socio-political supremacy, and it is imperative for the proletariat's liberation.[9] Vlassova's realization of this has given her a new social vocabulary with which she can speak the language of the workers. She no longer sees herself as only a mother of a working son; having discovered her true identity, she finds herself united to a class. This discovery is the first stage in her ascent from the "Lower World" of bourgeois confinement. However, she must articulate this identity in a more conscious manner if she is to participate in freeing her class from its social bondage. Such an understanding will require knowledge of political tactics and of her class's historical tasks. She still requires what Marxism calls "class consciousness."

The Grammar: Class Consciousness. The sixth episode is one of the most important in the play, for here the mother learns the basic tenets of Marxism and how she can use them for future agitation and eventual revolution. Brecht skillfully juxtaposes Marxism — expressed in three lyrical passages — with the conservative ideology of a country school teacher — outlined in the dramatic dialogue. Arguing with the mother, the teacher maintains that learning about class conflict is worthless since human nature is unchangeable. The mother and her worker friends claim just the opposite, and in stark contrast to the teacher's conservatism, a fundamental Marxian principle emerges: the notion of class consciousness.

Marxist theory is logically developed through the ordering of the lyrical sequences in this episode. Interspersed throughout the conversation among the mother, her friends, and the teacher, all three lyrics build on each other, progressively explaining Marxism. In the first song, "Praise of Communism," the mother responds to the accusation that communism is a crime. Marxism is dialectically defined through the song's poetic antitheses; what it is, is made possible only by the concurrent disclosure of what it is not. Hence, we see that communism is not a crime, "it is the end of crime" (p. 73). The mother continues: "It is not madness, but the end of madness. It is not chaos but order" (p. 73). The poem's active voice emphatically defines Marxism, with the lyric's subject — "It" (communism) — rigidly being described through the precision of the continually used verb, "is." Brecht attempts to show us the simplicity of Marxism through this seemingly strict definition. But it is still in a fairly abstract and theoretical form and must yet be expanded to illustrate how Marxism is used in social practice. Brecht hints at the difficulty of this next step in the last line of the song: "It is the simple thing so hard to bring about" (p. 73).

The second song expands Marxism's definition by indicating that the acquisition of knowledge is needed for social revolution. "Praise of Learning," sung by the mother and her friends, illustrates that Marxist theory can be applied to social action only through studying and questioning: "Go search some knowledge, you who freeze! You who starve, reach for a book: it will be a weapon. You must prepare to take command now!" (p. 79). A "book" metaphorically becomes a "weapon" which the proletariat must use in order to liberate itself. Marxism's emphasis on action is accented here, as every line in the song is in the imperative form. It is further stressed at the end of each refrain, with the song repeatedly reminding the workers of the underlying reason for learning: "You [the proletariat] must prepare to take command now!" In this way, the lyric reveals that the historical success of the proletariat depends upon its ability to learn so that it can take leadership of society in the future.

The concepts of Marxism find their fullest development in the final lyric that the mother recites as she reflects on the whereabouts of her son. Her personal concern about what Pavel may be doing moves to a broader discussion of a revolutionary's activities. Here, we are shown different ways Marxism can be translated into or utilized for agitation. First, a revolutionary must deal with both the daily activity of the worker as "he organizes his fight around wage levels," as well as with the overriding struggle for "power in the state" (p. 80). Secondly, he should critically question society, "ask[ing] of property: where do you come from? . . . [and] . . . of opinions: to whom are you useful?" (p. 81). Through these questions, he can demystify society's ideological deceptions which keep the worker in an oppressed condition. Finally, the revolutionary must "speak out" "wherever silence is" (p. 81). And, he must take social responsibility by being willing to "name names" "where oppression rules" (p. 81). In this final lyrical passage we are shown how the theoretical definition of

Marxism, presented in the first song and elaborated in the second, can be manifested in actual practice. Brecht thus illustrates the socio-political usefulness of Marxian knowledge for carrying out the proletarian revolution.

Taken separately, the three lyrical sequences may appear somewhat unrelated, ranging from a straightforward delineation of communism to a description of the son's activities. But once they are understood as a logical development of Marxian theory, their seemingly unconnected messages teach the mother class consciousness and reveal a comprehensive theoretical plan for revolutionary action. Besides helping her discover her proletarian identity, these passages provide the mother with a Marxian set of rules or "grammar" for her future political activities. And, they offer us an historical framework, without which the dramatized events would simply be viewed as part of the biographical development of Vlassova's life. Further, the mother's learning effectively refutes the conservative view initially maintained by the teacher, proving that human nature can indeed be changed. Aesthetically, the comic mode is sustained, as the three sequences gradually bring us closer to the fulfillment of the play's quest: liberation of the proletariat.

Ascent to a Higher World

The Syntax: Social Function of Theory and Practice.   In the previous two sections, we have seen how the mother, learning a "lexicon" and "grammar" of Marxian theory, has discovered her identity as a worker. In accordance with Marxism, however, she must now attempt to recover the identity of her class as a whole. But more than class consciousness is needed for the mother's ascent to a "Higher World" of freedom for the workers. In fact, Marxism holds that comprehension of the world is valid and meaningful only insofar as it can change the world. Brecht shows us this in the next episodes (7 through 11) where we see how Vlassova's newly acquired knowledge becomes a vehicle for shaping and changing reality.

In applying the theory underlying Marxism to its practice in daily life, the mother orders or arranges her knowledge for use in society. That is, she identifies Marxian "syntactical" principles which govern the relationship between theory and practice; thought and reality are no longer conceived of as separate and distinct. The mother organizes her ideas so that they can help in her struggle for class unity—a struggle which ultimately will lead to the emancipation of the proletariat and its recovery of identity. As the dramatic action moves toward a more desirable classless society where all mankind will be liberated, a strong comic mood is produced. Yet, a somber tragic tone casts its shadow over these episodes depicting the mother's personal sufferings, establishing further evidence for the necessity of her class's ascent to a "Higher World."

In episode seven, the mother visits Pavel in prison to obtain political information, and we are given the first example of how she uses Marxian knowledge. To prevent the prison guard from knowing her purpose, she carries on a "double dialogue" with her son. In a loud voice, meant for the guard to hear, she speaks like an old, useless woman, uninterested in politics, as she says to her son: "We have nothing in common" (p. 88). But in soft whispers interspersed throughout, she asks for the names and locations of political sympathizers. In contrast, this voice reflects her political consciousness; she is working for a common cause with Pavel, and she successfully gets the information she needs from him. Brecht gives us two attitudes through these voices. The first sees a generation gap between the young and old, preventing the possibility of class unity. Here Brecht discredits the liberal assumption that a generation gap exists — a view which had wide influence in Expressionist art of Weimar culture.[10] The other attitude, however, holds that young and old alike must work together. It is this second view — unity through class — that prevails and is emphasized and developed in the remaining episodes of the play.

The mother's actions in this episode give a new political significance to her relationship with Pavel. No longer passively dependent upon him, she actively participates in the class struggle herself. When the mother leaves the prison, Pavel sings of the proletariat's inevitable victory in the face of powerful bourgeois opposition, thereby relating Vlassova's singular effort to the entire struggle of their class. The Marxist notion of class unity thus clearly emerges.

The conceptual motif of class solidarity is further elaborated in episode eight when the mother arrives in the country to find farm laborers on strike. But the farm household workers, including the butcher, are not striking because their pay has not been cut. Once again Vlassova utilizes her political knowledge, this time to provoke the butcher into recognizing his class position. Through the mother's suggestive prodding, he begins to understand the political reasons why he must exercise class solidarity and support his fellow workers in their strike. The spectator is shown that the mother's agitation is not based on the spreading of dogma, but on inducing self-consciousness in others.[11]

Episode nine provides a third example of how Vlassova integrates Marxism into her life. After a long separation, mother and son briefly meet. But this reunion is not laden with the typical emotional overtones one would expect. Instead, Brecht portrays it in terms of their sharing political activities, as Pavel helps his mother print illegal leaflets. In a poem the mother recites — "Praise for the Common Cause" — she characterizes her relationship to Pavel through Marxism:

> . . .
> How have I kept [my son]? Through a third, the cause.
> He and I were two; the third it was,
> the common cause commonly driving us, that is what
> united us.
>
> (p. 105)

Traditional family ties wane in importance as we see that mother and son, striving toward a common goal, are united through class. Their new sense of fraternity sustains and builds the comic mood of the play.

A final and most poignant illustration of how the mother applies Marxism to her life comes in episode eleven with Pavel's execution. Throughout the drama, Brecht has created antithetical tensions between tragedy and comedy to ensure that the spectator does not follow only the personal chronology in the dramatized events, but also their historical expression of Marxism. Hence, in direct contrast to the comic mood of the previous scene, a tragic tone is interjected here. What would normally be seen as an individual tragedy and part of the story line, when viewed historically, can be interpreted as part of the workers' struggle in a capitalistic society. The chorus's song reports the circumstances of Pavel's death in such a manner that its lyrical message is transmitted as an appeal for proletarian solidarity. And, the mother, instead of mourning, draws on her understanding of Marxism and describes her son's death as a political consequence of bourgeois society. She thus transcends personal grief and preserves the history of her son's actions as part of the larger revolutionary struggle.

In episodes seven through eleven, Brecht has shown us how the mother applies Marxist theory to social practice. Vlassova has conceptually discovered an appropriate "syntax" to establish a Marxian meaning or "semantics" for her actions. Interpreting reality through this new perspective, she has helped escalate class conflict — a necessary prelude to revolution. This conflict will reach its peak in the next section, as it is elevated to an historical level with the onset of the proletarian revolution.

The Semantics: Historical Significance of Theory and Practice.   What is the historical goal of the class struggle and of Marxian theory and practice? The answer was given at the beginning of the play: the proletariat's seizure of the state. The comic resolution at the end of the play indicates the workers have reached this goal. In the drama's last four episodes, Brecht makes this historical significance of Marxism explicit by dramatizing the development of the Russian working class movement from the beginning of the war to the Revolution of 1917. Describing the mother's revolutionary activities within these greater social events, he outlines the various stages of the working class movement: disorganization, disintegration, renewed conflict, and victory.[12]

Brecht first shows us that the outbreak of the war leads to the breakdown of the socialist movement. The ruling class's nationalism to support the war effort suppresses the internationalism of the class conflict, disorganizes the working class movement, and finally destroys it (episodes 12 and 13). Yet, the proletariat begins the struggle anew. In dialectical terms, its disintegration is necessary for it to realize its potential unification. As class conflict is renewed (episode 14), the workers resume their task of overthrowing the state. In the play's final episode, their victory is proclaimed.

As these four stages of the working class movement are outlined, the dramatic action moves closer to the sphere of a "Higher World." Similar to previous episodes, this progression is not linear, for the workers' ascent is mixed with disappointment and defeat. Tragic events temporarily enter these episodes, such as when the mother discovers, in episode twelve, that the socialist movement has disintegrated. "There won't be any revolution. . . . See the world as it is" (p. 120), disillusioned workers advise her. But Vlassova's firm conviction in Marxism enables her to find a strategy to reunify the workers: she must revive and intensify the class conflict. With this realization, the drama's overall comic tone once again dominates.

Putting her strategy into practice, the mother appears at a government office where people, hoping to shorten the war, donate copper utensils to be recycled into armaments. The mother, however, claims these donations will really prolong the war, arguing that the production of more weapons will allow the nations to fight longer. When a worker insists she is against the war, Vlassova replies: ". . . And why should you be against the war? Who are you, exactly? All of us here are of the decent, better sort, if I am not mistaken. But you look like a worker. Are you or are you not a worker? I am waiting for your reply. Here you are, trying to slip yourself into our midst! Don't you ever forget there is a distance between your type of people and us!" (p. 127). The logic of the mother's argument is intended to divert focus away from the national war by identifying the real conflict — the one between the class[es].[13] By offering a different explanation for the utilization of copper, the mother instigates class tensions which exist in actuality but which have been subdued through the war's nationalism.

The drama reaches its conclusion with the outbreak of the Russian Revolution. Carrying a red flag and marching among workers fighting for a new society, the mother reflects: "I was disturbed many years ago to see how my son was not satisfied; at first I only felt despair. But that did no good. Then I helped him in his fight for the kopek. We were involved at the time in small strikes for better wages. Now we are in the midst of a huge strike in the ammunition factories, and we're fighting for power in the state" (pp. 130–31). As is typical of comedy, we have come to the end of the story only to return to the ideas expressed in the beginning. The final episode provides the solution the mother had sought at the start of the play. But now we can clearly see that these echoes of the past have helped shape the future, and although the drama, in a sense, makes a circle, we end up in a different place. Comedy has afforded us a higher level of consciousness by exposing and breaking bourgeois society's deceptions, which have served to perpetuate the workers' misery. What was once a fight for the kopek has become a revolutionary struggle for the state. We have come from a society controlled by arbitrary economic and social laws to one permeated with a new freedom.

As the play's story reaches its conclusion, Brecht shifts from the world of the drama to that of real life. Through a lyrical exode, the mother expresses the infinite potential of the proletariat to transform history: "The victims of today will be victors of tomorrow / And Never is changed into Today" (p. 131). The society emerging at the drama's conclusion portrays a future that is accessible to us all. Again, the spectator is asked to participate, and we see the play's ending paralleling its beginning. Having been invited to understand his economic dilemma in the opening scene, the spectator is now urged to realize his potential to overcome it. The unfolding of the drama, with its presentation of a Marxian "lexicon," "grammar," "syntax," and "semantics" has provided the spectator with a revolutionary language to do this. Marxism's radical imagination has created for us a present, where the contradictions between past history and future possibilities beg for a political resolution. Thus, art attempts to reach out beyond its aesthetic boundaries, seeking completeness in reality.

To understand *The Mother* most fully, we have seen that it must be viewed both historically, through Marxism, and aesthetically, as a tragi-comedy. Brecht interweaves these two levels in a complementary fashion that affords his play its rich theoretical and artistic texture. To interpret this drama either on one or the other level alone would distort its meaning. In fact, it is the dramatic structure of *The Mother* as a tragi-comedy that permits the language of Marxism to be articulated. On the level of tragedy, we have seen how society's economic organization (the Base) depicted the workers' oppression in a capitalist society. On the level of comedy, however, the proletariat's consciousness of its class identity and its use in society (the Superstructure) has allowed it to transcend the old social structure and define a new and more just use value for man.[14] By analyzing this tragi-comic structure, we have been able to see how Marxian knowledge is incorporated into and in fact helps shape drama, and how drama, through particular aesthetic techniques, translates this knowledge into radical artistic communication.

Notes

1. For the purpose of my analysis, I relied on the first edition of Bertolt Brecht's *Die Mutter* (Berlin: Kiepenheuer Verlag, 1933); for quotations in this paper, I have used Lee Baxandall's translation of *The Mother* (New York; Grove Press, Inc., 1965). Page numbers within parentheses in the text refer to this translation.

2. Two valuable analyses of Marxism's dual time-sense can be found in Georg Lukács' *History and Class Consciousness* (Cambridge, Mass.: MIT Press, 1971) and in Ernst Bloch's *A Philosophy of the Future* (New York: Herder and Herder, 1970).

3. This interpretation of tragedy and comedy follows the line indicated by Northrop Frye in his *Anatomy of Criticism: Four Essays* (New York: Atheneum, 1968).

4. Brechtian criticism, which focuses mainly on the playwright's social theory, has failed to recognize aesthetic elements of *The Mother*, especially its plot structure. Rainer Steinweg, for example, sees the play as a "biography." On the other hand, Werner Mittenzwei argues that the drama is similar to the Learning Plays, Brecht's most abstract dramatizations of Marxian theory. My analysis of *The Mother* hopes to resolve this controversy in the secondary literature. For an overview of this problem, see Mittenzwei's "Die Spur der Brechtschen Lehrstücktheorie. Gedanken zur neuern Lehrstück-Interpretation," in Steinweg, ed., *Brechts Modell der Lehrstücke — Zeugnisse, Diskussion, Erfahrungen* (Frankfurt/Main: Suhrkamp, 1976), pp. 225–54. Steinweg's argument is found in the above text, but see also his *Das Lehrstück, Brechts Theorie einer politisch-ästhetischen Erziehung* (Stuttgart: Metzler, 1972).

5. See Roland Barthes' "An Introduction to the Structural Analysis of Narrative," *New Literary History*, VI, No. 2 (Winter 1975), 237–72, for his argument on the function of chronological and logical sequences in the structure of narrative.

6. Frye, p. 192.

7. Karl Marx and Friedrich Engels, *The Communist Manifesto* (New York: Pathfinder Press, 1973), pp. 27–33. See also Marx's "Toward the Critique of Hegel's Philosophy of Right," in Lewis S. Feuer, ed., *Basic Writings on Politics and Philosophy: Karl Marx and Friedrich Engels* (New York: Doubleday, 1959).

8. Hayden White, in *Metahistory: The Historical Imagination in Nineteenth-Century Europe* (Baltimore: Johns Hopkins University Press, 1973), uses these aspects of language to analyze Marx's theory. I have found White's schema useful and have adapted it in a new way for my analysis of this play.

9. Brecht is closely following Marx here; see *The Communist Manifesto*, p. 16.

10. A good account of the generation conflict in Expressionism is given in Peter Uwe Hohendahl's *Das Bild der bürgerlichen Welt im expressionistischen Drama* (Heidelberg: Universitätsverlag, 1967), pp. 80–95.

11. See Marx's argument about heuristic development of social consciousness in Dirk J. Struik, ed., *The Economic and Philosophic Manuscripts of 1844* (New York: International Publishers, 1973).

12. These stages of the Russian workers' movement, often referred to by historians, can be found in Isaac Deutscher's *The Prophet Armed* (New York: Vintage Books, 1965), *I*, 211–49.

13. The strategy to turn the "imperialist war into a civil war" was proposed by V. I. Lenin during the Zimmerwald Conference (1915) in Switzerland and is found in his "Die Aufgaben der Linksradikalen (Oder der Linken Zimmerwaldisten) in der Sozialdemokratischen Partei der Schweiz," *Werke* (East Berlin: Dietz Verlag, 1972), *23*, 135–47.

14. For an insightful argument on the relationship between Base and Superstructure, see Raymond Williams' *Marxism and Literature* (Oxford University Press, 1977), pp. 75–82.

The Private Life of the
Master Race

Eric Bentley*

. . . Many have enjoyed Brecht's plays and left it at that, but did these people — the crowds who flocked to *The Threepenny Opera* — really enjoy anything more than Brecht's biting wit or Kurt Weill's tunes? Brecht has a theory of drama and, if his words are not to be misread and his gestures misinterpreted, the theory must be examined — at least by those who try to judge Brecht's plays from their armchairs.

The history of drama affords many clear examples of the life and death of a form which at first satisfies the needs of the age and later does not. Greek tragedy, for instance, implies a particular attitude to the universe, and to fate in particular, and once that attitude disappeared the art form which went with it died out. The same is true of Elizabethan tragedy. The tragic view of life has in fact only had any apparent validity at one or two points in history, and attempts to revive it at other points have only yielded such results as the music drama of Wagner and the hortatory exercises of Nietzsche.

The bourgeois epoch has had its own nontragic drama. The serious, noncomic, nontragic drama of Diderot, Lessing, Dumas *fils*, and Ibsen was the major theatrical product of the period and survives today in the well-made Broadway play. It is based on two psychological factors: the *illusion* that the actors are real people and *suspense* used as a magnet by which the interest of the audience is drawn.

This drama Brecht believes to be bankrupt. To it he opposes Epic Theater, a type which lacks the careful centralization of Ibsen, the identification of the spectator with the chief characters, the sympathy — or empathy (*Einfühlung*) — with the fortunes of the protagonist, "all the illusion," as Brecht once put it, "which whips the spectator for two hours and leaves him exhausted and full of vague recollection and vaguer hope." To *Einfühlung* Brecht opposes *Verfremdung*, the making strange or alien, a word we may roughly translate as "distancing." The drama of sympathy, pity, and intimate, largely passive suffering has sacrificed greatness in theater to naturalness, and from Aristotle's "pity and terror" the second term has been either removed or debased to mere sensationalism. We are now — audience, actor, dramatist, director — so far conditioned to the well-made play of pity, sympathy, illusion, and suspense that distance can only be secured by the most drastic means. And Brecht has been drastic.

In a play called *The Measures Taken* . . . he offered to his audience none of the enticements and titillations which have come to be considered "good theater" but a play which is a study in the same sense as Czerny's

*Reprinted by permission from *The Brecht Commentaries, 1943–1980* (New York: Grove Press, 1981), 29–37. "*The Private Life of the Master Race*" copyright 1945 by New Directions.

studies for the piano, a play therefore which would help to train the audience and the actor in dramatic method (not to mention politics). The scene is a tribunal. Three comrades have returned from China to report on their activities there. In a nondescript setting, with the help of chorus and orchestra they tell their story by acting it out before the tribunal, playing not only their own roles but those of all who enter into the narrative. This device is characteristic of the Brechtian theater.

The meaning of the device is, in a word, *Verfremdung*. The audience is put at a distance from the events related, is prevented from identifying itself with any character because each actor is all the time shifting roles; it must therefore observe what passes critically and not — as in the older theater — with such excited empathy that it ceases to be conscious of anything but narrative and excitement itself. The characters quote themselves, so to speak, in rehearsing what they formerly experienced, and just as quotation in an essay gives the quoted passage distance, allows one to see it in the different light of a new context, so quotation of whole episodes imparts the required distance to the action of a play. From the simple "quotations" of *The Measures Taken* is but a step to the "quotations" in *The Private Life of the Master Race*, notably in "The Chalk Cross," where the worker gives his real opinions while pretending to act out a game, and in "The Jewish Wife," where the actual conversation of husband and wife, which is so far from explicit, is preceded by a series of "unreal" speeches, namely, three telephone conversations and several interrupted monologues.

Brecht does not claim to have discovered the drama of the future but to have tried out several types of Epic Theater, one of which is the *Lehrstück* or Didactic Play [Play for Learning] — *The Measures Taken* is an example — another of which is the Documentary Play, *The Private Life of the Master Race* being a prime instance of this type. These are not experimental plays in the sense in which the term was used twenty years ago. But they are experiments, made in the conviction that drama from Diderot to Ibsen is one completed epoch, and that now we have to go elsewhere, not merely on account of the exhaustion of technique but also because of changes in society and in men. If we knew the exact nature of these changes we might be able to chart the future of the drama. Guessing, Brecht writes Epic Theater for an audience different from that of Sophocles, which presumably gazed in awe at the workings of inexorable fate, and different from that of Diderot, which wept in sympathy for the unhappy lot of one's neighbor who was also oneself. Greek tragedy demands some pity, some terror, and much impotent contemplation; the older modern drama demands pity and surrender of the self to the current of excitement and suspense; both Greek and modern types confer a kind of catharsis, and are, in plain terms, a laxative of the soul. Brecht foreshadows a drama with a different interest and a different result. He sees the dramatist making an analysis of society, not portraits of individuals.

He sees the audience as active, inquisitive, noncontemplative, in the spirit of our pragmatic, nonmetaphysical age. A great philosopher of this spirit, William James, found words about music much like Brecht's on drama: "Even the habit of excessive indulgence in music, for those who are neither performers themselves nor musically gifted enough to take it in a purely intellectual way, has probably a relaxing effect upon the character. One becomes filled with emotions which habitually pass without prompting to any deed, and so the inertly sentimental condition is kept up. The remedy would be, never to suffer oneself to have an emotion at a concert, without expressing it afterward in some active way."

But, besides audience and author, there are two other factors in drama without which there can be no production: acting and staging. The Brechtian theater has few technical demands to make. It needs neither naturalistic paraphernalia nor expressionistic hocus-pocus. Readers of *The Private Life* will see that aside from one extraordinary item — the Panzer — the whole thing can be done with platforms, screens, and economical lighting. Nor can much be said of the director in Brechtian production: he must be an artist of intellect, taste, and active, social interests. All the emphasis in Brecht is on the actor, and from him a special technique is required in accordance with the principles of Epic Theater. Again the negative idea is the avoidance both of naturalism and of stylization: all real style is neither stylized nor natural. In a piece by Brecht the actors should be cool but not mannered, accomplished and subtle but not ostentatious and artificial. They should not squander all their art on the single trick of pretending to *be* the character they are portraying; nor, if they are actors at all, can they remain themselves in every role. Modern actors who have been trained in the school of *Einfühlung* will have to give most of their attention to the art of *Verfremdung*.

Such is the Brechtian theater. It has aroused a good deal of opposition among German critics. To Thomas Mann, who once described Brecht as "very gifted, unfortunately," the whole Brechtian world is distasteful. An anonymous writer (it was Hermann Kesten) in Thomas Mann's journal, *Mass and Wert*, raised six specific objections:

1. That Brecht's work is "propaganda for propaganda's sake."

2. That actually *Fear and Misery of the Third Reich* [*The Private Life*] is defeatist.

3. That all Brecht's characters are the same. There is, says the critic, neither differentiation of personality nor of levels of consciousness. The Brechtian drama is flat.

4. "The Brechtian characters are without hate, without love, without ambition or desire for revenge. All Shakespearian passions cease to exist."

5. "His people have no memory either. They are the opposite of Ibsen characters. Everything happens without looking back to the past. There are no cracks through which the past presses in."

6. Brecht claims on the one hand to be scientific, objective, cool; on the other hand he argues for didacticism. The contradiction is complete.[1]

The first two points cancel each other, and the truth behind them is that, while Brecht's drama embodies his own ethics, it does not, like most propagandist art, underestimate the enemy. The third objection is unjust. The characters of *The Private Life* are differentiated psychologically, socially, and — something the translation does not show — regionally. Objection four was perhaps true of Brecht's early plays with their quasi-vegetative, passive people and the atmosphere of dreamy bewilderment, but it has no application to *The Private Life*, as the most casual reader can attest. Objection five also is not quite true of *The Private Life* since many of the characters (see "The Box" and "The Man They Released") are and will be deeply affected by memories. In fact the memory of "the old days" before 1933 is a leitmotiv of the play.

Objection six merely reiterates the fact that Brecht is not Ibsen, Shakespeare, or Sophocles. Brecht is objective *and* didactic in the same way as a doctor. His works are diagnoses; but with the diagnosis come proposals for cure. Of course the objectivity of an artist is not the same as that of a scientist; but among artists Brecht can portray society with rare analytic power and detachment. Compare his Nazis with those of Hollywood. The political proposals of a poet do not have the status of a doctor's prescriptions, but we are surely beyond the stage where we regard concern with practice and politics as something incompatible with objectivity.

I have the impression that Brecht's critics are die-hard defenders of the Ibsen tradition against all comers, and/or that they think Brecht is trying to replace drama that is all *Einfühlung* with drama that is all *Verfremdung*. That is not so. Such a scene as "The Jewish Wife" immediately arouses sympathy and compassion; misinterpretation would arise only if an actress played the scene for these emotions alone. Then the fine balance and interplay between *Einfühlung* and *Verfremdung* which Brecht's theater aims at would be upset, and the result would be a touching but by no means extraordinary one-act play. Aristotle said: pity *and* terror. Brecht says: sympathy *and* distance, attraction *and* repulsion, tenderness *and* horror. The tension of the two contrary impulses is the tension — so different from that of suspense — and of the Brechtian theater.

The article in *Mass und Wert* is called "The Limits of the Brechtian Theater."[2] Fair enough. Brecht — like all modern artists of any integrity — is content to be limited. Unlike Shakespeare and Sophocles, but not unlike Mann, Rilke, Yeats, Kafka, and the rest, Brecht has his own small tract of territory and sticks to it. Why must one compare him with Shakespeare or even Ibsen? This is not an age of greatness and fulfillment. It is an age of crisis and therefore at best a seedtime, an age of premonition. Brecht's theater consists of hints and premonitions. They must remain hints and premonitions — perhaps even so they sound pretentious — until they can be tried out, rejected, modified, or developed in an environment that offers real opportunity to serious dramatists and serious actors. It is better that they should remain hints and premonitions until they make or break themselves in the theater itself.

No single work of Brecht's is more important than *Fear and Misery of the Third Reich*,[3] of which *The Private Life of the Master Race* is the stage version.[4] Both for its intrinsic merits and for its interest as a portrait and interpretation of Nazi Germany it will probably be his best-known piece. Already it has been published in French by the *Nouvelle Revue Française*.[5] We hear of performances of "The Jewish Wife" before Red soldiers at Leningrad and of a projected movie version by Pudovkin. Yet the piece will be widely misunderstood unless it is interpreted as Epic Theater.

I have heard it said after productions of "The Jewish Wife" and "The Informer" that Brecht "has abandoned his early experimentalism and, like the Soviet dramatists, has returned to naturalism." This opinion is convincing enough to those who have seen these scenes as one-act plays (which they are not), presented out of their context, and acted in the naturalistic manner. But it is wrong. *The Private Life* is Epic Theater, but Epic is not a "pure" type, exclusive of naturalism, expressionism, and all other styles. On the contrary, Epic is of its nature impure and hybrid. The very name is a challenge — like calling drama undramatic. The point was that epic, dramatic, and lyric elements could *all* be used. So could all styles the dramatist needed. The dialogue of the scenes in *The Private Life* is naturalistic but the play is not naturalism. Within the scenes are many nonnaturalistic devices such as the "quotations" mentioned above. More important: the spectator cannot be carried along on the surfboard of suspense, since there is no continuous plot, no turning point, no centerpiece of any sort. He might as well sit back, self-possessed but emotionally and intellectually alert, to take note of the succession of historical documents which constitute the play. The framework, with its recitations, songs and placards, is not meant to provide an illusion of unified structure. It is a system of interruptions which break up the play into the atomic elements of which it consists. Interruption is for Brecht a dramatic device of the first importance.

Brecht's audience must be intellectually alert, but the alertness is not that required by the untheatrical Poetic Theater which an audience has to strain every nerve to follow. It is an alertness much commoner in everyone's experience than the sweaty, emotional indulgence of the sensationally dramatic. It is the alertness of everyday curiosity, discussion, and activity. The facts are such and such; if they are presented with a lively appreciation of contradiction and dialectic in the material, and a lively appreciation of the moral urgency of the problems, the audience may not be intoxicated — intoxication produces first irrational behavior and then sleep — but they will be awakened and enlivened. Perhaps Brechtian plays are propaganda, but they are very different from the "passionate indictments" which have had such a vogue in the theater of the past generation.

Drama with so much theory attached to it, drama with so strong a didactic flavor, drama so analytic, objective, circumstantial, so lacking in thrills and "human" sympathy — is it a bore? It is a bore to those who are so busy observing the lack of Ibsenite qualities that they cannot observe the Brechtian qualities. And since Brechtian qualities are frequently more authentically good theater than those which pass for such, one can but regret the fact that Brecht has to be given to the public only in book form with a long theoretical exegesis. A man laughs somewhere at the back of the theater, a grotesque, half-hysterical laugh. His neighbors, snatched out of their trance, look angrily round and hiss: "sh!" But in a Brecht performance such a man is usually right. The scenes set up the strangest pressures. There is a constant pulling this way and that (read "In Search of Justice") and the result may very well be grotesque laughter. Brecht's repudiation of the sentimental theater is not a repudiation of theater.

The reader of *The Private Life of the Master Race* should regard himself as the director of the play. Then he will interpret the Horst Wessel verses not as Brecht's poetry but as a Nazi song, the Woman's Voice not as declamation but as ballad, the verses of The Voice as dramatic commentary. In the theater of the mind, he will supply the rumbling of the Panzer, the strange vision of the twelve soldiers, the many pictures of Misery and Fear. Without stylization the Brechtian drama seeks to give back to gestures something of the force they have lost through the "naturalness" of current fashion. Repeatedly a hand jumps half-clenched to the face: a head turns abruptly round: what is wrong? It is the Fear of the Third Reich. Repeatedly a figure stands limp and still: it is the Misery of the Third Reich. Some scenes are conceived almost entirely in plastic terms — "Physicists," for instance, in which the whole effect is that of nervous movement, sudden opening of doors, speaking so as not to be overheard, speaking so as to *be* overheard. This is pure theater in the best, though not in the Broadway, sense. So is that special invention of Brecht's — doubtless suggested by movies — the tiny but complete scene of five or six lines. Where did Dumas, or even Ibsen, show a finer economy of means than Brecht in "The Two Bakers"? The style is new, to many, puzzling at first, to some, flat as a text for reading. But the cumulative effect can be dramatically every bit as strong as the unilinear development of a well-made play.

The effect is one of sheer accumulation. In Part One we see workers shortly after the Nazis came to power, a worker betraying a comrade, a worker debating with an S.A. man, workers in a concentration camp, in a factory, at home. We see the strength of the Nazis, and in "Prisoners Mix Cement" we see their opponents united, but too late. In Part Two we see several segments of German bourgeois life, scientists, judges, doctors, teachers. The picture is dark, sustained in longer scenic units, a masterly sequence of analyses. Part Three recovers the swift tempo of Part One in a series of quick shots of Misery and Fear, extending the analysis of Germany from one cell in the social organism to another until, in the final scene, Hitler enters Vienna.

But this is not the adventurous story of the rise of a villain-hero. The story is framed, "distanced" by being presented in retrospect. The date is 1941. The rise of Hitler is now only a "story"; but in Hitler's first five years of power — depicted in the inset scenes — is the whole truth of his career. To tell this story rather than that of 1938 to 1941 is further evidence of Brecht's desire to present beginnings, causes, essentials, rather than ramifications, spectacular results. The play ends with the Nazis singing of failure to the tune of their victory hymn. What should one feel when the play is over? Not, certainly, "full of vague recollection and vaguer hope," but more critical, more aware, not as one is more critical and aware after reading a blue book but as one feels after a perusal of Goya's *Disasters of the War*. Here is the record, with Goya's almost *demure* superscriptions, the record presented with the matter-of-factness of a genius who does not need to shout and of a subject that renders exaggeration unthinkable. I sometimes wonder if the French title of Brecht's work is not the best: *Scènes de la Vie Hitlérienne*.

Notes

1. [Ed. note: Anon., "Grenzen des Brecht-Theaters," *Maß und Wert* 6 (July/August 1939):837–41.]

2. [Ed. note: see n. 1, above. The article followed that by Walter Benjamin, referred to in n. 3, below.]

3. [Ed. note: in his prefatory remark Eric Bentley states: "In this essay [written in 1943/1944] I came close to letting Brecht ghostwrite or rather to letting his girl friend [Ruth Berlau] be the ghost. . . ." Bentley was also influenced by and borrowed from Walter Benjamin's essay, "What Is Epic Theatre" [second version], that was first published in *Maß und Wert*, 2, no. 6 (July/August 1939):831–37. See Walter Benjamin, *Understanding Brecht*, trans. Anna Bostock (London: Verso Editions, 1983), 15–22.]

4. [Ed. note: *Furcht und Elend des III. Reichs* (13 scenes) was first published in Moscow (1941); 24 scenes were published by the German–language Aurora Verlag, New York (1945). A German-language production took place in New York City on 28 May 1942 (four scenes) and 14 June 1942 (five scenes); Eric Bentley translated seventeen scenes as *The Private Life of the Master Race* (© New Directions, 1945). The (unsuccessful) English-language production of the play opened on 12 June 1945 in New York City; it was preceded by another production at the University of California at Berkeley. See James K. Lyon, "Off-Broadway, 1945: *The Private Life of the Master Race*," *Brecht in America* (Princeton, N. J.: Princeton University Press, 1980), 132–41.]

5. [Ed. note: actually, only three scenes were published under the title, "Grand'peur et misères du troisième Reich," trans. Pierre Abraham, *Nouvelle Revue Française*, 52 (June 1939):924–34.]

The Earth Stands Still
[Review of *Life of Galileo*]   Irwin Shaw*

There has been considerable discussion, some of it quite acrimonious, about the propriety of having an institution called the Experimental Theatre put on a work in which an actor of Charles Laughton's standing plays the leading part. . . . According to the critics of the enterprise, it would seem that nothing a well known actor can do on a stage can properly be considered an experiment. This, of course, is nonsense, and the sponsors of the project are to be congratulated for fulfilling handsomely, in Bertolt Brecht's *Galileo*, the promise of the organization's title.

The play is noble in theme, relentlessly unconventional in execution, and it permits Laughton to escape, if only for six performances, the absurd, minor warblings which have recently been his lot in Hollywood. Equipped with an abstract set, a fluttering gauze curtain that is drawn at the end of each scene by a small boy with a pole, projections of Renaissance drawings and paintings, and intermittent choruses with music by Hanns Eisler, sung by three choirboys, it could hardly be called a standard Broadway performance.

Aside from its technical innovations, the story of Galileo's martyrdom by Authority is bitterly apposite for today's audiences. The heresy hunters are almost as busy today in Washington as they ever were in Florence, and recantations fill the air in a medieval blizzard of fear. *Time, Life* and Hearst have replaced the rack, and the Representative from New Jersey has donned the Inquisitor's dark satin. The sobbing "I was wrong" of the matinee idol is now to be heard, instead of the "I have sinned" of the old astronomer, but the pattern, as Brecht bleakly points out, is the same. Truth dies with conformity, this year or last.

Cool demands.   Brecht's method of saying these things, in accordance with his theories of the "Epic" theater, is abstract, cold and didactic. He assumes the air of the passionless teacher lecturing to students who are not so bright as they should be. He disdains all emotionalism; scornfully, he refuses to amuse us with the usual dramatist's tricks. His characters are symbols, not people; his action the functioning of huge forces, not the clash of human beings. The final effect is interesting, but aggravating. We get the unpleasant feeling that Brecht regards the human race, or at least that part of it which goes to the theater, as animals equipped with only the most rudimentary ability to reason. His Olympian condescension is bound to annoy us, even when we agree with him most heartily.

Joseph Losey's staging meets, I suppose, with Brecht's cool demands, but it is only in three magnificently searching and eloquent scenes in the second half that the play comes really alive. One is in a garden, in which a

*Reprinted from the *New Republic*, 29 December 1947, 36–37.

young monk tells Galileo the reasons of conscience for which he is giving up the study of physics; another is in the Pope's robing room, in which the humanitarian prelate is forced by the logic of his position to agree to the limited torture of the scientist; and the third is the last scene of the play, in which Galileo explores the most profound and complex depths of compromise, cowardice and treachery.

It is in this scene, seated quietly on the almost empty stage, that Laughton gives us one of the most memorable moments of the recent theater. With a stony and scientifically accurate self-knowledge he appraises himself and the world. Tragically clear, half-victor, half-victim, the old giant delivers himself of a monumental monologue, and for a time, on the stage of the Maxine Elliot, we seem to be at the very core of truth.

It is devoutly to be hoped that the commercial theater will rise to the challenge of *Galileo* and put it on the boards where all may see it.

History and Moral in Brecht's
The Life of Galileo   M. A. Cohen*

For those who seek clear-cut literary definitions, historical drama is an elusive category. The many plays to which this description might be applied vary greatly in their degrees of historical involvement. Roughly, a play is "historical" if it contains characters and situations based upon actual persons and events, but it may do so without being primarily historical in its preoccupations. A possible example is Büchner's *Danton's Death*, which arguably attributes personalities and motives to Danton, Robespierre, and Saint-Just sufficiently removed from the historical evidence for a recent critic to put the play in the category of tragedy rather than "history."[1]

However, in *The Life of Galileo*, historical pretensions are clearly central. The play is perhaps best regarded as a "history" in something like the Elizabethan sense. Irving Ribner believes the essential feature of the Elizabethan historical play to have been that it fulfilled what the Elizabethans considered to be the purposes of history, and that the purposes of history in this case were mainly didactic: "The purpose of a history . . . was not to present truth about the past for its own sake; it was to use the past for didactic purposes, and writers of history, both non-dramatic and dramatic, altered their material freely in order better to achieve their didactic aims."[2] Ribner later remarks that plays based on factual material but not serving such ends did not come into the category of history plays as the Elizabethans conceived them.[3]

*From *Contemporary Literature* 11, no. 1 (1970):80-97. Reprinted by permission of the University of Wisconsin Press.

The situation of modern historical drama is obviously very different. There are no generally agreed views on the meaning of history. Insofar as there is any accepted criterion of merit in historical studies, it is precisely the one which, in Ribner's view, the Elizabethans regarded as comparatively unimportant — truth to "the facts." If then a modern dramatist assumes the functions of an historian in an Elizabethan manner and subordinates the facts to his historical message, he may be confronted with an audience whose views on the facts come between them and the play. The work may even be assessed on purely factual grounds as we have seen in some of the reactions to [Rolf] Hochhuth's two plays. And yet, to some extent, Hochhuth invites this kind of assessment, as does Brecht in *Galileo*. On the one hand the historical details are considerable, on the other hand Brecht is assuming, like his Elizabethan counterparts, that the function of history is didactic: we have both a modern preoccupation with authenticity and a neo-Elizabethan desire to use the past to point morals for the present. There is a clear suggestion of "this is what actually happened" about the play, but there is also a very personal interpretation of real events and a certain amount of pure invention. Spalter describes it as "an uneasy mixture of authenticity and special pleading,"[4] though it would be difficult to think of any historical play to which this description might not be applied.

Galileo is so firmly grounded on historical re-creation that it is not always easy to separate the special pleading from the authenticity. We may agree that "it does not so very much matter whether the play is historically accurate, the moral is what counts,"[5] and yet find it difficult to isolate the moral from the history. Indeed it is arguable that the most important message of the play is essentially historical, that moral and history coincide, though what Brecht is most essentially "saying" in the play has been interpreted in a variety of ways. Whatever view we come to take, it seems likely that an analysis of the crucial manipulations of accepted fact in *Galileo*, of the points where Brecht most clearly exceeds his historical brief, is a useful accompaniment to an exploration of the moral.

That Brecht strove hard to obtain authenticity in many areas of the play is well known. The background reading and consultations which he undertook have been described,[6] especially his attempt to think his way back into the Ptolemaic world picture. Much of the biographical matter is reasonably authentic too, despite the obvious omissions and distortions made in the interests of Brecht's characterization of the great scientist. This applies even to the most striking misrepresentation, the depiction of Galileo's family. Instead of three children he is given one daughter, whose engagement to the wealthy Ludovico is entirely invented. A crucial moment comes when Galileo determines to resume his prohibited astronomical researches at all costs, causing Ludovico to break off the match. It would seem that here we have truth to fact entirely subordinated to the portrayal of character and motive, but this aspect of the play is not without foundation in an approximate sense. The real Galileo did not actually break off a daughter's engagement — he simply prevented such a situation from ever arising by putting his daughters in a convent, much to the distress of the younger daughter. His behavior in this has been characterized as verging on cruelty even by so sympathetic an authority as Geymonat.[7] A touch of the real man also seems to be present in the dramatic character's financial opportunism, if we are to believe the story that Galileo accepted a pension from the Pope which had been turned down by both his son Vincenzo and his nephew because of the religious exercises attached to it.[8]

Comprehensive fidelity to fact would of course be an unreasonable demand to make of a play. Hochhuth quotes Schiller's view that "the playwright can use no single element of reality as he finds it so that his work in all its aspects must be the work of an Idea if it is to possess reality as a whole."[9] He also remarks that the theater cannot hope to compete with the newsreel in the mere recording of facts. It is partly a matter of what Shaw called the "stage limits of historical representation," of the exigencies of dramatic form and theatrical production. He pointed out that *Saint Joan* condensed into three and a half hours a series of events which had in fact taken years. In addition he could not claim more for his dramatization of Joan's contemporaries than that they were quite like the originals: Dunois would have done equally well for the Duc d'Alençon, but, by lumping them together, he had succeeded in saving the theater manager "a salary and a suit of armour."[10] By leaving out two of Galileo's children, Brecht saved producers of his play two salaries and two seventeenth-century costumes.

If the portrayal of Galileo's relationship with the daughter of the play has a grain of historical truth, there are other aspects of the real man which Brecht did not attempt to depict, even in an approximate sense. A highly sympathetic feature which is — wittingly or unwittingly — ignored is the self-sacrifice with which he cared for his mother, younger brother, and sisters, paying large sums for their debts and dowries.[11] A less attractive side which also finds no place in the characterization is Galileo's bitterness in controversy, what Koestler calls his "cold sarcastic presumption" and "futile pernicious feuds."[12] Even authorities better disposed toward Galileo than Koestler concede that there is some truth in this.

Interesting though Brecht's manipulations of the facts of his hero's private life are, it is the rendering of Galileo's relationship to his society which has greater bearing on the meaning of the play. As he himself said: "It is not so much the character of Galileo that invites interest as his social role."[13] We note first that Galileo's age is seen as one in which reason might have begun to control human affairs, a new age. In the first version of the play, Brecht had been attracted to the period as a time which, like the twentieth century, had abounded with discoveries and liberating possibilities for mankind, but which had disappointed expectations rather in the way that the twentieth century had disappointed him when the Nazis had perverted the very idea of a new age.[14] But though the play shows the ultimate betrayal of the new age by Galileo's recantation, the initial picture of the period is idealized, the tone being set by Galileo's long speech in Scene 1, where a vision of astronomy reaching the marketplaces and the people welcoming the freedom and movement of the new world picture is painted:

> And the earth rolls happily round the sun, and the fishwives, merchants, princes and cardinals and even the Pope roll with it.
>   Overnight the universe has lost its centre, and next day it has countless ones. So that now each — and none — is regarded as its centre. For suddenly there is plenty of room. . . .
>   What does the poet say? "Oh happy morning of beginning. . . .
>   (Stücke 12; Plays 234)

It is interesting to speculate on what relation this depiction bears to what is, after all, late Renaissance Italy. Certainly it contrasts sharply with the conception of the period in a study of Galileo written in the same year as the first version of the play:

> It must not be thought that Galileo, born in the same year as Shakespeare, was born into the same brave world of expanding knowledge, wealth and genius. Rather did he encounter a corrupt and sterile society, whose influence may account for much of what we might wish to see expunged from his record. . . . The morals of Machiavelli and the cheerfully avowed villainies of Benvenuto Cellini may afford a measure of the tone of sixteenth century Italy. . . . Such, then, was the background of a scientific man in the late sixteenth century — an expanding world, a repressive Church, and a corrupt society.[15]

The analysis here does not go very deep, but the passage does indicate aspects of Galileo's world which Brecht minimized. Sagredo is present to counter Galileo's naive optimism about the reaction of the authorities to his discoveries but, on the whole, the corruption and repression of the time are played down. In fact Brecht states that he did not wish to make a case against the Church, even though he believed that the evidence was available to do so: "In the present play the Church functions, even when it opposes free research, simply as Authority," and hence "the play shows the temporary victory of Authority, not the victory of the priesthood" (Stücke 207; Plays 341). Brecht went on to say that he had ignored the whole question of possible falsifications to the protocol of 1616 by the Inquisition (he appears to have regarded this as fully established by Emil Wohlwill and other German historians), his lack of concern for such questions implying no reverence for the Church of either the seventeenth or the twentieth century but rather a wish not to divert attention from present-day Authority.[16] It is certainly true that the play does avoid the pitfall of presenting the Church as a simple villain in the affair, an approach which

would have been dramatically weak, quite apart from historical considerations. But dramatic factors apparently were not uppermost in Brecht's
mind here. What he wished to do was to show parallels for the present age
about the attitude of Authority in general: "what society extorts from its
individuals" (*Stücke* 205; *Plays* 340). We could compare this with Shaw's
attitude to the trial of Saint Joan. True, Shaw appears to have believed
that his presentation of the trial as comparatively fair by modern standards was also in accordance with the facts,[17] but it seems likely that, even if
he had had access to the virtually conclusive indictment of the trial made
by Régine Pernoud,[18] he would have retained his interpretation, rather in
the way that Brecht ignored discreditable possibilities about the Church's
behavior in the interests of his. The interpretation suited the attack on
modern complacency that Shaw wished to make and also his conception of
what was universally tragic about the affair. Joan had been burned by
"normally innocent people in the energy of their self-righteousness."[19] It
was necessary, moreover, to the generalized theme of heterodoxy versus
orthodoxy, which Shaw regarded as as much a modern as a medieval one.
Similarly, Brecht suggests a universal theme: Authority versus the Individual and his freedom of inquiry.

However, it would be difficult to reconcile the experience of the play
itself with so generalized a moral. It may be that Brecht chose to present
his work in this light in order to protect it against over-literal historical
evaluations, but most of his other remarks encourage a different kind of
response, and one which seems more relevant to the sort of play *Galileo* is.
We find ourselves pondering the meaning of his claim that the recantation
was "the 'original sin' of modern sciences" and that the atomic bomb was
"the classical end-product of his contribution to science and his failure to
society" (Stücke 204-205; *Plays* 340). The play itself directs us more
strongly toward specific historical morals than to universalized ones,
though the latter are also open to interpretation. Martin Esslin, for
example, finds a generalized comment on science: "science itself . . . is
shown as being merely another of man's basic, instinctive urges, just as
deeply rooted in the irrational as the instinct for procreation."[20] This is not,
in our view, the most important point that Brecht seems to have wanted
his audiences to retain about science, however.

An essential strand in the play's meaning is Galileo's relationship with
the people; he believes in them as the future standard-bearers of science —
astronomy will be talked about in the marketplaces and will be welcomed
there. Against Sagredo, who accuses him of confusing the people's
"miserable cunning" (*Stücke* 48; *Plays* 254) with reason, Galileo invokes
the everyday common sense of "the mariner who, when laying in stores,
thinks of storms and calms ahead" or "the child who pulls on his cap when
it is proved to him that it may rain . . ." (*Stücke* 48-49; *Plays* 254). These
are his hope because they all listen to reason (Scene 3). In Scene 9 Galileo
explains why he wants to write his works in the vernacular for the people

who work with their hands: "Who else wants to learn about the origins of things? Those who see only the bread on the table don't want to know how it is baked; that lot would rather thank God above than the baker. But those who make the bread will understand that nothing moves which isn't moved" (*Stücke* 137; *Plays* 302).

It has been pointed out that here Brecht misunderstood the significance of the new physics. The idea that nothing moves which isn't moved really belongs to "the commonsense Aristotelian theories which Galileo was in the process of superseding by groping toward the concept of inertia."[21] Moreover, consciously or unconsciously, he gave a distorted picture of the real Galileo's relationship with the people. It corresponds to fact that the real man respected the craftsmen of his age, especially the mechanics and artisans of the Venetian Arsenal, and it is true that he was a pioneer in publishing scientific works in the vernacular. But he does not appear to have had the dramatic character's faith in the common sense of the common people in general. According to Santillana, the idea that Galileo wished to appeal to the people is a misrepresentation, for Galileo had considered it unwise to make such an appeal.[22] A passage from his letter to Grand Duchess Christina seems to bear this out: "It is sufficiently obvious that to attribute motion to the sun and rest to the earth was necessary lest the shallow minds of the people should become confused, obstinate and contumacious."[23] It would seem that the real Galileo's faith was not so much in the lower classes as in people in all walks of life who were capable of thinking for themselves, especially people of influence. Geymonat describes Galileo's "cultural program" as aimed at "cultured persons" and "the higher Venetian authorities."[24]

There is some evidence for the kind of humanistic optimism about people which Brecht attributes to his Galileo in the real man's writings about the people of Florence: "The steps of the Santa Maria del Fiore swarm with men of every rank and every class; artisans, merchants, teachers, artists, doctors, technicians, poets, scholars. A thousand minds, a thousand arguments; a lively intermingling of questions, problems, news, of disputes, of jokes; an inexhaustible play of language and thought, a vibrant curiosity. . . . And this is the pleasure of the Florentine public."[25] But we do not note in the list the fishwives and Campagna peasants with whom Brecht's character is so concerned. It seems that his enthusiasm for Galileo as a man who wanted to bring science to the people was justified in some respects, but the flavor of the dramatic character's pronouncements on this question is often a twentieth-century Marxian one. Brecht may have been influenced by Leonardo Olschki's picture of Galileo as a Renaissance leader.[26] But while Olschki sees Galileo as the last great leader of the Renaissance, Brecht depicts him as a forerunner of modern scientific and social revolutions, who often expresses more what science allegedly *ought* to be for the twentieth century than what it was for the seventeenth, though the influence of Bacon can be detected in some of his utterances.

Brecht's moral begins to emerge as more *for* the modern proletariat than *about* their seventeenth-century counterparts.

The drama's Galileo wants more than to spread scientific knowledge to the people. He also wants to spread the spirit of doubt, and doubt appears to be the central feature of scientific thinking for Brecht. Galileo believes that such doubt, combined with the new methods of manufacturing, portends a social revolution:

> And because of that a great wind has arisen, lifting even the gold-embroidered coat-tails of princes and prelates, so that the fat legs and thin legs underneath are seen; legs like our legs. The heavens, it has turned out, are empty. And there is a gale of laughter over that.
>
> But the waters of the earth are driving our new spindles and in the dockyard, in the rope and sail shops, five hundred hands are moving together in a new way of working. (*Stücke* 11, *Plays* 233)

The point is driven home in Scene 12 when the Inquisitor describes the popularity among the people of Aristotle's prophecy that "When the weaver's shuttle weaves on its own and the zither plays of itself, then the masters will need no apprentices and the rulers no servants" (*Stücke* 158; *Plays* 314).

It has been argued that Brecht does not in fact present Galileo himself as wanting the subversion of the cosmic order to be followed by that of the social order, but rather as a moderate who, according to his daughter Virginia in Scene 11, deplores the twist given to his astronomy by the ballad singer and the carnival crowd in the immediately previous scene, and that this is reasonably faithful to the facts about the real Galileo, who would certainly have deplored the crowd's picture of him as a "Bible Buster."[27] Indeed, Galileo does declare himself a true son of the Church in the confrontation with Bellarmine and Barberini (Scene 7), and proves himself Barberini's match in the battle of Biblical proverbs. He also makes the essential point in the real man's case for reconciling the Bible with the new world picture: "But, gentlemen, man can misinterpret not only the movements of the stars, but the Bible too" (*Stücke* 101; *Plays* 283), and in Scene 14 we find him declaring his abhorrence for "cheap lucidity in sacred matters" (*Stücke* 174; *Plays* 323). All this is very much in historical character. The actual Galileo's letter to Castelli has been described by a Jesuit biographer as showing "an acquaintance with the Bible and the interpretation of the Fathers of the Church, especially Augustine's *De Genesi Ad Litteram*, quite extraordinary in a man whose interests lay in a very different field,"[28] and Galileo is rated as having been "better acquainted with recent commentators on the Scriptures than Bellarmine himself."[29]

If such moments were typical of the play as a whole we should be justified in agreeing with the assertion in the Notes that "it corresponds to the historical truth in that the Galileo of the play never turns directly against the Church. There is not a sentence uttered by Galileo in that sense" (*Stücke* 207; *Plays* 341). However, closer examination reveals that to accept Brecht's statement would be very much a case of trusting the teller rather than the tale. Scene 3 shows Galileo arguing that God is "in us or nowhere" (*Stücke* 47; *Plays* 253), and his reply when asked by the Little Monk to accept that the decree forbidding the propagation of the Copernican teachings showed maternal compassion toward the peasantry on the Church's part, must surely count as an attack on the institution itself:

> Why is the orderliness in this country merely the order of an empty cupboard, and the necessity merely that of working oneself to death? Among bursting vineyards, beside the ripening cornfields! Your Campagna peasants are paying for the wars which the representative of gentle Jesus is waging in Spain and Germany. Why does he put the earth at the hub of the universe? So that the throne of Saint Peter can stand at the hub of the earth. (*Stücke* 113; *Plays* 289)

The point at which Galileo most clearly identifies the cause of science with that of social revolution is in Scene 14. The full implications of Galileo's long speech here are seldom recognized in comments on the play. Spalter, for example, dismisses the speech as "extrinsic" to the work as a whole, on the grounds that it contradicts the characterization of Galileo which has been developed previously. Spalter sees Galileo as a person whose "distinction is precisely that nothing can make him subordinate his lust for pleasure to categorical imperatives," his scientific activities being simply another expression of the "same basic drive for pleasure that makes Galileo a connoisseur of food and wine." Hence Galileo's final affirmation of the need to put the social responsibilities of the scientist before self-interest is unconvincing, because "one cannot build up a persuasive pattern of episodic detail and then expect to add a climax unprepared for by such detail without confusing the issue."[30]

It is difficult to reconcile the final version of *Galileo*[31] with Spalter's description. The bulk of his most interesting study is devoted to a tradition in German drama which he relates to Brecht's work, that of Lenz, Grabbe, Büchner, Wedekind, and Kraus. Brecht's early plays seem to fit in well, but it would seem that, in order to assimilate the later ones too, Spalter has, among other things, oversimplified Brecht's characterization of Galileo and perhaps underestimated the revision of the original conception by the third version of the work.[32] In the play as Brecht left it, in *Stücke*, VIII, there is no question of the speech in Scene 14 being "extrinsic" nor of Galileo's nature being adequately defined in terms of "lust for pleasure." Galileo's sensuality, hedonism, and occasional dubious ethics (as in the matter of the telescope) are merely some facets of a many-sided character. We also meet the idealist whose faith in human reason strikes the sceptical Sagredo as naive: "I believe in mankind, and that means I believe in its commonsense. Without that belief I should not have the strength to get up from my bed in the morning" (*Stücke* 47-48; *Plays*

253). Then there is the optimistic humanist who tells the Little Monk that science and industry will provide ample substitutes for the lost faith of common people if the spirit of doubt is allowed to spread (Scene 8). Above all, there is the Galileo who affirms: "I say to you: he who does not know the truth is merely an idiot. But he who knows it and calls it a lie, is a criminal" (*Stücke* 120; *Plays* 293). The fact that Galileo goes on to recant his beliefs proves not his lack of an ethical imperative but his human frailty, and this is underlined in the description of his return from the Inquisition, "altered by his trial, almost to the point of being unrecognisable" (*Stücke* 167; *Plays* 319). Galileo's self-condemnation is a valid development of the character who has been established in the earlier stages of the play, a contradictory one it is true, but then most dramatic characterizations which go beyond the superficial encompass contradictions.

In his self-castigation, Galileo begins by arguing a view of the purpose of science to counter Andrea who, from being the first to condemn the recantation, has come to see the matter differently on discovering that Galileo has used his time under house arrest to write the *Discorsi* and to make a secret copy of it. When Galileo assures him that he recanted from fear of physical pain rather than from the calm calculation of a new ethics, he is disappointed but declares: "Science knows only one commandment: contribute to science" (*Stücke* 183; *Plays* 328). Galileo, however, feels that it is science which he has betrayed. He argues first that the wool merchant is concerned with both his own profits and the general health of the wool trade and, similarly, a scientist must hold himself responsible both for advancing knowledge and for promoting the development of science in the community. By science he seems to mean not only pure science but also the spirit of scepticism: "Making knowledge about everything available for everybody, science strives to make sceptics of them all" (*Stücke* 185; *Plays* 329). In his time the spirit of doubt had arisen for the first time among people who had been kept "in a nacreous haze of superstition and outmoded words" (*Stücke* 185; *Plays* 329) but who now saw hope when they turned their telescopes on their tormentors: "These selfish and violent men, who greedily exploited the fruits of science to their own use, simultaneously felt the cold eye of science turned on a thousand-year-old, but artificial misery which clearly could be eliminated by eliminating them" (*Stücke* 185; *Plays* 329). The clinching point in the first half of the speech comes with:

> The movements of the stars have become clearer; but to the mass of the people the movements of their masters are still incalculable. The fight over the measurability of the heavens has been won through doubt; but the fight of the Roman housewife for milk is ever and again lost through faith. Science, Sarti, is concerned with both battle-fronts. (*Stücke* 186; *Plays* 329-30)

So far from being an extrinsic attitude in the play, this is the culmination of a theme which runs through the whole work, from the first major speech with its reference to the common people's discovery that the rulers have legs like their legs, to the rejoinder made to the Little Monk in Scene 8, and later the important speech made by the Inquisitor [about the social relevance of science].[33] . . . Thus Galileo's opponents also see the issue as the potential subversion of the social order by science.

The historical validity of this theme of a social revolution bound up with an astronomical revolution is, of course, open to question. What, for example, is the historical warrant for attributing such thoughts to carnival singers in 1632?

> For now the Creatio Dei
> Shall turn the opposite way.
> Now the mistress must obey
> And turn around her maid.
> (Stücke 143; Plays 305)

Both Marjorie Hope Nicolson and Santillana testify to the popular excitement and celebration in verse and prose attending the publication of Galileo's Sidereus Nuncius (1610).[34] The existence of popular ballads drawing revolutionary conclusions from the new astronomy in the 1630s appears less likely, though the importance of this kind of carnival procession for the expression of popular thought is not in doubt.[35] But something close to the basic idea of the ballad was undoubtedly current in seventeenth-century thought. That the new cosmology implied social disorder and anarchic individualism is very much the theme of a famous passage from the Anatomy of the World:

> 'Tis all in pieces, all coherence gone;
> All just supply and all relation:
> Prince, Subject, Father, Son, are things forgot,
> For every man alone thinks he hath got
> To be a Phoenix. . . .

Thus it is arguable that even if the carnival episode is "un-historical" in the sense that no such particular carnival took place, Brecht was not making a travesty of history by imagining such an event: something like this was a potential if not an actual episode and therefore we can allow him the same kind of license here that Schiller demands in Maria Stuart by creating an imaginary confrontation between Elizabeth and Mary.

In any case the moral again takes precedence over the historical representation. But what conclusions are we invited to draw about the carnival? According to Zimmermann, Brecht intended to arouse an ambivalent response to the scene. The episode is alleged to show the consequences of doubt among the masses as anarchy, and Galileo's reported condemnation of the spirit of carnival (Scene 11) is seen as Brecht's own position. Hence the self-indictment in Scene 14 must be taken with reservations, for the discriminating spectator ought to bear in mind the consequences of scepticism among the ignorant and feel that the Galileo who recanted was more realistic than the Galileo who wishes he had stood firm.[36]

That Brecht might have had reservations about the attitude of the ballad is likely — for one thing he might not have identified revolution with the simple, anarchic inversion pictured in it. That he would have wished us to endorse the recantation is out of the question, as any number of his own statements show. For example, in the postscript to the American version he rejected those physicists who had said to him that the recantation was portrayed as being sensible because it enabled Galileo to get on with his work: "The fact is that Galileo enriched astronomy and physics by simultaneously robbing these sciences of a greater part of their social importance" (*Stücke* 204; *Plays* 339-40). Second, the view that scientific scepticism could and should have been allowed to spread through society is very much in line with what Brecht wrote elsewhere, not long after the American version, in the *Short Organon for the Theater* (1948), which contains important echoes of the play:

> The reason why the new way of thinking and feeling has not yet penetrated the great mass of men is that the sciences, for all their success in exploiting and dominating nature, have been stopped by the class that brought them to power . . . from operating in another field where darkness still reigns, namely that of the relations which people have to one another during the exploiting and dominating process. . . . The new approach to nature was not applied to society.[37]

Or again, "The bourgeois class . . . knows very well that its rule would come to an end if the scientific eye were turned on its own undertakings. And so that new science which was founded about a hundred years ago and deals with the character of human society was born in the struggle between rulers and ruled."[38] It would seem, then, that what Galileo has betrayed in the play is partly science in the sense of the science of society, which, in Brecht's view, meant Marxism. Pure science triumphs as Andrea smuggles the *Discorsi* over the border, but the penetration of social relations by scientific thinking, a potential age of reason, has been postponed. We do not have to endorse Brecht's equation between Marxism and social science to appreciate that his point about Galileo is a subtle one. When he speaks of the atomic bomb as the end product of Galileo's contribution to science and failure to society, he is holding Galileo responsible for two reasons: first, he contributed to the science that made the bomb; and second, he failed to help the cause of scientific thinking about social relations, which could have created an idealized age of reason in which the bomb would never have been made.

It is not uncommon for critics to represent the play's judgment on Galileo as historically simplistic: "the point of *Galileo* is that men do not today live in an age of reason simply because at a particular moment in the

seventeenth century Galileo recanted . . . ."[39] or again, "Brecht does imply
at this instant that a whole epoch of European history turns on one man's
failure."[40] But, after all, Brecht merely speaks of an age of reason that
could have *begun*, of Galileo's as only the *original* sin of modern science
(and therefore, presumably, not the only one) and of the atomic bomb as
the end product rather than the direct result of his action. And if he asserts
that there was a setback to science as a result of the affair, he is correct, at
least so far as Italy was concerned. Santillana claims that this marked the
decline of the "whole scientific movement in Italy" and the vanishing of
Florentine civilization from history but concludes that "as for the fate of
science itself, his (Galileo's) concern was justifiably less."[41] Of course, for
Brecht, the issue was larger than an Italian one, and there was more to
science than "science itself."

Ultimately, insofar as so brilliant a theatrical vehicle can be reduced
to *the* point, the point is more for the present than about the past.
Confronted by the drama in performance, we meet Galileo's dilemmas as
our own and are not allowed to be either simply censorious or simply the
reverse: "Confronted with such a situation, one can scarcely wish only to
praise or only to condemn Galileo" (*Stücke* 205; *Plays* 340). And there is
an aspect of the moral which even the bitterest opponent of Brecht's
politics, or the most detached critic of his naiveté, may regard as a telling
one. In Scene 14 Galileo laments his failure to help the poor in their battle
for milk and cannot be consoled by his success in pure science. This is not
without relevance to an age which has made great strides in the exploration of space but in which the majority go hungry. When Andrea is held
up at the Italian frontier in the final scene, he finds time to obtain a jug of
milk for an old woman and tries to dispel the idea that she can be a witch.
As a good historical drama should, *Galileo* ends by leaving us at one of our
own frontiers rather than in the past.

Galileo, like its Elizabethan predecessors, is a didactic history play
which demands detailed exploration of its message. Unlike the Elizabethan histories, it also has pretension to a degree of historical authenticity
in the modern sense. No amount of factual support for its historical
interpretation will make it a better play nor necessarily make the moral
more acceptable, but, since the historical claims are made, and since so
much of the moral content is historical moral, it is desirable that the
history should not be a travesty. We hope to have gone some way to
showing that the history in the play is not a travesty and to have made a
case for the moral as more complex and thought-provoking than it is often
represented as being, complex and thought-provoking enough to be both a
literary and an historical virtue.

Notes

1. Max Spalter, *Brecht's Tradition* (Baltimore, 1967), p. 78.

2. *The English History Play in the Age of Shakespeare* (Princeton, 1957), p. 10.

3. *Ibid.*, p. 26.

4. Spalter, p. 193.

5. Ronald D. Gray, *Brecht* (London, 1961), pp. 85–86; published in the United States as *Bertolt Brecht* (New York, 1961). [Ed.note: also published as *Brecht. The Dramatist* (Cambridge: Cambridge University Press, 1976).]

6. Ernst Schumacher, *Bertolt Brechts Leben des Galilei und andere Stücke* (Berlin, 1968), pp. 40 ff.

7. Ludovico Geymonat, *Galileo Galilei: A Biography and Inquiry into His Philosophy of Science*, trans. Stillman Drake (New York and London, 1965), p. 55.

8. Karl von Gebler, *Galileo and the Roman Curia*, trans. Mrs. George Sturge (London, 1879), p. 118, fn.

9. "Historical Sidelights" to *The Representative (Der Stellvertreter)*, trans. R. D. MacDonald (London, 1963), p. 269; original (Hamburg, 1963), p. 229.

10. Preface to *Saint Joan* (London, 1946), pp. 36–38.

11. Geymonat, pp. 6, 19.

12. Arthur Koestler, *The Sleepwalkers* (London, 1959), pp. 354, 362.

13. Quoted by K. Rülicke, "Leben des Galilei, Bemerkung zur Schlußszene," *Sinn und Form, Zweites Sonderheft Bertolt Brecht* (Berlin, 1957), p. 282.

14. See Brecht's "Notes on 'The Life of Galileo,' " trans. Desmond I. Vesey, *Plays*, I (London, 1961), 335–36. All English quotations from the play and Brecht's notes are from Vesey [cited as *Plays*], and their German originals [not supplied here] are from *Stücke*, VIII (Berlin, 1957) [cited as *Stücke*]. [Ed. note: see also Bertolt Brecht, *Gesammelte Werke in 20 Bänden* (Frankfurt am Main: Suhrkamp, 1967), 3:1229–1345, and *Collected Plays*, ed. Ralph Manheim and John Willett (New York: Vintage Books, 1971–), 5:1–98, 213–305.]

15. F. Sherwood Taylor, *Galileo and the Freedom of Thought* (London, 1938), pp. 7–8.

16. See *Stücke* 209; *Plays* 341.

17. [Shaw,] Preface to *St. Joan*, pp. 36–38.

18. Régine Pernoud, *St. Joan* (London, 1964), pp. 169–218.

19. Shaw, Preface [to *St. Joan*], p. 63.

20. *Brecht: A Choice of Evils* (London, 1959), p. 226 [4th, rev. ed. (London: Methuen, 1984)]; published in the United States as *Brecht: The Man and His Work* (New York, 1960).

21. F. R. Jevons, "Brecht's 'Life of Galileo' and the Social Relations of Sciences," *Technology and Society*, IV (1968), 27.

22. Giorgio de Santillana, *The Crime of Galileo* (Chicago, 1955), p. 17.

23. Quoted by James Brodrick, *Robert Bellarmine* (London, 1961), p. 366.

24. Geymonat, p. 156.

25. Stillman Drake, ed., *Discoveries and Opinions of Galileo* (Garden City, N.Y., 1957), pp. 70–71.

26. See "Galileo und seine Zeit" in *Geschichte d[er] neusprachlichen wissenschaftlichen Litteratur*, III (Berlin, 1927).

27. W. Zimmermann, "Brechts 'Leben des Galilei'," *Beihefte zu Wirkendes Wort*, XII (Düsseldorf, 1965), 34.

28. James Brodrick, *Bellarmine*, p. 352.

29. James Brodrick, *Galileo, the Man, His Work, His Misfortunes* (London, 1964), p. 79.

30. Spalter, pp. 289 ff.

31. The text used here is the final version, published in *Stücke*, VIII, after Brecht's death in 1956. Before that there were, of course, the American version (1946–47) and the first, written in Denmark (1938–39).

32. For comments on differences between the various versions, see Schumacher, *Leben des Galilei*, especially pp. 242–46, on differences between the third and the American version; Rülicke's paper as a whole; Gerhard Szczesny, *Das Leben des Galilei und der Fall Bertolt Brecht* (Berlin, 1967), pp. 47–53. Szczesny includes the texts of Scenes 8, 9, and 13 in the first version and those of the corresponding scenes—9, 10, and 14—in the third. [Ed. note: the scenes are not included in the reissue of Szczesny's book under the title *Bertolt Brechts "Leben des Galilei": Dichtung und Wirklichkeit* (Bonn: Bouvier, 1986) and in Szczesny, *The Case Against Bertolt Brecht, With Arguments Drawn from His "Life of Galileo,"* trans. Alexander Gode (New York: Ungar, 1969). The American version (translated by Charles Laughton) was first published in 1952; it may also be found in Brecht, *Collected Plays* 5:403–467. All three versions are available in Bertolt Brecht, *Werke. Große kommentierte Berliner und Frankfurter Ausgabe*, 30 vols., ed. Werner Hecht, Jan Knopf, Werner Mittenzwei, and Klaus-Detlef Müller (Frankfurt am Main: Suhrkamp, 1988–), 5:7–289.]

33. See *Stücke* 157; *Plays* 313–14.

34. In *The Breaking of the Circle* (New York, 1962), p. 119; Santillana, p. 9.

35. Schumacher cites various authorities: *Leben des Galilei*, p. 394.

36. *Wirkendes Wort*, XII, 34–35.

37. Bertolt Brecht, "Kleines Organon für das Theater," *Schriften zum Theater*, VII (Frankfurt am Main, 1964), 17–18. [Ed. note: see also "A Short Organum for the Theatre," trans. John Willett, in *Brecht on Theatre* (New York: Hill & Wang, 1964), 184.]

38. *Ibid.*, p. 19.

39. Harold Hobson, [London] *Sunday Times*, June 19, 1960.

40. Gray, p. 86.

41. Santillana, pp. 305, 306.

Mutter Courage und ihre Kinder [*Mother Courage and Her Children*]

Keith A. Dickson*

Brecht began working on the idea for a play on the subject of the Thirty Years War in 1939, just as C. V. Wedgwood was completing her own scholarly study of the same historical phenomenon. In her foreword to the 1949 reprint she wrote of her book: "It was written . . . under the advancing shadow of the Second World War, and it may be that the apprehension of those years can be felt vibrating from time to time in its

*From *Towards Utopia: A Study of Brecht* by Keith A. Dickson (Oxford: Clarendon Press, 1978), 97–109, 315–16. Reprinted by permission of Oxford University Press. © 1978, Keith A. Dickson.

pages." Brecht might well have said the same of his own account. Throughout the thirties he had turned out one work after another denouncing the German variant of Fascism, showing that its pernicious *Weltanschauung* leads inevitably to war. In the autumn of 1939, with Austria, Czechoslovakia, and Poland already under the Nazi yoke, it was all too clear that Hitler's foreign policy was about to plunge Europe into war on an unprecedented scale. Although theoretically the First World War might have furnished a more vivid illustration of Brecht's point, he was doubtless aware that it was still much too close to attempt an objective assessment. The Thirty Years War, the nearest thing to a world war before 1914, facilitated a more dispassionate analysis in that spirit of "smoking observation" that Brecht sought to foster in his form of theatre.[1]

"The Thirty Years War," Brecht wrote in his notes on the play, "was one of the first large-scale wars that capitalism brought upon Europe."[2] For him war belonged to that same process of economic exploitation that allegedly characterizes all class-based society, "the continuation of business by other means" (17:1138). This explains why, although all histories of the Thirty Years War to date have ranked it amongst the most fanatical religious wars in history, Brecht exonerates religion from any part in the conflict of interests. In Scene 3 Mother Courage, who exploits both sides without compunction, offers her assessment of the war to the cook and the chaplain: "To hear the big shots talk you'd think they make war for fear of God and all things bright and beautiful. But if you take a closer look, they're not so stupid. They make war for profit. And ordinary folk like me wouldn't join in for any other reason, either" (4:1375).[3] Mother Courage does not know the whole truth about this war, but she is certainly at this point articulating Brecht's Marxist attitude.

The elimination of the religious motive is an exaggeration rather than a falsification. It is true that Frederick V wrote in 1619: "My only end is to serve God and His Church,"[4] but it is equally true that James I said, "I mean to make use of all religions to compass my ends."[5] Even of Gustavus Adolphus, the most devout of the Protestant princes, it has been said, "He was in sober fact the protagonist of Swedish expansion on German soil."[6] Other assessments of his role have been more generous, but it is a fact that the God of all the combatants in this unusually sordid imbroglio became conveniently identified with dynastic interests, territorial greed, and sheer egomania. Of Gustavus, for instance, another historian writes: "In point of fact both the political and religious aims were inseparably connected in the King's mind. . . . His political enemies were at the same time his religious enemies; it was the religious differences which gave the political differences such a keen edge and such deeper significance."[7] As for the troopers, their motives were still less idealistic, most armies being "a mere collection of mercenaries without religion, without pity and without remorse."[8] At any rate there is no room in Brecht's chronicle for discussion of a complex religious conflict that involved not only Protestants and

Catholics, but also Jesuits, Capuchins, and Utraquists on the one side and Lutherans and Calvinists on the other. For Brecht this was all a matter of the ideological superstructure of history, not its actual driving force.

Brecht's historical researches appear to have been, as usual, conscientious, and since he aimed neither at allegory nor at a tale of private woe, the seemingly arbitrary limits he has imposed on his account of the Thirty Years War invite careful attention. A comprehensive study of the war would necessarily involve an analysis of the European situation prior to the outbreak of hostilities. The mutual antagonism of Habsburg and Bourbon, the Dutch problem, the emergent sense of national identity in Bohemia and Hungary, the rivalry of Denmark and Sweden, the formation of League and Union: all this and more is what sparked off the conflagration. Even if Brecht had begun his survey in 1618 he might reasonably have been expected to allude to the Bohemian crisis, the division into two main power blocs, the dashing of Protestant hopes at White Hill [in 1620] and the ensuing stalemate.

Brecht ignores all this. The first scene is set in a remote province in Sweden, where, as the recruiting-sergeant complains, there has been no war for years, and where men are in consequence happy but undisciplined. Sweden was more heavily committed than most countries after 1630 but it remained one of the few European countries the war never reached. The year too is interesting. After six years of bitter fighting 1624 was more a year of respite than of war, following [Elector of the Palatinate] Frederick's enforced armistice with [Emperor] Ferdinand. But it was not without importance. It was the year of Mansfeld's visit to London to drum up recruits and subsidies — to the nearest month contemporary with Brecht's opening scene; it was a year of tension in Austria as anxious eyes were kept on the precarious balance of power in Bohemia; Urban VIII, newly elected, was making his anti-Habsburg policies felt, thus providing moral support for the foxy antics of Richelieu, another newcomer to the power game in 1624; John George of Saxony recognized Maximilian's Electorate [of Bavaria] in the interest of German solidarity; it was also the year of Wallenstein's spectacular land-grab in Bohemia. Any of these incidents might have introduced Brecht's anatomy of the war, but he turns instead to peaceful Dalarne, almost as far from the nerve-centre of the war as he could have got, and ignored by all the standard histories. It is a historical fact that a three-year truce, a temporary breathing space in the protracted dynastic struggle of the Vasas, was nearing its end. This was followed by four years of intensive campaigning, during which Gustavus, obsessed with the dream of the Baltic as a "Swedish lake," secured a valuable foothold on the Continent and muzzled the Habsburg's faithful watchdog, Sigismund III [King of Poland]. Gustavus's contemporaries saw little significance in his invasion of the Continent at the time and were obliged to look up Sweden in their atlases, while for the Emperor it was "halt a Kriegel mehr."[9] Gustavus had in fact only been biding his time until Germany would be forced to accept his offer of intervention. All this is indisputably history, but it seems to belong to a different chapter. Few histories of the war can afford to trace so remote a connection between a recruiting-campaign in Dalarne and the war in Germany, let alone follow the fortunes of Gustavus in Poland as Brecht does in the second, third, and fourth scenes of his play.

The new perspective created by Brecht's opening gambit suggests that sooner or later war affects the whole world and directly or indirectly finds its way into the remotest valleys. Perhaps Brecht had Sweden's traditional neutrality in mind, for in such a war as this no country is truly neutral, and even if armed conflict never reaches its borders, its manpower and its economy will not be immune for long. The most important effect of Brecht's opening, however, is the implication that the familiar division into "periods," "phases," and "spheres of influence" is a mere textbook convenience which has little to do with the reality of war. S. R. Gardiner notes that 1648 marks the end simultaneously of the Thirty Years War of Germany and the Eighty Years War of the Netherlands, whereas "for France 1648 is hardly a date at all,"[10] since peace in one quarter for her merely meant she could devote greater energy to the continuing conflict with Spain. If at times even the historian admits that wars are blurred at the edges, for Brecht it is an axiom that affects the very structure of his play.

Towards the middle of the piece, and with no attempt at continuity, Brecht's own history of the war and that of the traditional historian momentarily overlap. We are made eyewitnesses of the sack of Magdeburg, the most sensational atrocity of the whole war, for which, Schiller said, "history has no language and poetry no brush."[11] But Brecht's scene is in a very low key. We remain on the periphery of the event, seeing only its impact on the lives of Mother Courage and Kattrin, nor is there any indication of the criminal blundering that led to it or of the reprisals that followed. Again, we watch troops dodge the funeral of Tilly, who had been mortally wounded in a skirmish with the Swedes near Ingolstadt. It is emphasized that his death will not alter the course of the war in the slightest. When Mother Courage asks the chaplain anxiously whether this means the end of the war (and thus her financial ruin) he replies cynically, and entirely in the spirit of Brecht's own attitude to heroism: "Because the general's dead? Don't be childish. They grow by the dozen, there'll always be plenty of heroes" (4:1401; *Plays* 5:178). Similarly, we almost encroach upon the "real" scene of the war again after the Battle of Lützen, which must on any reckoning be accounted one of its major events. Even Ferdinand is said to have grieved over the death of his most formidable and chivalrous adversary, but no tears are shed for Gustavus in Brecht's play. His death causes only a temporary "outbreak of peace," as Mother Courage describes it, during which the impetuous Eilif faces a firing-squad for committing an offence that only a few scenes earlier had been rewarded as an act of heroism. After passing thus close to the centre of gravity of the war we leave it again and move into its "last phase," as the historians usually call it, with no explanation of the shift of emphasis from the Sweden–Habsburg axis to the predominantly Bourbon–Habsburg conflict, which can be dated roughly from the arrival in Brussels of the French declaration of war on Spain in May 1635. The action of the play passes on into war-torn Saxony where the Imperial Army mounts an unsuccessful attempt to storm Halle, which changed hands so many times that historians do not bother to keep the score. This insignificant Protestant victory costs only one life, but Brecht includes it in his survey of the war because it is the life of Mother Courage's last remaining child.

The last three scenes reflect faithfully the growing sense of confusion and despair, which drained the war of whatever idealism and sense of purpose it may once have had for at least some of the contestants. Mother Courage comments on the appalling results of famine and pestilence, those seasoned camp-followers of both armies, which culminated in reliably documented outbreaks of cannibalism. "The war reveals a spectacle of purposelessness and hopelessness," writes one historian of this phase, "a general fatalism and cynicism in wickedness seem to deepen as the war drags its interminable length."[12] Brecht's army cook says simply: "It's the end of the world" (4:1423; *Plays* 5:196), and this is very much the impression left by the last few scenes of the play. At the end of the last scene, with Mother Courage now bereft of all her children, it still seems as though the war has a long life ahead of it, as the chaplain cynically predicted a few years earlier (4:1402), and the armies march on. The final chorus prophesies that the war will last a hundred years. That the prophecy is wrong by exactly eighty-eight years is not the point, for war in Brecht's sense is continuous, an ineluctable condition of pre-revolutionary society. By choosing this particularly degrading, destructive, and protracted war as the subject of his play, and by readjusting the historical focus, Brecht has succeeded in suggesting a war that has no geographical boundaries and no clearly definable beginning and end. It bursts the artificial limits imposed on it by the historian, reaching right down to our own century and beyond.

Brecht's second major reinterpretation affects the characters and it parallels the method he adopted for the novel on Caesar. The period of the Thirty Years War was not in any case particularly rich in attractive personalities. Neither the military exploits of its Mansfelds and Torstenssons nor the statesmanship of its Eggenbergs and Oñates offer much scope to a dramatist, to say nothing of the weathercock politics of the aristocracy. But few students of the period have failed to respond to the energetic Gustavus Adolphus, the inscrutable Wallenstein, the dashing duc d'Enghien, or even the dogged Tilly. Brecht is one of the few. After providing the historical framework of the first four scenes, *il re d'oro* dies unsung in a laconic sub-title to Scene 8; Oxenstjerna, his aide and successor, is reduced to a synoptic heading in the first scene; Wallenstein is not so much as mentioned. No historically authenticated character is in fact allowed on the stage. The historian's heroes are kept in the wings and the stage is dominated by a resourceful camp-follower and her children, a cynical padre, a scoundrelly cook, a whore, and an amorphous mass of anonymous peasants and troopers. Brecht's Lukullus [in *The Trial of Lucullus*] is amazed to find in the Underworld that nobody has heard of him. His military successors are threatened with the same fate in *Mutter Courage*. Off stage in Scene 6 we hear a roll of drums and the strains of a funeral march as the hero of Magdeburg is borne by his more conscientious followers to his grave. On stage, Mother Courage is making an inventory of the wares with which she seeks to wrest a living for her children from the chaos and destruction of the war, and says all in one breath: "It's a shame about the general — socks: twenty-two pairs — I hear he was killed by accident" (4:1399–1400; *Plays* 5:177). Not hers to sit upon the ground and tell sad stories of the death of kings, or their generals, but to see that the raw materials of war are still intact. At the end of the same scene, when Kattrin, already handicapped by a war-experience in her childhood, returns after a brutal assault has been made on her, the padre, hearing the artillery honour the dead general, mutters reverently: "This is a historical moment." Mother Courage replies: "To me it's a historic moment when they hit my daughter over the eye" (4:1408; *Plays* 5:184), and for the first and only time in the play she curses war.

The fluctuating fortunes of the common man, of whom the orthodox political historian has so little to say, are for Brecht the real stuff of history. History faintly recalls a nameless peasant who exclaimed, "I was born in war. I have no home, no country and no friends, war is all my wealth and now whither shall I go?"[13] Here is the historical counterpart of Mother Courage as she appears in the final scene, though Brecht's character is less querulous about it as she straps herself to the wagon and moves on despite everything. Or again: "The young girl, who in better times would have passed on to a life of honourable wedlock with some youth who had been the companion of her childhood in the sports around the village fountain, had turned aside, for very starvation, to a life of shame in the train of one or other of the armies by which her home had been made desolate."[14] This is almost detail for detail the story of Yvette Pottier. For the historian such things can be nothing but a brief illustration, a deviation from his main purpose, in pursuit of which the suffering of the anonymous masses remains largely statistical. He may supply facts and figures, historical maps, graphs showing population-losses and the like, but these do not amount to the reality of suffering. Aware of the inadequacy of his medium in this respect, Gardiner asks at one point, "How is it possible to bring such scenes before our eyes in their ghastly reality?"[15] It is precisely to this question that Brecht as a dramatist has an answer unique to his craft, and what has been said of Fontane as a historical novelist is equally true of

Brecht: "He has written the history which the historians cannot remember."[16]

Brecht's worm's-eye view does much more, however, than dramatize the sufferings of the poor at the expense of the historian's heroes. It is bifocal. Not only are some of the outstanding events of the war discussed in the course of the dialogue. They also appear in the projected synopses, which often pin them down to a specific date and location, in the manner Brecht had pioneered in his adaptation of Marlowe's *Edward II*. These projections contribute toward a radical *Verfremdung* [estrangement] of history which is now seen as the repercussion of world-historical events on the lives of a representative cross-section of the unremembered masses. Conversely, their unrecorded exploits are transformed into events of historical moment. Before the Magdeburg scene the projected text reads: ". . . Tilly's victory at Magdeburg costs Mother Courage four officers' shirts" (4:1396). In the version first performed in Zurich in 1941, Mother Courage grudgingly sacrifices the shirts for bandages; in the revised version written for Berlin eight years later they are removed on the sly by Kattrin, but either way textbook history has undergone an alienation-effect. The fall of Magdeburg is said to have cost some 25,000 citizens their lives: it costs Mother Courage four shirts, despite the fact that she is on the winning side. As she has said earlier, victory and defeat are equally expensive for the little man (4:1379).

There is an additional interest in this particular caption in that it shows that the play offers more than sympathy with the underdog. The underdog is also criticized for his passivity and for his stubborn and unrealistic belief in his ability to exploit the historical situation to his own ends.

The soldiers in Brecht's play are largely passive, but this does not make them the innocent victims of circumstance. Mother Courage gives an ironical account of their passivity, in which Brecht's philosophy of history transforms persiflage into serious criticism:

> I feel sorry for such a general or emperor. There he was p'raps, thinking as how he was doing something special, something people will be talking about in times to come, and thinking they'll build him a statue. He goes and conquers the world, for example, now there's an ambition worthy of a general, he can't ask for nothing better. In short, he works himself to a standstill and then it all comes to nothing because of the ordinary folk what p'raps want a mug of ale and a bit of company, nothing grander than that. The best plans have come adrift along of the pettiness of them as are supposed to carry 'em out, for of course the emperors can't do nothing for themselves, they rely on the support of their troops and the folk as happen to be around at the time, ain't I right? (4:1400–1401)

In *Schweyk im Zweiten Weltkrieg* [*Schweyk in the Second World War*; *Plays* 7:63–134] Hitler's grandiose plans for world domination founder on the pusillanimity of the Schweyks in his millenial empire. At the end of Scene 8 of *Mutter Courage* the heroine sings another strophe of her theme song, the second quatrain of which says of war:

> Though steel and lead are stout supporters
> A war needs human beings too
> Report today to your headquarters
> If it's to last, this war needs you!
>
> (4:1421)

Eric Bentley's translation of the last line [above][17] recalls Kitchener's famous recruiting-poster of the First World War. The unspoken corollary is that if the soldiers refuse to rally round the war-mongers, there will be no war. This endorses the ironical impression the audience receives from the foreshortening effect of the first scene, that the Thirty Years War cannot begin again at all without Eilif.

The complicity of Mother Courage herself is much more active. The war did not catch her unawares. In the first scene not the least of the many ironies created by the unusual choice of location is that Mother Courage, who says she cannot afford to wait for the war to reach Bamberg, her home town, has traversed the whole of Europe in search of business. A situation created by the war at many removes is there as the play begins, and into this situation rolls the covered wagon of a small-time opportunist. Even the death of the horse did not deter her and, significantly, when we first see her wagon it is drawn by her two strapping sons. The Berliner Ensemble's official programme shows a picture of this wagon and on the opposite page there is a photograph of its modern counterpart with the caption: "1933–1945. Railroad trucks of the American Standard Oil Company, whose profits in peacetime (1939) amounted to $55,800,000, in wartime (1945) $100,400,000, i.e. almost double." Fair comment. But Brecht's potent symbol, which dominates the stage from beginning to end, expresses more than this over-explicit programme-note. It demonstrates Anna Fierling's tragic dual function in the play: that of a mother, for whom the wagon is a mobile home, and that of a profiteer, for whom it is a valuable investment. Brecht wrote of his heroine: "Mother Courage . . . recognizes, in common with her friends and guests and just about everyone else, the purely commercial nature of war: that is precisely what attracts her. She believes in war to the very end" (17:1150). In one of her songs, in a strophe written specially by Brecht for the Berlin production in a vain attempt to inhibit the sympathy Therese Giehse's Mother Courage had elicited in Zurich, she sings: "A war is only what you make it. / It's business, not with cheese but lead" (14:1409; *Plays* 5:185).

If audiences stubbornly continue to admire this attitude despite the changes Brecht made in the text, it is not, as he seems to have thought, that they fail to see in her a "hyena of the battlefield," as the padre calls her (4:1414). It is rather that they see and admire the selfless motive behind her brazen attempt to beat the capitalist warmongers at their own game: "My aim in life is to get through, me and my children and my wagon" (4:1406; *Plays* 5:183). This is what she tragically fails to do. She arrives in Dalarne to make money and protect her children from the war: she makes half a guilder and loses a son. She sacrifices all her children to an inexorable Moloch, each one the price of a commercial enterprise: Schweizerkas because she haggles too long over his ransom, and Kattrin because she is too preoccupied with a fluctuating market to keep her out of harm's way during a crisis. She retains the courage that earned her her nickname, but also her blind obstinacy in thinking she can turn the war-game to her advantage. What she fails to grasp is, as the chaplain picturesquely puts it, that anyone who wants to breakfast with the Devil needs a long spoon (4:1414). Someone is certainly making a fortune out of this war, but it is demonstrably not Mother Courage, whose wagon gets steadily more dilapidated.

But Mother Courage's assessment of the war is at least partially right. It is man-made, not the work of fate or what insurance policies still quaintly call an act of God. Brecht specifically warned against any fatalistic interpretation of history: "*Historical conditions* may not be conceived . . . as inscrutable forces . . . : they are created and maintained by man" (16:679). This is where Anna Fierling differs so strikingly from Maurya in John Synge's *Riders to the Sea*, the play to which both *Die Gewehre der frau Carrar* [*Señora Carrar's Rifles*] and *Mutter Courage* were a kind of "counter-project" (*Gegenentwurf*), to use a term Brecht coined later.[18] The sea destroys Maurya's children, whereas Eilif, Schweizerkas, and Kattrin are the victims of a man-made conflict to which their own mother contributes more than most.

Despite Brecht's warning there is a strong sense of fatality in the play, and critics persisted in speaking of it as a Niobe tragedy. This is because within the historical limits of the Thirty Years War Mother Courage has no viable alternative. Collectively men are seen to be the executors of their own doom and the whole course of history is determined by their action or inaction. The opportunities presented to them for turning it to their own advantage, however, are brief and rare. In 1688, 1789, 1871, and 1917 their chance will come in one place or another, but in the meantime there is little they can do. Anna Fierling can either wait passively for the war to destroy her and her children, as it destroys the citizens of Magdeburg, or she can harness her wagon to it in a vain attempt to exploit the exploiter. Tragically, she services the machinery of destruction.

To the consternation of Friedrich Wolf, who mildly rebuked Brecht in an interview for not making her see the error of her ways,[19] Mother Courage learns nothing from her tragic experience, no more, Brecht said, than a guinea-pig learns from the experiment of which it is part (17:1150). Brecht was too much of a realist to play at make-believe with history. Like Tolstoy, whose realism he guardedly admired, Brecht can stand far enough back from the historical process to see that it is men who make it, but he can see just as clearly as the great Russian realist that whilst they are making it they are "the involuntary tools of history, performing a task which is concealed from them, although comprehensible to us."[20] If there is anagnorisis in *Mutter Courage* it does not take place on-stage, as in the Aristotelian tradition, but in the auditorium of Brecht's Epic Theatre. It is not Mother Courage as a tragic character, but those who study her fate, who must be taught to see how history works.

Nothing distinguishes Brecht's method as a historical dramatist so sharply from that of more conventional Communist writers as this aspect of *Mutter Courage*, quite apart from the wide divergence of theatrical techniques. Marxism is committed to the dogma of historical optimism, and its literature, according to the prescription in the *Great Soviet Encyclopedia*, must be imbued with its "life-asserting force, consciously reflecting the inevitability of victory of the new over the old, the revolutionary over the reactionary."[21] J. R. Becher, the poet laureate of orthodox German Communism, rounds off his *Winterschlacht* (one of the few non-Brecht plays adopted by the Berliner Ensemble) with a rousing apotheosis of the Red Army, in which he had himself fought against his own countrymen during the war. . . . The Stalingrad disaster becomes retrospectively a victory for German freedom since it heralds the end of Nazi tyranny. The Red Army as deus ex machina represents the victorious life-asserting force of the Revolution, in the face of which Hitler's reactionary regime is inevitably doomed.

Brecht was no less committed than Becher to the dogma of historical optimism, but the lesson he hoped his audiences would learn from *Mutter Courage* is much more subtle than anything in Becher's pious doggerel. The life-asserting force in this play is not that of triumphant socialism, of which there is not the faintest hint. It is to be found in the reactionary figure of Mother Courage, whose indomitable will to survive is prone to tragic error but is the real guarantee of ultimate victory. Brecht's chronicle from the Thirty Years War teaches that man will make history "under conditions of his own choosing," to use Marx's famous phrase,[22] only when he has learned from bitter experience to harness to his own needs Anna Fierling's stubborn courage, her protective instinct, and her mis-spent energy.

Notes

1. Bertolt Brecht, *Gesammelte Werke in 20 Bänden* (Frankfurt am Main: Suhrkamp, 1967), 17:992. [Ed. note: subsequent references in the text will be to volume and page(s).]

2. *Materialien zu "Mutter Courage und ihre Kinder,"* ed. W. Hecht (Frankfurt, 1964), 92. [Ed. note: see also *Brechts Mutter Courage und ihre Kinder,* ed. Klaus-Detlef Müller (Frankfurt am Main: Suhrkamp, 1982), and *Mother Courage and Her Children, Collected Plays,* ed. Ralph Manheim and John Willett (New York: Vintage Books, 1971–) 5:133–210, 331–94 (Notes and Variants). Hereafter cited as *Plays.*]

3. [Ed. note: translations from the German (omitted here) are by the author unless otherwise indicated.]

4. C. V. Wedgwood, *The Thirty Years War* (1956), 98.

5. Ibid., 190.

6. Ibid., 281.

7. Georg Winter, *Geschichte des Dreißigjährigen Krieges* (Berlin, 1893), 349.

8. S. R. Gardiner, *The Thirty Years' War* (1874), 205.

9. Winter, *Geschichte*, 339: [just an additional little war.]

10. Gardiner, *Thirty Years' War*, 216.

11. Schiller, *Geschichte des Dreißigjährigen Kriegs*, Säkularausgabe, xv, 182.

12. David Ogg, *Europe in the 17th Century*, rev. edn. (1954), 167.

13. Wedgwood, *Thirty Years War*, 505.

14. Gardiner, *Thirty Years' War*, 213.

15. Gardiner, *Thirty Years' War*, 183.

16. H. B. Garland, "Theodor Fontane," in *German Men of Letters*, ed. A. Natan (1961), 222.

17. In Bertolt Brecht, *Plays*, vol. ii (1966), 66.

18. *Gesammelte Werke*, 5:2*.

19. The interview was published under the title "Formprobleme des Theaters aus neuem Inhalt" (17:1142–47).

20. R. F. Christian, *Tolstoy's "War and Peace." A Study* (1962), 93.

21. The phrase (*zhizneutverzhdayushchaya sila*) occurs in both the *Malaya* and *Bolshaya sovyetskaya entsiklopediya* in the articles on Socialist Realism.

22. Karl Marx und Friedrich Engels, *Werke* (Institut für Marxismus-Leninismus beim ZK der SED). Dietz Verlag, Berlin, 1956–68, vol. 8, 115.

Revolution from the Right: Bertolt Brecht's American Gangster Play *The Resistible Rise of Arturo Ui*

Ernst Schürer*

In recent years we have witnessed a renaissance of interest in two phenomena of our recent past: the Mafia and its most noteworthy representative, Al Capone, and National Socialism and its "Führer." Scores of books, films, and television features have fueled the popular imagination — suffice it to mention *The Godfather*, *The Last Ten Days*, and Joachim Fest's biography of and film about Hitler. One wonders whether the love of violence and perverse admiration of great criminals or the desire to seriously examine the social and cultural conditions that give rise to such "leaders" are the reasons behind this infatuation.

*Reprinted by permission from *Perspectives on Contemporary Literature* 2, no. 2 (November 1978):24–46. © 1978 by the University Press of Kentucky. The essay was revised and somewhat abridged by the author for publication in this volume.

Bertolt Brecht was one of the first writers who saw a connection between Al Capone and Adolf Hitler. In *The Resistible Rise of Arturo Ui*, written in 1941,[1] Brecht uses Capone's rule over Chicago as a model for the portrayal of Hitler and his henchmen.[2] In early 1941, the second year of World War II, Hitler's power stood at its zenith and his military might was threatening all nations. In contrast, in March 1941 Brecht and his family, refugees from Hitler's Germany, were in Helsinki, Finland, anxiously awaiting their visas that would enable them to enter the United States. Brecht had felt particularly desperate when, in April 1940, Denmark, where he had spent the years from 1933 to 1939 in exile, and Norway were invaded by German troops and he had to flee to Sweden and then to Finland. The Nazi army seemed invincible and irresistible, as Brecht noted with regard to the fighting in Greece: "One had expected months of battle, it took only days. . . . One gets the impression that only this army can move."[3] Helsinki no longer seemed a safe place; yet in this atmosphere of fear and suspense Brecht drafted his new play: "In the middle of all the excitement about the visas and the possibility of leaving, I am stubbornly working on the new gangster history" (*AJ* 1:269).

In penning the play, Brecht had a specific audience and a specific didactic purpose in mind: *Arturo Ui* was written for the American stage and aimed at an American audience to instruct it, in 1941, about the dangers of fascism.[4] In view of Brecht's intent to continue the fight against Hitler and the Nazis in the United States with all the weapons at his command, it is strange indeed that *Arturo Ui*, a play featuring one of the noteworthy Brechtian characters,[5] was neither published nor performed until after his death in 1956 — a fact that possibly accounts for the play's long neglect by the critics.[6] Apart from tracing the genesis of the play, pointing out some of its sources, and commenting on Brecht's artistic means, I hope to provide an answer to the vexing question why Brecht did not make any attempt to have it produced in the United States.

Since the German historical background that Brecht alludes to — such as the *Osthilfe* scandal, the burning of the *Reichstag*, the trial of Van der Lubbe, the murders of Röhm and Dollfuß, and the *Anschluß* of Austria — has been sufficiently discussed,[7] I wish to concentrate on the similarities between Al Capone and Hitler that Brecht observed. After all, Brecht wanted to familiarize *American* theatergoers with the reasons for the rise of Hitler and the dangers threatening democracy, dangers that were not posed by left-wing forces as most Americans assumed at that time, but by conservative, right-wing groups.

It has been asserted by critics that Brecht did not know the United States and that his portrayal of the Nazis as gangsters neither does justice to the impact they had on modern history nor adequately conveys an understanding of their unprecedented crimes. "Brecht knew Hitler; he knew very little about Chicago," Martin Esslin asserts;[8] and Frederic Ewen notes: "Gangsterism is scarcely a phenomenon that could adequately describe Nazism and its atrocities."[9] This is certainly true, but in 1941 those atrocities were not known to the world; furthermore, the gangster-ism of the twenties was not "an accepted phenomenon in modern life, a part of the structure of modern society."[10] It must also be stressed that Brecht did not write a historical documentary drama about Hitler, as many critics seem to think, but the story of a Chicago gangster. He therefore cannot be faulted with not mentioning such facets as racism that Brecht in *Roundheads and Peakheads* interprets as a diversionary tactic on the part of the ruling class. Rather, *Arturo Ui* is "an attempt to explain to the capitalistic world the rise of Hitler by placing him in a familiar milieu" (*GW* 17:1176). At the same time, Brecht's attack in *Arturo Ui* is in part directed against the often fanatical cult of the charismatic and demonic, heroic and invincible great leader upon whom millions of Germans looked for the solution to all their national problems as well as their personal salvation.

Actually, Brecht's interest in America predated his knowledge of Nazism. His first play with an American setting, *In the Jungle of Cities*, was performed in 1923, the year of Hitler's Munich putsch. Chicago in particular captured Brecht's imagination; to him this dynamic and ruth-less city became a symbol for the modern metropolis and served as a setting not only for *In the Jungle* but also for *Happy End* (1929), *Saint Joan of the Stockyards* (1932),[11] and *Arturo Ui* (1941).

In his youth, Brecht saw America as an exotic and romantic country, the home of hardy pioneers and the land of the future. The skyscrapers of New York, the technical inventions, the spirit of its people fascinated him as they did most Europeans. After his study of and conversion to Marxism in the late twenties, he stressed America's capitalistic aspects, the suppres-sion of the labor movement and the brutality of the captains of industry. During the years of the Weimar Republic the German papers were filled with stories about the America of the "Roaring Twenties," its manners and morals, its fabulous wealth, its new inventions, its movies, music and literature, its sports events and beauty contests, and, last but not least, its Prohibition, racketeering, gangsters, and political corruption. America exerted a powerful influence on German industry and politics, and Brecht was such an avid reader of news from the United States that he considered himself an authority on things American. In some of his poems he alludes to current events such as the hurricane of 1926, the flood caused by the Mississippi, the flight of the Okies to California, and the boxing world championship in 1927, "one of the 'great, [almost] mythical amusements of the gigantic cities across the ocean' " (*GW* 17:948). After the stock market crash in October of 1929, Brecht voiced his disenchantment with the American Dream in his poem, "Late Lamented Fame of the Giant City of New York" (*GW* 11:475–83).[12]

During his Danish exile Brecht's interest in America increased; in 1935 he visited this country for the first time to assist in the New York production of *The Mother,* a play that is based on Gorky's novel.[13] With his friend, the composer Hanns Eisler, Brecht went to the movies almost daily;[14] it is likely that he saw far more gangster films than *Public Enemy* (1931), a treatment of the life of John Dillinger specifically mentioned by Eisler.[15] The genre that had got its start in the late twenties with *Underworld* (1927, directed by Ben Hecht with whom Brecht later became acquainted in Hollywood), and *Racket* (1928), reached its peak in the early thirties with classics such as *Little Caesar* (1930), the above-mentioned *Public Enemy* (1931), *Lady Killer* (1933), *The Little Giant* (1933), *G. Men* (1935), and finally, towards the end of the decade, *The Roaring Twenties* (1939). These were action movies with a quick pace; they refrained from moralizing. Some of these films were based on the life of Al Capone and one bore his nickname *Scarface.* It was also billed as *The Shame of the Nation,* a title which must have seemed very appropriate to Brecht when applied to Hitler and Germany.

During his 1935 visit to New York City, Brecht seized upon the idea to write "the gangster play we know," since it would "call back to memory certain events with which we are all familiar" (*AJ* 1:249),[16] that is, the Nazis' rise to power. Brecht, an admirer of Charlie Chaplin, later saw the latter's *The Great Dictator* (1939), a political satire that influenced his own portrayal of Hitler.[17] And in Finland, in January 1941, he saw a gangster movie entitled *Invisible Chains.*[18] Although Brecht's interest in films was surpassed by that in English detective and crime novels, it was the gangster movies rather than the detective novels that influenced his play.

Upon his return to Europe from New York in January 1936 Brecht continued working on other projects and finished some of his plays such as *Mother Courage and Her Children* (1939) that subsequently were to make him famous. But in March 1941 his thoughts turned to the American stage, and he quickly developed a plan for eleven or twelve scenes of a "gangster play," a "gangster history," or a "historical farce," as he called it variously (*AJ* 1:249, 250, 274). To avoid traditional genre classifications Brecht later subtitled *Arturo Ui* a "parable play."[19] At any rate, Brecht, aided by his co-worker Margarete Steffin and his son Stefan, worked furiously and completed the play in early April. He felt so elated that he considered writing "*Ui* Part Two: Spain/Munich/Poland/France,"[20] a plan that did not materialize.

In order for the parable to be successful, the playwright had to enable the audience to recognize the play's historical background. Conversely, the gangster plot required a life of its own so as not to induce the audience to constantly search for historical parallels. To prevent such speculation on the audience's part, Brecht stipulated that, at the end of each scene, a few sentences be projected on the curtain — a kind of writing on the wall — that establish the analogy between the happenings on stage and past political events in Germany. However, such projections tend to undermine the autonomy of the plot, particularly since most characters' names are easily recognizable as renderings into Italian of Nazi leaders' names. "Arturo Ui" is obviously intended as a composite of Adolf Hitler and Al Capone—he is mentioned twice in the text—and the name has the Italian sound that Americans are wont to associate with the Mafia. More importantly, Brecht based plot episodes on the exploits of Al Capone who had become a folk hero and an almost mythical figure by the end of the 1930s.

Thus Arturo Ui describes himself twice as a plain son of the Bronx, without a job, who came to Chicago with only seven proven men to bring peace to the vegetable market. These statements allude to the Nazi myth of the 1920 founding of the Nazi party by the first seven members of the German Workers' Party (DAP)—Hitler being the seventh member. They also refer to Hitler's constant profession of his desire for peace while engaging in a huge military buildup and committing acts of aggression against Germany's neighbors. In 1920 Al Capone, then completely unknown and hailing from Brooklyn rather than the Bronx, had been called to Chicago by Johnny Torrio, a Sicilian gangster, who wanted to organize bootlegging. Later Capone liked to stress that he was a peace-loving, law-abiding citizen and family man. But in his business dealings he was utterly ruthless. Both Capone and Hitler were social upstarts; on the one hand, they adopted the ostentatious lifestyle of the parvenu: they drove around in huge cars, surrounded themselves with a large number of bodyguards, and built sumptuous villas. On the other, they declared themselves to be "regular guys" and benefactors of society. Thus they assumed the typical pose of the petty bourgeois parvenu;[21] both the Nazis and other rightist organizations drew their main strength from the petty bourgeoisie.

The ratification of the Eighteenth Amendment and the passing of the Volstead Act for the enforcement of the amendment introduced Prohibition in 1920, and it provided Johnny Torrio and his lieutenant Al Capone with the opportunity to establish a liquor business on a grand scale. It seems likely that Brecht had read such books as Fred D. Pasley's *Al Capone* (1930)[22] and Frederick Lewis Allen's *Only Yesterday* (1931),[23] since the bribing of elected officials, blackmail, extortion, and even the training of the body guards, as described in these books, are used by him in his play. Al Capone's aim was to be the dictatorial ruler of Cook County to gain a monopoly in the liquor traffic in Chicago and its suburbs, and he used his political influence as well as brute force to expand his territory. In the spring of 1924 he conquered Cicero, a suburb of Chicago, after having been asked by the Republican committeeman from that town, Konvalinka, to assure the election of his ticket. By bribery, intimidation, terrorism, slugging, kidnapping, and plain murder in open daylight, Capone did just that, and to him fell the spoils: he now had a safe base from which to operate without being molested by the police. In 1926 he decided to gain control of bootlegging in other cities and then across the nation, a plan which resulted in more warfare and killings, until finally in

May of 1929, the warring factions signed a nonaggression and mutual aid pact like so many statesmen. Just as Nazi aggression was caused, among other things, by the hunger for more land and trade, so gang wars usually erupted because territorial rights had been infringed upon and a rival gang like the Gennas or the O'Banions tried to "muscle in" ("reinstiefeln"; GW 4:1799) on a competitor's trade zone. Although Brecht did not treat this aspect in his play, he perceived the Western powers as an alliance of commercial rivals rather than partners; hence he considered writing a counterplay ("Gegenstück") to Arturo Ui, "The Market of Nations," intended to expose the ineptitude and corruption of allied leaders (AJ 1:396).

Capone exerted great influence on the elections in Chicago, and many of the influential ward leaders were in his pay. Thus in Arturo Ui old Dogsborough is referred to as "Wahlboss" (ward leader; GW 4:1727). Capone's influence was not confined to politics, it also extended to the business world. After their start in the liquor trade, the gangsters ventured into racketeering. By 1930 there were more than a hundred different rackets in Chicago, and rackets were spreading to other cities mentioned by Brecht. Arturo Ui's racket is the vegetable trade. He sells legitimate businessmen "protection" against burglaries, robberies, and the like and resorts to violent means, including murder, if they refuse to pay. Conversely, gangsters would endeavor to keep their customers solvent; in the garage racket, for example, they would puncture tires to provide work for the garage owners. Recourse to the police was often to no avail; the authorities had either been bribed or intimidated and did not intervene.

Bribery, a favorite means of the gangsters to corrupt and influence people, is also evident in Arturo Ui. Old Dogsborough receives as a present the majority of stock in a shipping company and a lakeside estate to make him receptive to the troubles of the cauliflower trade. In a different vein, the trial against Fish for arson is not only patterned closely after Van der Lubbe's trial in the Reichstag arson and his brilliant defense by Dimitrov,[24] it also refers to the many trials against Capone and other gangsters who were seldom prosecuted because they always had an alibi. In murder after murder, Capone openly flouted the authorities and the courts by producing witnesses who testified to his having been in Cicero or in Florida at the time of a killing in Chicago. If the police in rare cases succeeded in dragging a gangster into court, he usually won an acquittal. Prosecution witnesses were openly gunned down like Bowl in the fifth scene of the play, or they were cowed into silence, while members of the juries as well as prosecuting attorneys and judges were bribed or threatened. Bowl is also being punished according to Mafia law for being a traitor, since he first helps Ui against Dogsborough and then turns to the authorities in the inquiry against Dogsborough who is now under the protection of Ui. The reign of terror in Chicago lasted with differing intensity for fourteen years, from 1920 to 1933, when Prohibition was finally ended by the

Nineteenth Amendment and citizens' groups and the federal government crushed the gangsters.

Roma's plot against Givola and Giri in scene ten is based on the killing of the Irishman Dion O'Banion in 1924, at that time the most powerful gangster in Chicago.[25] A skillful florist during the day, at night he was an accomplished bootlegger and hijacker. Brecht alludes to the latter practice when he has Givola and the trust complain to Ui about Roma whose boys have shot at trucks from the Caruther Garages that belong to the trust.[26] Brecht paid attention to the smallest detail; both the flower shop owner Givola (Goebbels) and O'Banion had a crippled foot. Torrio, Capone, and O'Banion got along well at first; but when the latter refused to engage in a business deal with the former, he was marked for assassination. The assassins came to O'Banion's flower shop, ostensibly to order wreaths for the funeral of the influential president of the "Unione Sicilione" — an association that Capone used in a fashion corresponding to Hitler's employment of the SA, the Storm Troopers. When others — presumably friends of the deceased — arrived, the ordinarily very cautious O'Banion came trustingly forward to shake their hands. But while one man held O'Banion's right hand in a tight grip, his companions gunned him down. Via this assassination and his control of the "Unione Sicilione" "Capone was enabled to establish his gunman dictatorship of Chicago."[27] In a similar manner, Roma seeks to persuade Ui to allow him to take Dogsborough for a ride — a favorite assassination method of gangsters — kill Giri in the process, then order wreaths in Givola's flower shop, and "pay in cash" (GW 4:1802) by shooting the owner. However, Roma never gets the opportunity to put his plan into effect since Giri and the trust succeed in changing Ui's mind and in turning the tables on Roma. Ui and Givola then use the method employed by the enemies of O'Banion, the "handshake murder,"[28] to kill Roma. The elimination of Roma and his men is also patterned after the infamous St. Valentine's Day murder of seven members of the Moran gang — a massacre in which some participating members of the Al Capone gang were disguised as policemen. When they entered the garage of the Moran gang, the Morans, in the belief that a routine police raid was taking place, willingly lined up against the wall to be searched, whereupon they were mowed down by fire from a Thompson submachine gun.[29]

Finally, Dullfeet in Brecht's play represents the press, which indeed was very powerful in Chicago. But it was also infiltrated by gangland. When in 1930 Alfred Lingle, an influential police reporter for the *Tribune*, was shot, it was thought at first that he had been murdered because he knew too much, but later it was established that he had connections to most gangsters in town and had aided them. Dullfeet is represented in the play as an honest man, but the figure of Ted Ragg, the reporter of the *Star*, may well be modelled after Lingle. After the murder of Dullfeet, Ui, Giri and Givola attend his funeral; they even carry "large wreaths in their hands" (*GW* 4:1802). Brecht here points to the custom of the gangsters to bury their murdered colleagues with great pomp and circumstance—a custom that began with the O'Banion funeral. Although questioned by the police and closely watched by the O'Banion gang, the prime suspects Torrio and Capone attended the funeral.

There are further details that attest to Brecht's familiarity with the Capone story: Capone's headquarters hotel, the Metropole, is renamed the Mammoth—presumably to ridicule the Nazis' predilection for monumental architecture. Emmanuele Giri wears a "carnation in his buttonhole" (*GW* 4:1741); Brecht here alludes to the gangsters' flair for gaudy dressing as well as Göring's infatuation with uniforms and decorations that made him the butt of many jokes.

So far I have referred only to actual events in Chicago, but Brecht's aim was to show the relationship between politics and the economic sphere, between fascism and capitalism. His son Stefan, who knew about "the connections between the world of the gangster and the administration" (*AJ* 1:250),[30] helped him. Both Pasley and Allsop repeatedly draw attention to the interaction between economics, politics, and crime in Chicago: "A perceptible pattern of bold collaboration between politics, business and gangsters was becoming apparent, and the attention of the whole nation was drawn to the harum-scarum cowboy mayor and his New Frontier roughneck rule by the roar of bombs and the bark of guns."[31] Indeed, "Capone and the others . . . were the executives and technicians. The city was being run by the politicians and by City Hall, and the big bosses weren't interested if the gangsters killed each other providing they kept delivering the money."[32] Hence the big bosses used Capone, and Capone in turn used the little people for his own purposes and as cannon fodder.

One cause of racketeering was the warfare between organized labor and the businessmen. Labor leaders at times employed violence to state their demands more emphatically.[33] Conversely, big plants and trusts hired their thugs to protect themselves or to take the offensive by breaking up strikes, killing labor leaders, and running them out of town. Substitute communism for unionism and "great industrialists" for "big business" and the analogy that Brecht posits is clear: Hitler's rise to power had been accomplished with the help of the German industrialists who feared socialism/communism as threatening their profits and believed they could manipulate the despised upstart Hitler in whose politics they did not entirely concur.[34] Brecht's admittedly one-sided view of Hitler's success corresponds to his emphasis on Ui's function as a tool of the trust through scene twelve; only after the murder of Dullfeet does he assert his independence.

Brecht ignores another facet that does not fit his theory: the vast majority of Chicago's inhabitants, especially the German and Italian immigrants, were against Prohibition and indirectly supported Capone, who supplied a commodity they wanted: beer for the poor and whiskey for the rich. The acquiescence of the population and its support in Capone's fight against the Volstead Act allowed him in turn to completely corrupt the authorities and establish his reign of terror. Undermining of the laws in general because of one senseless law, hope of economic gains, and fear were the factors leading to the terror. In Germany the population was against the Treaty of Versailles and supported Hitler's fight against it; this equivocal attitude of the people towards the Nazis created a political climate which enabled Hitler to set up his dictatorship. He was then able to corrupt the laws and the authorities to such a degree that they would do his bidding unquestioningly.

In Chicago, the gangster was not only "protecting" other business-men; he considered himself to be a businessman. "We're big business without high hats,"[35] O'Banion told a friend. Capone justifiably claimed that he was merely supplying goods that were in popular demand, and he ran his enterprise in a strictly businesslike fashion "with a complete auditing system, maintained by a clerical staff."[36] The bootleggers had received some of their initial capital from former brewery owners eager to lease their plants; five former breweries were controlled by the Capone syndicate. Actually, on account of their virtual monopoly the gangs could set prices for all alcoholic beverages at artificially high levels and coerce innkeepers to buy products of inferior quality. Brecht compared the exploitation of the small shopkeepers by the cauliflower trust — in collusion with the Ui gang — with the fate of small nations in 1941 (AJ 1:256). The dispossessed shopkeepers and the middle class turned to the Nazis, how-ever, not to the communists or democratic parties, as Brecht would have us believe. Capone imitated captains of industry and statesmen by combining the ruthlessness and philanthropy of a Morgan and Carnegie with the philosophy of von Clausewitz, who had postulated that warfare is a continuation of politics via other means. Resorting to guns and bombs is actually indicative of the gangsters' origin — mostly immigrants from backward societies where feuds are settled violently. In contrast, the modern gangster shuns brute force and avails himself of more subtle economic and social forces to destroy his opponents.[37] Obviously, the Nazis with their blood and soil ideology and their appeal to brute force catered to the same primitive instincts in people.

The alliance of politicians and gangsters in Chicago was common knowledge: "Chicago politicians are in league with gangsters, and the city is overrun with a combination of lawless politics and protected vice."[38] Capone controlled many of Chicago's most influential political figures; he helped them during election time or contributed to their campaign funds, thus enjoying their protection as a reward. He also tried to install his own men in key positions to gain control of patronage, jobs, and budgets. When the leaders of the cauliflower trust in Brecht's play attempt successfully to get a loan from the city, ostensibly to build docks, they only follow a time-honored practice in Chicago. Naturally they divide the money among themselves, and the docks are never constructed. In 1930, Chicago, because of overspending, was totally bankrupt, a condition that could be only partially blamed on the Depression, "the times [that] are bad" referred to at the beginning of Brecht's play (*GW* 4:1724). Pasley asserts: "Entering 1930, the municipality, in a political sense, was a moral bankrupt; a financial bum; flat broke; literally a panhandler on the doorsteps of its bankers."[39] The same conditions prevailed in Germany in 1930; the result in both cases was a situation approaching anarchy, the best breeding ground for dictators. If, particularly during an economic crisis, the people's trust in politicians is destroyed and the whole political process becomes repugnant to them, they tend to call for a strong man who will clean up the Augean stables and restore order.

Ample proof has been offered that Brecht based the plot of *Arturo Ui* on actual events in Chicago during the Capone era; the contention that he did not know America is thus unfounded. The announcer's concluding lines in the prologue strongly allude to the American audience's familiarity with Capone: "But everything you'll see tonight is true. / Nothing's invented, nothing's new / Or made to order just for you. / The gangster play that we present / Is known to the whole continent" (*CP* 6:198–99). However, Brecht did not succeed in resolving the difficulty of separating the two strands of the plot, the "*gangster- und nazihandlung*" (*AJ* 1:251). Moreover, the assertion that Chicago gangsters would not speak and behave like their counterparts in *Arturo Ui* is valid. But then Brecht did not want to present Al Capone and his associates in a naturalistic way; rather, the parodistic treatment was intended to bring into sharper focus the conditions alluded to on stage. The rise of Al Capone, accompanied by violence, had a melodramatic and sensational quality that reminded Brecht of the *Bänkelsang* ("popular journalistic balladry in Germany"),[40] the yellow press, and the plays of his great model Frank Wedekind. Naturally, Brecht also thought of Hitler and the Nazis' love for theatrical actions and the circus atmosphere at their mass meetings.[41] He therefore developed a framework for his gangster story that is "reminiscent of the fairground and the wax-work museum"[42] and employs, in nonrealistic fashion, "cartoons" (*AJ* 1:390) in vivid colors and a naive style as a fitting background for the sensational depiction of the Prohibition era.

The framework of the play — the announcer's prologue,[43] the projection of newspaper headlines, and the introduction of the characters — is based on the easily understood forms and language of popular literature. The short plot summary in the prologue eliminates suspense, but in the following fifteen scenes Brecht uses more sophisticated means of estrangement (*Verfremdung*) such as the "elevated style" (*AJ* 1:249) that the announcer claims for the production (*GW* 4:1722). The grand style of the Elizabethan theater, of classical German plays, and the perverted grand style of the dictator, as shown by Chaplin, are exhibited; thematic allusions and iambic verse are a means to achieve parodistic effects as well as estrangement. In fact, in theme, structure, and language *Arturo Ui* is very much indebted to *Saint Joan* so that Brecht could write the former play in a comparatively short time.[44] *Saint Joan* depicts the fight of the Chicago meat packers among themselves and against the workers during an economic crisis;[45] Joan Dark attempts to help the unemployed — but in the end she dies like the heroine of Schiller's *Maid of Orleans* (1801), a classical drama that Brecht parodied.

Parody is also fully evident in *Arturo Ui*[46] — especially in the two garden scenes from Goethe's *Faust*. In scene twelve of *Arturo Ui* Givola, Ui's Mephistopheles, threatens Dullfeet in veiled terms and predicts his future death, while Ui (Faust) is unable to put Betty (Gretchen) at ease about his religion and his handling of the social question. These idealistic concerns are secondary to the real issue, the attempt to create a cauliflower trust, but they conveniently obfuscate and embellish the real question.[47] Scene thirteen is based on the courting scene (I.2) in Shakespeare's *Richard III*[48] — referred to in the prologue — in which Richard proposes to Lady Anne shortly after he has murdered her husband. In similar fashion Ui has murdered Betty's husband; whereas Richard attempts to win Lady Anne's love, Ui endeavors to gain Betty's business. Both men are successful — although Betty at first refuses Ui's offer of friendship with a ringing "Never! Never! Never!" (*GW* 4:1826). But, ironically, her later actions in support of Ui speak louder than her words that are merely a means of saving face. Brecht employs this method of exposing the difference between appearance and reality in several scenes; figures of apparently steely resolve frequently turn out to lack character. For example, Dogsborough answers Ui's attempt to blackmail him with "Never!" (*GW* 4:1755) — but then hires him nevertheless. When Ui is urged to betray his loyal follower Roma, Ui responds with the ringing phrase: "I know my duty" (*GW* 4:1805) — but in the next scene he has Roma murdered. These ironic twists at the end of scenes create an element of surprise and demonstrate that the promises of political leaders are not to be trusted.

Scene fourteen, in which Roma's ghost predicts Ui's eventual destruction,[49] is patterned — without parodistic intent — after *Richard III* (V.3), that is, the scene preceding the battle in which the ghosts of Richard's victims appear to him to announce their revenge. Among the victims is Buckingham, who may have served as a model for Roma.[50] When Ui takes speech lessons,[51] he uses Mark Antony's speech from *Julius Caesar* (III.2) as his text. Ui learns to use the language of demagogy and the ringing phrases of false pathos; in addition, he is tutored on how to walk, stand, sit, and talk in "the grand style" (*GW* 4:1768). But later on, Ui's speeches to the merchants are not effective, and he has to resort to violence to convince them of the necessity for his protection.[52] And Ragg, a reporter rather than a gangster,[53] parodies verses from dramas by Schiller, notably *Wallen-*

stein.[54] Since Caesar, Richard III, and Wallenstein are heroic figures who came to a sad end, Brecht is strongly suggesting that Ui's rise is "resistible." However, Brecht does not want to equate Ui with the characters of Shakespeare's and Schiller's plays, since his concept of man is basically different from that of classical drama. The protagonist in a classical play is determined by his character; his tragic fate is the result of his hubris and caused by metaphysical forces. Brecht wants the audience to realize that Ui is not such a great character, a mythical leader sent by God to save the people, but simply a gangster who has imposed his regime upon them by brute force with the help of the capitalists. Brecht despised the romantic view of history that was prevalent in bourgeois society; his intention was to destroy the aura of greatness surrounding dictators, statesmen, politicians, who were often no more than political criminals. The people had to lose their admiration and respect for these leaders, recognize their methods of operation, and learn to laugh about them. Yet Ui should not be portrayed as a hysterical clown:[55] "Just as the failure of his undertakings does not make Hitler a fool, so the size of these undertakings does not make him a great man" (*GW* 4:1177), Brecht wrote much later. He did not share the opinion of his friend Lion Feuchtwanger and other refugees that Hitler was a clown, an actor, a phony; rather, a "deep dramatic portrayal" of Hitler as the leader of the petty bourgeoisie did not seem possible to him without acknowledging "that he is a real national figure, a 'popular leader,' a clever, vital, unconventional and original politician" who, to be sure, showed "extreme corruption, inadequacy, brutality, etc." (*AJ* 1:380). Brecht sought to overcome the romantic view of history by an encompassing portrayal rather than by replacing an old myth with a new one.

Brecht intended to shock the (German) audience that was accustomed to listening to blank verse in the plays of Schiller and Goethe— plays extolling the harmony of the classical ideal, the categorical imperative, ethical idealism, and the death and transfiguration of their respective heroes. By putting classical meter in the mouths of ruthless capitalists and murderous gangsters, Brecht hoped, a critical audience would realize the "inadequacy of their lordly behavior" (*AJ* 1:258) in that they used the philosophy of idealism as a means of obscuring the real political issues and hiding their criminal deeds.[56] "The verses make it possible to judge heroism" (*GW* 4:3*), Brecht opined. After the fall of the Third Reich he added an epilogue warning of the danger of continuing fascism. In 1941, when Hitler was at the height of his power, the play ended with Ui planning new conquests. This open ending required the audience to deduce that Ui's rise was, after all, "resistible."

Despite the fact that he was not completely convinced by his assistant Margarete Steffin's argument concerning the unsuitability of his deliberately uneven and rough meter for the projected English translation of *Arturo Ui* that was to precede its eventual American production, Brecht regularized the verse (*AJ* 1:258). Whatever the merits of Steffin's contention that an uneven rhythm would weaken the estrangement effect, Brecht claimed that in *Arturo Ui* double estrangement was at work via his choice of the gangster milieu and the grand style. Yet the gangster milieu is predominant in that it provides the setting for the parable; the connection between the world of the gangster and Hitler is established by analogy.[57]

Brecht finished the play on 12 April 1941. Before he left Finland on 15 May, he wrote that he was taking along to America a new play that "really ought to stand a chance over there."[58] On 21 July Brecht arrived in the United States and settled in Santa Monica, where he encountered many friends. He endeavored to have some of his plays produced — an effort that did not extend to *Arturo Ui* even though he continued revising the play.[59] In the fall of 1941, Erwin Piscator, Brecht's collaborator in Berlin, refugee from Nazi Germany, and director of the Dramatic Workshop in New York, wanted to stage some of Brecht's plays, including *Arturo Ui.*[60] For the latter play Piscator had engaged a translator, H. R. Hays, and had agreed with Brecht that exiled actor Oskar Homolka would be an excellent prospect for the lead role. To Piscator's great frustration Brecht then apparently refused to comment on the translation, and the project fell through. Critics have explained Brecht's strange indifference to having *Arturo Ui* — written explicitly for the American stage — staged in New York by asserting that "the gangsters of *Arturo Ui* were far too unlike the originals to give that ambitious play a chance."[61] Yet this was not the case at all; rather, Brecht was motivated by political considerations of a complex nature. Despite maintaining — in his unread statement intended for the House Committee on Un-American Activities — that he had refrained from engaging in any political activities, including those "in a literary form,"[62] Brecht had attempted to have other anti-fascist plays such as *The Private Life of the Master Race* staged. But in this country Brecht may have realized that the American public's attitude towards Al Capone, who was still admired and respected by many Chicagoans as late as 1960, was markedly different from his attitude towards Hitler. Thus, once Al Capone had been convicted for tax evasion and had served his sentence from 1932 to 1939, most Americans no longer considered him a threat to the democratic system. In fact, they might be inclined to think that Germans should have taken care of Hitler in a similar fashion. Furthermore, Brecht advocated a united front against fascism; hence he supported the United States that were helping England and, indirectly, the Soviet Union in their war against Nazi Germany — without, however, losing sight of his ultimate goal, a socialist society. Since *Arturo Ui* did not only attack fascism but also capitalism, the effect of the play might have been politically inopportune and detrimental to a united, anti-Nazi front. Finally, after the Japanese attack on Pearl Harbor on 7 December 1941 and the German declaration of war against the United States, the production of the play seemed no longer a necessity. Perhaps artistic reasons contributed to Brecht's seeming disinterest in *Arturo Ui*: the reception of Brecht's *Galileo* is indicative of the American audiences' preference for well-constructed plays with the traditional five-act structure; their unfamiliarity with Brechtian dramatic innovations and aversions to political topics most likely would have resulted in a cool reception.

As a matter of fact, the play was not staged until 1958. The Stuttgart production by Brecht student Peter Palitzsch was followed by that of the Berliner Ensemble on 23 March 1959 — three years after Brecht's death and eighteen years after the play had been written in Finland. Since then the play has become one of the classic pieces in the repertory of the Berliner Ensemble; owing to its lacking raison d'être in a socialist state, *Arturo Ui* has been performed as a historical spectacle and has become static. However, in 1960 the Berliner Ensemble production won first prize at the Paris "Théâtre des Nations" festival;[63] a French adaptation by Jean Vilar and Georges Wilson at the "Théâtre National Populaire" in Paris was even more successful.

During the last few years the political and economic situation in the United States has caused theaters to take a renewed interest in the play. With Watergate and a new depression at hand, with inflation and rising unemployment, with stress on law and order by rightist forces, with an ever-increasing defense budget and the ability of government and the supertrusts to manipulate and oppress the individual citizen and the population in general, Brecht's play with all its strong and weak points, its correct assumptions and its mistakes, takes on a new meaning. It is indeed relevant for our times, and we should ponder its message that a revolution from the right is a greater possibility than one from the left — and that this revolt must be resisted in its beginnings, before it is too late.

Notes

1. Bertolt Brecht, *Gesammelte Werke in 20 Bänden* (Frankfurt am Main: Suhrkamp, 1967), 4:1719–1839. Hereafter cited as *GW. Collected Plays*, ed. Ralph Manheim and John Willett (New York: Vintage Books, 1971–), 6:195–303. Hereafter cited as *CP*. Unless otherwise indicated, English translations are my own; I wish to thank James K. Lyon, University of California, San Diego, for his useful suggestions. Helfried W. Seliger, *Das Amerikabild Bertolt Brechts* (Bonn: Bouvier, 1974), reaches similar conclusions; however, his book was published after the completion of the original version of this article.

2. See Hans Magnus Enzensberger, "Chicago Ballade. Modell einer terroristischen Gesellschaft," *Politik und Verbrechen* (Frankfurt am Main: Suhrkamp, 1964), 135–36.

3. Bertolt Brecht, *Arbeitsjournal*, 2 vols., ed. Werner Hecht (Frankfurt am Main: Suhrkamp, 1973), 1:257. Hereafter cited as *AJ*.

4. See Johannes Goldhahn, *Das Parabelstück Bertolt Brechts als Beitrag zum Kampf gegen den deutschen Faschismus dargestellt an den Stücken "Die Rundköpfe und die Spitzköpfe"' und "Der aufhaltsame Aufstieg des Arturo Ui"* (Rudolstadt: Greifenverlag, 1961), 98.

5. See *AJ* 1:274, 390; 2:592, 652.

6. Older and recent studies include: Goldhahn, *Parabelstück;* Edouard Pfrimmer, "Brecht et la Parodie: *Arturo Ui*," *Etudes Germaniques* 26, no. 1 (1971):73–88; Burkhardt

Lindner, *Bertolt Brecht: "Der aufhaltsame Aufstieg des Arturo Ui"* (Munich: Fink, 1982); *Brechts "Aufhaltsamer Aufstieg des Arturo Ui,"* ed. Raimund Gerz (Frankfurt am Main: Suhrkamp, 1983).

7. See especially Lindner, *Brecht*, 49–73.

8. Martin Esslin, *Brecht. The Man and His Work* (Garden City, N. Y.: Doubleday, 1961), 306. Esslin does not realize that Brecht uses the setting of Chicago in much the same way as in his early plays about which Esslin makes some excellent comments (see 109).

9. Frederic Ewen, *Bertolt Brecht: His Life, His Art and His Times* (New York: Citadel Press, 1967), 375.

10. Ewen, *Brecht*, 374.

11. See Patty Lee Parmalee, *Brecht's America* (Oxford: Ohio State University Press, 1981). [Ed. note: see also Reinhold Grimm, "Bertolt Brecht's Chicago — A German Myth?," in this volume.]

12. Bertolt Brecht, *Poems 1913–1956*, ed. John Willett and Ralph Manheim with the co-operation of Erich Fried (New York: Methuen, 1976), 167–74.

13. [Ed. note: see Petermichael von Bawey, "Dramatic Structure of Revolutionary Language," in this volume.]

14. Klaus Völker, *Brecht Chronicle*, trans. Fred Wieck (New York: Seabury Press, 1975), 76.

15. Hans Bunge, *Fragen Sie mehr über Brecht. Hanns Eisler im Gespräch* (Munich: Rogner & Bernhard, 1970), 233.

16. See also Brecht's fragmentary narrative, "Die Geschichte des Giacomo Ui" (*GW* 11:252–62, The History of Giacomo Ui), that was begun in 1934.

17. See Robert Brustein, *Seasons of Discontent* (New York: Simon & Schuster, 1965), 144.

18. Völker, *Brecht Chronicle*, 101.

19. Hans Kaufmann, *Bertolt Brecht: Geschichtsdrama und Parabelstück* (Berlin: Rütten & Loening, 1962), 131, refers to *Arturo Ui* as a "satirical-comical" play.

20. See Kaufmann, *Brecht*, 260.

21. Pfrimmer, "Parodie," 78.

22. Fred D. Pasley, *Al Capone. The Biography of a Self-Made Man* (n.p.: Ives Wasburn, 1930). Pasley relates Capone's life through 1930; the continuation is provided by Kenneth Allsop, *The Bootleggers and Their Era* (Garden City, N. Y.: Doubleday, 1961).

23. Frederick Lewis Allen, *Only Yesterday. An Informal History of the Nineteen-Twenties*. 1931 (New York: Harper & Row, 1964).

24. See Brecht's poems about Dimitrov (*GW* 8:420; 9:458).

25. In Brecht's 1929 film story "[Happy End]" that takes place in Chicago, O'Banion appears as William Cracker. See Bertolt Brecht, *Texte für Filme* (Frankfurt am Main: Suhrkamp, 1969), 320–28.

26. Pasley, *Al Capone*, 70, uses the terms "supertrust" and "syndicate" in reference to the gangsters.

27. Pasley, *Al Capone*, 228.

28. See Pasley, *Al Capone*, 56.

29. See Pasley, *Al Capone*, 114. Brecht translates "Thompson gun" as "Thompson-kanone," a slang expression for Thompson "Maschinenpistole." He further uses unwitting irony when he contrasts "typewriters" with "Thompson guns" (*GW* 4:1753) since the gangsters referred to the latter by means of the former.

30. Ewen, *Bertolt Brecht*, 372, incorrectly considers "Steff" to be an abbreviation for Margarete Steffin. See also *AJ* 1:222 for a list of titles Brecht might have consulted.

31. Allsop, *Bootleggers*, 207. The reference is to William Hale Thompson, mayor of Chicago (1915–1923; 1927–1931). See also Pasley, *Al Capone*, 247–48.

32. Allsop, *Bootleggers*, 250.

33. See *AJ* 2:836. Despite the fact that Brecht points out that gangsters were used by labor unions and industrialists alike, Goldhahn, *Parabelstück*, 77–78, mentions only that gangsters were employed by trusts to suppress the workers—obviously an ideologically motivated misreading.

34. See, e.g., Brecht's poem "Ballade vom 30. Juni" (*GW* 9:520–24).

35. Pasley, *Al Capone*, 46.

36. Pasley, *Al Capone*, 70.

37. Allsop, *The Bootleggers*, 233–34.

38. Report of the Better Government Association to the United States Senate. See Pasley, *Al Capone*, 98.

39. Pasley, *Al Capone*, 151.

40. Sammy K. McLean, *The "Bänkelsang" and the Work of Bertolt Brecht* (The Hague: Mouton, 1972), 15.

41. See the series of pictures, "Hitler Dances" (*AJ* 1:104–15). The theatrical aspects of both the gangsters and the Nazis lent themselves to being treated in the manner of Brecht's epic theater. See *AJ* 1:50.

42. Enzensberger, "Chicago Ballade," 101.

43. See McLean, *The "Bänkelsang,"* 217, 149: The words of the prologue "relate to the Bänkelsang in its character as *Neue Zeitung*"; "The announcer . . . is reminiscent of both a fairground barker and the Bänkelsänger as Zeitungssänger."

44. Günter Hartung, "Brecht und Schiller," *Sinn und Form* 18 (1966):743–66, points to Shakespeare's *Richard III* as the common model for both *Saint Joan* and *Arturo Ui*.

45. [Ed. note: see Patty Lee Parmalee, "*St. Joan of the Stockyards*," in this volume.]

46. See Pfrimmer, "Parodie." Volker Klotz, *Bertolt Brecht. Versuch über das Werk* (Bad Homburg v.d.H.: Gehlen, 1967), 108–10, provides a definition of Brechtian parody that can also be applied to *Arturo Ui*.

47. See Pfrimmer, "Parodie," 82–83; Goldhahn, *Parabelstück*, 113.

48. See Pfrimmer, "Parodie," 83–84; Rodney T. K. Symington, *Brecht und Shakespeare* (Bonn: Bouvier, 1970), 138–40; Reinhold Grimm, *Brecht und die Weltliteratur* (Nuremberg: Hans Carl, 1961), 27; Goldhahn, *Parabelstück*, 113–14; Helge Hultberg, "Bertolt Brecht und Shakespeare," *Orbis Litterarum* 14.1 (1959):92–93. I do not agree with Hultberg's assertion that Brecht, in addition to parodying Shakespeare, attacks him.

49. See also Brecht, "Ballade vom 30. Juni," n. 34, above.

50. Symington, *Brecht und Shakespeare*, 140.

51. See Gudrun Schulz, *Die Schillerbearbeitungen Bertolt Brechts* (Tübingen: Niemeyer, 1972), 154, who remarks on Hitler's studying the "grand style" with a Munich actor for the conduct of both criminal and political affairs—a method reminiscent of Al Capone.

52. See Pfrimmer, "Parodie," 80–81.

53. Schulz, *Schillerbearbeitungen*, 154, misidentifies Ragg.

54. See Schulz, *Schillerbearbeitungen*, 154–58; Goldhahn, *Parabelstück*, 114.

55. Ekkehard Schall's portrayal of Ui at the Berliner Ensemble production tended in this direction. See also Herbert Ihering, "Bemerkungen zu Theater und Film," *Sinn und Form* 11, no. 2 (1959):312–19.

56. Brecht considered the blank verse ill-suited for German, anachronistic, and feudal.

If modernized, it would take on the appearance of a parvenu — hence both Ui and the language he uses are classified as parvenus. See AJ 1:258.

57. See Kaufmann, Brecht, 132, for a definition of political comedy in general.

58. Letter to Mordecai Gorelik, quoted in James K. Lyon, Bertolt Brecht in America (Princeton, N. J.: Princeton University Press, 1980), 27.

59. See Lyon, Brecht, 34.

60. See Herbert Knust, "Piscator and Brecht: Affinity and Alienation," Essays on Brecht: Theater and Politics, ed. Siegfried Mews and Herbert Knust (Chapel Hill: University of North Carolina Press, 1974), 56–57; Lyon, Brecht, 99–100.

61. Esslin, Brecht, 69.

62. See Esslin, Brecht, 80.

63. See Agnes Hüfner, Brecht in Frankreich 1930–1963. Verbreitung, Aufnahme, Wirkung (Stuttgart: Metzler, 1968).

Herr Puntila and His Servant Matti
Klaus Völker*

> The attempts by someone who has fallen into a swamp to reach solid
> ground are not, of course, experiments. To want something new is out of
> date, what is new is to want something old.[1]

"These clear nights are very beautiful. Just before 3 o'clock I got up, because of the flies, and went outside. The cocks were crowing but it had never been dark. And I do so love to urinate in the open" (AJ, 1:130). The days when he swam in lakes and rivers as he wandered with his Augsburg friends along the Lech or drove into the Allgäu, never again seemed so close as they did in the summer of 1940 on the Marlebaek property in Kausala. The lakes and streams full of fish, the birch woods, the smell of berries and the clanging of milk cans filled him with a happiness, of which he could not feel ashamed but which, nonetheless, seemed wrong when he thought of the war. While the Battle of Britain was raging, and the Nazis were preparing their campaign against the Soviet Union, he was intoxicated by the summer nights in Finland and wrote a comedy about a rich farmer who is only human when he is drunk, "because then he forgets his own interests" (AJ, 1:159). The title character and the framework of the plot were taken from a farce by his hostess Hella Wuolijoki. Brecht's task, as he saw it, was to "tear down" the psychologizing talk of this comedy of manners in order to "make room for tales of Finnish national life or for opinions, to give dramatic expression to the contrast between 'master' and 'servant,' and give back to the subject its poetry and comedy" (AJ, 1:164).

*From Brecht: A Biography by Klaus Völker, trans. John Nowell (New York: Seabury Press, 1978), 273–81. Reprinted by permission of the publisher. English Translation © 1978 by the Continuum Publishing Company.

In contrast to *Refugees in Conversation,* which was written immediately after *Herr Puntila and his Servant Matti (Herr Puntila und sein Knecht Matti)*[2] and in which the author divided his personal views and experiences between the bourgeois scholar and the worker, he here puts everything personal into the character of the rich farmer. In the "Nocturno" scene, which was entirely new, Brecht makes Puntila rhapsodize: "I could never live in a town. Why? Because I want to walk straight out and urinate in the open, under the stars. Otherwise what do I get out of it? They tell me it's primitive to do it outside, but I call it primitive to do it in a piece of china" (*GW*, 4:1695). The practice of literature turned out to be far removed "from the centres where all the decisive events are taking place." Brecht had to admit that "*Puntila* means almost nothing to me, the war everything; I can write almost anything about *Puntila* but nothing about the war" (*AJ*, 1:171). Just how important Brecht felt this comedy to be and how greatly affected he was while writing it by the discrepancy between art and reality — a discrepancy he constantly noted down — can be seen from the fact that when he was in Zurich, on his return from America [in 1947], he immediately produced it and also chose it for the opening performance of the Berliner Ensemble. The outward incentive to write *Puntila* was a competition for a "Volksstück," or folk play, which Hella Wuolijoki wanted to enter with Brecht. When the latter told her of his Setzuan play,[3] which he had just finished, and of the girl in it who led a double life as a good and as a wicked person, she remembered her comedy about the rich farmer who makes promises in his cups that he cannot keep when he is sober. This story of a drunkard with two sides to his nature was based on a true incident, the mad driving-escapade of her uncle Roope, which in the mid-nineteen-twenties had caused something of a sensation in Kausala. She had also used the subject for a film script, with the title *The Sawdust Princess.* What disturbed Brecht was not the play's construction, in the form of a farce, but simply the conventional dramatic technique with which the subject was presented. When he first published *Puntila* in 1950, in the tenth volume of the *Versuche,* Brecht commented: "It is a folk play and was written in Finland in 1940; it is based on stories and the outline of a play by Hella Wuolijoki." Both these originals, however, were complete dramatic works and had been preceded only by a short sketch in prose.[4] There are no stories among Hella Wuolijoki's works. What Brecht was referring to were stories which his hostess used to tell him and which impressed him far more than her literary work; he often got Margarete Steffin to take them down. When she told stories she was "an entrancing epic poet" (*AJ*, 1:164); but in her plays he missed any observation based on reality, he could find no trace in them of her rich experience of life.

Hella Murrik, who was Estonian by birth, had gone to Helsinki in 1904 to study philology, and while there had married the lawyer and social democrat politician Sulo Wuolijoki. Before starting to write plays she had been manageress of various timber firms as well as a diplomat and journalist. She spoke six languages. She had remarkable stories to tell of Finland's "heroic" days during the civil war of 1918. Her sympathies were with the "reds," her manner when telling stories was that of a woman of the people: "everything was biblically simple and biblically complex" (*AJ*, 1:164), was how Brecht put it. But in her approach to art she belonged to a different world, to the class of society she wanted to fight. By supplementing Hella Wuolijoki's play with her stories Brecht hoped to make her artistically a socialist too. Although he incorporated many elements of the plot, almost all the characters and some actual phrases, the new play, which took him barely three weeks to write, was radically different from the original.

The central character of Hella Wuolijoki's *Sawdust Princess* is Eva, the daughter of a farmer named Puntila, who has in mind for his daughter's husband a man from the upper classes. To the father a socially acceptable son-in-law is worth a dowry of a saw-mill. At the Kurgela estate, which is financially dependent on him, Puntila drinks heavily with the local bigwigs and sets out to serenade his hostess Aunt Hanna. To prevent things getting out of hand the women hide the bottles. In protest at the forcible removal of the alcohol the humiliated farmer decides to go and get some illicit schnaps. The newly engaged chauffeur, Kalle, uses the time when he is away to court Eva. When Puntila, on his return, announces that all men are his brothers, tells of his engagement to five women and distributes currency notes, Kalle seizes the opportunity to try to come to an agreement with his employer on the subject of Eva. As a reward for helping his master to dispossess himself of his fiancées, who are now claiming their rights, Puntila agrees. To show his loved one that it is not the dowry he is after, Kalle tells her of the romantic bliss of a poor life and tries to abduct her. When his master, who is now sober again, wants to dismiss him, Kalle discloses his real identity as Dr. Vuorinen, so that nothing any longer stands in the way of a respectable marriage. Puntila, for his part, submits to the strict regimen of Aunt Hanna.

As this brief summary shows *The Sawdust Princess* is a comedy like a thousand others, devoid of genuine incongruities; all the conflicts are amicably resolved. One cannot help being struck by its similarity to Carl Zuckmayer's comedy *Der fröhliche Weinberg*, in which the wealthy owner of the vineyard, Gunderloch, wants to marry his daughter Klärchen to the university Student Knuzius, but in the end is glad for her to get the honest sailor Jochen. And there is even a fine strapping woman for Gunderloch. As Hans Peter Neureuter has pointed out, the play is also a variation, in comedy form, of the battle of the sexes in Strindberg's *Miss Julie*.[5] Brecht left intact the comedy scheme of his model, changing only the perspective of the story. In his play the class differences remain intact throughout the comedy. Kalle really is a chauffeur, a man very much to the taste of both Eva and Puntila — only he is not socially acceptable. Master and servant like each other, but they can have no personal relationship: "Because in this life the corn does not thresh the flail, and because oil does not mix with water."[6] Puntila is no longer a man "torn in two," who is overcome by remorse and ill-humour when he is sober but a man with twin natures that throw into relief the division into human being and representative of his class imposed on him by social conditions. According to Brecht's first sketch, entitled "The twin natures of Herr Puntila or Rain always falls down": "Herr von Puntila has twin natures. When he is drunk he is a human being, but when he is sober he is a rich farmer. When he is sober, he beats his chauffeur, but when he is drunk he engages a chauffeur who refuses to put up with that sort of treatment. When he is drunk he marries any woman who gets up early and deserves a good life, but when he is sober he does not want to part with his money, and asks indignantly if he is supposed to give an annuity to every dairy maid he sleeps with. When he is drunk he promises his daughter to the chauffeur, but when he is sober he gives her to the attaché to marry. Drunk once more he disowns her for obeying him. Drunk he blames his housekeeper for ill-treating the servants, sober he marries her. He has a servant who knows all this and proves to him that all the things he wants when he is drunk are impracticable in real life."[7] When he wrote the play Brecht kept to this sketch. The housekeeper, whom Puntila finally marries and who was based on Aunt Hanna, was the only character he eventually dropped. He confined himself to a determined manageress and an Aunt Klinkmann who never appears.

The servant Kalle acts as the mouthpiece of plebeian intelligence, making sure that class antagonisms are not simply ignored. He adds the dimension of social categories to the rich farmer's thinking. As a human being Puntila is not affected by this, on the contrary his intoxication is supposed to have something about it of "divine, Dionysian drunkenness." Brecht, however, does not regard Kalle but the women of Kurgela as the true key figures representing an opposing social viewpoint. It is they who tell the stories which Hella Wuolijoki did not think capable of literary treatment. In her play there had been room only for "upper class" anecdotes and witticisms, such as the attaché, provost, judge and advocate had at their command. But in her case they were introduced for their own sake, not for that of the "Sprachgestus" or underlying attitude.

Out of the farce about a marriageable daughter whose father when drunk plays some mad pranks which he later regrets, come scenes about "Tavast drunkenness." Brecht's first version contains more stories than the later ones. Kalle, who is later given the name Matti, is also rather more talkative; he strives still harder for equality with Eva and Herr Puntila, being the latter's social conscience rather than his social critic and opponent. A "Gesindemarkt," or fair where servants could be hired, held in the vicinity of Marlebaek, gave him the idea for the scene of this name which he added to the manuscript.

To work from Brecht used a new version of Hella Wuolijoki's Puntila comedy, which she had made after talking the play over with him and had dictated in German to Margarete Steffin. The Finnish authoress was considerably upset by the greater artificiality of the new play, by its narrative elements and by the fact that the points she made in it had been discarded. But Brecht succeeded in convincing her to some extent that his alterations made sense and in persuading her to start translating it into Finnish. By and large Hella Wuolijoki accepted Brecht's version and, although she did not keep exactly to the text, she retained the scenic structure almost unaltered. She added Herr Kurgela (in other words Klinkmann) because she was clearly unenthusiastic over Brecht's idea of making Puntila think from time to time of marrying Kurgela's widow in order to save his wood. In her version she also dispensed with the "Nocturno" scene and the great story of Emma the smuggler.

The Finnish version, published by Hella Wuolijoki in 1946, was called *Squire Iso-Heikkilä and his Servant Kalle*, the name Puntila being omitted for personal reasons, because the manor belonging to Uncle Roope's stepfather was called Puntila and the landowner portrayed under this name was still alive. Apart from cuts and slight alterations the play remained essentially unchanged until 1948. In Zurich Brecht wrote the poem "The Plum Song" ("Das Pflaumenlied") for Therese Giehse, who played the part of Emma the smuggler. Because Puntila engaged people's sympathies too strongly, and in order to give added force to the social criticism voiced in the play, Brecht added the character of Surkkala, a red, for the production by the Berliner Ensemble, in order to give Matti, who is merely his master's servant, the support of a genuinely proletarian character. The addition was made chiefly because it was thought that the political background, with the rich farmer, had become historic in the context of the new social realities of East Germany. The intention was to show something of the history of the class struggle. A further addition was the Puntila song, performed, while the scenery was being changed, by the actress who played the cook; it was meant as a comment "from the kitchen" on what went on on the Puntila estate.

Along with *The Threepenny Opera, Herr Puntila and his Servant Matti* must today be Brecht's most frequently performed play. It is considered to be his funniest and seems to be "indestructible." While its social criticism is regarded as out of date, it is praised for its universal human qualities as exemplified by sex and drink. At last a play that is not epic, that parades no theory, but is simply a superb comedy of human types. The farce, which the play was originally designed to refute, seems to be visible once more through the back door. Is Puntila really dated? In his book *Letzten Endes* Fritz Kortner has answered this question with an emphatic "no":

> To prove how valid it is, transfer the setting to Texas, for example,
> dress Puntila as a Texan and make Matti black. The play would then be

condemned as a flagrant piece of literary engagement by the very people who now complain that it has no topical interest. . . . Be that as it may, in some recent productions the Puntilas of the day have been transferred to *Der fröhliche Weinberg*, the social monsters acclaimed as jovial drunkards and the guilty sybarites not been pilloried for what they are: smarmy spongers, robber barons at the expense of the public good, drinking companions for whose drinking the public has to pay, descendants of those Junkers who said fatherland when they meant my estates, who allied themselves to big business and, in order to protect this unholy alliance, introduced compulsory military service to preserve and extend their estates.[8]

Kortner's arguments in favour of a Brecht text not being a libretto and against rendering it harmless by turning it into a farce are valid; he is also right to resist the all too transparent political complaints that Brecht is out of date. But to make the play topical in the way he suggests is to ignore completely the human traits undeniably inherent in the character of Puntila. Politically a play against Puntila, the Junker, no longer has much to say to us. The equation of landowner with capitalist is convincing only if we set the play in the Finland of 1940. As we see it today the landowner type portrayed by Brecht appears politically dangerous, but not representative, and on its way out. Of much greater interest are the autobiographical, Baal-like elements of the character, all the things, in fact, about the man Puntila that are "worth preserving." The tendency of the audience to identify itself with the more complete, more vital, character of Puntila, and to dismiss Matti as insipid, should be exploited. How far is it possible to go with Puntila, and how far is it not (any longer) possible to go with Matti?

There is nothing wrong with the basic construction of the comedy. It demonstrates "what servitude is in relation to authority" (Hegel). Matti's servitude is his apprenticeship. With the sure instinct of a man who longs for authority, he senses that the unpredictability of his master and his attacks of humanity can harm him. Matti fears those moments when his master addresses him as a human being and in this way might quite irrationally bind him to him. By forgetting that he needs his servant, Herr Puntila prevents the latter from developing his "servile awareness." But this, as Hegel attempts to show in his *Phenomenology of Mind*, is the prerequisite for true independence.[9] In Diderot's novel *Jacques le Fataliste* the servant, being a fatalist, remains faithful to his master; he is content merely to know of the freedom to get along without him. Brecht's Matti is an optimist. He wants not only authority but power as well. He wants to be his own master. One suspects that he is looking for a new place only with a master for whom he is more than a match. He is prepared to wait until the Surkkalas have brought about a revolution or, to bring it more into line with the social realities of our own day, to profit by the economic reasoning that will rationalize Puntila's estate away.

Puntila owns an estate, a saw mill, a mill and ninety cows. He is a big landowner, an influential man in Kausala and is anxious to acquire more influence with the government in Helsinki. Hence his idea of marrying Eva to the attaché. The planned union is even worth a wood to him. And this wood could be saved if he were to marry the attaché's aunt, who has had her eye on him for a long time. But the old woman is disagreeable, a termagent and hideously ugly. The human being in Puntila rebels against all these manipulations and marriages of expediency. He much prefers to get engaged without ulterior motives and as often as he feels like it. When drunk his human qualities come out and he speaks almost like a communist. When sober he is repulsive, a man who has "gone wrong." To enjoy things is easy when one has money, that is obvious! It is all very well for Herr Puntila to praise the cows and become intoxicated with the sound of milk cans, the cowman sees it differently; the lumberman will only be able to curse the trees that do not belong to him, whereas Herr Puntila's heart is warmed by the sight of them. Yet this Puntila is no drunken drone, no social monster, he is a great national figure, a "Tavast Bachus." There is something biblical, something godlike about him. He is certainly not a "money-grubber"; he is not a Sternheim character nor a George Grosz type. Puntila, and one must not try to hide the fact, is a reactionary numskull, a member of the Finnish *Heimwehr*. As a politician he can still afford to indulge in a certain drunken anarchy; nevertheless he is more sober than drunk. We must not be blind to the dangerous side of Puntila, but what makes him sympathetic and important to us is his ability to give free play to his imagination, his charm, his gift for enjoyment.

Puntila is an irrational person, like Herr Quitt in Peter Handke's play *Die Unvernünftigen sterben aus (Irrational People are Dying Out)*. He is going to die out too because he does nothing to safeguard his property, to save his estate in the new age. If he knew anything about earning power and profits, the most sensible thing he could do would be to bind Matti to himself and the estate by tying him to Eva. Matti is the only one who is in a position to manage the estate as an economically profitable concern, the only one who has any experience of machinery. If he were to give Matti a share in his possessions, his problems of economic survival would be over. But any cooperation between the vital giant and the ascetic functionary and technocrat is out of the question. Puntila gradually realizes that Matti is not the man he took him to be at first. Red Surkkala would be much better suited to him, a man "who will do anything for his convictions" (*GW*, 4:1703).

Matti is a rebel but he is no revolutionary. He is a Schweyk character, the prototype of the little man who makes his way in the world with a certain cunning, and always knows in good time when he must accommodate himself to changed conditions. The qualities in Matti that grate on one are, above all, his inability to enjoy himself and his rather stuffy morality. His attitude to Eva is petit-bourgeois pure and simple and is seen at its most unpleasant in his idea of what a good working-class wife should be.

In his *Working-Diary (Arbeitsjournal)* Brecht wrote of Puntila: "It is a fat little calf of a play. More of the countryside in it than in any other of my plays, except perhaps *Baal*" (*AJ*, 1:172). Puntila is even more reminiscent of *In the Jungle of the Cities* than of *Baal*, the comedy being like a cheerful paraphrase of the early play. The relationship between Puntila and Matti reminds one of the fight between Shlink and Garga. When Matti leaves Puntila he is giving up the fight, because he realizes that his own hour has come — he assumes power, though not at Puntila's side. The new age simply passes Puntila by. Matti will clear things up and put the estate in order, where things are going increasingly to rack and ruin.

When he was working out the scenes involving the women of Kurgela, who are the real heroes of the play and the bearers of the people's hopes, Brecht noted: "For the lower classes we have only mawkishly sentimental models and ones prior to 1848. Sympathy leads to everything being seen in a good light, to the popular (or folklorist) affability of romanticism."[10] So Brecht sketched out a coarsely sensual, wonderfully comic, group of four women to whom Puntila, drunk, immediately becomes engaged. These engagements can also be seen as anticipating subsequent consent (*Einverständnis*), which is destined to be lasting and in which all who spring from the Finnish countryside, and are tied to it, unite. Puntila thus belongs to these women, whereas Matti emerges as the enemy of this picture of happiness. Matti simply represents the state, he can never know the anarchy of happiness.

Notes

1. Bertolt Brecht, *Arbeitsjournal*, 2 vols., ed. Werner Hecht (Frankfurt am Main: Suhrkamp, 1973), 1:188 (16 October 1940). [Hereafter cited as *AJ*.]

2. [Ed. note: Bertolt Brecht, *Gesammelte Werke in 20 Bänden* (Frankfurt am Main: Suhrkamp, 1967), 4:1609–1717. Hereafter cited as *GW*. The play has been translated as: *Puntila and Matti, His Hired Man, Collected Plays*, ed. Ralph Manheim and John Willett (New York: Vintage Books, 1971–), 6:105–194. Hereafter cited as *CP*. Hans Peter Neureuter, *Brechts "Herr Puntila und sein Knecht Matti"* (Frankfurt am Main: Suhrkamp, 1987), informs about the origin of the play.]

3. [Ed. note: *The Good Person of Szechwan, CP*, 6:1–104.]

4. [Ed. note: see Neureuter, *Brechts "Herr Puntila,"* 20–41, for these versions.]

5. Hans Peter Neureuter, "Herr Puntila und sein Knecht Matti. Bericht zur Entstehungsgeschichte," *Mitteilungen aus der Deutschen Bibliothek Helsinki* 9 (1975):7–42.

6. [Ed. note: Neureuter, *Brechts "Herr Puntila,"* 51.]

7. [Ed. note: Neureuter, *Brechts "Herr Puntila,"* 51–52.]

8. Fritz Kortner, *Letzten Endes* (Munich, 1971), 90–91.

9. Georg Friedrich Wilhelm Hegel, *Phänomenologie des Geistes* (Frankfurt 1970), 150 ff.

10. Bertolt Brecht Archiv 566/09.

Brecht's *Caucasian Chalk Circle* and Marxist Figuralism: Open Dramaturgy as Open History

Darko Suvin*

The opus of the German poet and playwright Bertolt Brecht (1898–1955) is a particularly clear case of concern for the historical fate of Man informing and shaping a highly significant aesthetic whole of our times. It has been sufficiently noted by criticism of Brecht[1] how deep-seated that concern was. I have myself argued elsewhere that all of his major plays evince a strong tension between the implied "look backward" from the historical vantage point of an anticipated friendly, classless humanity and his intimate understanding of the bloody history of the 20th Century with its class and national warfare; I have argued that Brecht's basic stance is a utopian blend of intellectual and plebeian alienation from the inhuman contradictions of our times.[2] From such a point of view he effects his whole system of "estrangements" (*Verfremdungen*). From its heights he judges the world that forces a truly good person to develop a tough competitive Alter Ego that will protect the tender and friendly Ego (*The Good Woman of Setzuan*), the world that uses the humor and shrewdness of a mother only for the petty pursuits of a "hyena of the battlefields" trying — and failing — to nourish her own family by cooperating with the warmongers (*Mother Courage and Her Children*),[3] the world that forces a passion for reason into officially approved channels of an exploitative science (*The Life of Galileo*).[4] That is why all major plays by Brecht contain an explicit or implicit judgment scene: the basic stance of the author is thus thematized and brought clearly into the open.

However, even among Brecht's major plays, *The Caucasian Chalk Circle* (further *CCC*) has, I contend, a privileged position. It shares the concern for history as manmade destiny, the tension and the utopian "look backward" described above, with his other plays. But it was written in 1944, at the brightest and most open moment of history in the last 50 years — the moment of victory over Nazism. Only in *CCC* — and in *The Mother*,[5] his play of the early 1930's, written during the decisive battle of the German Left against Hitler's rise to power — is an approximation to Brecht's utopian standpoint concretized on the stage at any length, and brought into explicit and victorious collision with inhuman history.

CCC is thus a glaring exception among Brecht's plays that realistically could not but be plays of stark defeat. However, it also poses complex exegetic problems. These do not seem to have been dealt with fully by Brechtian criticism, and yet they are basic to an understanding of how his open dramaturgy relates and is complementary to his vision of an open

*Reprinted by permission from *Clio: An Interdisciplinary Journal of Literature, History, and the Philosophy of History* 3 (1974):257–76.

history. I propose therefore to examine first the basic motifs which constitute the play into a meaningful unity, and then Brecht's philosophy of history which makes sense of such a composition — and is therefore not a body extrinsic to literary analysis but central to it. This should enable a final discussion of the relationship between Brecht's dramaturgy and historiosophy to be based on the evidence of the play itself; it should also enable reaching toward some general conclusions about the import of the Brechtian method that blends historiosophy and aesthetics into a significant creative method.

At first glance, *CCC* has an unusually complicated fable, consisting of three stories distributed in two levels, plus a number of epico-lyrical interventions by the Singer and his accompanying Musicians as well as several "songs" by some other characters. We can distinguish the opening "kolkhoz story," the "Grusha story" and the "Azdak story," the latter two coming together in the "chalk circle judgment." The kolkhoz story is supposed to happen at the end of World War II, it is chronologically nearer to the audience, and it acts as a frame to the "chalk circle" nucleus which is supposed to happen in the depth of [the] Middle Ages.

The center toward which the play converges is indicated by its title: it is the legendary decision about the future of a Noble Child, placed between a false and a true mother. However, in a subversion of dominant social ideologies — such as the one affirmed in the Biblical story of Solomon's sword judgment in an analogous dispute — the theme of motherhood in the "Grusha story" is used to demystify the alleged primacy of the "call of the blood," of the biological motherhood represented by the rapacious upper-class bitch Natella, in favour of the "social motherhood" of the dumb servant Grusha, who at a time of political upheaval saved the Noble Child left at the mercy of killers by its biological mother. Yet if this were the whole import of the play, it is scarcely explainable why it would be necessary to supplement this plebeian fairy tale with the whole history of the judge who hands down the wise chalk-circle judgment. Still less is it clear why this whole nucleus must be performed as a play-within-the-play presented for and by the kolkhoz litigants over the use of a valley. And in fact, the bourgeois theatre has often treated the Grusha story as a sentimental fable, supplemented in a pseudo-Shakespearean way by the comic relief of a hammy Azdak; logically, the kolkhoz story was then seen as a piece of "socialist-realist" propaganda on the virtues of Soviet society and performed with great embarrassment or completely dropped. I want to argue here that such a sundering procedure is false, since it violates the basic presumption of unity and economy in a significant work of art.

In order to show the unity of the play, it is necessary to analyze more closely the themes of the various "stories" and see whether they have a common set of references. To go back to the Grusha story, we saw that even a first attempt at formulating its theme was impossible without entering into the universe of social relationships in that story. That

universe is, right from the beginning, clearly identified as a world of
topsy-turvy human relations passing for normal and indeed hallowed,
where basic human values are polar opposites to the official ones:

> In olden times, in a bloody time
> There ruled in a Caucasian city —
> Men called it the City of the Damned —
> A Governor.
> His name was Georgi Abashwili.
> He was rich as Croesus
> He had a beautiful wife
> He had a healthy baby.
> No other governor in Grusinia
> Had so many horses in his stable
> So many beggars on his doorstep
> So many soldiers in his service
> So many petitioners in his courtyard.
>
> (27)

This world is a world of war, of class oppression of the poor and powerless
by the rich and powerful, and of internecine Hobbesian warfare of each
against each in the upper class, engendering a system in which the lower
class also has to choose between kindness and survival (for example — the
peasant selling milk to Grusha, or her brother). Grusha saves the infant
because she is, as Brecht noted, an exceptional "sucker" — that is, she
responds to norms of human kindness although they threaten her with
death in the unnatural class society. Obviously, behind the old legend the
basic Brechtian questioning of what is "normal," of the alienating effect of
social power-relations on human potentialities, insidiously reemerges.
Appearances deceive, the reality is fraught with murderous contradictions, and any peaceful moment is only an interlude:

> The City lies still
> But why are there armed men?
> The Governor's palace is at peace
> But why is it a fortress?
> And the Governor returned to his palace
> And the fortress was a trap . . .
> And noon was no longer the hour to eat:
> Noon was the hour to die.
>
> (33)

When Grusha succumbs to the "terrible temptation of goodness" to help a
helpless human being, though she is helpless herself, she has to flee
through the Northern Mountains, encountering in that epic anabasis all
kinds of trials and surmounting them by means of a slowly developing
sense of motherhood. To the killings of the princes and the egotist
insensitivity of Natella she opposes a principle which is as important as the
all-pervading destructiveness of the upper classes: the principle of *produc-*

tivity or *creativity*. If it were not sufficiently clear from the language and style of the play, its use of stylized scenery, masks for the upper-class characters, etc., even this first approach to the fable might be sufficient to show that Grusha's actions, putting as they do into question the norm (e.g., of "true motherhood"), are super-individual. As other major figures of Brecht's, she is both a precisely personalized character and allegorical in a sense yet to be explored, but more akin to the Shakespearean synthesis of allegory and realism than to the Individualist 18–20th Century drama. Thus, a child in Brecht's plays usually carries his basic motif of *posteri*, the future generations whose forebears we are. The tug-of-war between the biological upper-class mother and the plebeian "social mother" over the Noble Child is an *exemplum*, standing for a decision which social orientation shall prevail as the parent of posterity, future ages (see the song "Had he golden shoes," 125). Grusha's social maternity is characterologically earned by her labors and dangers, but it is also the sign of a potential coming into existence of a new set of human relations, a new normality, which is attained by standing the topsy-turvy universe of the Chalk Circle nucleus on its head—i.e., by subverting it.

Thus, the maternity motif is here—as different from other plays by Brecht such as *The Good Woman of Setzuan*—explicitly collocated within the theme of a reasonable and humanized *ultimate goal (telos) of history*[6] envisaged as a system of human actions and interactions. The goal toward which class history is moving is, in fact, the main theme of the whole play. Therefore, developing the "Azdak story" at some length is not only autonomously enjoyable but also essential in order to bring out its theme of an advent of Justice as a *temporary* reversal of historically "normal" (i.e. alienated) power and jurisprudence. As an intercalary short-lived exception at the time of a power-vacuum, Azdak can rid the chalk-circle judgment of a non-cognitively fantastic or fairy-tale character. Placed into the Saturnalian tradition of the Oriental and European Lord of Misrule, "Roi pour rire," whose interregnum momentarily replaces and cancels out the class world and its inhuman laws, the "Azdak story" validates the outcome of the "Grusha story" (and by that token itself too) as more than escapism—as an incident, exemplary by its very exceptionalness, and thus in a roundabout but logically unassailable way reintegrated into a theory which sees history as the development of humanity through class conflicts. The combination of Grusha and Azdak, plebeian emotion and plebeian intelligence, revolt against old laws and power over the enforcing of new laws, is necessary for a cognitively credible outcome of the chalk-circle test as an interaction of human wills—where man's destiny is man.

The parallels between the Grusha and Azdak stories, which happen simultaneously but are developed successively on the stage, show up their similarities and differences. Both derive their function from an initial impulsive, "abnormal" humanist action (the saving of the child and of the Grand Duke). This lands them first into trouble, so that they try to

backslide into their old ways, but finally educates them into true motherhood and judgeship respectively. As opposed to the upper class, both
Grusha and Azdak show by such acts that they are in harmony with
nature, outer or inner. Grusha extends her awakened maternal feeling to
the wind:

> GRUSHA   *(turning to the Child):* You mustn't be afraid of the wind. He's a
> poor thing too. He has to push the clouds along and he gets quite
> cold doing it. *(Snow starts falling.)* And the snow isn't so bad
> either, Michael. It covers the little fir trees so they won't die in
> winter.   (61)

Azdak, on the other hand, is an Epicurean, in the double sense of hedonist
and of a radical intellectual for whom his own sensual nature, perceptions
and concepts are the only genuinely human touchstone remaining in the
desensualized, calculated, brutal world around him. Both Grusha as the
herald of a new Nature and Azdak as the herald of a new Wisdom could
fail only by selfishness or cowardice, and they both grow by having
assumed responsibilities contrary to such temptations of conforming.
Without Azdak, Grusha would have been simply a somewhat more violent
and expressive Kattrin from *Mother Courage and her Children*, barely
beginning to speak and reverting to mutism at times of complex stresses
involving both emotion and rationality — a frustrated and barren Mother
of the New. Without Grusha, Azdak would be only a Saturnalian Falstaff,
Schweik, or Groucho Marx supplying anarchist entertainment but having
no significant, historical "bearing on our problem" (as the peasant woman
in the kolkhoz scene defines the compositional method of the play) — a
freak without insertion into historical processes. As it is, Azdak can be
remembered by the people as an anti-judge whose term was "a brief
golden age, / Almost an age of justice." Azdak's anabasis is a flight *toward
power* (the Ironshirts) used in a new way, complementary to Grusha's
flight *from power* used in the old way. During it, Azdak has grown from a
disaffected bohemian, first to somebody reducing the old justice to its
absurd conclusions by anarchist parody, and finally to the allegorical
herald of a new justice, of the new and coming Golden Age which shall
"transform justice / Into passion" (Brecht's *Address to Danish Worker-
Actors*).[7]

The hypothesis that this is a play thematically centered on a theory
which sees history as a conflict of social alienations with strivings toward
de-alienation, can also account for the unusual "kolkhoz story" and
framework. Its "new wisdom" of peaceful resolution of the dispute over
the valley finds a common denominator with the subversive "old wisdom"
of Azdak's decision in the concluding verses:

> That what there is shall go to those who are good for it:
> Children to the motherly, that they prosper.

Carriages to good drivers, that they be driven well,
And the valley to the waterers, that it yield fruit.

This also makes of the central action of *CCC* a performance for an exemplary audience, poetically validating its settling of conflicts of interest without the violence of each against each by inserting it into a historical and philosophical sequence. As Aristotle knew, poetry is more philosophical than historiography.

Brecht's philosophy of history and the compositional method in this play is *Marxist figuralism*. In his essay "Figura," Erich Auerbach has outlined the medieval figural interpretation of history. A *figura* was a real historical person or event of the Old Testament reaching fulfillment in another real historical person or event of the New Testament — say Moses and Jesus. Neither figure nor fulfillment were spiritualist moral allegories; the allegorical aspect in this process was the *intellectus spiritualis* which recognized figure in fulfillment. Augustine refined this to the point where things and people could "prefigure" abstract fulfillments — e.g., Noah's ark prefigured the Christian church, or the pair Hagar-Sarah prefigured the opposition Old Testament vs. New Testament, also *civitas terrena* (terrestrial Jerusalem) vs. *civitas Dei* (heavenly Jerusalem). Brecht does the same when the boy Michael prefigures the future, so that his redemption from class bondage of his "terrene," biological mother is *figurally* connected with the fate of the valley redeemed from private property and its concomitant warfare-type settlement of disputes.

In Auerbach's definition "figural interpretation establishes a connection between two events or persons, the first of which signifies not only itself but also the second, while the second encompasses and fulfills the first. The two poles of the figure are separate in time, but both, being real events or figures, are within time, within the stream of historical life."[8] This is an allegorical approach which retains and encourages the historicity of events but inserts them within a formal process participating both of historiographic facticity and of utopian expectation. Auerbach observes that "figural interpretation is a product of late cultures, far more indirect, complex, and charged with history than the symbol or the myth"; on the other hand, complementary to the interpretation of venerable, indeed legendary matter, it is "youthful and new-born as a purposive, creative, concrete interpretation of universal history" (57). These observations seem to me to apply with full force to Brecht's theory of history in *CCC*. Just as the Christian figural interpretation absorbed characters from the Old Testament as well as from lay authors (*teste David cum Sibylla*, as the *Dies irae* has it) down to the Grail legends, so Brecht's Marxist figuralism absorbed configurations from the New Testament and the old folk legends, generally recognized as the two principal sources of his tradition. It is not difficult to find in the Grusha story the archetype of the hierogamic Holy Family, blasphemously complete with a virgin mother (*figlia del tuo figlio* — Dante, *Paradiso* 33) an exalted child, an official father (or two) who does not know how he came by the child, a flight from soldiers sent to massacre the child, etc. In the same way, Azdak's decision is a forerunner of a subversive final judgment. If Michael has overtones of the Christ Child, Azdak finally assumes overtones of Christ as the messianic fulfiller of Moses' leading his people out of bondage: he is beaten and stripped, he tours the country with the sacrament of a new Law —

> And he broke the rules to save them.
> Broken law like bread he gave them,
> Brought them to shore upon his crooked back . . .
>
>   (107)

As for the folk legends, the use of the Chinese chalk-circle story, the Egyptian Song of the Chaos, the Judgment of Solomon and the legend-imbued location on Caucasus may be sufficient testimonials.

No doubt, differences between the Medieval Christian and the Marxist figuralism are no less pronounced, and homologous with the differences in the main import of these two major systematic non-individualistic philosophies of our civilization. Christian figuralism aims at a super-temporal, theistic resolution, where horizontal temporal prefiguration is possible only because all times refer vertically to divine providence, in whose eye past [and] future are simultaneous. Marxism takes from secularized (rationalist and Hegelian) historiography a real pluritemporality; the orientation toward earthly historicity that began with the Gothic and Renaissance ages grows into the axiological sovereignty of earthly, human reality, in all its sensory and historically differentiated multiplicity. Following Feuerbach, Marxism stood the god-man relation on its ear: god is an emanation made in the image of man. Therefore, instead of an incarnation of the Word (Logos), a Marxist dramatist will start from a verbalization and rationalization of the flesh, from a canonization of ethically exemplary human relations where the sensual and the visionary are not sundered. Grusha and Azdak behave thus: Grusha's motivation for picking up the child is dumb in terms of Individualist experience (each for himself and the devil take the hindmost), but it affirms a radical humanist *sapientia* as touchstone for the whole play:

> OLDER WOMAN (amiably): Grusha, you're a good soul, but you're not very bright, and you know it. I tell you, if he had the plague he couldn't be more dangerous.
>
> GRUSHA (stubbornly): He hasn't got the plague. He looks at me. He's human!
>
>   (44)

Parallel to Grusha, Azdak can unite the dramaturgic function of a figure of new Justice with the character of a comically sensual, anarchistic parodist of old justice. In short, radical religious prefiguration is in Brecht replaced by radical humanist prefiguration, whose historiography is taken from the *Communist Manifesto* with its succeeding stages of class society identified as human "prehistory" which should lead to a classless and warless brotherhood of man on earth. The specific ideational characteristic of *CCC* is the encounter of this historiography with radical Marxist and Anarchist anthropology in the tradition of young Marx and Rimbaud (forgotten by much official Marxism).

The Marxist theory of history can be envisaged as a Hegelian synthesis fusing the useful aspects of the feudal and bourgeois historiosophies. As in the medieval Christian theory of history, the Marxist one has a privileged point of convergence in the future which is the saving *telos* of human history (thesis); but as in the rationalist-liberal theory of history (antithesis), this point is to be reached by a chain of development based exclusively on human interactions (synthesis). The anticipated Golden Age or Terrestrial Paradise is prefigured by a series of more or less short-lived revolutionary and utopian endeavours and visions throughout history from the equality of tribal society (the "primitive communism" of Marxist historiography) through lower-class revolts (such as the one of Spartacus, Wat Tyler, or the German Anabaptists) and through artistic, scientific, religious, or philosophical prefigurations, to revolutions such as the Bolshevik one. The sequence in the play: the Persian Weavers' revolt — Azdak's judgeship — cooperative socialism of Soviet kolkhozes, is an obvious example of such prefigurational, humanist salvation-history.

However, this is not to be taken to mean that the kolkhoz scene is the final privileged point of convergence, a static utopia of perfection. Beside Brecht's reserves on the development within the Soviet Union, the usual static confrontation of two (only sometimes three) points in Christian history (figure and one or two fulfillments) is here replaced by a dynamic development along an infinite curve of succeeding prefigurations hopefully ever closer to fulfillment. On this asymptotic curve, the chalk-circle point and the kolkhoz point serve merely as dramatically powerful examples and determinants. The "chalk-circle," inner part of the play has to be much longer than the kolkhoz frame because it focuses on the human potentialities of Grusha and Azdak as opposed to powerful social alienations in the barbaric class system; their success can then be transferred *a fortiori* to the more rational kolkhoz situation. But the quote from Mayakovsky characterizing the kolkhoz situation says: "The home of the Soviet people shall also be the home of Reason," prefiguring a further future (the German original "soll auch sein" is formally an imperative but also with future-bearing function). Then too, and more obviously, as in the inner play there is still war in the kolkhoz story (although it is a just one, as opposed to the unjust one about which Azdak sings the "Song of Injustice in Persia"). Also, the frame story itself is a dispute about stewardship of possessions which recalls the fierce ownership battle around the Noble Child, the inheritor of the Abashwili estates (although the battle is now fought with a pencil and not with a pistol). The social differentiation between the direct producers (the peasants and the artist) on one hand and on the other a centralized State apparatus, represented by a Delegate from the nearby town, still exists — and Brecht was very aware of its degenerative potentialities. In fact, the type of decision reached by the kolkhoz villagers without a court situation and by mutual agreement, which acts as a fulfillment of the unorthodox Azdak judging, would be illegal in the Soviet Union of 1944, as of today (though not of 1920), as the Soviet critics of Brecht have clearly stated. Another pointer is the deliberate onomastic mixture: Grusha is a Russian name with Dostoevskian (or anti-Dostoevskian) echoes of the humble being exalted, Azdak an Iranian one with radical and salvational echoes.[9] Also, the mixture or indeed mix-up of mostly Grusinian place-names with Russian and Azerbaidjani ones makes out of the kolkhoz situation a very stylized reality indeed (in "real life" the Nazi army came only to the border of the Grusinian Republic, and never to Azerbaidjan). The kolkhoz in the play is thus more of a model-like fulfillment of the legendary Azdakian Golden Age than a "socialist-realist" reflection of 1944 Transcaucasia. This too is of a piece with the figural method. As Auerbach noted, there is always a certain contradiction between figure and history: history (*historia* or *littera*) "is the literal sense of the event related; *figura* is the same literal meaning or event in reference to the fulfillment cloaked in it, and this fulfillment itself is *veritas*" (47). The human relationships in the Grusinian kolkhozes are thus not to be taken either literally or as a final truth, but as Auerbach's "middle term" (47) between their historical literality and dynamic fulfillment: they are themselves another, more advanced figure.

In the same way, the figural parallels of the disputed valley to young Michael are clear: the fruit-growers have a better right to it partly because they fought for it against the Nazis, just as Grusha did against the Ironshirts and other vicissitudes, but mainly because they propose to use it more productively. The question which Azdak decides in the chalk-circle judgment is not at all who should "possess" Michael, and by implication "own" the future. As his questions and the final verse show, the decision hinges on who will be better *for the child*. Not the child to his mother, but the child "to the motherly," the maternal ones, says the Singer in the quoted conclusion — a stylistic device taken over by Brecht from the Luther-Bible style which substitutes the nominalized adjectival quality for a static, fixed substantive. The child and the valley-area are not objects to be allocated to subject-possessors — they are entities, subjects in their own right, and the users have only rights of stewardship over them in the name of human productivity. The formal analogies to the medieval theory of property and just dealing in the name of divine justice are clear. Such analogies are not syllogistic proofs, since a prefigurational parallel is never complete: a certain tension between *figura* and fulfillment is immanent to this approach. Yet, like the fruit-growers, Grusha too had to earn her right to motherhood, and indeed part II and III of the Grusha story show the birth of Grusha as a "motherly one." Her nascent capacities for feeling are criminal in the chaotic world around her:

> She sat too long, too long she saw
> The soft breathing, the small clenched fists,
> Till toward the morning the seduction was complete
> . . .
> As if it was stolen goods she picked it up.
> As if she was a thief she crept away.
>
> (46)

Yet such feelings grow into a justification of Grusha's right to be the noble child's parent—hers is the true nobility, and the blood-and-water baptism of Michael and changing of his clothes are initiation rites for Mother Grusha:

> . . .
> SINGER: And in her flight from the Ironshirts
> After twenty-two days of journeying
> At the Foot of the Janga-Tau Glacier
> Grusha Vachnadze decided to adopt the child.
> CHORUS: The helpless girl adopted the helpless child.
> *Grusha squats over a half-frozen stream to get the*
> *Child water in the hollow of her hand.*
> GRUSHA: Since no one else will take you, son,
> I must take you.
> Since no one else will take you, son,
> You must take me.
> O black day in a lean, lean year,
> The trip was long, the milk was dear,
> My legs are tired, my feet are sore;
> But I wouldn't be without you any more.
> I'll throw your silken shirt away,
> And wrap you in rags and tatters,
> I'll wash you, son, and christen you in glacier water.
> We'll see it through together.
> *She has taken off the child's fine linen and wrapped it in a*
> *rag.*   (57–58)

The *telos* of Marxist figuralism is indeed, notwithstanding dogmatic vulgarizations, not to be found in any particular, arrested point. Though in its dynamic theory of historical equilibrium the direction of humanity is always clear, each point should also be the starting point for new contradictions and resolutions: Judgment Day is also Genesis. It might seem curious that Brecht at some moments insisted that the inner play in *CCC* is not a parable—though its story is told in order to clarify the kolkhozes' decision about the valley—but another (undefined) kind of exemplary narration, to whose "practicability and also genesis" the kolkhoz story "assigns a historical localization."[10] In fact, this is an aesthetic correlative to a salvational perspective in which history has no end, so that the "kolkhoz story" is simply a *presently possible* society in which Azdak's exceptional drawing of a chalk circle has become the normative or dominant use of pencils instead of pistols.

The curve of prefiguration leads thus not only from the chalk circle nucleus to the kolkhoz frame, but also from the Singer's final verses to the temporal point of the audience—1974, or any time at which the prefiguration of a Golden Age has not been fulfilled although it is felt as absolutely necessary. The play is fully relevant only for such an audience, and it becomes clear why for an audience with a different attitude it must seem a chaotic mixture of fairy tale, clowning and propaganda. It is no accident that the first prefiguration of such a fulfillment has been written by Brecht in 1944, at the most promising moment of modern history, the moment of the victory of the anti-fascist coalition, and that he placed at least the frame story into the year in which he wrote it (an extraordinary exception rarely paralleled in modern drama). Drama and history touched in a privileged moment, an epiphany, that lent its effulgence to both. History is here shown as open-ended though clearly not value-free: there is a fixed provisional goal, but it will be reached only if the spectators learn what it means to become parents of the New, of the Future (as Grusha and Simon learned), and if they realize that the victory of the Golden Age of justice depends on the ability of later Grushas to act and later Azdaks to be in the arbiter's seat. Whether the historical horizon of a just, classless humanity will be reached depends on a further powerful conjunction of subversive emotion and subversive reason. For this change of the times ("thou hope of the people," 35) the play is a dynamic *exemplum*. Fittingly, its structure as an open drama exemplifies its message of an open history.

The open structure of the play is communicated through a number of devices. I have already touched on some effects of the play-within-the-play form which results in two audiences. We watch the kolkhoz both act out the chalk-circle story and function as its audience, in a prefiguration of the participatory or doing-your-own-thing theatre, of politics as theatre rather than theatre as politics; and we see the kolkhoz members obtaining insights which justify their decision about the valley as a step in the necessary humanization of humanity. By watching this, we as the "outer" audience gain not only the "moral of the story" but also the reasons why and ways how it is moral. We see, as Brecht wrote in his *Address to Danish Worker-Actors* that "only he who knows that the fate of man is man / Can see his fellow man keenly with accuracy";[11] and we see this cognition presented as delight.

One could embark upon a discussion of songs, and many other devices in the play, but I want finally to consider here only the Singer-narrator. He seems to me to be much more than a formal trick, in fact a semiotic model which not only signifies but is significant in his own right as showing Brecht's theatre esthetics in action. As with almost all major modern dramatists (and indeed artists in general) the theatre's reflection about life is at the same time a reflection about itself. The play—and its performance—is a seduction to goodness in the exemplary type of Grusha, and to justice in that of Azdak. It seduces through a method uniting in its allegorizing the corporeal and spiritual (in)-sight, *eros* and *agape*; it warns against the difficulties on the road to goodness and justice presented in Grusha's archetypal flight and Azdak's tempestuous up[s] and downs, the small-scale landlocked *Odyssey* and *Iliad* of this stage narration.

Parallel to this, the Singer personifies the right type of theatre for an audience interested in the delightful didactics of history; the Chalk-Circle nucleus which he narrates and his approach to its narration and performance are supposed to represent the proper message and the proper style of a plebeian, liberating theatre. The Singer is the only stage figure participating in both the kolkhoz frame (as character) and the chalk-circle nucleus (as narrator and commentator). He mediates between the stage and the audience (both the stage audience and the "real" one); he makes it impossible to forget that the kolkhoz audience is (that we are) seeing the exemplary reality of a performance and not illusionistic slices of life. Like a novel narrator, he manipulates time and space rhythm at his will, he knows the motives and thoughts of all characters. His comments suggest to the audience the most economical attitude proper to the play and its unified understanding. Similar to a Greek chorus, or to Hamlet in the Mousetrap play-within-a-play, he unites epic coolness and lyrical emotion, such as in "O blindness of the great":

> O blindness of the great!
> They go their way like gods,
> Great over bent backs,
> Sure of hired fists,
> Trusting in the power
> Which has lasted so long. But long is not forever.
> O change from age to age!
> Thou hope of the people!
>
> (35)

Compared to Bob Dylan's "The times they are a-changing" this singer-narrator (*cantastorie*) is obviously better trained in philosophy and sociology, but he is turned much in the same direction. His arsenal of devices ranges from narrative interjection to the equivalent of operatic arias such as the one just quoted, and encompasses the stichomythic questions and answers he exchanges with his attendants and gnomic fixations of panto-mimic events such as Grusha's seduction by the Child. With Grusha and

Azdak, the Singer is the third, and perhaps central character of this rich tapestry in time and space: he too, beside being Arkadi Cheidze, is the New Theatre—a male plebeian Thalia, an open, liberating dramaturgy which has assimilated manifold devices of written and oral literature, spectacle and cinema, in order to present us with a useful and delightful lesson about our existence.

The basic tension between utopia and history, humanity and class alienation, results here in a vision of open history transmitted through open dramaturgic structures. I have discussed above how history can be open yet meaningful in a mature Marxist figuralism. The dramaturgy is open in a double sense. First of all, it openly shows its artificial nature, from the fact that it is an art-form consisting of scenic signs of reality and not reproducing it, right to the particular techniques used—beginning with the fact that a particular kind of people (actors) portray other "iconic" people (characters). Further, its structure is open toward the spectators' reality, in which such drama finds its culmination and resolution. It becomes a significant unity only by its effect on the spectators' reality, whose change it wants to help along by esthetic exemplarity. Based on a similarly grand sweep of historical and philosophical horizons as the medieval drama, the Brechtian one differs from it mainly in the imaginary ideal onlooker for whom it is written. In the Middle Ages, that ideal onlooker was he to whom all unfamiliar events were familiar because he saw their eternal essence through surface differences—i.e., God. For *CCC*, the ideal onlooker is he to whom all familiar events are unfamiliar because he looks for the unrealized potentialities in each historical stage of man's humanization—i.e., a Man prefiguring the ethics of a blessed classless Future. The ideal onlooker is both demanded and shaped by Brecht's play. Showing us an open drama correlative to open history, the play itself contributes to such opening.

Notes

1. See Reinhold Grimm's excellent bibliographical handbook *Bertolt Brecht*, 3d ed. (Stuttgart: Metzler, 1971). A long select bibliography which I contributed to *Brecht*, ed. Erika Munk (New York: Bantam, 1972) indicates perhaps how conscious I am of trying to stand on the shoulders of other viewers of Brecht's opus, beginning with his own. Yet to total drowning in a sea of footnotes I have preferred the *terra firma* of concentrating on the text and the implicit performance, trusting that my use of insights by, say, Ernst Bloch, Hans Mayer, Reinhold Grimm, Hans J. Bunge, Bernard Dort, or Albrecht Schoene is readily apparent. This essay was first presented as a lecture at Toronto University in 1970, and then as a paper in the Forum "Perspectives of Marxist Scholarship" on the margins of the 1972 MLA meeting. I am grateful to my colleagues Don Bouchard and Yehudy Lindeman from McGill University and David Stratman from Colby College for suggestions how to improve it. All quotations from *The Caucasian Chalk Circle* are from Eric Bentley's translation (New York: Grove, 1972), and will be indicated by page number in parentheses. [Ed. note: see also *The Caucasian Chalk Circle, Collected Plays*, ed. Ralph Manheim and John Willett (New York: Vintage Books, 1971–), 7:135–229. The present essay was also published in *Weapons of*

Criticism, ed. Norman Rudich (Palo Alto: Ramparts Press, 1976), and Darko Suvin, *To Brecht and Beyond* (Totowa, N. J.: Barnes & Noble, 1984).]

2. See D. Suvin, "The Mirror and the Dynamo: On Brecht's Aesthetic Point of View," in *Brecht*, ed. Munk, [80–98]. I have tried to examine a crucial phase of Brecht's arriving at such a stance in an essay on Brecht's *Saint Joan of the Slaughterhouses*, in print in [*Essays on Brecht: Theater and Politics*, ed. Siegfried Mews and Herbert Knust (Chapel Hill: University of North Carolina Press, 1974), 114–40. Both essays were republished in Suvin, *To Brecht and Beyond*.]

3. [Ed. note: see Keith A. Dickson, "*Mutter Courage und ihre Kinder*," in this volume.]

4. [Ed. note: see M. A. Cohen, "History and Moral in Brecht's *The Life of Galileo*," in this volume.]

5. [Ed. note: see Petermichael von Bawey, "Dramatic Structure of Revolutionary Language: Tragicomedy in Brecht's *The Mother*," in this volume.]

6. Georg Lukács's definition in *History and Class Consciousness* supplies a Marxist approach pertinent to this discussion: "The ultimate goal (*Endziel*) is rather that relation *to the totality* (to the whole of society seen as a process) through which every aspect of the struggle acquires its revolutionary significance. This relation *dwells within* every moment in its simple and sober ordinariness, but it only *becomes real by becoming conscious*, and . . . raises the moment of daily struggle to *reality* out of *mere factuality*"—*Geschichte und Klassenbewusstsein* (Berlin: Malik, 1923), pp. 36–37, trans. D. S. (see also the translation by Rodney Livingstone, London: Merlin, 1971). This opposition between factuality and an ontologically and axiologically more significant "reality" seems analogous to the medieval opposition between *historia* and *figura*, just as the "ultimate aim" is analogous to the fulfillment which is the only real truth or *veritas*—see later discussions in this essay, and Auerbach's discussions in the work cited in note 8. An argument parallel to Lukács's but better known to Brecht is in Karl Korsch, *Marxismus und Philosophie* (Leipzig, 1923; rptd. Frankfurt a.M.: Europäische Verlagsanstalt, 1966).

7. [Ed. note: see Bertolt Brecht, "Speech to the Danish Working-Class Actors on the Art of Observation," *Poems 1913–1956*, ed. John Willett and Ralph Manheim with the co-operation of Erich Fried (New York: Methuen, 1976), 238.]

8. Eric[h] Auerbach, "Figura," *Scenes from the Drama of European Literature* (New York: Meridian, n.d.,), p. 53; further quoted in the text by page number in parentheses.

9. Mazdak was a communist Zoroastrian heresiarch and leader of a plebeian revolt in 6th Century Iran—see Firdusi's epic *Shah-name*, also A. E. Christensen, *Le Régne du roi Kawadh I et le communisme Mazdakite* (Copenhagen, 1925), N. Pigulevskaia, *Goroda Irana v rannem srednevekov'e* (Moskva-Leningrad: AN SSSR, 1956), and on Mazdak's later influence Ziia Buniatov, *Azerbaidzhan v VII–IX vv.* (Baku, 1965), and Dzhamel Mustafaev, "Priroda sotsial'nykh utopii stran Blizhnego Vostoka," *Voprosy filosofii* no. 8 (1968), 115–24.

10. Brecht's note in *Materialien zu Brechts "Der kaukasische Kreidekreis,"* ed. Werner Hecht (Frankfurt a.M.: Suhrkamp, 1966), p. 18, trans. D. S.

11. [Ed. note: See Brecht, "Speech," 237.]

ON OTHER ASPECTS

The Poet of Dark Times [Review of *Poems 1913-1956*]

Stephen Spender*

In his preface to this impressive selection of Bertolt Brecht's poetry,[1] John Willett speculates on why Brecht is only today beginning to be appreciated as a poet of major stature — perhaps a greater poet even than playwright, as Auden believed him to be. His early poems, which appeared in the 1920's, were overshadowed by his plays and later forced out of circulation by the Nazis. Then came the burning of the books. Exiled to Los Angeles, Brecht felt himself to be practicing a vocation and writing in a language made alien by his surroundings:

> Teaching without pupils
> Writing without fame
> Are difficult.

> It is good to go out in the morning
> With your newly written pages
> To the waiting printer, across the buzzing market
> Where they sell meat and workmen's tools:
> You sell sentences.

He wanted to be able to sell his poems like commodities to people who needed them, and where they were not foreign.

When Brecht went to live in East Germany after World War II, he was regarded as a kind of poet laureate of Marxism — a situation made all the more onerous by his reluctance to appear before his public in the role of poet. Mr. Willett tells us that when, in 1928, he was asked by the novelist Alfred Döblin to give a reading of his poetry, he refused on the ground that "my poetry was the strongest argument against my playwriting activities. Everyone heaves a sigh of relief and says that my father should have put me into poetry and not into the business of writing plays."

The great majority of Brecht's poems were not published during his lifetime. This translation of roughly 500 poems comprises less than half his work, but even in translation and without parallel German texts it shows

*Reprinted by permission from the *New York Times Book Review*, 10 February 1980, 1, 24. © 1980 by The New York Times Company.

convincingly that his oeuvre is one of the major poetic achievements of the present century. The editors, John Willett and Ralph Manheim, who compiled *Poems 1913–1956* with the assistance of Erich Fried, deserve our gratitude. The editing, with excellent notes, excerpts from Brecht's own views about poetry and Mr. Willett's concise introduction, is exemplary. Most important, the translations by 35 poets, among them H. R. Hays, Peter Levi, Christopher Middleton and Naomi Replansky, maintain a high standard of accuracy and often convey a very clear idea of the texture and feeling of the German. Many — notably Michael Hamburger's translation of the famous "Of poor B. B." — seem beautiful as English poetry.

The extent of Brecht's range is amazing. There are the ballads, which in their simplicity, direct idiom and lack of archaism, must have influenced Auden's ballads; the Rimbaudesque prose poems called Psalms; the political vehemence of the Epistles; and the sonnets, luminous as pictures painted on glass, with their concrete portraits of characters and situations. Then there are free verse journal poems in which the poet writes down ideas or records impressions that are as immediate as today's news. There are prose poems — entitled "Visions" — that are really parables, like some of Tolstoy's short stories. One has the impression of spontaneous responses to events, and yet of the poet being slyly conscious of the models that inform his writing: Arthur Waley's translations from the Chinese, the Old and New Testaments, the Greek Anthology, Virgil's Eclogues, the Odes of Horace, medieval ballads, Goethe.

Like most poets who become Marxist converts, Brecht was disparaging about his early pre-Marxist poems. He sees them as symptomatic of a stage of "dehumanization," the recognition of which led him to Marxism. This is how he writes in his journal of 1940 about "Devotions for the Home" (1920-25)[2]: "This is where literature attains that stage of dehumanization which Marx observed in the proletariat, along with the desperation which inspires the proletariat's hopes. The bulk of the poems deal with decline, and the poems follow our crumbling society all the way down."[3]

Brecht despised the reader who liked these early poems of his, which were "branded with the decadence of the bourgeois class"; such a reader would find his later "Sven[d]borg poems" a "staggering impoverishment." Indeed there *is* impoverishment when he adopts the stance of a poet who thinks the times demand that he write like a political commissar. But the odd thing about him is that while the ideological Brecht deprives his poetry of all but the politics of necessity, the man Brecht remains unredeemed — or at any rate identifies himself with the ugly, the sordid, the corrupt and sly.

> Pushing hair down from his forehead
> Seaweed-like across his face
> Does he hope to hide his horrid

Clinkered insolent grimace?
Watch his nasty naked features
Twitching: is that to persuade
God to save one of His creatures
Or because he is afraid?

That is early Brecht. He is not writing about himself later on when he begins a poem: "I'm dirt, From myself / I can demand nothing but / Weakness, Treachery and degradation . . . " And yet the tone of voice is the same: he identifies with the damned and the decadent as well as siding with the insulted and oppressed. This is his special note. In the end it is what gives him integrity. Deep down, under the comradeship and party discipline — a superstructure he adopts to cover over bourgeois decadence — he remains the same person, the lowest common multiple of humanity.

This indeed is what gives Brecht his humanity: all his conscious talk about it. And this is where he seems unlike all the "moderns," the esthetes who turn the poem into a verbal object, a means of escaping from the personality, the self. In his best poetry (and a good deal of his writing is simply very adroit compressed journalism, or propaganda) he is inescapably that self which identifies with the lowest of the earth. In this respect the poet he most reminds me of is Theodore Roethke in Roethke's early poetry, when he seems to identify completely with the larval life, the slugs in the tanks of his father's greenhouses.

Brecht, though a poet of urban life, the asphalt city, has Romantic appurtenances. He can be romantic about pine forests and the flesh of women — even, in a rather Edward Learish way, about Alabama and Chicago.[4] What he can never be romantic about is Bertolt Brecht. There is no feeling in him that being a poet provides spiritual redemption for the evil in him. He certainly sides with the poor and the oppressed, he hates tyranny and injustice; he is on the side of the comrades. All this makes him sociable, talkative, a backroom boy:

Towards evening it's men that gather round me
And then we address one another as 'gentlemen.'
They're resting their feet on my table tops
And say: things will get better for us. And I don't ask when.

Not asking when is of course what distinguishes him from the others, combining idealism with a secret conviction that it is all a lot of nonsense. And underneath all the real camaraderie is that despair which perhaps he alone feels — though there is always death: "Of those cities will remain what passed through them, the wind!"

In the moving "An Inscription Touches Off Sentimental Memories," Brecht contemplates the photograph of an old flame (who is described more cynically in the diaries):

A photograph. Inscribed on which I see
The words PURE, LUCID, EVIL, through a mist . . .
That was her. My God, I wish I had
An inscription like that on my tombstone: Here lies B. B.
PURE, LUCID, EVIL.
I'd sleep all right with that on top of me.

Brecht takes his ultimate stand on being lucid, knowing pure evil, at moments even being it. Yet he does not regard himself as exceptionally wicked, a villain. It is merely that he knows everyone's wickedness in himself, better than others do. And his real humanity starts from there: from his consciousness of himself as the lowest common multiple of the human race. Upon that, one can build a new society, where men will be better than Bertolt Brecht. As a human being he can dream, have romantic experiences, be a part of nature as well as of society; but that is secondary, peripheral to the lucid knowledge of evil.

He lives in a time of mass killings, the tyranny and murders of Hitler, the "house painter"; he becomes an exile within a materialist America where no one speaks the language of his thoughts and poetry, and later returns to the East Germany that ought to provide the fulfillment of his aspirations. He records impressions in poems and diaries, sometimes reflecting the official aims and optimism of the society around him, but relapsing, when he is disappointed, into that cynicism which is almost a matter of principle to him, since it implies the acceptance of himself as identical with disillusioning and disillusioned humanity. John Willett raises what might be called the Gulag Archipelago question:

"The dark times. . . . " There were plenty of other poets who lived in them or died because of them, but none to whose writings they seemed so central. One of the most desperate moments of the world's history . . . was also a high point in this man's work. Yet how does his own poem about them, "In dark times," conclude? "They won't say: the times were dark / Rather: why were their poets silent?" Once given the full significance of this concept for Brecht . . . the question becomes a double-edged one. The times had darkened for him, we now see, even where they had turned red; so why was he himself silent wherever the dark places of the USSR and international Communist movement were concerned?

There are several answers to this question. One—however inadequate—is that he did voice some politic objections to censorship; after workers in East Germany rioted against the Communist government in June 1953, he asked the pointed and witty question:

After the uprising of the 17th June
The secretary of the Writer's Union
Had leaflets distributed in the Stalinallee
Stating that the people

Had forfeited the confidence of the government
And could win it back only
By redoubled efforts. Would it not be easier
In that case for the government
To dissolve the people
And elect another?

But this is really only Berlin cafe sharpness. A more weighty answer would be that in choosing the Communists he had — from his point of view — chosen the people, and that to choose the other side on account of Stalin would be to betray the people and their confidence in him.

The deep answer, though, one implicit in this poet of desperate cynicism and willful choice, is that the best lines of his poetry revealed the characteristic Brecht: lucid about himself, but never under any obligation to disclose his thoughts about politics, and perfectly prepared to play games with evil for the sake of some ultimate conditioning good. He never pretended to be other than ugly, sly and cunning. He put himself on the workers' side in a struggle where there were only two sides anyway: Communism and capitalism. Too bad his side turned out as it did, but he did not feel called upon to change sides. Underneath it all, he remained truly himself, B. B. Besides, he was dying.

Notes

1. [Ed. note: this article is a review of Bertolt Brecht, *Poems 1913–1956*, edited by John Willett and Ralph Manheim with the co-operation of Erich Fried (New York: Methuen, 1976).]

2. [Ed. note: Brecht's *Hauspostille* is also available in English as *Manual of Piety*, bilingual edition, trans. Eric Bentley (New York: Grove Press, 1966).]

3. [Ed. note: Bertolt Brecht, *Arbeitsjournal*, 2 vols., ed. Werner Hecht (Frankfurt am Main: Suhrkamp, 1973), 1:153 (20 August 1940).]

4. [Ed. note: see also Reinhold Grimm, "Bertolt Brecht's Chicago — A German Myth?", in this volume.]

The Poet Beneath the Skin   Claude Hill*

. . . [I]n 1971, John Willett opened a lecture with the following sentence: "At the end of it all we come back to the poet, because you cannot really appreciate the playwright Brecht, or even perhaps the theatrical director, let alone the theoretician, without realizing that he was a poet first, last, and all the time."[1] Willett was then speaking as the

*From *Bertolt Brecht* by Claude Hill (Boston: Twayne Publishers, 1975), 161-80, 191-92. Reprinted by permission of G. K. Hall & Co. © 1975 by G. K. Hall & Co., Boston.

editor of a forthcoming first full English selection of Brecht's poems. . . .[2]
Brecht's *Collected Works* in German contain more than twelve hundred
different poems on almost eleven hundred pages, not counting the rejected
earlier versions and hundreds of verses discarded by their creator before
publication.[3] These startling figures are indicative of the sad fact that an
Anglo-Saxon reader who does not know German is in no position to
appreciate and evaluate the poet Brecht adequately. And yet, many
scholars and critics consider his to be the most powerful German lyrical
voice since (or even including) Rilke. Leading poets of our time, such as
Auden, Spender, and Pasternak, felt drawn to translate him; Willett comes
to the conclusion that it is precisely Brecht's poetic genius that also gives
his plays whatever distinction they may have. He only reiterates what the
influential German editor Willy Haas had already expressed in the
twenties and what Hannah Arendt repeated in the sixties. The playwright
was, above all and foremost, a poet at heart, or, to borrow Willett's
felicitous title of the above-mentioned lecture: "A Poet Beneath the Skin."

Although Brecht published many poems in magazines and newspapers scattered all over Europe, he only prepared three selections in book
form, and it is remarkable how much material he withheld altogether
during his lifetime. Since it was the wild young man who burst upon the
literary scene with a vengeance, so to speak, the mature and older Brecht
is still considerably less known and recognized as a poetic voice, both in
Germany and abroad; and the reasons for this neglect are mainly political.
In trying to do justice to the achievement of a poet who not only was
amazingly prolific at every stage of his career but also went through
recognizable phases of literary development and growing maturity, I shall
treat Brecht's poetry under three headings, which, in rough chronological
order, indicate the main phases of his topical concerns and stylistic
endeavors. If in my presentation, the first one tends to overshadow the
others, the almost total absence of the older Brecht's poetry in translation
is the obvious reason. Since I do not feel apt to render Brecht's poems into
adequate English myself, I must depend on the available work done by
Bentley and Hays, which, while highly laudable, falls considerably short
of approximating the stark uniqueness of Brecht's original language.[4]

In the Shadow of Baal

Willy Haas, editor of *Die literarische Welt*, Germany's most prestigious literary journal in the twenties, after discussing the beginnings of
Brecht's dramatic career, adds the following significant sentence: "Let us
take a deep breath now, because in 1927 there appeared a little book
which established Brecht's lasting fame as a very great poet: a small and
yet great book, the book of poems and songs with the title *Die Hauspostille*." A little later he adds the rhapsodic statement: "In this small
volume there are cantos and verses which are as great, as mysteriously

great as anything ever sung by man."[5] Haas only expresses a sentiment shared by many German scholars and critics as well as by Eric Bentley, who says in the preface to his own bilingual edition of *Die Hauspostille* (Manual of Piety): "Arguably, it is one of the best of all books of modern poems and certainly it is Brecht's best book of poems."[6] The original German title is indicative of two tendencies, both characteristic of the early Brecht and the period in which the book first appeared. Historically, a *Hauspostille* is a book of prayers and other devotional literature for use in the home; the title was obviously chosen to mock religion and shock the bourgeois. Furthermore, it suggests the subordination of personal poetry to a communal purpose, i.e., a functional use, similar to the operatic efforts of Hindemith and Weill and the goals of the Bauhaus Movement in the twenties. Accordingly, the book is divided into sections such as "Supplications," "Spiritual Exercises," "Chronicles." It is here where the wild and anarchistic young Brecht, who projected himself into the fictitious Baal on the stage, fully released his lyrical voice. Not only does the book contain the "Chorale of the Man Baal" from the play, but we now know that Brecht and his youthful gang literally lived some of its scenes in and around Augsburg and that all poems in the book precede — and many accompany — the first and second drafts of the play. The shadow of Baal clearly lingered over Brecht's first selection of poetry.

Thematically, one may distinguish among three different types of poems in *Die Hauspostille*, with the ballads and legends forming the first group. The influence of Kipling and Villon is most noticeable, and to a lesser degree that of Wedekind. The heroes are the damned and rejected, the outcasts of society, viewed with affection, compassion, and also envy. Sometimes the tone is factual, even deliberately dry and impersonal like a newspaper account, as in "Von der Kindesmörderin Marie Farrar" (Concerning the Infanticide, Marie Farrar), which opens as follows:

> Marie Farrar, born in April,
> No marks, a minor, rachitic, both parents dead,
> Allegedly, up to now without police record,
> Committed infanticide, it is said,
> As follows: in her second month, she says,
> With the aid of a barmaid she did her best
> to get rid of the child with two douches,
> Allegedly painful but without success.
>> But you, I beg you, check your wrath and scorn
>> For man needs help from every creature born.
>>   [Translated by H. R. Hays][7]

The affinity to Neo-Factualism is, of course, unmistakable here, just as it was in the third version of *Baal* in 1926. At times, the style of journalistic reportage may become mocking, as in the poem about another murderer, the boy Jacob Apfelböck, who killed his parents without apparent motive:

In the mild daylight Jacob Apfelböck
Struck his father and his mother down
And shut them both into the laundry chest
And he stayed in the house, he was alone.
[Translated by H. R. Hays]

The subtitle "Oder die Lilie auf dem Felde" (Or the Lily of the Field) with
its biblical allusion makes clear that a deliberate parody was intended.[8]
Most often, however, the legends, ballads, or chronicles in Brecht's first
book of poetry are hymnical and ecstatic evocations of the spirit of
adventure, glorifying the strength and cruelty of nature and the exuber-
ance of living at the edge of the abyss. There is the adventurer, "sick from
the sun, and gnawed at by the rainstorms," who is forever seeking "the
country where there is a better life"; and there is the sailor,

Naked and with his sharks and without a hat.
He knows his world. He has looked into that.
And he has one desire left: to drown.
And he has one desire: not to go down.
[Translated by E. Bentley]

The world which is revealed by the poet in his first book of verse is
neither kind nor nice nor comfortable, but brutal, often dangerous, and
always precarious; it is largely an outdoor world for tough men: soldiers,
sailors, pirates, and adventurers. These men are what they are because
they live close to nature, which to them *is* the world. Consequently, we
find in the *Hauspostille*, next to the ballads, many poems with nature
mirroring and symbolizing the transitoriness of all life, doomed to end in
rot and decay sooner or later. If there are any idyllic times, they are
significantly experienced while "you must just lie in ponds or rivers like
water-plants in which pike make their home"; i.e., by swimming through
waters polluted by algae, mud, and seaweed, or by nakedly climbing in
trees: "Slowly and blackly in the evening air. / And in the foliage await the
nightfall / With wraith and bat hovering about your brows." Inspired by
Rimbaud,[9] the poet finds relief by imagining himself to be a ship, of which
he sings: "Swimming through clear waters of many seas / Beneath red
moons, beside the sharks, I freed / Myself from gravity and destination."
Idyllic moments, however, are rare and brief in a world in which every
living creature is ultimately doomed to be devoured by nature. After
Cortez's men died exhausted by their futile battle with the jungle, "the
forest ate the meadows up in a matter of weeks." A man desperately
holding on to a tree in his defiance of death "Died like a beast with its
claws in the roots," and of the ship, mentioned above, fishermen said,
before it went down: "Something was moving, bright with seagull dung, /
Full of algae, water, moon, dead objects, / Silent and broad toward the
washed-out sky" [translated by E. Bentley]. Nowhere did the young Brecht
voice his lament about the eternal decay of life and nature's propensity for

changing everything into carrion in more perfect lyrical terms than in the poem "Vom ertrunkenen Mädchen" (On the Drowned Girl), the last stanza of which reads:

> When her pale corpse rotted in the water
> Very slowly God forgot her bit by bit:
> First her face; her hands then; then last of all her hair.
> In carrion-carrying rivers she was carrion.
>   [Translated by E. Bentley]

It is not only the drowned girl that God forgot; again and again these poems express the young Brecht's bitter notion of the bad memory of Heaven. With sadness, at times with bitterness, and most often with defiance and cynicism, the poet sings of a world forgotten and forsaken by God. I am, therefore, inclined to consider religion the third theme of *Die Hauspostille;* even though it comes across only implicitly at times. It seems inconceivable to me that a writer who is in the habit of evoking the name of God, who reveals an intimate familiarity with the Bible, who models individual poems after hymns, prayers, and psalms, should be labeled nonreligious or indifferent to religion. Even violent renunciation would seem to indicate a concern that the true agnostic lacks. When Brecht parodied a well-known Protestant church hymn and carefully (i.e., ironically) started each stanza with "praise ye" while in reality meaning "woe," he cried out in a spirit which can only be called religious, as, for instance, the third stanza reveals:

> Praise ye the tree that from carrion shoots
>   whooping toward Heaven!
> Praise ye the tree!
> Carrion that feeds it, praise ye!
> But never cease to praise Heaven.
>   [Translated by E. Bentley]

Sometimes, the religious implication is veiled, as in a poem about a "man in violet" who sucks blood like a tick. Only after pondering the last stanza will the casual reader conclude that the man in violet is, of course, no other but a priest, of whom it is said:

> The bed he loves to sit at
> Is a bed of death.
> The man in violet
> Haunts your final breath.
>   [Translated by E. Bentley]

Whether mocking, lamenting, or renouncing, the voice of the young poet is directed against those who try to avert man's attention from the misery (and glory) of this world and wish to console him with a better afterworld. He preaches instead:

> Don't let them lure you into
> Exhaustion and duress!
> Why all the trepidation?
> You die like all creation.
> And after: nothingness.
>   [Translated by E. Bentley]

It should be added that a division of Brecht's early poems into three thematic groups is both simplistic and also to some extent arbitrary. It leaves out, for instance, one of the most beautiful love poems Brecht ever wrote. "Erinnerung an die Marie A." (Memory of Marie A.) is based on a Breton lay of Marie de France (*ca.* 1100) which, in turn, became the model for Ezra Pound's "La Fraisne" of 1909. Brecht used for his version a rather vulgar popular World War I song which, according to the playwright Carl Zuckmayer, he succeeded in transforming into a genuine folk song.[10] This is not a true love poem but rather a poem about nature, in which a white cloud sparks the memory of a girl the poet once kissed under a plum tree. Her face and fate are now forgotten, but it is the image of the cloud that is still in his mind:

> Even the kiss would have been long forgotten
> If that white cloud had not been in the sky.
> I know the cloud, and shall know it forever,
> It was pure white and, oh, so very high.
>   [Translated by E. Bentley]

In addition to this unexpectedly tender and formally perfect poem at least one other, which also does not quite fit into the three groups outlined above, ought to be singled out, the "Chorale of the Man Baal," because it best exemplifies both the philosophy and tone of Brecht's first lyrical phase. Here it is the stark hammering rhythm, suggestive of the young poet's extraordinary power and his hunger for life, which gives the poem its almost hypnotic appeal from the very first lines, "Als im weissen Mutterschosse aufwuchs Baal" (When inside the white maternal womb grew Baal), to the end, when the dead Baal rots beneath the earth: "Large as ever was the sky and still and pale / Young and naked and almost miraculous / As Baal used to love it when Baal was" [translated by E. Bentley].

In 1927, when *Die Hauspostille* appeared, German poetry was highly individualistic, refined, sophisticated, aristocratic, and generally withdrawn from the profane business of everyday life. The recognized masters were Stefan George, Hugo von Hofmannsthal, and Rainer Maria Rilke, and the latter's widely read *Das Stundenbuch* (Book of Hours) had initiated a tendency toward writing lyrical prayers, so to speak. The new fashion was also imitated by the Expressionists, and since Brecht scorned their soul-baring efforts as well as poetry he felt was too personal and esoteric, he may deliberately have set out to do the opposite in his first collection of verse. This accounts for his choice of the ballad, the least individualized genre of lyrical expression, the folk-song quality of his poetry, and the mocking parodistic tone of the introductory "Guide to the Use of the Individual Lessons." In a retrospective assessment of his lyrical beginnings, Brecht stated:

> In almost every genre I started conventionally. In poetry I began with songs accompanied by the guitar and composed the verses simultaneously with the music; the ballad was an ancient form and in my time nobody who wanted to be somebody wrote ballads anymore. Later I changed to other and less old forms, but I reverted from time to time, even making copies of old masters and translating Villon and Kipling. The type of song which came to this continent after the war like a folk song of the big cities already had developed a conventional form when I used it. I started with it and later went beyond it.[11]

Notwithstanding the strongly parodistic element in *Die Hauspostille*, these words show an unexpected respect for tradition on the part of the young rebel poet, because without mastery of, and familiarity with, the old forms, nobody would or could attempt parodies. In short, the poet Brecht was neither an inventor of new lyrical forms nor an explorer of as yet unprobed levels of consciousness. If his first book of verse nevertheless charmed, enthralled, startled, electrified, stunned, and excited unprofessional lovers of poetry as well as the most expert and blasé literary critics, we must look for other qualities. These are, first, an almost hypnotic rhythmic originality and, second, a strongly sensual and concrete imagery combined with a rather unique color typology. The sky may be mauve or "pale as apricot" or drunk (starkly blue); and at night it "grows dark like smoke," or the poet may sing of opal heavens and violet horizons. A tree "sways like a drunk monkey," and the autumn may bring "a day of blue September." Cities are black and their inhabitants "black beasts of the pavements," while an old leaky ship "vomits salt in remorse. It makes water in fear." Drunkards have "lips of violet"; adventurers are "sick from the sun, and gnawed at by the rainstorms," and a pirate "had hair like a mole" while sailing through "absinthe seas." In *Die Hauspostille*, Brecht broke through the thin veneer of the used-up German literary language of his day and away from the highly intellectualized and introspective poetry of his contemporaries, associated with the development of modern German literature and with that of all other countries. It is this combination of stark language, metaphorical sensuality, and extraordinarily variegated rhythm that caused Bentley to call the book "one of the best of all books of modern poems."[12]

In the Service of Society

While the first collection of verse by the young Brecht revealed an outsider, a rebel, and an anarchist, who had composed his ballads and songs in the meadows and under the trees of his native town and had sung them to his friends in rural taverns, the urbanizing influence of the big city of Berlin, which became his new domicile in the early 1920's had a taming effect on him. The difficult and tough conquest of Germany's theatrical capital by the young man from the provinces coincided with the urban orientation of the latest literary fashion: the new sobering voices of Neo-Factualists replacing the ecstatic utterances of the Expressionists. Partly preceding and partly coinciding with the study of Marx, a new awareness of urbanization directed the poet's attention to societal concern and responsibility, however begrudging and reluctant at first. Significantly, Brecht gave to the cycle of new poems written after *Die Hauspostille* the title of *Lesebuch für Städtebewohner* (Reader for City Dwellers). The poet's change of emphasis corresponds to the playwright's shift from Baal's anarchic defiance to Galy Gay's adjustment to life in the army and Garga's realization, at the end of *Im Dickicht der Städte*, that "the chaos is used up now." The new city dweller, while tough and cynical, is aware of the transitoriness of the steel and concrete surrounding him and of the necessity to live as cautiously as possible in order to avoid trouble. It is here where the poet can help him. "Do not show your face," he advises him, and "Do not open the door," and "He who was not there and did not say anything, how can he be caught?" Although Brecht, sobered-up, resigned, and cynical, was now far removed from Baal's hymnic evocations of nature's bliss and power, he equally welcomed the industrial environment and singled out for his lyrical statement objects and experiences of the man in the big city. There are songs about cranes for coal mining, an ironical poem about the power of money, a "memorial tablet" for twelve middle-weight boxing champions, a hymn to an oil tank, a poem in praise of automobiles, bitter reflections on economic inequities and unemployment. After the depression of 1929, the once highly praised and welcomed example of America was conspicuously lamented in a long elegy about "Verschollener Ruhm der Riesenstadt New York" (Forgotten Fame of the Giant City of New York). The new mood and the new tone of the urban Brecht is perhaps best summed up by the "Sang der Maschinen" (Song of the Machines), of which the poet sings:

> This is no wind in the maple-tree, my boy
> This is no song to the lonely star
> This is the wild howl of our daily labor
> We curse it, yet we like it, too
> For it is the voice of our cities
> It is the song that pleases us
> It is the language we all understand
> And soon it will be the mother tongue of the world.
> [Translated by C. Hill]

While it would be an overstatement to ascribe these lines, and similar poems written between 1926 and 1930, to a consciously experienced social concern, they nevertheless reveal a new, totally un-Baalian, tolerance of, and even solidarity with, the insignificant little everyday urban man of today. The real impetus for placing his poetic talent at the service of society came, of course, from Brecht's simultaneous political involvement. His didactic plays are full of poems which, even when removed from their context, are often memorable for their power and simplicity, such as "Lob des Lernens" (Praise of Learning) from *Die Mutter* [*The Mother*], the middle part of which reads:

> Seek out the school, you who are homeless!
> Sharpen your wits, you who shiver!
> Hungry man, reach for the book: it is a weapon.
> You must take over the leadership.
> [Translated by H. R. Hays]

Or the poet reveals his Marxist view when he raises, in "Fragen eines lesenden Arbeiters" (A Worker Reads History), sly questions like: "Who built the seven gates of Thebes?" followed by "Was it kings who hauled the craggy blocks of stone?" And after many more irreverent questions he ends with the laconic statement: "Every ten years a great man, / who paid for the expenses? / So many reports. / So many questions." In addition to writing poems in free verse, Brecht also succeeded in composing truly proletarian songs, set to music by Eisler and others and intended to be sung by marching workers, such as "Keiner oder Alle" (All of Us or None), which begins:

> Slave, who is it who shall free you?
> Those in deepest darkness lying,
> Comrade, these alone can see you,
> They alone can hear you crying.
> Comrade, only slaves can free you.
> [Translated by H. R. Hays]

Just as the fight against Hitler shifted the focus of Brecht's drama from pro-Marxist *Lehrstücke* [plays for learning] to antifascist plays, the poet Brecht subordinated his lyrical talent to the active fight of Nazism, and that to an even higher degree. If his antifascist poems considerably outnumber the pro-Marxist poems, the circumstances of his life, and especially of his exile, are undoubtedly responsible. Brecht fought Hitler with his pen to the limits of his capacity. His poems turned out to be powerful weapons, whether published in countries adjacent to Germany, recited over the radio by the BBC in London or by Radio Moscow, smuggled across the border by partisan trucks, or dropped by Allied airplanes. Since writing *against* something results as much from a sociopolitical motivation as fighting *for* a cause, we must consider Brecht's anti-Nazi poems part of a service to society that could only be achieved at the expense of the poet's persona, forced to remain mute until the hated foe had been defeated. In a poem with the revealing title "Schlechte Zeit für Lyrik" (Bad Times for Lyrics) he stated:

> To use rhymes in my song
> Would almost seem to be presumptuous.
> Inside of me there is a struggle:
> To be inspired by the blooming appletree
> or horrified by the speeches of the paperhanger [Hitler].
> Only the second one
> drives me to the writing desk.
>
> [Translated by C. Hill]

And this, indeed, did happen on an unprecedented scale. Literally hundreds of poems owe their origin to Brecht's hatred of Hitler and his regime—some of them mediocre, as most purely topical writing often is, but many of them powerful and original within the given limitations of political poetry. The elegy "Deutschland" of 1933, for instance, is in the highest German literary tradition, reminiscent of Friedrich Hölderlin, when it begins:

> O Germany, pale mother!
> How soiled you are
> As you sit among the peoples.
> You flaunt yourself
> Among the besmirched.
>
> [Translated by H. R. Hays]

One of Brecht's finest ballads, the very long and touching "Kinderkreuz-zug 1939" (Children's Crusade 1939) about a group of Polish children, roaming through the war-torn countryside, abandoned, and finally lost in a snowstorm, also owes its origin to his war service with the pen. The stark simplicity Brecht achieves here he also used with great effect in his so-called "Hitler Chorales," a number of biting satirical poems composed to the melodies of well-known Protestant church hymns in the style first tried in *Die Hauspostille*. There are also numerous other types of polemic poems, ranging from short epigrams to ballads, soldier songs, chronicles, marching songs, satires, sonnets, and long elegies. They show a poet whose societal concern had imposed on him the conviction that "to speak of trees is almost a crime, for it is a kind of silence about so many horrors."[13]

In the Company of the Classics

Although Brecht possessed an extraordinary talent for rhyming (which does not come through in the English translations of Bentley and Hays) and was equally at home in the traditional simple four-line stanza, as well as in the more formal schemes of the triplet and the sonnet, he tended more and more to a special kind of free verse as he grew older. In an essay written in 1938, he explained that he came to his "Rhymeless

Verse with Irregular Rhythms" as a dramatist searching for an idiom suitable for showing "human dealings as contradictory, fiercely fought over, full of violence."[14] Just as Brecht's theory of the epic theater simultaneously developed with the discovery of Marx, as we have seen, the newly sought poetic language had to correspond to the discordances and inconsistencies in people's social life. The oily smoothness of five-foot iambic meter, for instance, would no longer do. It is here that the term "gestus," . . . which includes considerations of language, comes in. As Brecht formulated it: "The sentence must entirely follow the gestus of the person speaking," and "it seems to me at present that irregular rhythms must further the gestic way of putting things."[15] What Brecht meant may perhaps best be illustrated by another look at [*Saint Joan of the Stockyards*] the plot of which follows the classical economic crisis in capitalistic society according to Marx. . . . We may now add that the language of this first Brechtian poetic drama in the grand manner is fashioned after the same societal principle: Joan's gestus demands the rhymeless verse with irregular rhythms that Brecht was beginning to develop in those years. It is only logical that, as the playwright Brecht became a sociopolitical writer, an *ecrivain engagé*, the poet Brecht would also tend to abandon rhyme and regular rhythm. It is for this reason that the bulk of his lyrical output consists of free verse, which has found a wide following among younger German poets, while *Die Hauspostille* has remained the unique testimony of a young anachronistic and inimitable genius.

Just as Marxism remained the firm philosophical basis of the mature and aging playwright, even after he had outgrown his rigid didactic and doctrinaire middle phase, so the irregular rhythm of Brecht's poetic voice, which he felt had to correspond to his notion of an erratic society, continued to dominate his profuse lyrical production. To this, however, we must add the increasing influence of a lifelong association with the classics.

Brecht's love for Latin goes back to his school days, . . . and among the most frequently handled and annotated books in his library at the time of his death were editions of Latin classics, his special favorites being Horace and Lucretius. It was the figure of Coriolanus that caused the playwright Brecht to attempt a complete adaptation (really a new version) of Shakespeare's drama; it was the Roman general Lucullus who became the focal hero of a radio play and opera; and it was Brecht's interest in Caesar that made him write one of his very few novels, *Die Geschäfte des Herrn Julius Cäsar* (The Business Deals of Mr. Julius Caesar). His admiration for the great Latin poets sparked one of the strangest projects in the history of versification: a long-considered free recasting of the *Communist Manifesto* in hexameters, which grew to about four hundred lines before he gave it up in 1945. In itself it was to be only the second part of a long didactic poem modeled after Lucretius' *De Rerum Natura* with the tentative titles of "Lehrgedicht von der Natur der Menschen" (The Didactic Poem on the Nature of Man) or "Über die Unnatur der bürgerlichen Verhältnisse" (On the Nonnaturalness of Bourgeois Relations). Above all, however, it was Horace whom Brecht loved and who became one of his spiritual guides as the following short poem (1953) reveals:

> Even the Deluge
> Lasted not for ever.
> There came a time when
> The black waters stopped.
> Yet how few
> Lasted longer!
> [Translated by C. Hill]

Lifelong influences and habits are likely to leave a trace, and when a dead language like Latin was—and to some extent still is—retained in the curricula of European high schools to inculcate in pupils a sense of logic and orderliness and to improve their grasp of grammar, a poet with a similar indoctrination is bound to show the latinizing effect upon his style. In addition to the frequent use of the imperative and the question mark so characteristic of the teacher's role that the older Brecht appeared to assume increasingly in his poetry, his striking (and relatively non-German) preference for the present participle is undoubtedly derived from the structure of Latin grammar. Brecht himself made joking reference to it when he said: "The present participle should only be used by a person who had, as I did, a '1' in Latin."[16] As the German scholar Walter Jens correctly pointed out, the employment of the present participle instead of a subordinating clause customary in German and introduced by the appropriate conjunction presupposes an intelligent reader, because it is he who will have to decide whether an adversative, a causal, or a temporal meaning is intended.[17]

Brecht did not only keep company with his beloved Latin classics but also deliberately learned from Oriental models. The playwright had already benefited from Japanese No-plays in his didactic phase; the theorist had observed the style of Chinese acting before he formulated his estrangement effect; now the poet's growing interest in Chinese philosophy and literature also enriched the colors on his lyrical palette. Lao-Tze, for instance, is the central character in one of Brecht's finest ballads, dealing with the transmission of politically useful knowledge, a subject doubly dear to him after he had personally experienced censorship and sealed borders.[18] Ten years later, while back in Berlin (1949), he still felt provoked to wrestle with Chinese poetry; this time it was Mao Tse-tung's "Thoughts while Flying over the Great Wall" that he tried to render into German. If one tries to assess the effect of Brecht's old-age love for things Chinese in general, and poets in particular, upon his own lyrical style, two things seem to stand out. On a philosophical level, the ideals he strives for and praises in his poems have become qualities of restraint, mellowness, and self-disclipline, such as wisdom, goodness, friendliness, and politeness. On the level of language, a new austerity, shunning excessive wordage and attributive richness while avoiding the aridity of the earlier didactic phase, can be felt in Brecht's poetry of his third and most mature period, and by no means only in the lyrics specifically concerned with Chinese topics or models. New poems for children, a few new love poems, and a new type of very brief, epigrammatic, didactic verse also testify to Brecht's finally reached posture of a classic poet who has succeeded in compressing a maximum of meaning into a minimum of words.

Brevity alone is not a sign of high quality unless it is augmented by other evidence of formal mastery. In the case of Brecht, it is his unique ability to condense and contract lines and phrases in such a way that the reader's intelligence will have to supply the logical conclusions through his own substitution of missing words and thoughts. An epigrammatic poem of 1940 may serve as an example:

> From the library halls
> Emerge the butchers.
> Pressing the children to their sides
> The mothers stand and full of horror search
> The sky for the inventions of the scholars.
> [Translated by C. Hill]

Only when we realize that the scholars who come out of the library will have become the inventors and designers of bombs and missiles for which the mothers are searching the sky in times of war do we understand the poem and, thus, retroactively grasp the otherwise unintelligible second line. Or a charming children's song of 1952 retells the German legend of a tailor who jumped to his death from the steeple of Ulm cathedral with self-made wings because, as each of the two stanzas states, "No one will ever fly, / The Bishop said to the people." This time it is the reader who will have to write his own third stanza, as it were, in order to conclude that (1) the tailor crashed because the wings were inadequate, and (2) the bishop was wrong, and man will eventually learn to fly.[19] Most of the characteristics we have just discussed, such as brevity, utmost simplicity, irregular rhythm, the ability to elicit an intellectual response by a technique of contracting, a distant and cool temperament, a measure of contentment, a longing for friendliness, can be found in Brecht's last small cycle of poems, which he wrote and published under the title *Buckower Elegien* (The Buckow Elegies) in 1953.[20] Nature, banned during the middle years of polemic writing, is now readmitted to his lyrical world; but instead of being a threatening and all-devouring danger to man, as it appeared to Baal, it is now domesticated and only seen in terms of its functional value for man. A flower garden is praised because ingeniously selected planting provides for continuous bloom from March until October; it makes the poet wish that "I, too, in good weather and bad, may show this or that which is pleasant." Nature without relation to human civilization is no longer of any interest. Observing smoke rising from the chimney of a little house on the lake, Brecht makes the significant comment that "if it were missing / how wretched then would be / the house and trees and lake." The poet has gone full circle; the shrill lament of anarchy has been subdued to the muted song of civilization; Baal has become Horace.

If we look back to Brecht's beginnings, follow the full range of his lyrical statements, and compare him with his contemporaries, we can now conclude that he occupies a rather exceptional place in his own native literature. While the traditional development of a German poet starts with an appreciation of Greek culture, continues along the milestones of Goethe and Schiller and the Romantic movement, and finally leads — mainly by way of Nietzsche and the French Symbolists — to an extremely individualistic and intellectualized lyrical idiom, Brecht's preference for Roman civilization, his love for Anglo–Saxon writers and places, his Chinese orientation resulting in a conscious adoption of aloofness and ceremonial politeness place him outside of the mainstream. I cannot agree with H. R. Hays when he states: "His genius for absorption is phenomenal and yet, at bottom, he is a traditional German poet still keeping alive the spirit of Heine."[21] While it is true that the early Brecht, like Heine, frequently used folk songs for his own adaptations and also came to the same painful rejection of the German Romantic spirit, Hays ought to know that it is precisely such a similarity that would exclude Brecht from being "a traditional German poet." It is a fact that Heine has remained suspect to German professors for political as well as racial reasons until today — witness the recent decision by the civic leaders of his native Düsseldorf *not* to name the new university after him. Brecht and Heine are the only two first-rate German poets who were also politically motivated to a high degree; they even shared the rare distinction of paying for their convictions with the hardship of exile abroad.

Looking beyond Brecht's native bonds and trying to assess his poetry from the perspective of world literature, we find that his very extensive, politically inspired verse-making makes him just as unique as he appeared to his countrymen. With few exceptions, the voice of the modern poet is highly personal and individualistic, generally sophisticated and intellectual, often metaphysical and esoteric. This is as true of the non-Germans Valéry, Eliot, Pound, Pasternak, E. E. Cummings, Auden, and many others, as it is of Hofmannsthal, George, Rilke, and Benn in Austria and Germany. Therefore, I agree with Hays when he continues: "Brecht is almost the only social poet writing today, the only social poet whose form and matter coincide, the only political poet in the proper sense of the word."[22] Commenting on the songs Brecht composed, either to his own tunes or set to music by renowned composers like Weill and Eisler, and sung by marching workers in many countries, Hays sums up Brecht's extraordinary contribution by adding: "They have enjoyed a popularity nothing short of amazing in an age in which poetry has tended to become more and more the concern of a few specialists."

There is another quality which, in my opinion, distinguishes Brecht's poetry from [that of] most other modern writers; it is to some extent already implicit in what was just stated. I am referring to his concept of functional poetry, first observed in the introduction to *Die Hauspostille* and symbolizing the subordination of the poet's persona to a higher purpose. This tendency, at first only mockingly admitted under the disguise of parody, gradually became stronger and more deliberate. It betrays a willingness to suppress the idiosyncrasies of the ego, a conscious effort to curb the excesses of bourgeois individualism which are felt to become obsolete in the expected and hoped-for times to come. The adoption of rhymeless verse with irregular rhythms by an eminently musical poet who possessed a natural facility for easy rhyming; the relentless search for a neoclassic style devoid of purely decorative wordage; the self-denial of metaphoric richness and linguistic beauty by a master of the German tongue without contemporary equal; epigrammatic concise-ness achieved by a new thought-compressing technique; the deliberate avoidance of the purely personal and autobiographical as he grew older — all these characteristics of Brecht's mature verse make him a unique phenomenon in contemporary world literature. He is the first consciously and intentionally nonindividualistic poet of our time. Future historians will have to decide whether this label will make Brecht the iconoclastic outsider in a highly individualistic and bourgeois tradition or the pioneer-ing genius of a less individualistic future age with a more collective consciousness. Nobody, however, will deny that he was always motivated by deepest societal concerns and wielded his pen with the strength of moral conviction and extraordinary poetic inspiration. . . . Willett's prediction is likely to become true: "This may well be the most surprising thing of all for the English-language reader: to find that Brecht, whom Anglo-Saxons have been brought up to think of as a rather limited writer, has such a thoroughly equipped verse workshop under his hat."[23] As is to be expected, it was the master himself who best characterized the desired effect of his poetry with a few lines of utmost simplicity. Contemplating a picture of dried roots of Chinese tea plants which resembled the shape of a lion, Brecht wrote, three years before his death:

> The bad ones are fearful of your claws.
> The good ones are delighted with your charm.
> Something like this
> I would like to be said
> Of my own verse.
>   [Translated by C. Hill]

Notes

1. John Willett . . . ["The Poet Beneath the Skin,"] *Brecht Heute — Brecht Today*, Jahrbuch der internationalen Brecht Gesellschaft II (1972), pp. 88–104.

2. [Ed. note: Bertolt Brecht, *Poems 1913–1956*, ed. John Willett and Ralph Manheim with the co-operation of Erich Fried (New York: Methuen, 1976). See also Stephen Spender, "The Poet of Dark Times," in this volume.]

3. [Ed. note: Bertolt Brecht, *Gedichte*, vols. 8–10 of *Gesammelte Werke in 20 Bänden* (Frankfurt am Main: Suhrkamp, 1967); see also *Gesammelte Werke*, Supplementband III–IV: *Gedichte aus dem Nachlaß* (Frankfurt am Main: Suhrkamp, 1982); and the forthcoming *Gedichte*, vols. 11–15 of *Werke. Große kommentierte Berliner und Frankfurter Ausgabe*, 30 vols., ed. Werner Hecht, Jan Knopf, Werner Mittenzwei, and Klaus-Detlef Müller (Frankfurt am Main: Suhrkamp, 1988–).]

4. Brecht, *Manual of Piety*, bilingual edition, trans. Eric Bentley (New York: Grove Press, 1966), and Bertolt Brecht, *Selected Poems*, trans. H. R. Hays (New York: Grove Press, 1959), now a Brace paperback. [Ed. note: the present essay was written before the publication of *Poems* (see n. 2, above).]

5. This and the preceding quotation from Willy Haas, *Bertolt Brecht* (Berlin: Colloquium Verlag, 1958), p. 41. My translation. [Ed. note: see also Willy Haas, *Bert Brecht*, trans. Max Knight and Joseph Fabry (New York: Ungar, 1970).]

6. Bentley in *Manual of Piety*, p. xi.

7. [Ed. note: the German originals have been omitted here.]

8. A more penetrating analysis of this poem, linking it with a similar "Moritat" by Wedekind and the use of the grotesque, is to be found in an article by Ulrich Weisstein in *The German Quarterly*, XLV (March 1972), pp. 295–310.

9. Brecht got to know Rimbaud's poem "Le bateau ivre" through K. L. Ammer, who had translated it as "Das trunkene Schiff." Ammer's translation of Villon had inspired many songs of *Die Dreigroschenoper* [*The Threepenny Opera*]. . . .

10. Carl Zuckmayer, *Als wär's ein Stück von mir* (Frankfurt: S. Fischer, 1971), p. 375.

11. Brecht, *Über Lyrik* (Frankfurt: edition Suhrkamp No. 70), p. 14. My translation.

12. Bentley in *Manual of Piety*, p. xi.

13. Brecht, lines 7 and 8 of the poem "An die Nachgeborenen," written in 1938. . . .

14. "On Rhymeless Verse with Irregular Rhythms," in John Willett, *Brecht on Theatre* (New York: Hill & Wang, 1964), p. 116.

15. *Ibid.*, p. 117.

16. Reported by Walter Jens in his edition of *Ausgewählte Gedichte* (Frankfurt: edition Suhrkamp No. 86, 1964), p. 89.

17. *Ibid.*

18. The complete translated title of this ballad, one of Brecht's finest, would read: "Legend about the Origin of the Book *Taoteking* on Lao-Tze's Road into Emigration."

19. The false statement by the bishop can also be seen as Brecht's application of the estrangement effect to his poetry: the startled reader must supply the correct conclusion.

20. The aging and ailing Brecht often relaxed and recuperated in his lakeside cottage in the suburban village of Buckow.

21. Brecht, *Selected Poems*, trans. H. R. Hays, p. 8.

22. *Ibid.*, p. 3.

23. John Willett, "The Poet Beneath the Skin," in *Brecht Heute — Brecht Today*, II (1972), p. 103.

Epic Theatre: A Theatre for the Scientific Age

Arrigo Subiotto*

The most common term used to characterize Brecht's dramatic theory and practice is "epic theatre," one that Brecht himself defined and promoted from the late 1920s. In subsequent years he attempted to vary and refine this description, partly because of the broad generalizations it engendered, partly because of shifts in his own attitudes to theatre. "Dialectical" and "scientific" were adjectives he introduced from about 1938 to adumbrate his modified and more sophisticated theatrical practice from then on. Yet "epic" does adequately embrace the major premises of Brecht's theatre. This seeks, through careful choice of theme and formal structural means, to inculcate in the audience the detached, distancing attitude of the historian towards the events portrayed. The intention of epic theatre is thus not only to present a situation but to surprise the audience into a fresh and critical appreciation of the causes and processes underlying what is enacted.

"Epic" is, of course, a generic label for a mode of literature that has always been contrasted, for convenience, to the lyric and dramatic forms. Though it is manifestly impossible to say that a piece of writing must be purely lyrical or narrative or dramatic — there are many celebrated works that mingle the genres — it is helpful to bear in mind the dominant characteristics of a genre that particularly reflect the perspective of the author and influence the formal structure of what he writes. Thus the lyrical mode is subjective, focusing on the poet's personal feelings and reactions to external reality. The dramatic aims at the enactment of incidents and events between individuals, generally structured to involve a conflict and its solution. The author is excluded in so far as the action is cast totally in dialogue between the characters. The epic mode is regarded as the most objective; the author excludes himself from the work but is present in the form of a narrator who conveys events through description and comment. The tense of the epic tends to be past, its span often of considerable length, both in narrated and narrative time. From the *Gesta Romanorum* and the medieval lays to the modern novel the epic has appeared to be the most objective literary representation of external reality positing, as it does, an author and audience in a detached, observing relationship to the events and characters portrayed. Dictionary definitions tend to emphasize the narrative aspect with its concomitant distance from the action. In common parlance, too, the use of the epithet "epic" implies a large-scale, panoramic span of events often covering a person's life or even several generations; essential to this is the vantage-point of the spectator standing outside the action and able to see it in its totality.

*From *Brecht in Perspective*, ed. Graham Bartram and Anthony White (London and New York: Longman, 1982), 30-44. Reprinted by permission of the publisher.

The formal aspects of epic detachment and narration are, however, only starting-points for the fundamental changes Brecht and others wished to achieve in the drama. He recognized and appreciated the tradition of epic narration in a dramatic context, from Shakespeare to crude fairground presentations of historical personages and their deeds. But these were still only a matter of technique, not of deliberate and systematic intention; that is to say, representation — not illumination — was still the aim. In 1938 Brecht wrote as the opening sentence to his important essay, *The Street-Scene: Basic Model for an Epic Theatre:* "In the decade and a half that followed the World War a comparatively new way of acting was tried out in a number of German theatres. Its qualities of clear description and reporting and its use of choruses and projections as a means of commentary earned it the name 'epic.' " (*GW* 16:546; *Theatre* 121, adapted).[1] It is true that Brecht consistently acknowledged the immense debt of the epic theatre to the pioneering work of the Naturalist movement a generation earlier, particularly in making social and political questions the explicit theme of literature. The impetus derived from the new topics of the great French bourgeois novelists began to penetrate the stage. Nevertheless, Naturalism never went beyond a surface realism and simply replaced "fate" by "heredity and environment": "A crude and superficial realism which never revealed the deeper connections. . . . The environment was regarded as part of nature, unchangeable and inescapable" (*GW* 15:214).

The systematic experimentation in the 1920s aimed at a coherent use of theatre as a social art and to that end the epic drama was most actively promoted in Erwin Piscator's political theatre. Brecht almost certainly had Piscator's productions in mind when he wrote the opening sentence of *The Street-Scene*, but although he often praised them he never perhaps sufficiently indicated how they pioneered many elements of his own drama. The reason for this may indeed lie in the fact that Piscator was solely a producer, while Brecht, as a dramatist, viewed theatrical presentation more as the creator of imaginary persons and situations. Piscator's concept of political drama was clear and forcefully formulated and practised: the task of the theatre was "to intervene actively in contemporary events" by instructing and altering the audience. He saw three stages in this process of opening the spectator's eyes — *Kenntnis, Erkenntnis, Bekenntnis* (knowledge, understanding, conviction) — and, like Brecht, he sought fresh formal means of dramatic presentation to achieve this goal. The aim of exposing "objectively" the workings of society, the desire to alter the spectator's consciousness, and shared political convictions made for close parallels between Piscator's political and Brecht's epic theatre.

Brecht's first and best-known contribution to a systematic theory of epic theatre appeared in 1930 in his notes to the opera *Rise and Fall of the City of Mahagonny*.[2] This was the culmination of his prolonged polemic against the established theatre that, in his opinion, was solely interested in selling superficial, mindless entertainment and side-stepped the serious concerns of the day. He called this theatre "culinary," as it was no more mentally stimulating than was the eating of food. At this stage, and unlike Piscator who identified the function of epic theatre in a more aggressively political manner, Brecht concentrated on differentiating between the modern epic theatre and the "dramatic" theatre he wanted it to oust. Thus, in his famous tabulation in the *Mahagonny* notes he compiled a list of contrasts between Aristotelian and non-Aristotelian forms of drama that, despite his cautionary footnote that these were not mutually exclusive characteristics but rather "shifts of accent," was taken to be the assertion of a new dramatic dogma. In 1938 Brecht had to revise his tabulation "because of possible misunderstandings," toning down the starkness of his initial formulation but with no radical alteration. If one remembers Brecht's caution that he was not promulgating total rejection of the "dramatic" theatre, these notes do offer a lucid outline of the tendency in epic theatre towards an "open" form that differed in a marked degree from the "closed" structure of traditional classical theatre. The contrasts relate to three main areas: the "hero" or human being as the subject of drama, the structure of the play, and the spectator. With unerring theatrical instinct Brecht unconsciously identified the crucial aspects of a drama (theme, presentation, reception) and centred his proposed changes on these. The principle that linked all three aspects into a coherent whole was the idea of *process*, that nothing is determined, absolute and fixed, but subject to influence and change. Thus Brecht attacked the prevailing conception that the hero (and all human beings) possess innate characteristics that cannot be altered by circumstances, a nature that determines his behaviour ineluctably. The consequent irresolvable conflict between the "fixed" hero and the world, which is the stuff of classical drama, was rejected by Brecht as inappropriate and unrealistic; in its place he posited a hero subject to alteration and development, adapting to society but also by his actions changing society. The notion that "social being determines thought" with all its consequences derives of course from Marx's premise that being determines consciousness and not the reverse, as in classical Kantian philosophy.

Brecht created a dramatic form to match this view of the hero by breaking down the "evolutionary inevitability" of the classical play. Instead of the inextricable interrelation of scenes where none could be omitted — a sort of organic absolute entirely enclosed in itself — Brecht allowed each scene or episode to stand independently as evidence of a process taking place rather than a psychic revelation of character. The autonomy of the separate parts of a play enabled Brecht to select such material as offered an "assembled" explanatory presentation of people's behaviour. Instead of embodying or simulating a situation, the stage was to narrate it, with all the detachment that this implies. Indeed, it was this detachment that perhaps most concerned Brecht and has been commonly taken as the hallmark of his theatre. Certainly, Brecht castigated the established bourgeois theatre in the 1920s for encouraging the spectator to leave his reasoning powers with his hat and coat in the cloakroom and enter the darkened auditorium simply to engage in a trance-like orgy of feeling, as if he were drugged. Brecht blamed the overemphasis on empathy for this, since it led to the pretence that the events and feelings being purveyed on the stage were real and encouraged the spectator to identify totally with them; he would wallow in emotions and would leave the theatre no more enlightened than before. Brecht had far more active designs on the spectator: he wanted him to use his critical faculties in assessing what was being enacted, and gain insights from this process that would influence his own further thinking, that is, alter his consciousness. Thus Brecht sought in the first instance to inculcate in the spectator the attitude of the observing historian who, however excited he may be by them, can stand back from the passions of personalities, register events and evidence, and come to a reasoned conclusion about a situation. But he also viewed the spectator as a person to be influenced and changed, so that the educative, instructive thrust of epic theatre, which was deliberately designed to convey an understanding of the causes underlying what was depicted, opened into a wider perspective than the play itself and aimed at "arousing the spectator's capacity for action" or, in other words, altering his consciousness.

By the time Brecht came to revise his table of contrasts he no longer needed to define his type of drama by setting it against the Aristotelian model. After five years of exile he had lost contact with the live German theatre and was embarking on a period of intensive theoretical writing. In that same year he set out in *The Street-Scene* his view of the essentials of epic theatre. Whereas earlier it could be inferred that the epic theatre was clearly best suited to dealing with social and political problems, public matters, Brecht now went further, unequivocally defining its function and purpose entirely in a political context: "Supporters of this epic theatre argued that the new subject-matter, the highly involved incidents of the class war in its acutest and most terrible stage, would be mastered more easily by such a method, since it would thereby become possible to portray social processes in their causal relationships" (*GW* 16:546; *Theatre* 121, adapted). But he adds that these experiments raised a number of substantial difficulties for aesthetics. *The Street-Scene* seems therefore to have been written to establish a close link between the practical goals of epic theatre and the expectations of traditional aesthetics. As an example of completely "natural" epic theatre Brecht takes " . . . an incident such as can be seen at any street corner: an eyewitness demonstrating to a collection of people how a traffic accident took place. The bystanders may not have observed what happened, or they may simply not agree with him, may 'see things a different way'; the point is that the demonstrator acts the behaviour of driver or victim or both in such a way that the bystanders are able to form an opinion about the accident" (*GW* 16:546; *Theatre* 121).

It is evident that this mundane scene that can happen spontaneously far from the aura of "theatre" nevertheless has, as Brecht claimed, a fundamental theatrical structure: the demonstrator (actor) re-enacting to bystanders (audience) an accident (dramatic event) so that they may make an assessment and judgement of it, displays all the ingredients of Brecht's epic theatre. If the theatre wished to widen its field and show the driver in other situations besides that of the accident it would in no way exceed its model, but merely create a further situation on the same pattern. The addition rather than integration of scenes is characteristic of epic theatre, as is "the direct changeover from representation to commentary," and a predominant role in this is assigned to the actor. His counterpart in the street-scene, the eyewitness, must eschew perfect imitation and not seduce the bystanders by his "Verwandlungsfähigkeit" ("powers of transformation"); he must also avoid creating pure emotions and engendering illusion, so that his audience is fully aware that here is a repetition, not a pretence of the real thing. Coupled with this is the natural attitude adopted by the demonstrator in two senses: he *is* himself *showing* the behaviour of the driver. It is also typical of the epic theatre that the demonstrator must derive his characters entirely from their actions. What aspects of the character's behaviour he gives, how thoroughly he has to imitate, is determined by his purpose; and it is his point of view (a "committed" one, because he sees the accident in a certain light) that gives the perspective on what features of the driver's behaviour are to be picked out. In this respect the demonstrator assumes the functions of both playwright and actor in a theatrical context.

The final element that concludes this basic model of epic theatre is its practical aim. It is by no means thought of as an autonomous event giving gratuitous pleasure, rather it is intended to convey information and produce a result. The street-scene might, for instance, be transferred to a court room (and how often is the pattern of a court case the core of a Brecht play!) where a judge and jury hear evidence, weigh it up and reach a decision as to the apportionment of blame and punishment. The concluding sentences of *The Street-Scene* stress the practical social application of both the compact street-corner vignette and the complex inventions of epic theatre on the stage:

> Our street-corner theatre is primitive; origins, aims and methods of its performance are close to home. But there is no doubt that it is a meaningful phenomenon with a clear social function that dominates all its elements. The performance's origins lie in an incident that can be judged in different ways, that may repeat itself in different forms and is not finished but is bound to have consequences, so that this judgement has some significance. . . . The epic theatre is a highly skilled theatre with complex contents and far-reaching social objectives. In setting up

the street-scene as a basic model for it, we pass on the clear social
function and give the epic theatre criteria by which to decide whether
an incident is meaningful or not. (*GW* 16:557-58; *Theatre* 128,
adapted)

One of the key elements of epic theatre that was to become indissolubly
associated with Brecht's theatre and a commonplace of twentieth-century
drama in general, the alienation effect [estrangement effect],[3] was first
described in 1935 in Brecht's essay, *Alienation Effects in Chinese Acting*
(*GW* 16:619-31; *Theatre* 91-99), although it had been part and parcel of
his practice from much earlier (e.g. in the prologue and epilogue spoken
by the actors in *The Exception and the Rule*, 1929). In *The Street-Scene* it
is given one of many later formulations, as "a technique of taking the
human social incidents to be portrayed and labelling them as something
striking, something that calls for explanation, and is not to be taken for
granted, not just natural. The object of this 'effect' is to allow the spectator
to criticize constructively from a social point of view" (*GW* 16:553;
Theatre 125, adapted). As a technique the alienation effect can be easily
identified, especially in Brecht's later plays, for it emerges in the major
areas of the theatrical experience: in the play's structure, the disposition
and contrasting of scenes and episodes; in the language, the conflict of
dialogue and the contradictions highlighted between the speech and
actions of the characters; in the actor's effort to play at being and to stand
outside a character; and in the handling of "sister" arts such as music,
lighting and scenic design in a stage production. But the alienation effect
in Brecht's theatre is not confined to formal techniques, a vehicle for the
author's message (it was exploited in this mechanical way, as Brecht noted,
by assorted playwrights like Thornton Wilder and Paul Claudel); it is
simultaneously the content itself, namely the matter the author is structur-
ing and his perspective on it. The social content that operates in the same
way as the technique of alienation is the *Gestus*, a term Brecht devised to
denote the essential theme of an incident, a scene, a whole play, and
which he also defined in the mid-1930s: "Not all gests are social gests. The
attitude of chasing away a fly is not yet a social gest, though the attitude of
chasing away a dog may be one, for instance if it expresses a badly dressed
man's continual battle against watchdogs . . . the social gest is . . . the gest
that allows conclusions to be drawn about the social circumstances" (*GW*
15:483-84; *Theatre* 104, adapted). Later, in . . . [*A*] *Short Organum* [*for
the Theatre*] (*GW* 16:661-700; *Theatre* 179-205) Brecht indicated how the
Gestus arises from the interaction of people, their attitudes and behaviour
towards each other. The "hands up!" *Gestus* in *Arturo Ui* as a sign of fear,
surrender and total agreement or acquiescence, the figure of Shen Te
"split" into pregnant woman and bloated capitalist in *The Good Person of
Szechwan*, the predictably unpredictable behaviour of the drunk-sober
Herr Puntila are examples of alienations that denote the social *Gestus*
exposing the contradictions in society. Thus the integration of content with

the formal means of presenting it is the distinguishing feature of the alienation technique in Brecht's works.

As Brecht in exile became more and more conscious of the complexities of human behaviour and the grey rather than black-and-white tones of social contradictions, the term epic theatre satisfied him less and less and he began to talk of the "dialectical" theatre or theatre of "contradictions." As early as 1930 he had tentatively broached such a title — *Die dialektische Dramatik* — but had found that the appellation "non-Aristotelian" better described at that time his general quarrel with traditional drama. Brecht's intensive study of Marx's dialectical materialism in 1926 bore fruit for his drama in the classic Marxist categories deployed in *S[ain]t Joan of the Stockyards* (1929-30), and — more interestingly — the *Lehrstücke* of the same period. These didactic "learning" plays were an experiment in articulating social and political issues in a simple, lucid but schematic form for the benefit of the performers, not for an audience. The participation of the actors in enacting and discussing a situation was a form of political self-instruction fully in accord with the intentions of epic theatre. But this unique type of drama (unique despite its echoes of the Jesuit instructional play of the seventeenth century) was ahead of its time and not easily transferable to the traditional theatre, and Brecht was clearly not yet ready to launch his drama into a new phase after dropping the ballast of the past. He needed the confidence and authority of experience to cut loose into fresh ground and propose a new general theory. This came at the time of writing his cluster of major plays between 1938 and 1943 with the bulk of the *Messingkauf* dialogues (1939-40),[4] subsequently more succinctly ordered in the *Short Organum* of 1948. In an addendum to the *Short Organum* in 1954 and in *Dialectics in the Theatre* (1956; *GW* 16:867-941), Brecht referred repeatedly to the imprecision and rigidity that the term "epic" theatre now suffered from and the need for a more adequate label: "The attempt will be made here to describe the application of materialist dialectic in the theatre. It appears increasingly important to elaborate on the content implicit in the term 'epic theatre.' . . . An effort is now being made to move on from the epic theatre to the dialectical theatre. In our view and according to our intention the epic theatre's practice — and the whole idea — were by no means undialectical. Nor would a dialectical theatre succeed without the epic element" (*GW* 16:923).[5] Brecht was clearly aware that epic theatre had come to be associated almost exclusively with formal aspects, focusing particularly on structural differences from traditional plays. His concern was to re-establish the significance of contradiction and dialectics in the content as well as the external mechanics of drama. Dialectics shifts the centre of gravity back to the ideas of society (political, economic, sociological) that see society as an organic process of men's living together in continual flux and change. Hence the less dogmatic, more flexible and ambiguous structures of the plays Brecht wrote after he left Germany compared with the relatively rigid illustrations of Marxist theory he favoured in the late Weimar Republic.

A further designation that Brecht used increasingly was "theatre of a scientific age," though he felt that this, too, was not broad enough and perhaps already "verschmutzt" ("contaminated") by the problem of the social and moral responsibility of science. In the prologue to the *Short Organum* Brecht calls for scientifically exact representations of human society in the theatre and several times later refers to contemporary men as "the children of a scientific age," for our life has come to be determined by the sciences to a new and formidable extent. Sections 15 and 16 describe tersely the broad sweep of technological invention that has enabled man to make great strides towards the mastery of his environment. But Brecht accuses the bourgeoisie, brought to power by science, not only of appropriating the wealth generated by technological progress but of actively preventing the application of the sciences to the study of society, " . . . another area where darkness still reigns, namely that of the relations between people involved in the exploitation and conquest of nature. . . . The new approach to nature was not applied to society" (*GW* 16:669; *Theatre* 184). Thus the technological ability to make this planet fit to live on has outstripped its social structures, and the bourgeois class knows very well ". . . that its rule would come to an end if the scientific eye were turned on its own undertakings. And so that new science which was founded about 100 years ago and deals with the character of human society was born in the struggle between rulers and ruled" (*GW* 16:670; *Theatre* 185). Science, for Brecht, is now *social* science; here he refers unambiguously to dialectical materialism, first formulated by Marx in the mid-nineteenth century and claimed by its adherents to be the most comprehensive "scientific socialism." Brecht looks to the working classes, the "true children of the scientific age," to apply the tool of political and sociological investigation and achieve an advance in the organization of society.

Although Brecht argued that it was no longer possible to devise accurate "representations of men's life together" without an understanding of the social sciences, he was careful not to shackle the dramatist. The roles of science and art are complementary in contributing to the well-being of mankind, "the one setting out to maintain, the other to entertain us" (*GW* 16:670; *Theatre* 185). With this Brecht introduces a dominant theme which pervades the *Short Organum* and his later pronouncements: the need for *Genuss* (enjoyment) in the theatre, that echoes and reinforces the enjoyment of thinking, of teaching and enquiring, of solving problems, of mastering reality. The moment of "enjoyment" was always latent in his work, but emerges unequivocally in the *Short Organum*, associated closely with the idea of *Produktivität*: "What is that productive attitude in face of nature and of society which we children of a scientific age would like to adopt for our own pleasure in our theatre? The attitude is a critical one.

Faced with a river, it consists in regulating the river, . . . faced with society, in turning society upside down" (GW 16:671; Theatre 185, adapted).

The productive critical approach that the theatre's models of reality must arouse in the audience is like "that detached view, . . . both difficult and productive" with which Galileo observed a swinging chandelier. Needless to say, this is achieved "by a technique of alienating the familiar" which, as Brecht had earlier described in New Technique of Acting (1940; GW 15:341-57; Theatre 136-47), science had developed for the purpose of analysing the familiar and achieving results, and which could be as productive in art. In contrast to his earlier more passive definitions of the alienation effect as a formal means of facilitating understanding of a situation, Brecht now stresses the impulse to intervention that it carries: "The new alienations are only designed to free socially conditioned phenomena from that stamp of familiarity which protects them against our grasp today" (GW 16:681; Theatre 192). Brecht's aim is not simply to release the "intimidated, credulous, hypnotized mass" from its thraldom in the auditorium of the traditional theatre, but actively to affect its presuppositions, assumptions, thinking processes.

There is thus an important distinction to be drawn between the detached, observing, "clinical" attitude of the natural scientist and Brecht's ideal critical stance of the spectator in the theatre. To illustrate this distinction, Brecht on more than one occasion referred to the phenomenon known to physicists as the Heisenberg Uncertainty Principle, which he understood as acknowledging the impossibility of obtaining totally "natural" conditions in which to conduct experiments: the very presence of instruments and observer affects the object under scrutiny and any measurement of a system must disturb the system under observation, with a resulting distortion and lack of precision in measurement. Brecht sees this instead as a positive virtue in his dramatic representations of reality. In the Messingkauf dialogues the Philosopher describes the phenomenon and relates it to the observation of society: "This is what happens when instruments observe, what could happen when human beings are the observers?" (GW 16:576-77; Dialogues 50, adapted). And in The Refugee Dialogues too Brecht has his physicist Ziffel describe the Heisenberg Uncertainty Principle and ironically make the connection between the physical and social worlds: "There appear to be similar phenomena in social life. The investigation of social processes does not leave these processes untouched but influences them quite strongly. It operates without doubt in a revolutionary manner. This is probably why influential groups are so slow to encourage deeper investigations in the social field" (GW 14:1420). Undoubtedly Brecht strove to induce in the spectator a detached, observant approach to the depiction on stage, but it was only objective in that it depended as much on the spectator's reasoning faculties as his emotions. A major intention of the Short Organum is to indicate ways in which Brecht's "scientific" theatre can be harnessed to change the consciousness of the audience and hence facilitate the altering of the reality that is reflected on the stage.

The keynote of this scientific theatre is then change. Whereas the theatre as we know it shows the structure of society depicted on stage as incapable of being influenced by society (in the auditorium), Brecht calls for a type of theatre that generates new thoughts and feelings in the spectator and leaves him productively disposed, even after the spectacle is over. The uncertainty principle that would have a deleterious, distorting effect in scientific observation is positively striven for as an active corrective in Brecht's theatre—the desired aim is that the audience *should* intervene in the processes of society and should itself change its own thinking. The renowned detachment of the spectator in epic theatre has in the first instance the quality of the historian's critical view of events: he reenacts them through description and indicates their relevance and significance through comment. This bifocal perspective is retained by Brecht through the manipulation of his material by means of alienation techniques; but while the insight into society is being mediated, the emancipatory dimension simultaneously comes into play and the audience is encouraged to adopt an actively critical stance towards the representation on stage. The audience is put into a position to see more than the protagonists, to grasp the wider context, to assess the evidence presented and adopt an attitude as to its significance. The spectator is thus not regarded as just the passive recipient of a description of circumstances, however naturalistic, but as an active and integral component of the total process of a play.

The dismemberment of social processes which lies at the core of Brecht's idea of scientific theatre rests, of course, on his confident belief in the causal nexus in society and in the possibility of analysing all social phenomena and explaining them rationally. From about 1926 Brecht had clearly agreed with and incorporated into his own arsenal Marx's postulate (formulated in the sixth Feuerbach thesis) that the human being is the sum of social circumstances ("das Ensemble der gesellschaftlichen Verhältnisse") and that there is a dialectical relationship between the individual and his social context leading to continual reciprocal change in both: "The concept of man as a function of his milieu and of the milieu as a function of man, in other words the resolution of the milieu into relationships between people, is the product of a new kind of thinking—historical thinking." The historical or dialectical materialism of Marxism Brecht here refers to envisages the human being only in a specific historical context, and it can quickly fall into the trap of a rigid mechanistic view of the interaction of individual and society and lead to a behaviouristic, socio-economic determinism, leaving no room at all for the essence of life, individual difference and unpredictable human actions. While retaining his faith in the rational analysis of social relationships,

Brecht did nevertheless modify a tendency around 1930 to attribute socio-economic explanations to all human actions, and acknowledged in his later work idiosyncratic contradictions in the behaviour of individuals. The complex reactions of Azdak, Grusche, Shen Te, Mutter Courage, Puntila, Galileo to their situations and fellow human beings are rich in contrasts that defy resolution by causal explanations of society.

Brecht's later plays have little to do with historical authenticity and nothing whatever with naturalism. Indeed, his dominant preoccupations became the parable form and realism which, paradoxically, are intimately connected. In a revealing work-diary entry of 30 March 1947 Brecht went to the lengths of setting out in tabular form — as he had done for epic and dramatic — some contrasts between naturalism and realism, the former being merely a "surrogate" realism.[6] Some of these distinctions illuminate Brecht's dramatic thinking and methods. His predilection for the parable, for instance, facilitated the "stylization" of reality and gave him the freedom to devise models of society that, unhampered by historical facts, could be structured at will to incorporate the didactic message with maximum impact. While the parable lacked the force of actual historical concreteness, Brecht was well aware that it had a vicarious authenticity that accommodates the author's intent, namely a clarification of the "system." In the last year of his life Brecht vigorously defended this quality of the parable in conversation with Ernst Schumacher: " . . . while abstracting it is nevertheless concrete since it opens our eyes to what is essential."[7] For all that he denied that there was an aesthetic dimension to theatre independent of its social content, Brecht recognized and exploited the fact that a fictional representation exercises the imagination and breadth of perspective more readily than the circumscribed real event. The aesthetic moment does indeed figure prominently in Brecht's dramaturgy and the *Short Organum* is permeated by the twin purposes of *Unterhaltung* and *Unterricht* (the classical "dulce et utile," "plaire et instruire"); the attaining of these goals by engaging both the intellect and the emotions of the audience is the enjoyment of realism generated by the theatre.

Time after time Brecht defined realism as a productive, "scientifically" analytical attitude towards reality rather than a recognizable imitation of the world, and he formulated specific guidelines of realistic art: "laying bare society's causal network / showing up the dominant viewpoint as the viewpoint of the dominators / writing from the standpoint of the class which has prepared the broadest solutions for the most pressing problems afflicting human society / emphasizing the dynamics of development / concrete and so as to encourage abstraction" (*GW* 19:326; *Theatre* 109). The clarity of the definition does put into relief one of the limitations of Brecht's epic theatre, in practice if not in theory, namely that it depends entirely on the acceptance of a particular political philosophy, Marxist dialectical materialism; any other springboard would result in a purely formalistic employment of epic techniques. Brecht himself admitted in 1955 that actors and audience needed to share the Marxist politics of the dramatist for the epic theatre to make sense. The question then has to be asked: is the epic theatre limited to refining and reinforcing the already existent historical approach, the realistically critical attitude of a Marxist audience? A further constraint of the epic theatre is its necessary predilection for "public" subject-matter that facilitates the exposure of the social structures and processes, with a consequent denial or disregard of private concerns and the intractable behaviour of individuals. Brecht's avowed practical aim of changing society by influencing the audience also restricts the constructs of reality presented on stage: "The epic theatre is chiefly interested in the attitudes which people adopt towards one another, wherever they are socio-historically significant (typical). It works out scenes where people adopt attitudes of such a sort that the social laws under which they are acting spring into sight" (*GW* 15:474; *Theatre* 86).

These programmatic limitations are both a weakness and a strength of Brecht's theatre. On the one hand, he deliberately eschewed traditional psychological drama, the delineation of the subtle interplay of personal relationships for their own sake; this he saw as the nugatory business of the bourgeois "entertainment emporia." On the other, he strove to realize his vision of an audience gripped by the scientific, objective logic of the truths about society elicited by him on the stage, an audience exercising its intellectual faculties to understand and be enlightened by the manner and matter of the telling, and revelling in the enjoyment of both thought and feeling aroused by the images of society set forth before it. The vision and the reality may be poles apart, for the statistics show that by far the most popular Brecht plays in East German theatres since 1945 have been *Señora Carrar's Rifles*, *The Threepenny Opera* and *Herr Puntila and his Servant Matti*, all with considerable "entertainment" value and none an obvious model of scientific theatre. It is indisputable, however, that at the theoretical and exemplary level at least Brecht has powerfully influenced drama wherever it is socially and politically conscious, as the widespread currency of the epithet "Brechtian" testifies.

Notes

1. [Ed. note: volume and page references are to Bertolt Brecht, *Gesammelte Werke in 20 Bänden* (Frankfurt am Main: Suhrkamp, 1967), hereafter cited as *GW*. Quotations from Brecht's major theoretical writings in the original have been omitted here, notes have been revised and expanded, and titles of works are generally given in English; English translations are mainly taken or adapted by the author from *Brecht on Theatre. The Development of an Aesthetic*, ed. and trans. John Willett (New York: Hill and Wang, 1964), hereafter cited as *Theatre*.]

2. *GW* 17:1004–16; *Theatre* 33–42. See Ladislaus Löb, "German Drama before

Brecht: From Neo-Classicism to Expressionism," *Brecht in Perspective*, ed. Graham Bartram and Anthony White (London and New York: Longman, 1982), 11–12.

3. [Ed. note: for the proper translation of the term *Verfremdungseffekt*, see, for example, Ernst Bloch, "*Entfremdung, Verfremdung:* Alienation, Estrangement," *Brecht*, ed. Erika Munk (New York: Bantam Books, 1972), 3–11.]

4. *GW* 16:500–657. Bertolt Brecht, *The Messingkauf Dialogues*, trans. John Willett (London: Methuen, 1965). Subsequently cited as *Dialogues*. Willett also provides valuable explanatory notes and dating.

5. See also Bertolt Brecht, *Versuche* 15 (Frankfurt am Main: Suhrkamp, 1956), 78.

6. Bertolt Brecht, *Arbeitsjournal*, 2 vols., ed. Werner Hecht (Frankfurt am Main: Suhrkamp, 1973), 2:780.

7. Ernst Schumacher, "Er wird bleiben," *Erinnerungen an Brecht*, ed. Hubert Witt (Leipzig: Reclam, 1964), 336. [Ed. note: see also *Brecht as They Knew Him*, ed. Hubert Witt, trans. John Peet ([East] Berlin: Seven Seas, 1974), 225.]

Brecht's Dream-Playing: Between Vision and Illusion

Herbert Knust*

In drawing on various sciences to cope with the complexities of twentieth-century life in his art, Brecht was receptive also to modern psychology;[1] but to the chagrin of some critics he favored behaviorism to the exclusion of psychoanalysis, a neglect that cost him an important element of reality, hence: his credibility.[2] Such findings, however, have not prevented critics from psychoanalyzing Brecht and his work.[3]

It is not my intention here to join the psychoanalysts in examining subconscious patterns in Brecht. Rather, I should like to survey Brecht's conscious and frequent use of the dream motif in the various genres of his writing.[4] This aspect has been neglected perhaps *because* of the common association of dreams with the irrational, of dream interpretation with psychoanalysis. In his strategy of revealing the mechanisms of human responses to economic conditioning, introspection means little or nothing to Brecht. As a rationalist pedagogue he appears to have brushed aside the power of the subconscious, as other rationalists had done before him. But even in Freud's theories social strictures play a role in man's psychic conditioning and overt conduct, and Freud himself was a rationalist by virtue of his attempt to analyze subconscious processes in the minutest detail with a view to changing human attitudes by appropriate therapy. As reflexes *and* as stimuli, dreams can be looked at even in "behaviorist" terms.

We may well ask, then, whether the strange nature of dreams, which

*This essay was written specifically for this volume and is published here for the first time by permission of the author.

Freud was the first to investigate scientifically (as he repeatedly claimed), contributed nothing at all to Brecht's theory of estrangement. Even if he doubted the scientific quality of psychoanalysis in general and some of its findings in particular, his specific criticism was directed not so much at analysis as at the professional therapists. From different angles Brecht as well as the psychoanalysts dealt with alienation, censorship, suppression, distortion, and the necessity for a changed consciousness. But whereas Brecht directed such shifts of perception toward a challenge for social change, the therapists, in his view, merely bargained for an awareness that would help to reintegrate the maladjusted into an unchanged society. There, to Brecht, was the rub; there the nightmare did not end but continued, and thus his view of psychotherapists as charlatans and servants of the bourgeoisie.[5]

What, then, about Brecht's use of dreams? Obviously he knew different kinds, conveying good, bad, and mixed experiences. Some are brief and some are elaborate, ranging from single metaphor to complete story in prose or in dialogue. Furthermore, the language of these dreams varies widely, from plain realism and clearcut allegory to ambiguous and seemingly confused symbolic representation requiring different skills of interpretation. Some of the criteria of modern dream analysis (such as censorship, wish fulfillment, day residue, condensation, displacement, dramatization, and elaboration) would also seem to yield insights into Brechtian dream scenes. Indeed, some of Freud's statements on dreamwork sound similar to Brecht's statements on epic technique;[6] yet it is apparent that Brecht's dream scenes are not burdened by overly complicated connections between "manifest"and "latent" dream content. By and large his dreams are overt and appear in logical contexts, conveying specific messages rather than suggesting obscure transfigurations. Still, his dreams confused the critics.

In using dreams as literary devices and in exploring the poetic and pedagogic potential of dream messages for his own purposes, Brecht not only looked at recent scientific findings (many facets of which were not so new after all), but, like a good scientist, he also viewed the historical development of dream interpretation. He could look back—as could Freud—on a long and complex tradition of dream theory nourished by popular beliefs, philosophical speculation, medical interest, and literary imagination. This widespread interest focused on such important issues as religion and superstition, knowledge of the past and prophecy of the future, possibilities and limits of human cognition, assurances of individual and social health and happiness, and on various perceptions of truth and reality.

What must have appealed most to Brecht's own ideological bent were the social implications of dream visions and their dialectic nature both as wishes arising from certain social conditions and as possible guides for future social action. If the "wild beast" theory from Plato to Freud—that

is, dreams as the eruption of man's irrational nature—was unpalatable to
Brecht, and if the enduring "nonpsychological" "mantic" view of dreams
as supernatural visitations was equally suspect to him, then there was still
a long line of thought employing rational and natural criteria to explain
the dream phenomenon and its relation to waking reality, past and future.
On the one hand we have the "materialistic" reasoning on external stimuli,
physiological syndromes, somatic and nervous conditions of dream formation and dream prognosis—from Aristotle via humor theory, Hobbes,
Voltaire to Bergson and post-Freudian dream experimentation. On the
other hand there are the no less challenging arguments about the continuity and coherence of productive mental activity throughout waking and
sleeping stages that allow for heightened awareness and insight through
dreams both retrospectively and prospectively. According to these views,
dreams may lead to vital cognitions and trigger useful thought processes,
not only *despite* but even *because* of the proverbial dream distortions.[7]
Indeed, there was hardly any "enlightened" dream commentator from
Graeco-Roman times through the so-called Age of Reason to our modern
Age of Science who did not include or emphasize the rational capacity of
the dream phenomenon in its interplay with waking reality.

The fundamental alternatives that have marked dream theory from
its earliest documentation to its most recent proverbial usage have qualified dreams as either true or false, depending on their origin. In most
sources seemingly contradictory views exist side by side, even in the more
differentiated typologies of the dream book genre. Most of the Brechtian
evidence plays with the ambiguous nature of dreams between illusion and
prophecy. Illusions are either exposed within the dream itself or after
awakening; visions (and disillusionments) need to be tested, concluded or
acted upon. That is, dreams, mostly emerging from specific causes such as
strife, stress, or distress, are real enough in their visual substance and
concrete experience, but what they project as wish or consequence is
questioned and may become deceptive or curative. Some examples in brief
outline must suffice to indicate the several stages and various techniques in
Brecht's use of the dream motif.

Symptomatic of Brecht's early fascination with visions are the two
versions of "Vulture Tree" (*GW*, 8:31–33; *GW*, 11:13–14). The ferocious
life-and-death battle between tree and vultures causes both sides, in utter
exhaustion, to dream of the tree's immortality—but with a difference: the
tree's vision of hope is the vulture's phantom of horror. At the verge of new
blossoming the tree dies under the leaden weight of vultures and turns into
a spooky dream image. The meaninglessness of the struggle for life in the
face of mortality appears to be the young Brecht's nightmare, whether
expressed in haunting images, stated with nonchalance, or absorbed in
vegetation metamorphosis. It is the shadowy side of the daydream of
resurrection among the "persecuted" and "tired" in his "Holy Saturday
Tale" (*GW*, 8:9), a poem dedicated to the orphaned. Even Baal, whose

unsatiable craving for life develops a sexual leitmotif first introduced in the dream of the inhibited Johannes,[8] answers a wish-dream out of repression. He, too, can trick the vultures of death only temporarily.[9] The dreams of Brecht's early adventurers and solitary drifters end in disillusionment.[10] Consequently, in a state of utter despondency or decay, dreams cease to exist altogether.[11] Or dreams take the form of nightmares, as with the visions of the tortured "Tsingtau Soldier" (GW, 8:11–12); the infested dreams of humanity in "About Fellow Man" (GW, 8:190–92); the depressing dreams of alienation and elimination in the poems from "A Reader for Those Who Live in Cities" (Poems, 131–59 [GW, 8:281]); all of which culminate in an echo from Dante's Inferno: "Give up your dream that they will make an exception in your case" (Poems, 138 [GW, 8:274–75]). But precisely the recurring "infernal" dream scene would undergo a significant change and become a challenge.

With Brecht's emerging ideology and developing literary technique in the late twenties, his wish-dreams and nightmares reflecting unsatisfactory reality or traumatic experience could be politicized and endowed with provocation for change. While specifying social repression as a cause of dreams, Brecht became increasingly interested in their anticipatory function. Dreams arise from situations of suffering such as deprivation, social misery, harassment, persecution, war, and exile. Although Brecht uses the dream motif occasionally for those in power who lust for more — or fear loss of — power, the typical dreamers are not the upper class but the underdogs: the worker, the kitchen maid, the servant, the farmer's wife, the water-seller, the fugitive, the prisoner, the beggar, and the cripple. Apart from revealing the sociopsychological mechanism of these dreams (including internalization of conflicts), their messages now evoke and modify the tradition of dream prophecy. They occur at crucial points within given contexts; for instance, Joan's rebellious dream in Saint Joan of the Slaughterhouses (GW, 2:733–34);[12] the kitchen maid's dream of defiance (GW, 13:945–46), and Fewkoombey's dream of revolt and judgment in Threepenny Novel (GW, 13:1151–65);[13] or the worker Jen's dreams of protest in the fragmentary Tui novel (GW, 12:617–21).

In the dream visit with the banished poets of the past (GW, 9:663–64), Brecht used the old epic motif of the terrifying but instructive descent to the underworld, where the voices of the dead offer advice and warning to the living. In The Trial of Lucullus (CP, 5:99–131) Brecht has transposed and changed the people's "judgment" concerning the field marshal from the elaborate dream scene of the prose version (GW, 11:304–14) to the authoritative verdict by the shadows of the netherworld who represent the authentic voices of history (GW, 4:1445–85). At one point in The Refugee Dialogues Ziffel calls emigration the best school for dialectics. Fugitives, he says, are the best dialecticians, for they are exiles because of change, hence they study nothing but change (GW, 14:1462). Ziffel's formula can be stretched to accommodate Brecht's literary strategy at large, but it seems particularly suitable for pinpointing the dialectic nature of Brechtian dream scenes as stages of productive alienation between past and future—alien in content and estranging in effect. In these dreams, buried or subdued voices speak out and significant messages are revealed: the gravestone of the unknown soldier of the revolution (*Poems*, 227 [*GW*, 9:547]) begins to speak; the dreams of the exiled prisoner revive obscured images from the past (*GW*, 9:591); the exiled fugitive, awakening from a "German" nightmare with relief, comes to the double awareness: "I was in a foreign land" (*Poems, 348* [*GW*, 9:818]); the voices of dead friends in a dream surprise the conscience of the survivor (*Poems*, 392 [*GW*, 10:882]); and so forth.

The most "telling" dream scene in Brecht's exile poetry, next to the poets' voices from the other world, is the "Dream About a Great Grumbler" (*Poems*, 294–95 [*GW*, 9:694–95]). It projects a political warning in bizarre but poignant dramatization, using dream distortion for satirical effect. At a time of great food shortages there arises the vision of a huge potato, whose voice competes with Hitler's rhetoric and shows by rapid shrinking what will happen if Hitler is elected. This is "epic theater" within a dream: concrete, instructional, and provocative. The scene of the vanishing potato as the rationalizing, narrative demonstrator on the public square in juxtaposition to Hitler's emotional raving in the opera not only challenges a curative awakening but also exposes the operatic theater scene as a deception. In the "estranging" dream prophecy the potato appears as a secularized soothsayer, as an economic message from the underground, and as the voice for the people.

From this satiric dream scene it is only a short step to Brecht's dream dramaturgy, the contradictory nature of which it helps to explain. In his programmatic poem "The Theater, Home of Dreams" (*Poems*, 340 [*GW*, 9:775–76]), Brecht exposes emotional theater at large as a heedlessly concocted drug-dream. He calls it a false world sadly distorted by wishes and fears, a theater of escapist visions perpetuating a bad life instead of provoking change by decisive action. It is, we gather from his elaborate theories, the entire so-called Aristotelian theater that Brecht here deprecates as the theater of dreams. However, the poem refers especially to the American scene that Brecht endured in exile: Los Angeles, the city of marketable dreams (*GW*, 10:858); the dream factories of Hollywood founded by the descendants of gold diggers (*Poems*, 380 [*GW*, 10:849]). Hollywood produces the venal escapist dreams, the unproductive dream illusions consumed in darkened houses, dreams on dimly lit stages lulling the viewers into drowsiness, or—to borrow a Freudian phrase: dreams as protectors of sleep. "But we need the audiences's / Wakeful-, even watchfulness. Let them / Do their dreaming in the light," exclaims the activist Brecht (*Poems*, 426 [*GW*, 9:795]). He sees this vigilant dreaming in brightness as a product of stage illumination and work elucidation, alerting an enlightened consciousness. It is Brecht's rationalizing "epic" dramaturgy that allows us to dream in the light, "to dream without being dominated by dreams" (*GW*, 12:566).[14] If the dream motif itself was already part of a theme treated by Brecht, he did not fail to adapt it to his own dramaturgic ends, as in his various versions treating Joan of Arc, *Schweyk*, *The Good Person of Szechwan*, or in his film scripts "Caesar's Last Days" and "All Our Yesterdays." The affinity of dream and film scenes had caught Brecht's eye long before he wrote for Hollywood. While his friend and collaborator Lion Feuchtwanger and the prospects of a screen version may have influenced the elaborate dream scenes in *The Visions of Simone Machard*, which feature certain similarities with the dream scenes in Feuchtwanger's psychologizing novel *Simone*,[15] they also need to be seen in connection with Brecht's own dream episodes in crucial contexts.

In his first "Joan" play, the economic battles of a slaughterhouse world were largely modelled after the heroic epic. Joan's religious dream mission that is blended with her descent to the lower region, once again echoes the epic hero's cognitions in the underworld — here secularized into the freezing social hell of the starving lower class. The protagonist's prophetic vision of masses of people changing history (*GW*, 2:734) is clear in its revolutionary impulse, but still uncertain and even mistaken in its political strategy. In her dream Joan speaks a language she does not yet understand; after she awakens, she first interprets her vision wrongly, for she still sees herself as a humanitarian leader rather than a link in the net of political solidarity. In a chain of progressive steps of understanding, Joan's dream, both "true" and "false," is a dialectic link to the harsh awakening of her final realization.

This progressive awakening to political incentive, mingling idealistic impulse with sobering actuality, is also brought out in Simone Machard's dream sequences, which transform past and immediate experiences through a process of alienation into subsequent action. These are not dreams set against waking reality, but dreams blending and contrasting different historical perspectives. By tracing the seemingly confused yet highly revelatory dream montages — the condensed results of Simone's intense attention to the "Book" on France's legendary heroine *and* to her own immediate social and political surroundings — we are able to reconstruct details of her "dreamwork." This dreamwork functions as a critical screen to expose not only deceptions, lies, and latent motives of those in power, but also contradictions, pretenses, and lack of solidarity among the exploited.

It took the critics a while to discover that, subjectively, Simone's "naive" or even "naturalistic" dream visions were, at the same time, objective, sophisticated epic theater,[16] that is, dream play as anti–dream theater in Brecht's programmatic sense. The recurrence of dreams cannot exclusively be explained by the child's uninhibited fantasy or dreamy disposition, for dream sequences are a frequent phenomenon of deep, if not desperate concern over excruciating, unsolved problems. In this sense, the dream sequences of a harassed and exploited, yet genuinely caring Simone have their parallels in the progressive dream sequences of other figures in comparable circumstances, as for instance in "The Four Dreams of the Worker Jen" in the *Tui* novel, or the five dreams of Wang in *The Good Person*.

The displacement of religious-patriotic visions by Brecht's sociopolitical dream sequence offers its own revelations. Simone's sensitivity and her exploitation by all sides turn her visions into a mixture of wish-dream and nightmare that are dramatized as plays within the play. They draw analogies between legend and reality, focus on contradictions, penetrate false facades, look behind masks, correct initial perceptions, and point to consequences that are, objectively, more fully perceived by the audience than, subjectively, by Simone herself. Still, these are her visions, and she acts according to what she thinks they tell her. Seeing that national interests are translated into class interests, but with dissimilar commitment from the opposing classes, she acts alone—an impressionable maid-servant turned resistance fighter. Her dreams and her actions were intended as lessons in criticism, no doubt. In her dream imagery not only persons and events, but also objects combine to comment on each other, as, for example, the bells of coronation and the empty soup pots pounded with ladles; or Joan's sword and Simone's key to the storehouse. These images, which to Freudian psychoanalysts might appear as subconscious symbols of sexuality, belligerently appeal to economic consciousness—a pun or counterpunch not uncommon in Brecht's work. Most telling is the secularization and political emancipation of the angel, the symbol of awakening, from the voice of God to the voice of the people. In the legend he was the divine messenger; in Simone's dreams he has the features of her brother, for whose life she fears; at the end the angel appears as a collective image of projected solidarity, reminiscent of other emblematic prophecies concluding Brechtian scenes.[17]

The visions in *Schweyk in the Second World War*, written shortly after *Simone*, may have been suggested by the dreams in Jaroslav Hašek's antiwar novel and its 1928 stage adaptation by director Erwin Piscator, Brecht, and George Grosz.[18] But those earlier nightmares focused satirically on the military chieftains, and in similar function they recur as interludes in the "higher regions" in Brecht's own version. However, Brecht added dreams of the "little man" in the "lower regions." Similar to Joan the little man finds himself at the low point of his existence, engulfed by ice and snow. His service, similar to Simone's, is exploited by both the upper and the lower ranks. In this situation, deep in the wintery steppes of Siberia, Schweyk has rosy and golden visions of his cozy hometown inn. They may be seen as wish-dreams but they are ambiguous in their value for survival. These pivotal dream scenes, seemingly less complex than Simone's, once again combine individual psychology with the contrasting techniques of epic theater. Not only are these visions, on closer inspection, full of paradoxes that must raise questions about the solidarity among the figures in the "lower region"; they also relate Schweyk's condition — he is near death — dialectically to his friends' feast at the inn. If the Balouns do not curb their appetites, the Schweyks will not survive to face the greater enemies. To put it differently: if the Schweyks allow themselves to be exploited by their friends, they stand little chance against their foes.[19] That is the message of the dreams' subjective illusion and objective prophecy.

The Good Person, reputedly one of Brecht's most "epic" dramas, but also one of his least accessible in terms of its sources, plays with dream on several levels: the dream within the play, the dream within the dream, and the play as counter-dreamplay to Strindberg's A Dream Play. Indeed, Strindberg had been claimed as a witness by Freud as early as the fourth reprinting of his Interpretation of Dreams.[20] Striking resemblances of plot and structure in The Good Person and Strindberg's play cannot be ignored.[21] At issue is the relationship between lofty gods and earthbound mankind. In both plays, good women of Oriental appearance — Indra's daughter Agnes, child of heaven, and Shen Te, angel of the suburbs, both symbols of love[22] — become divine test objects of the human condition through their involvement in worldly affairs, only to be split apart by the impossibility of combining love with justice and happiness. Indeed, the greatest difficulty, Strindberg said, is that one is forced to be bad to others if one wants to live.[23] This is also the major problem for Brecht;[24] but where Strindberg waxes metaphysical, Brecht secularizes, materializes, and politicizes the issue; he furthermore exposes the gods who in Strindberg's play still seem a potential source of help.

Although Brecht counted Strindberg among the "great educators of a new Europe" (GW, 15:4) whose dramas were important experiments in shaping the problems of the time for the theater (GW, 15:288), and although Strindberg's techniques have been found to include "epic" devices,[25] Brecht's criticism of A Dream Play points to political inconsequence and an all-too-smooth effect of the play's dream atmosphere. Having attended all of Max Reinhardt's rehearsals of A Dream Play in the early twenties, he wrote: "Went to the final rehearsal of The Dream Play and at last put my finger on the basic flaws that had been tormenting me, only I was numbed by the slickness of the scenes. It isn't a dream. Ought to be crooked, twisted, gnarled, horrible, a nightmare with something delicious about it, a divinity's nightmare. And proves to be something for the right-minded, not a curve in it."[26]

This highly interesting comment means in effect that Strindberg's A Dream Play was simply not estranging, not provocative enough to shake the viewers awake. What must have provoked Brecht in particular is the unmistakable way in which Strindberg himself resolved the connection between dream and waking by first giving to the dream a disturbing though passive reality, and then by inactivating it: when sleep (that is, dream) becomes not a liberator but a torturer, Strindberg says, the awakening reconciles the sufferer with reality. For no matter how agonizing real life may be, at this moment, compared with a tormenting dream, it is a pleasure.[27]

Advanced dramaturgy wasted on such joyous, pain-embracing philosophy must have stung Brecht to the quick; and his belated answer to Strindberg's *A Dream Play* is most pointed in the conclusion of his counterplay. Strindberg shows us a compassionate daughter of the gods, who, recognizing that "the human heart is split in two"[28] by uncertain emotions and contradictions, bids her farewell to humankind and promises them to carry their lament to the throne. In juxtaposition to this finale Brecht sets a torn human being who is split in two halves (*CP*, 6:100 [*GW*, 4:1603]) by the impulse to do good and the necessity to do evil and left alone with her burden by fading gods who bid their meaningless farewell from a throne of cloudy nothingness. The challenging reality of this harsh awakening from a golden legend is further activated by the epilogue's call to wakefulness: an appeal not to the gods but to the viewers as judges and helpers to find an answer to the questions left open.

The epilogue that comments on the "open" play by directly addressing the audience is of course not the only epic device. In contradistinction to Strindberg's superior narrator, in whose unifying consciousness "anything can happen; everything is possible and probable," without "incongruities, scruples or laws," and whose dreams therefore are an indiscriminate fusion of "reality, imagination . . . memories, experiences, unfettered fancies, absurdities and improvisations,"[29] Brecht projects the poor, abused water-seller Wang as a continuous narrator. His dream sequence in five interludes interrupts the action and functions as progressive distancing commentary, questioning and criticizing the gods' precepts as incompatible with the actual conditions of life. In these dreams, and in the parabolic dreams within the dreams (*CP*, 6:78, 93 [*GW*, 4:1577, 1595]) that heighten Wang's critical curiosity, the play's problems are reflected in terms of social ethics. As Shen Te's affliction materializes and grows,[30] the battered and demoralized gods retreat and vanish. Thus Strindberg's dreams within a dreamplay, intended to signify a poetic transcendence of a reality of conflicts,[31] are answered by Brecht's rationalizing dream dramaturgy that does not draw spiritual promise from the tortures of life but inverts this dialectic by a strategy of secular agitation.

Such strategy has its own poetics. Within the texture of Brecht's composite fable that alludes to a variety of sources, both historical and literary,[32] the Strindbergian connection is enhanced by even smaller details of counterpoint: the leitmotif of the mysterious door, behind which is sought the secret of existence, finds its counterpart in Brecht's entry to the hidden compartment in which Shen Te secretly changes into Shui Ta and vice versa. The shawl, which in Strindberg's symbolism wraps the accumulated pain of humanity, signifies, in Brecht's emblematic use, the economic base of goodness and beauty and thus explains love turned misery. The police, as instrument of the "right-minded" (or "righteous"), appear both in Strindberg and in Brecht as guardians of the mystery of the secret chamber and function similarly in yet another scene of class difference: chasing the poor who pick fruit from the tree of the rich. Indra's daughter, child of heaven, whose wings have been clipped through her involvement in a heavily burdened world, believes all the more in flying, as do the gods; and so does Shen Te, burdened angel of the suburbs, who through her own sacrifice wants to enable the flyer Sun to pilot human messages through the skies. I cannot list all the parallels here. But last and not least: the chrysanthemum, Strindberg's symbol of liberated spirituality, that blossoms forth from the castle of imprisonment and grows out of stable dung, reappears in Brecht's play. Brecht's chrysanthemum is a parodistic emblem of "spiritual" union sanctioning the meeting of souls between a scheming capitalist Shu Fu and a beleaguered angel of goodness turned Shui Ta, whose imprisoned but expanding labor force, housed in barracks behind cattle stables, grows from the mire of exploitation.

In more than one way, then, Brecht imbued his own play with what he had found lacking in Strindberg, including the "nightmarish" quality in the vision of a divine being and what he calls the "curve,"[33] the nonlinear, disrupting, provocative tack not for but against the "righteous" ones. Thus, by a metaphoric leap, his counter-dreamplay became a most disquieting dreamplay of its own, whose earlier concept of an opium rather than a tobacco business[34] was intended to underscore the hallucinatory and destructive side of such marketable divine "good(s)," but was dropped partly to avoid the "danger of Chinoiserie"[35] — now a moot point in view of the burgeoning Western drug scene. The *actual* Chinese influence on *The Good Person*,[36] however, is not lessened but gains meaning even through Brecht's encounter with Strindberg: whereas Strindberg conjoined Western and Eastern transcendental philosophy in a quest for spiritual liberation through suffering, Brecht blended Eastern and Western social wisdom in a plea for secular justice and happiness. The counterplay opens the bilateral argument into a multilateral discourse.

After exile and World War II the frequency of dream scenes in Brecht's work declines. Some variants of the motif in his late poetry take a perhaps not unexpected turn. After the early nightmares, followed by a complex dream strategy activating political awakening, this last stage is an optimistic version of Brecht's call for "dreaming in the light" — they are dreams within reach. This is best exemplified by the "bright" dream metaphors in "The Education of Millet" (*GW*, 10:979–92) and in the "Song of Happiness" (*GW*, 10:997–98) — both are golden socioeconomic dreams of the postwar period. The changed political circumstances as reflected in dream imagery come out more clearly if we recall the dream of Lucullus, so disturbing to the field marshal's sense of authority, but so beautiful to the philosopher Lucretius's sense of nature: a dream in which masses of soldiers of opposing armies, rather than fighting each other, unite in fighting a raging river in order to save the farmers' grain fields (*GW*, 11:304–14) — such was Brecht's antiwar wish-dream in 1939. But in 1950 there was a vision of the victory of communal cultivation of huge grain fields of millet that had been developed progressively since ancient times and that would yield, in reality and against the odds of war time, a sustenance for life surpassing even the most optimistic golden dreams of productivity. There is a jump and a sublimation of dream prognosis regarding grain provisions in hard times, a motif that harks back to Pharaoh's dream and Joseph's interpretation,[37] but which in Brecht's distant secularized echoes has passed from providential intuition to conscious simile. Whereas Lucullus is only subconsciously aware of the beauty of his dream, Lucretius calls it beautiful for its rational appeal. The historic thriving of millet, both in its economic and social aspects, is a metaphoric promise that is reiterated in the refrain of the legend and has finally come true through human circumspection, determination, and labor — a wish fulfillment turned into plan fulfillment. Along comparable lines, the sailor's dream of the good golden city in the "Song of Happiness" is a postrevolutionary vision of social happiness reachable through calculated joint industriousness — a late counterpoint not only to the disillusioned dreams of Brecht's early adventurers, but also to "The Song of the Futility of All Human Endeavor" in the last act of *The Threepenny Opera*.[38]

Yet skeptical dream visions prevail at the end. "The 17th of June has alienated all existence" wrote Brecht in 1953;[39] in his *Buckow Elegies* cryptic but intensive dream experiences prominently convey that alienation: in a dream he sees the broken fingers of workers pointing at him (*Poems*, 440 [*GW*, 10:1010]); in a dream he sees a storm tear down part of a construction scaffolding (*Poems*, 442 [*GW*, 10:1012]); in a dream his own construction tool is partly shattered by a shot (*Poems*, 445 [*GW*, 10:1015]). Symbolic images of public uprising against a rigid system[40] combine with subjective self-recrimination. Whether the dream device here offers "immunity from censorship"[41] is a moot point. Once again the ambiguous nature of dreams is invoked to project dialectic truth from contradictions. Disillusionment leaves a door open for prophecy on behalf of the people: knowledge and pliability will vouchsafe reconstruction.

Brecht's dream imagery thus moves from metaphors of doomed existence to cautious visions of social promise via provocative steps of transition, sifting alienation through estrangement. His "dream-playing" is more than free poetic association. Dreams were realistic to Brecht as common human experience, especially in conditions of hardship. He was aware of — and used — dream theories both in their retrospective and prospective value, as trials of cognition and impetus for action. He utilized the fact that literature as well as psychology had used the dream-as-theater comparison for analytic and didactic purposes. And he employed a strategy of counterplay for the sake of productive antithesis. Brecht's rationalizing use of dreams to probe social perspectives implies not a neglect of psychoanalysis but a confrontation with it — as an answer to the split between individual psychology and sociology.[42] By joining the "strangeness" of socioeconomic paradoxes to individual dream structures, Brecht relates psychic problems to social alienation, suggesting that the subconscious irrational is an internalization of the social irrational. True psychoanalysis to him is socioanalysis. What Brecht once glossed as the rivalry between sexual and economic determinants of all life[43] was not just a quip but a recurrent focus of his literary counterplay.[44] In his subtitle to *The Interpretation of Dreams*, Freud immortalized a line from the *Aeneid* (Book 7, line 312) to compare the subconscious to the underworld. This simile became stigmatic for a brand of psychoanalysis that treated infernal passions as a threat to superior order.[45] In his own association of disturbing dreams (via Virgil's and Dante's underworld) with the lower regions of the underprivileged, the depths of social hell, the outcasts under bridges, the limbo of exile, the voices of the dead, and all their rebellious visions and persistent demontage of the superior ones, Brecht himself seems to offer a critical reinterpretation of Freud's borrowed motto: "Flectere si nequeo superos, acheronta movebo": "If I cannot bend those above, I shall raise all hell for them."

Notes

1. For discussions of Brecht's differentiated concept of "psychology," see, for example, Reinhold Grimm, "Notizen zu Brecht, Freud und Nietzsche," *Brecht-Jahrbuch* (1974):34–52; Meinhard Adler, *Brecht im Spiel der technischen Zeit: Naturwissenschaftliche, psychologische and wissenschaftstheoretische Kategorien im Werk Bertolt Brechts. Ein Beitrag zur Literaturpsychologie* (Berlin: Nolte, 1976).

2. Carl Pietzcker, "Brechts Verhältnis zur Psychoanalyse," *Amsterdamer Beiträge zur neueren Germanistik* 17 (1983):275–317.

3. See, for example, studies such as Gerhard Szczesny, *The Case against Bertolt Brecht with Arguments Drawn From His "Life of Galileo,"* trans. Alexander Gode (New York: Ungar, 1969); Carl Pietzcker, *Die Lyrik des jungen Brecht: Vom anarchischen Nihilismus zum Marxismus* (Frankfurt am Main: Suhrkamp, 1974).

4. I gratefully acknowledge the assistance of Professor Steven P. Sondrup of Brigham Young University, who kindly conducted a computer search of the "dream" motif in Brecht's poetry.

5. See the appendix to Bertolt Brecht, *Flüchtlingsgespräche, Gesammelte Werke in 20 Bänden* (Frankfurt am Main: Suhrkamp, 1967), 14:1500–1505. Hereafter cited as *GW*.

6. In discussing the complicated psychic complex of dream thoughts (subjected to dreamwork and analysis), Freud states: "Die Stücke desselben stehen in den mannigfaltigsten logischen Relationen zu einander; sie bilden Vorder- und Hintergrund, Bedingungen, Abschweifungen, Erläuterungen, Beweisgänge und Einsprüche. Fast regelmäßig steht neben einem Gedankengang sein kontradiktorisches Widerspiel" [*Über den Traum*, 2d ed. (Wiesbaden: Bergmann, 1911), 23.]

7. An especially interesting spokesman in this respect is David Hartley (1707–57), who sees a wholesome effect of the dream's inconsistency on a fallacious, habit-forming consistency of waking reality: "The wildness of our dreams seems to be of singular use to us, by

interrupting and breaking the cause of our associations. For, if we were always awake, some accidental association would be so much cemented by continuance, as that nothing could afterwards disjoin them; which would be madness" (*Observations on Man* [London: Richardson, 1749], 389). See also Ralph L. Woods, *The World of Dreams. An Anthology* (New York: Random House, 1947), 400; Werner Wolff, *The Dream — Mirror of Conscience* (New York: Grune & Stratton, 1952), 28.

8. *GW*, 1:10. See also Bertolt Brecht, *Collected Plays*, ed. Ralph Manheim and John Willett (New York: Vintage Books, 1971–), 1:9–10. Hereafter cited as *CP*. Baal not only explains the dream image (the girl clasped by the tree) to Johannes, but he himself enacts the metaphor in a sequence of scenes in which vegetation imagery blends with copulation.

9. See the vulture metaphor in "Chorale of the Big Baal" (*CP*, 1:4 [*GW*, 1:4]).

10. See, for example, the following poems, only one of which has been translated in Bertolt Brecht, *Poems 1913–1956*, ed. John Willett and Ralph Manheim with the co-operation of Erich Fried (New York: Methuen, 1976) — hereafter cited as *Poems —*: "Nordlandsage" (*GW*, 8:56); "Ballade von den Abenteurern" (*GW*, 8:217); "Remembering Marie A." (*Poems*, 35–36 [*GW*, 8:232]); "Mein Bruder war ein Flieger" (*GW*, 9:647–48).

11. See "The Heaven for Disenchanted Men" (*Poems*, 10 [*GW*, 8:55]); "His End" (*Poems*, 180–81 [*GW*, 8:334]).

12. See also *Saint Joan of the Stockyards*, trans. Frank Jones (Bloomington: Indiana University Press, 1969).

13. First published in English translation as *A Penny for the Poor*, trans. Desmond Vesey and Christopher Isherwood (London: Hale, 1937), republished as *Threepenny Novel* (New York: Grove Press, 1956).

14. Other variants of Brecht's "bright dream" motif convey a rational climate, for example, dreams of freedom; young Keuner's dream of a girl as being so attractively reasonable ("*sehr vernünftig*"; *GW*, 12:412); Kin-jeh's dreams about art examinations, in which the element of condensation is used productively: only Kin-jeh (= Brecht) and four other (unknown) poets succeed in economizing their art, providing a maximum of observation within a minimum of space (*GW*, 12:525).

15. Whereas the Feuchtwanger-Brecht collaboration on the subject of "Simone Machard" has been mentioned frequently, a close comparison of novel and drama (as well as their sources) remains a desideratum.

16. See Jürgen Albers, "Die Gesichte der Simone Machard. Eine zarte Träumerei nach Motiven von Marx, Lenin, Schiller," *Brecht-Jahrbuch* (1978):66–86.

17. See, for example, the revealing of the sickle emblem, accompanied by the "Sickle Song" at the end of *Roundheads and Peakheads* — a play that supplied the leitmotif of "Rich birds flock together" (*CP*, 7:41 [*GW*, 5:1887]).

18. For details, see my *Materialien zu Bertolt Brechts "Schweyk im zweiten Weltkrieg"* (Frankfurt am Main: Suhrkamp, 1974).

19. For a more detailed interpretation of the dreams, see my article, "Brechts braver Schweyk," *PMLA* 88 (1973):219–32.

20. Otto Rank, "Anhang," Sigmund Freud, *Die Traumdeutung* (Leipzig: Deuticke, 1914), 376.

21. Marianne Kesting, in *Vermessung des Labyrinths: Studien zur modernen Ästhetik* (Frankfurt am Main: Fischer, 1965), 136, hinted at a close relationship between Strindberg's *A Dream Play* and Brecht's *The Good Person*. Then Manfred Karnick, in *Rollenspiel und Welttheater* (Munich: Fink, 1980), 214–30, argued that Brecht's play, conceived as a counterplay to Calderon's *Great Theater of the World*, also uses and criticizes Strindberg's play. While Brecht's general anti-Calderonian concept may indeed play a role, his specific anti-Strindbergian elements are more obvious and in need of further detailed discussion.

22. The names suggest similarities: Agnes means "holy," "pure," and Shen Te, according

to Antony Tatlow, *The Mask of Evil* (Berne: Lang, 1977), 269, "divine efficacy" or "divine virtue."

23. See Strindberg's letter to Emil Schering, 13 May 1902, *Strindbergs Werke. Deutsche Gesamtausgabe.* Unter Mitwirkung von Emil Schering als Übersetzer vom Dichter selbst veranstaltet. Abteilung I, 4th ed. (Munich: Müller, 1914), 8:234.

24. See Brecht's statements on how easy it is to be good but how difficult to be evil (if one also wants to be good to oneself): *Materialien zu Brechts "Der gute Mensch von Sezuan,"* ed. Werner Hecht (Frankfurt am Main: Suhrkamp, 1968), 6–7, 12, 14.

25. See Peter Szondi, *Theorie des modernen Dramas* (Frankfurt am Main: Suhrkamp, 1963), 40–57; Kesting, *Vermessung des Labyrinths*, 135; Fritz Paul, "Episches bei Strindberg?" *Germanisch-Romanische Monatsschrift*, N.F. 24 (1974): 323–39; Walter Benjamin, *Versuche über Brecht (1966;* Frankfurt am Main: Suhrkamp, 1971), 15.

26. Bertolt Brecht, *Diaries 1920–1922,* ed. Herta Ramthun, trans. John Willett (New York: St.Martin's Press, 1979), 150.

27. See *Strindbergs Werke*, Abteilung I, 8:144. See also the more complete version of the preface in August Strindberg, *Five Plays,* trans. Harry G. Carlson (Berkeley and Los Angeles: University of California Press, 1983), 205–6.

28. *Strindbergs Werke,* Abteilung I, 8:224.

29. *Six Plays of Strindberg,* trans. Elizabeth Sprigge (Garden City: Doubleday, 1955), 193; Strindberg, *Five Plays*, 205.

30. In her double role, Shen Te/Shui Ta ("Mater"/"Materialism") grows bigger (with child/with capital).

31. See the pertinent passages in the dialogue between Indra's Daughter and the Poet, *Strindbergs Werke,* Abteilung I, 8:201–12 (also 223).

32. See *Materialien,* ed. Hecht; Jan Knopf, *Brecht Handbuch. Theater* (Stuttgart: Metzler, 1980), 201–13; Jan Knopf, *Bertolt Brecht. "Der gute Mensch von Sezuan"* (Frankfurt am Main: Diesterweg, 1982); *Brechts "Guter Mensch von Sezuan,"* ed. Jan Knopf (Frankfurt am Main: Suhrkamp, 1982).

33. Brecht's expression "curve" (in the sense of nonlinear development) anticipates a dramaturgic term in his juxtaposition of "epic" and "dramatic" forms of theater (*GW*, 17:1010); what he wishes to improve in his "epic" *The Good Person* is "abschweifung und umweg." Bertolt Brecht, *Arbeitsjournal,* 2 vols., ed. Werner Hecht (Frankfurt am Main: Suhrkamp, 1973), 1:52; see also *Materialien,* ed. Hecht, 11.

34. See *Materialien,* ed. Hecht, 91–93; 101–4.

35. See Brecht, *Arbeitsjournal* 1:52; also *Materialien,* ed. Hecht, 11.

36. See Tatlow, *The Mask of Evil;* Yun-Yeop Song, *Bertolt Brecht und die chinesische Philosophie* (Bonn: Bouvier, 1978); Han-Soon Yim, *Bertolt Brecht und sein Verhältnis zur chinesischen Philosophie* (Bonn: Institut für koreanische Kultur, 1984).

37. An allusion to the biblical dream prophecy of the seven good years and the seven bad years even exists in Wang's speculation about the "economy" of rain and water for sale: "Just last night I dreamt that seven / Years went by without a rainfall / Rubbed my hands, gave thanks to heaven! / How they shouted: Give me water" (*CP*, 6:35).

38. Note the identical verse structure of the songs (*GW*, 2:465).

39. Brecht, *Arbeitsjournal*, 2:1109.

40. It has been generally accepted that the "iron" references allude to "Iron" Stalin, hence to the rigidity of Stalinism.

41. See Peter Whitaker, *Brecht's Poetry. A Critical Study* (Oxford: Clarendon, 1985), 211.

42. In recent studies that propose rapprochements of these opposites, Brecht is occasionally mentioned, for example, by Michael Schneider, *Neurose und Klassenkampf*

(Reinbek: Rowohlt, 1973), and Helmut Dahmer, *Libido und Gesellschaft* (Frankfurt am Main: Suhrkamp, 1973); but Brecht's position in the dialogue and his various strategies in addressing the issue more or less directly have not yet been dealt with satisfactorily.

43. See Ziffel's remark in *The Refugee Dialogues* (GW, 14:1504–05).

44. The *Threepenny Novel*, abounding in satire, is a particularly prolific case in point.

45. See Manfred Pohlen and Lothar Wittmann, *"Die Unterwelt bewegen": Versuch über Wahrnehmung und Phantasie in der Psychoanalyse* (Frankfurt am Main: Syndikat, 1980), esp. 34, n. 17. Not only the bourgeoisie but also some Marxists were worried about that unruly dark psychological underworld: see Helmut Dahmer, "Psychoanalyse und historischer Materialismus," *Psychoanalyse als Sozialwissenschaft* (Frankfurt am Main: Suhrkamp, 1971), 67.

Bertolt Brecht's Chicago — A German Myth?

Reinhold Grimm*

One need not be a specialist, nor even a Germanist, to know that the German playwright from the provincial Bavarian town of Augsburg, Bertolt Brecht, wrote about the city of Chicago. When the question about Brecht's Chicago plays is raised, the answer one normally receives from almost everybody is that, of course, Brecht composed a Marxist play, *Saint Joan of the Stockyards;* people more familiar with Brecht's work might add that both his early drama, *In the Jungle of Cities,* and his later parable on the ascent of Hitler, *The Resistible Rise of Arturo Ui,* are also located in the Windy City. Yet almost inevitably, the informant, whether an American or a Britisher, will conclude that the Brechtian image of Chicago is a typical "German myth."

Surely there is no denying that a few odd things do occur in these plays, especially in the one equating Chicago with a "jungle." We encounter a Malayan lumber merchant born in Yokohama; we find certain outlandish drinks no American would ever order; and the currency used in this befuddling city is a curious combination of the once almighty dollar, the English shilling, and the good old German *Groschen* or dime. Worse yet, steamships are leaving from Brecht's Chicago directly for San Francisco as well as Tahiti; as late as 1941, in *Arturo Ui,* Brecht's Chicagoans prefer to sail "to Frisco," as they put it, rather than to travel by train or to fly. On the other hand, it takes a migrating American family no fewer than fourteen days to get from Lake Michigan to Chicago; in a variant of the same story, they start in the "savannah" (Brecht's favorite word for "prairie") where they have been growing wheat, then move to San Francisco where they own a business selling motors and enjoy jazz,

*Translated, revised, and expanded by the author from *Brecht 85: Zur Ästhetik Brechts,* ed. Werner Hecht ([East] Berlin: Henschelverlag, 1986), 224–34, 411–12. Reprinted with the permission of the author.

after that to Massachusetts where they own an oil field and a drill, and, finally, to Chicago where they arrive with nothing.[1] Small wonder that critics, either with a sigh and a shrug or triumphantly, tend to point out such geographical eccentricities. According to Eric Bentley, for instance, Brecht's Chicago is situated on a continent that Christopher Columbus never set foot in: "The nickelodeon plays *Ave Maria:* a Salvation Army officer shoots himself after uttering the last words of Frederick the Great; and a lynch gang goes into action at the bidding of the police! It is the America that was discovered not by C. C. but by B. B."[2] Bentley's remarks are characteristic also in that they implicitly generalize by extending Brecht's "mythical image" of Chicago to stand for Brecht's "American myth" at large. There is hardly a critic or scholar who fails to concur: the Chicago of the Augsburg playwright as well as his America have been labeled "absurd," "exotic," "entirely abstract," and "vague"; they have been seen as an "outgrowth" both of his "poetic imagination" and his "Marxist ideology"; they have also been considered as "a fabulous, visionary domain, partly concocted out of reality, mostly built on fantasy," or simply as a mixture of "morass" and "mysteriousness" that is "madly unreal" to boot. In short, this Chicago and this America "do not exist"; they are a "phantasmagoria," a "transatlantic" German "myth" conceived in the Bavarian backwoods.[3]

Granted, "Most anything can happen in Chicago and usually does," as none other than Carl Sandburg, the great Chicago poet who certainly knew his city, assures us in his 1952 autobiography, *Always the Young Strangers.*[4] But Brecht's "shadowy," "grotesque," and, time and again, "mythical" Chicago appears to be very strong stuff indeed. If a critic is ill-disposed, Brecht's Chicago and, for that matter, his America will be termed a "caricature," called "incomprehensible," and even "unrecognizable"; conversely, if the critic is kind and benign, Brecht will be classified as a naive perpetuator of that "fantastic" image "which has little in common with the reality of the United States," but that has haunted the German mind ever since the so-called "Roaring Twenties" with their jazz, boxing, and plenty of bootlegged whisky.[5] Yet, all the same, the prevailing concept of Bertolt Brecht's Chicago as a German myth — not even the most circumspect and conscientious scholars have abandoned this concept altogether — is a grave misconception on several counts. In fact, when reading that "grim Chicago"[6] with its "omnipotent cold," "icy rains," "snowstorms attacking the huddled poor," and infernal "wind in the depths" is "not too far from the nethermost circle of Hell congealed by Lucifer's fawning" — then one has reason to suspect that Brechtians and Brechtologists rather than the Master himself are responsible for this Brechto-Chicagoan myth. Perhaps, one is tempted to ask, Brecht's mythical Chicago is itself a myth of sorts?

Interestingly, neither the city of New York nor that of Los Angeles, which also frequently appear in the Brechtian oeuvre, have been endowed with so blatantly mythical a status; nor have their images been expanded so unconditionally as to represent America, that is, the United States, as a whole. It seems to be the sole prerogative of Chicago to serve as a projection of Brecht's "German myth" in all its ramifications. But this intriguing geographical question will be dealt with later. After all, the playwright from Augsburg lived in Santa Monica for over six years and visited the Big Apple repeatedly in the 1930s and 1940s, whereas he merely passed through the Windy City, albeit a number of times. He must have cast at least a fleeting glance at the Chicago stockyards; but he never stayed in Chicago, not even overnight.[7] And yet, paradoxically, Chicago was and remained at the center of Brecht's American imagination as well as experience. Astonishingly though, Brecht's image of Chicago has been consistently misunderstood, both quantitatively and qualitatively, by scholars and critics alike. Granted, we do have three admirable monographs dealing with Brecht and — or in — America to which I am greatly indebted even though they themselves are not entirely free of certain aspects of the prevalent fallacy.

In fact, the Brechtian portrayal of Chicago and Chicagoans is in no way limited to the aforementioned plays that are commonly invoked: to wit, the triad of *Saint Joan*, *Jungle*, and *Arturo Ui*. Actually, Chicago provides the setting for, and Chicagoans make an appearance in, a whole series of dramas and dramatic fragments; they emerge in his poems and film stories; and the name Chicago occurs even in Brecht's theoretical tracts. In listing and briefly commenting on those various works, I shall proceed in Brechtian fashion and draw liberally on previous research.

Admittedly, the three Chicago plays mentioned above are fairly well-known; this applies in particular to *Saint Joan*. Nevertheless, recalling a modicum of facts about these plays is essential. The most enigmatic of all Brechtian works, *Jungle*, subtitled "The Fight between Two Men in the Gigantic City of Chicago," was written during the period 1921–24. This play was first produced in Munich in 1923 as *In the Jungle*; there are several extant versions. The version in Brecht's *Gesammelte Werke* abounds with meticulous dates and spans a period of roughly three years, from August 1912 to November 1915. The action itself, however, is all the more puzzling. In addition, the play contains dramatic constellations and crypto-quotations from a variety of authors and works, among them Arthur Rimbaud and his experimental prose; but, despite its bewildering and cryptic plot, the play's main concern is clearly discernible: humankind's total and insurmountable alienation in the big cities. "If you cramp a ship full to bursting with human bodies, they'll all freeze with loneliness," says Shlink. "Yes, so great is man's isolation that not even a fight is possible."[8]

Almost a decade after the production of *Jungle*, Brecht demonstrated in *Saint Joan* (composed 1929–1931) that a fight — that is, class struggle or a reaction against oppression and exploitation — was not only possible but both inescapable and mandatory.[9] The fierceness of this fight is indicated by the fact that the term *"Schlachthöfe"* in the German title, *Die heilige Johanna der Schlachthöfe,* can also be translated as "slaughterhouses." The play, although stimulated by, among other sources, Shaw's *Major Barbara* and Schiller's *The Maid of Orleans,* and incorporating ideas, figures, and scenes from these works, is set in the Windy City or, more specifically, the stockyards and commercial exchanges of modern Chicago. In this drama — which was not produced until 1959, three years after Brecht's death — there is nothing cryptic or enigmatic whatsoever; quite to the contrary. *Saint Joan,* a gruesome spectacle as well as an overtly didactic play, is more than explicit in laying bare the workings of capitalism and the furtherance they receive from institutionalized religion. The dying heroine Joan converts to atheism and socialism and proceeds to propound the playwright's message in no uncertain, indeed brutal, terms:

> Anyone . . . who says there is a God
> Invisible yet a helper of humankind
> Should have his head banged on the pavement
> Till he croaks. . . . For
> Only force helps where force rules.
> *(GW,* 2:787–83; my translation)

Brecht loved this work and ranked it among the very best he had written; many critics agree with him. Yet, ever so often, the stridency of its allegedly blasphemous mock-canonization as well as its ruthless and allegedly cynical parodies of such German classics as Goethe, Schiller, and Hölderlin, have vexed and embittered not only readers and playgoers but also Brecht scholars.

Conversely, his parable play of 1941, *The Resistible Rise of Arturo Ui,* is often shrugged off as too farcical a work because it is based on a seemingly strange equation: Hitler's seizure of power and rule over the Reich are compared to Al Capone and his bootlegging gangsters' terrorizing of Chicago.[10] But was Brecht's equation really so far-fetched? Capone was a celebrity after all; in fact, a jury of American journalists had named him, along with Albert Einstein and Mahatma Gandhi, "man of the decade" in the 1920s. Nor was Brecht the first and only one to perceive such similarities; as early as 1939, the American playwright Irwin Shaw, in a piece called *The Gentle People,* had equated his native gangsters with Nazism and fascism. In Brecht's parable, intended for a "kind of music-hall production on Broadway" that, however, failed to materialize, the correspondence of Cicero to Austria, or Cicero's Mayor, Dullfeet, to the Austrian Chancellor, Dollfuss, is as obvious as is that of Chicago to Germany. Also, the assorted historical events evoked in the play (such as the *Reichstag* fire) are no less easily identifiable. The play is not only located in and around Chicago; as in the case of *Saint Joan,* it is written in stately blank verse and shows an ironic sprinkling of textual and dramaturgical elements from both Goethe and Shakespeare.

Happy End, the fourth Brechtian play on Chicago, has been excluded from Brecht's *Gesammelte Werke*, for he denied his authorship, claiming that merely the songs had been penned by him. However, there can be no doubt that he contributed much more—the basic idea, the plot outline, the pithy language—to the 1929 piece that was set to music by Kurt Weill. Its kinship to Brecht's other Chicago plays, composed either before or after *Happy End*, is quite evident. The primary reason that this musical was created by Brecht and Weill is beyond dispute: the two of them hoped to cash in on their box office success of 1928, *The Threepenny Opera*, by providing a sequel of sorts. Yet *Happy End* proved to be an utter failure and provoked harsh criticism—hence, as most scholars argue, Brecht's disclaimer. John Willett has provided a summary:

> Bill Cracker, gangster and proprietor of "Bill's Ballhaus," falls in love with Lieutenant Lilian Holiday of the Salvation Army, who has come to his establishment with Lieutenant Hannibal Jackson to make converts. Lilian is thrown out of the Salvation Army; Bill, who fails his part in a robbery, out of the gang. Bill goes to an Army meeting to find Lilian, but the gang follow in order to murder him. The gang's mysterious leader, the Lady in Grey, recognizes Hannibal as her long-lost husband, and so the Army and the crooks join forces. Bill gets an Army uniform, and all unite to found a bank.[11]

It is true, *Happy End* sounds a bit simplistic; however, seen in the light of the preceding *Jungle*—and even more so, in the light of Brecht's subsequent *Saint Joan*—it is not as simple and silly as certain critics maintain. The satirical thrust and its target are, in any event, unmistakable.

As to the remainder of the Brechtian treatments and evocations of Chicago, I will, for the most part, content myself with a mere listing. They all share, in varying manner yet to an increasing degree, the themes of the big city and of people's struggle and alienation, as well as those of capitalism and its detrimental effects, both on its agents and, in particular, its victims. Thus, with increasing frequency, not only crime and poverty but also oppression and exploitation emerge as Brecht's Chicagoan topics. During the period 1921–22, for example, he planned to write a piece called, plainly enough, "Chicago," "Cold Chicago," or "The Play of Cold Chicago"—although the few scattered pages in the Berlin Brecht Archives do not tell us very much about his plans. Far more specific, important, and unequivocal is another sizable dramatic fragment, "Joe Fleischhacker" of 1926. The very title of the fragment, the name of a meatchopper and butcher, is indicative of its Chicago setting and its close relationship to *Saint Joan*. A third such fragmentary piece, "The Bread Store" (or "The Bread Shop") of 1929, was likewise to be situated in Chicago—Brecht even gave the precise year, "1923," and the exact area, "around 43rd Street"[12]—but the author then decided to relocate it in Berlin, a city that in his youthful letters he likened mockingly to "cold Chicago." Later on, during his exile in California in the 1940s, Brecht

harked back to both these momentous fragments; he was bent on combining them and making them into a unified play, "The Bread King of
Chicago." Similarly, in collaboration with his American friend, Ferdinand
Reyher, he drafted a screen version thereof, entitled "The King's Bread"
(also, "Joe Fleischhacker, or A Bread King Learns How to Bake"). There
are yet other pertinent film stories by Brecht, also penned or conceived in
conjunction with Reyher, such as "All Our Yesterdays," subtitled "Lady
Macbeth of the Yards," and, last but not least, "The Hamlet of the Wheat
Exchange." Without doubt, the theme and image of Chicago haunted the
playwright and poet from Augsburg; as indicated, Chicago appears in his
verse and pops up in his most divergent writings. Brecht's "Psalm Nr 6,"
for instance, which consists of a series of Rimbaud-like incantations and
identifications ("I am a snowy mountain peak . . ." / "I am a shipwreck at
the bottom of the sea . . .") starts out with the unambiguous statement: "I
am a band in Chicago. . . . I play the Marseillaise" (GW, Supplement
3:76). Another poem introduces "John Smith from Chicago" (GW, Supplement 3:155), while an unpublished one-act play or opera of 1919, called
"Prairie" and derived from a Knut Hamsun novella, reports on the "great
disastrous fire in Chicago," boldly decreeing that "It was arson."[13] Even in
Brecht's monumental theoretical treatise, Buying Brass [The Messingkauf
Dialogues], the longest and most ambitious of its kind, Chicago puts in an
appearance. Anticipating, around 1940, modern missile warfare, albeit of
comparatively modest dimensions, the author of this enormous dialogue
has one of his discussants reflect: "A man in Chicago might [some day]
launch a device [Apparat] that will crush twelve people in Ireland—or
12,000!" (GW, 16:526). Thus, similarly to Berlin, Chicago and the
Chicagoans symbolize the modern city and its inhabitants; in fact, they
symbolically represent the entire United States in economic, political, and
military terms. It therefore is no great surprise that Brecht's choices of
representative places for social upheaval and international class struggle
such as Glasgow and Lyon, Shanghai and Calcutta, also include Chicago—even in his Russian revolutionary play, The Mother. Indeed, there
exists a Brechtian "Epistle to the People of Chicago" that employs Chicago
as a fitting symbol not only of the big city and America as a modern jungle
but of humankind in its entirety on this our "planet" (GW, Supplement
3:124). What more can even the most devout and impassioned Chicagoan
wish?

     Finally, let us not forget that the Windy City and its people played a
decisive role in Brecht's intellectual and artistic biography; indeed they
were responsible for the most important turning point in his life and
career—that is, his conversion to Marxism. Retrospectively musing on the
abandonment of his fragment, "Joe Fleischhacker," the playwright pithily
declared:

     Years ago when I was studying the ways of the Chicago Wheat
        Exchange

I suddenly grasped how they managed the whole world's wheat there
And yet I did not grasp it either and lowered the book
I knew at once: you've run
Into bad bad trouble.

Brecht's confessional poem ends: "Much work and unrest / Awaited me" (*GW*, 9:567-68).[14] What is contained in the intervening lines, whether stated explicitly or not, is Brecht's intensive study of economics and the "system" in general — a study that ultimately led him to embrace Marxism; likewise, those lines comprise emblematically, as it were, his social and political struggle, his fight against Hitler, and his exile of fifteen years, six of which (1941-47) he spent in the United States. The same biographical facts and intellectual developments are expressed or hinted at in an autobiographical sketch and an essay on theater: both ponder Brecht's experience of Chicago and what it entailed.[15]

In sum, then, the Windy City in his life and work reveals itself as a towering presence, as all but overwhelming. Chicago and the Chicagoans constitute one of Brecht's most frequent as well as most poignant motifs and ideas; moreover, it is a sound guess that no other German, European, or non-American author has written more, and more unflaggingly, about this city and its inhabitants than has Brecht. Such attention may perhaps be regarded as an obsession — yet can its result be really termed a "myth"? It should be acknowledged that Brecht studied the functioning of the Chicago wheat exchange; but, from the very beginning, he also drew on a whole host of sundry additional sources, both literary and historical. Indeed, he gradually became totally engrossed in his subject. A brief enumeration of selected names, dates, and facts may suffice to illustrate both his fixation and the realistic basis on which it was built. Brecht read and made use of the following volumes, most of which he owned[16]:

1. George Horace Lorimer, *Letters of a Self-Made Merchant to His Son* (1902; in German translation, 1905; sequel, 1905). These delightful prose pieces by Lorrimer, the influential editor of the *Saturday Evening Post* for almost four decades, provide an authentic, near perfect, picture of shrewd and brutal Big Business in turn-of-the-century Chicago. Apart from German, they were translated into several languages; in fact, they proved to be more successful and popular than any American work since *Uncle Tom's Cabin*.

2. Frank Norris, *The Pit: A Story of Chicago* (1903; German translation, 1907). The "pit" is the wheat exchange, the Chicago Board of Trade around which the entire action revolves; Brecht was well-read in other writings by Norris, too.

3. Upton Sinclair, *The Jungle* (1906; German translation, 1906). Brecht called attention to Sinclair's work, a fictionalized reportage, in a theater review in 1920 and praised it highly at the expense of Schiller's play *Don Carlos*. Sinclair undoubtedly made one of the strongest and most lasting impressions upon the playwright and helped shape his obsessive image of Chicago.

4. Jack London, *The Iron Heel* (1906; German translation, 1927). The book has been characterized as a kind of "utopian science-fiction"; Brecht immediately adopted the phrase "The Iron Heel" for his fragment, "The Bread Store." London's novel is located in Chicago, and it deals explicitly with violence, the masses, and — as does Sinclair's novel — with the slaughterhouses or stockyards.

5. Johannes Vilhelm Jensen, *Das Rad* (1908; The Wheel). Unlike the majority of Brecht's sources, the Chicago novel of the Nobel Laureate — *Hjulet* in its original Danish — presents itself as an exuberant and totally uninhibited eulogy of the city and its teeming life: Chicago is extolled on account of its boundless ruthlessness and brutality.

6. Alfons Paquet, *Fahnen* (1923; Flags). The topic of this work, a "dramatic novel" or "epic drama," is the notorious Haymarket Affair or Haymarket Massacre that occurred in Chicago in 1886. Director Erwin Piscator, with whom Brecht was intimately associated, produced *Fahnen*; in fact, his staging of the play by the German writer and newspaperman Paquet has been hailed as one of the first significant productions of Piscator's "political theater."

7. Gustavus Myers, *History of the Great American Fortunes* (1910; German translation, 1916). The title of this voluminous tome sounds deceptively sober; in truth, however, Myers's book reads like a collection of exciting detective stories. For Brecht, at any rate, it turned out to be a real thriller because it contained a wealth of factual information on America in general and on Chicago in particular.

This listing of Brechtian sources is by no means exhaustive. Other names, titles, and dates include: Bouck White, *The Book of Daniel Drew* (1910; German translation, 1922); Theodore Dreiser, *The Titan* (1914; German translation, 1928); Sherwood Anderson, *Poor White* (1920; German translation, 1925); Ida M. Tarbell, *The Life of Elbert H. Gary: The Story of Steel* (1925); and Louis Adamic, *Dynamite: The Story of Class Violence in America* (1934). Since the latter two volumes were not translated into German, Brecht either studied them in English as a result of mastering the language before coming to this country, or he ploughed through them with the help of his secretary, Elisabeth Hauptmann, who knew English. Brecht used similar procedures with regard to the newspaper clippings about current American events from the *Chicago Daily News* and other newspapers that he collected along with other pertinent materials. As a matter of fact, he even procured a floor plan of the Chicago Board of Trade that has been preserved in the Berlin Brecht Archives. It is an enlightening document: "The floor areas for the different kinds of grain are indicated, and the accompanying text, underlined by Brecht, explains the techniques of trading, such as hand signals. The scenes of *Saint Joan* set in the cattle exchange take account of the buying and selling techniques, at the same time rendering them grotesque with biblical language."[17]

While Brecht's deliberately grotesque mode of presentation may have been conducive to the critics' impression of myth and irreality, what was actually presented by Brecht was anything but a myth. In essence, the Brechtian image of Chicago was an irrefutable reality even if most of the Brechtian sources that have been listed are works of fiction, and many a fault they decry has long since receded into the realm of history. To adduce but a single striking instance: Sinclair's *The Jungle* had a tremendous impact on public life in the United States; the facts it drew attention to were the immediate cause of federal legislation, that is, the enactment of the so-called pure food laws. Such things are well-known. Or should they be too little known nowadays? Should the accusation of being a "muck-raker," leveled not only at Sinclair but also at others who have been cited, still be rampant? Then, perhaps, we ought to remember that one of the most horrid incidents in *Saint Joan* stemmed directly from Sinclair's report: "A man had fallen into one of the rendering tanks and had been made into pure leaf lard."[18] In a letter of 8 February 1913, Carl Sandburg wrote: "Chicago . . . is unfamiliar with the truth, can not recognize it when it appears. . . ."[19] Surely this inability to recognize and face the truth is no longer the rule — or, at least, not in such crude and sweeping manifestations. Nor, for that matter, is it peculiar to the Windy City and its inhabitants. As late as 1955, in a letter of 14 May discussing the reaction of spectators in Germany, Brecht observed that "it is quite possible that they reproach the playwright and the actors with what they don't like about their city."[20] The historian, if only of literature, may on occasion find himself in the position of facing a similar reproach.

Anyhow, it has become evident that Brecht's Chicago can hardly be disposed of as a "myth" in the sense of something existing merely in the imagination or having been invented arbitrarily; there is no question that this "German myth" rests on too much solid "American truth." A more detailed demonstration of the underlying reality is provided by scholarly studies, notably Helfried W. Seliger's *Das Amerikabild Bertolt Brechts* (1974), James K. Lyon's *Bertolt Brecht in America* (1980), and Patty Lee Parmalee's *Brecht's America* (1981). All these works, plus a growing number of essays and articles, offer a veritable surfeit of proof[21] — although they differ considerably in their conclusions. As can be inferred from the titles of the works cited above, they tend to describe and evaluate an overall image of, or attitude toward, "America" — that is, the United States at large, including New York and Los Angeles. Only a brief and isolated study published in 1982 is explicitly and entirely devoted to Chicago — but not even remotely to Brecht.[22] Still, a summary of all the major assess-ments both of Brecht's Chicago and Brecht's America — they can scarcely be separated — is in order. Brecht's image of the Windy City is identical, to a high degree, with his image of the country in whose heart it is situated, and vice versa. In Brecht's intellectual and imaginative landscape New York and Los Angeles are, quite literally, marginal and peripheral locations: the former serves mainly as a symbol of doom and destruction, downfall and decay, while the latter symbolizes intellectual prostitution and degeneration, commercialized culture, and the commodity character of everything. Chicago alone, as is meet and proper, occupies the center; it is the core of Brecht's American imagination and experience, ideologically as well as geographically.

What, then, are the salient features of this remarkable locality, the focus and hub that in the eyes of the German author stood for America and the United States as a whole? On the one hand, we read: "For Brecht, Chicago epitomized the violent human relationships and the intrinsically corrupt nature of capitalism." In Brecht's opinion, according to the critic, the "somber city" once nicknamed "Porkopolis" is "one vast gulf of disorder" inhabited "by savages."[23] On the other hand, we hear: "After as well as before his Marxist conversion, Brecht continued to admire the gigantic, the powerful and even the brutal facets of Chicago. Even in crisis Chicago is great."[24] Or we are told that Brecht's attitude underwent a development consisting of two phases, one positive, one negative; that a fundamental change took place in his image, a shift from incipient enthusiasm and acceptance to ultimate rejection and wrath. More specifically, Brecht is said to have been "fascinated" during the early 1920s "by the energetic progressiveness of Chicago," but to have soon been appalled and enraged by "its complete absence of human values," and therefore, at the end of that decade, to have denounced and foresworn it for good.[25] Conversely, Chicago is seen as constituting two separate images: a *Schreckbild*, or image of horror, and a *Wunschbild*, or wishful image; according to such theories, the repulsive aspects have to be relegated to "naturalistic prose" in the novel, the enticing and desirable facets chiefly to "poetry."[26]

None of these explanations is devoid of astute insights, in particular as regards Brecht's development; yet each of them, even the concept of a "rise and fall," is too narrow and one-sided. After all, at the end of the 1920s, Brecht still admired "the city of Chicago with its breath-taking speed, its unrestrained vices, and its nerve-racking sensuality"; as late as 1945, in a letter to an American writer, he praised "the youth, the verve, and the sensitive vigor of your great cities," such as Chicago, and celebrated their "virtues."[27] Hence the few Chicagoan oddities and eccentricities that critics enjoy harping upon reveal themselves as trifles at best. They are either means of estranging Brechtian form, expressions of a sovereign contempt or *Wurstigkeit*, or altogether negligible. Brecht knew full well and proclaimed repeatedly that his Chicago, albeit *unwirklich* in its presentation (both "uncanny" and "non-naturalistic"), was nevertheless *streng wirklichkeitsgetreu* ("essentially true to reality") in its representation.[28] In this as in other respects, his own assessment of the Windy City and what it symbolized was "ambivalent"; the relations he entertained with it have rightly been defined as relations of a "love-hate struggle."[29] All this comes to the fore in yet another confessional poem. It is entitled

"Chicago"; in fact, it is addressed to Chicago, and its decisive lines run as follows:

> They tell me you are wicked and I believe them, for I have seen
>   your painted women under the gas lamps luring the farm boys.
> And they tell me you are crooked and I answer: yes, it is true I
>   have seen the gunman kill and go free to kill again.
> And they tell me you are brutal and my reply is: On the faces of
>   women and children I have seen the marks of wanton hunger.
> And having answered so I turn once more to those who sneer at this
>   my city, and I give them back the sneer and say to them:
> Come and show me another city with lifted head singing so proud
>   to be alive and coarse and strong and cunning.
> Flinging magnetic curses amid the toll of piling job on job, here is a
>   tall bold slugger set vivid against the little soft cities;
> Fierce as a dog with tongue lapping for action . . .

Of course, these lines are not by Bertolt Brecht; they are by my principal Chicago witness, Carl Sandburg, and appear in the opening verse of his famous collection of 1916, *Chicago Poems*.[30] But could they not as well have been written by Brecht? Do they not bespeak a similar ambivalence, indeed betray the same "love-hate" relation? Are not both Brecht's and Sandburg's portrayals equally Janus-faced? Admittedly, the latter moved, as he developed, in a direction opposite to that of the former. Yet, if Brecht's image of Chicago has to be a *myth*, then it is certainly not a German, but rather an American myth. Perhaps it is "the" myth of this country and her people, composed as it is of the American dream and the American nightmare, either of which has been shared by millions of Germans.

Notes

1. Patty Lee Parmalee, *Brecht's America* (Oxford: Ohio State University Press, 1981), 116.

2. Eric Bentley, "On Brecht's *In the Swamp, A Man's a Man*, and *Saint Joan of the Stockyards*," in *Brecht: A Collection of Critical Essays*, ed. Peter Demetz, 52 (Englewood Cliffs, N. J.: Prentice Hall, 1962).

3. See Frederic Ewen, *Bertolt Brecht: His Life, His Art and His Times* (New York: Citadel Press, 1967), 113; Thomas O. Brandt, "Das Amerikabild Brechts," in *Deutschlands literarisches Amerikabild; Neuere Forschungen zur Amerikarezeption der deutschen Literatur*, ed. Alexander Ritter, 451–67 (Hildesheim: Olms, 1977); Jan Needle and Peter Thomson, *Brecht* (Chicago: Blackwell, 1981), 28, 86; John Willett, *The Theatre of Bertolt Brecht: A Study from Eight Aspects* (London: Methuen, 1959), 114; etc.

4. Carl Sandburg, *Always the Young Strangers* (New York: Harcourt, Brace, 1952), 168. A copy of this book—dated, however, 1953—is contained in Brecht's library.

5. Ronald Gray, *Brecht the Dramatist* (Cambridge: Cambridge University Press, 1976), 24, 65.

6. Darko Suvin, "Saint Joan of the Slaughterhouses: Assumptions, Exchanges, Seesaws

and Lessons of a Drama Module," in *A Production Notebook to "St. Joan of the Stockyards"* by Bertolt Brecht, ed. Michael D. Bristol and Darko Suvin, 232 (Montréal: McGill University, 1973).

7. See James K. Lyon's *Bertolt Brecht in America* (Princeton: Princeton University Press, 1980); see also Lyon's *Bertolt Brecht's American Cicerone: With an Appendix Containing the Complete Correspondence between Bertolt Brecht and Ferdinand Reyher* (Bonn: Bouvier, 1978). In a letter to me of 31 May 1983, Lyon stated: "On four of his cross-country trips, Brecht passed through Chicago and had to change trains there. Since the railroad lines all pass through the Chicago stockyards (or did then), he saw first-hand the stockyards he had mentioned in *Die heilige Johanna* [*Saint Joan of the Stockyards*]. . . . Otherwise I have no record of his visiting anyone or staying in Chicago."

8. Bertolt Brecht, *Gesammelte Werke in 20 Bänden* (Frankfurt am Main: Suhrkamp, 1967), 1:187. Hereafter cited as *GW*. See also *Collected Plays*, ed. Ralph Manheim and John Willett (New York: Vintage Books, 1971–), 1:157.

9. [Ed. note: see also Patty Lee Parmalee, "*St. Joan of the Stockyards*," in this volume.]

10. See Burkhardt Lindner, *Bertolt Brecht: "Der aufhaltsame Aufstieg des Arturo Ui"* (Munich: Fink, 1982), 159. [Ed. note: see also Ernst Schürer, "Revolution from the Right: Bertolt Brecht's American Gangster Play *The Resistible Rise of Arturo Ui*," in this volume.]

11. Willett, *Theatre*, 30–31.

12. Quoted by Helfried W. Seliger, *Das Amerikabild Bertolt Brechts* (Bonn: Bouvier, 1974), 170.

13. Quoted by Seliger, *Amerikabild*, 21.

14. Bertolt Brecht, *Poems 1913–1956*, ed. John Willett and Ralph Manheim with the co-operation of Erich Fried (New York: Methuen, 1976), 263–64.

15. See *GW*, 20:46; 15:238.

16. For the following, see especially Parmalee, *Brecht's America*, and Seliger, *Amerikabild*. See also Carl S. Smith, *Chicago and the American Literary Imagination 1880–1920* (Chicago: University of Chicago Press, 1984), 152–55.

17. Parmalee, *Brecht's America*, 254.

18. See my *Bertolt Brecht und die Weltliteratur* (Nuremberg: Carl, 1961), 11.

19. *The Letters of Carl Sandburg*, ed. Herbert Mitgang (New York: Harcourt, Brace, and World, 1968), 98.

20. Bertolt Brecht, *Briefe*, ed. Günter Glaeser (Frankfurt: Suhrkamp, 1981), 745.

21. See nn. 1, 7, 12 above; see also Marjorie L. Hoover, "Ihr geht gemeinsam den Weg nach unten: Aufstieg und Fall Amerikas im Werk Bertolt Brechts?," in *Amerika in der deutschen Literatur: Neue Welt – Nordamerika – USA*, ed. Sigrid Bauschinger et al., 294–314 (Stuttgart: Reclam, 1975).

22. Walter Göbel, "Schreckbild Stadt: Chicago im naturalistischen Roman," *LiLi. Zeitschrift für Literaturwissenschaft und Linguistik*, 12, no. 48 (1982):88–102.

23. See Anne Clark et al., "Images of Chicago in Adamic, Mailer and London as compared to *St. Joan*," *A Production Notebook*, 63. See also Göbel, "Schreckbild."

24. Iring Fetscher, "Bertolt Brecht and America," *Salmagundi* 10/11 (Fall 1969–Spring 1970):246–72, 257. Granted, Fetscher says "America"; what he means is the United States or, more precisely, Chicago.

25. See Patty Lee Parmalee, "Brecht's Americanism and His Politics," *Beyond Brecht/ Über Brecht hinaus: Brecht Yearbook* 11 (1983):194. A similar view was already expressed by Seliger, *Amerikabild*, 243–45; see also Jürgen Schäfer, "Brecht und Amerika," *in Über Bertolt Brecht – Aspekte seines Werkes, Spuren seiner Wirkung*, ed. Helmut Koopmann and Theo Stammen (Munich: Ernst Vögel, 1983), 201–17.

26. Göbel, "Schreckbild," 101–2.

27. See BBA [Bertolt-Brecht-Archiv] 898/28, and Brecht, *Briefe*, 504.

28. See Bertolt Brecht, *Im Dickicht der Städte: Erstfassung und Materialien*, ed. Gisela E. Bahr (Frankfurt: Suhrkamp, 1968), 134; *GW*, 4:1723.

29. David Bathrick, "Brecht's Marxism and America," in *Essays on Brecht: Theater and Politics*, ed. Siegfried Mews and Herbert Knust, 209 (Chapel Hill: University of North Carolina Press, 1974).

30. Carl Sandburg, *Chicago Poems* (New York: H. Holt, 1916), 3.

Brecht's Women   James K. Lyon*

Photographs of Brecht fail to convey the uncanny attraction he held for women. A famous German actress once told a friend he was the most sexually exciting man she had ever met.[1] Losey, who associated closely with Brecht during his last year in America, remembers that he was always accompanied by two or three women, and that "he ate very little, drank very little, and fornicated a great deal."[2] A number of Americans who knew him well noted (or complained) that he was constantly surrounded by women — his "harem," his "female followers," his "lady admirers," and his "coterie of mistresses" are a few of their descriptions. These observations apply mainly to Brecht's last two years of American exile, especially while he was working on *Galileo*. Before that time, personal circumstances restricted his opportunities for such liaisons.

All his life Brecht had entered freely into sexual relationships without a sense of obligation or guilt. He rejected the bourgeois notion of love, which to him was an extension of capitalist notions of property ownership based on the feeling that two people "belonged" to each other. His alliances were motivated by a variety of reasons as simple as relaxation or help on his writing and as complex as fundamental ego needs and the desire for intimate human contact. Almost without exception the women he attracted were not beauties, but writers and artists themselves with highly independent personalities.

The consensus among friends is that Brecht's women were captivated by his genius. But speculation on the sources of his personal attraction is ultimately a futile exercise, just as it would be impossible to document the names of all the women with whom he had sexual liaisons in America. Doubtless there were a number of casual relationships, but they are not significant. In terms of his work, there were only two women in America who mattered — his wife Helene Weigel, and Ruth Berlau. His relationship to them mirrors some of the complexity of his makeup which permitted

*From *Bertolt Brecht in America* (Princeton, N. J.: Princeton University Press, 1980), 220-31, 375. Reprinted by permission of Princeton University Press. © 1980, Princeton University Press.

him to care for people without letting emotional considerations control him.

Ruth Berlau

A day after Laughton read the completed *Galileo* to Brecht's assembled friends in early December 1945, a vague journal entry mentions a long-distance call to New York: "At night I call R. and hear unfavorable things."[3] These "unfavorable things" pertained to Ruth Berlau's deteriorating mental state. A family history of mental illness, and the loss of the child she was expecting by Brecht in 1944, had left her more unbalanced than ever. As Christmas 1945 approached, her behavior became increasingly peculiar. On December 27th she became violent with her roommate Ida Bachmann, who called a doctor.[4] When the doctor arrived, Berlau attacked him, whereupon Bachmann called Brecht's friend Fritz Sternberg. Brecht placed one of his regular long-distance calls to Berlau's apartment while Sternberg was there, and the latter confirmed through "yes-no" answers that she had suffered a breakdown.[5] Brecht then phoned [his American friend, Ferdinand] Reyher, whom Berlau liked, and asked for help. The next day Reyher, a Dr. Gruenthal, and the police picked up Berlau and took her to Bellevue Hospital. On December 31st she was transferred to a mental hospital in Amityville, Long Island, where she spent a number of weeks undergoing electric-shock treatment.

Brecht, who was sick with severe flu and a high fever in January, could not come immediately. But sentences from a letter to Reyher reporting a telephone conversation with Berlau following her confinement show that his feeling for her ran deep enough to make an unusual confession: "They must allow her to call me here when she is able. That, too, would help her. . . . The fact that she is so far away and in strange hands naturally upsets me very much."[6]

Brecht's sole purpose for the cross-country trip which brought him to New York on February 10th was to care for Berlau. Hoping to have her released from the hospital, he accompanied [actress Elisabeth] Bergner and [producer Paul] Czinner to Amityville, only to discover she was still very ill. On one visit he told Berlau he wanted to take her home. She shouted that he would have to get enough cars for the thirty-two other patients there, whereupon she threw him out. Berlau later claimed he muttered something to Bergner about no one being as crazy as a crazy Communist,[7] but he continued to return until some time in March, when Berlau was well enough to be released to his care. In the ensuing weeks Brecht was preoccupied with looking after her in her 57th Street apartment. Only when she stabilized did he resume promoting his own theater projects.

Like Brecht's other female collaborators, Berlau was an alter ego who filled a need in his writing. In America, his need for her became particularly acute. After Margarete Steffin's death in Moscow in 1941, he had no other close female associate. Consequently he began to invest in Berlau the attention he normally shared with several at once. With the exception of Weigel, no person, male or female, played a more significant role in his life and works between 1941–1945 than Berlau, and few relationships at any time were more intense. In Brecht's words, her love "could make five continents happy."[8]

Berlau was a warm, spontaneous, and affectionate person. She was also a scolding, possessive, often hysterical individual who existed only in extremes and who could shift from one mood to the other without warning. Never secure in Brecht's affection, she made such excessive demands on him that at times she became his personal fury. Her insistence that he write her daily forced him to send more letters to her during his American years than to all other friends combined, and more than to any single person in his lifetime.[9] In them he reveals a private side that is seldom seen. One letter thanking her for cigars she sent (he had her buy El Capitan Corona cigars from a shop in New York) contains an uncharacteristically sentimental expression by Brecht, who describes walking in his garden in Santa Monica one evening: "A silver haze filled the evening sky, and no stars were visible. But I knew you were looking up, and I stood, so to speak, next to you."[10] Others show him as a concerned friend and lover who is solicitous of her health (she did not eat properly and drank excessively), reassuring about his feelings for her, and sometimes almost maudlin in expressing them. Brecht seldom apologized, but Berlau managed to extract repeated apologies from him for his irregular letters. Her constant reprimands were no doubt responsible for eliciting from him unusually direct expressions of affection. But it would be inaccurate to claim that Berlau extracted these reassurances from an unwilling subject.

If one can believe his letters, Brecht felt a genuine need for Berlau. Like a leitmotif, the phrase "I need you" recurs throughout them as his means of expressing feeling obliquely. And dozens of letters close with the abbreviation (and sometimes the complete words) of "I love you" in Berlau's native Danish tongue (*je elsker dig*) or with the abbreviation e.p.e.p. for the Latin *et probe et procus* (near and far). Yet these are not conventional love letters. In spite of the strong concern they express for her diet, her health, her writing, her discomfort in the New York heat, and financial circumstances, they more often resemble business correspondence instructing an agent how to deal with his works, requesting help, or seeking advice on collaborative projects. Brecht tried to structure their relationship that way. To compensate Berlau for losing her job with the Office of War Information in mid-1943 (her employers discovered that she was a Communist), he asked her to become his "New York office" and manage his affairs there. Quickly she assumed the role of his authorized agent. This required that his letters to her deal largely with business matters, thereby keeping emotional and private considerations in the background. Though he sent her money from time to time, he even tried to depersonalize this. In one letter containing two checks, he states that they are in payment for "six months work" and urges her to keep receipts "for tax purposes."[11]

It was also a sign of Brecht's need for and dependence on her that nearly everything he wrote in America, including poems, went to her for criticism and approval. In New York, in Santa Monica, or by mail, Berlau collaborated on *The Primer of War, Chalk Circle,* a long epic poem that includes part of the *Communist Manifesto, Schweyk, Setzuan,* and a number of lesser works. After the 1942 production of *Master Race,* he assigned her to send clippings and to communicate with the director about possible future performances. At the 1945 English production, she worked in the theater with him as his "production secretary" and photographed the rehearsals and the performances. On July 10, 1945, Brecht wrote out a formal power of attorney for her to act in his behalf.[12]

After becoming pregnant by Brecht early in 1944, Berlau returned to Santa Monica in June of that year. The removal of a tumor on September 3rd, which resulted in the premature birth of a male child, left further evidence of Brecht's concealed tender side. A note in an envelope of the Cedars of Lebanon Hospital addressed to her in room 314 reads: "Love, I am so glad that you are fighting so courageously. Don't think that I do not want to see you when you are ill. You are beautiful then, too. I am coming tomorrow before noon. Yours, Bertolt."[13]

After returning to New York in March 1945 Berlau did odd jobs, ranging from factory work and house cleaning to barkeeping. But jobs were only a means of subsistence; her life was essentially committed to Brecht and his works. Unselfish, generous to a fault, and self-effacing when it came to his works, but also domineering, histrionic, and brazen, she promoted him so zealously that she sometimes hurt his best interests. [Publisher James] Laughlin recalls her marching into the New Directions office in the summer of 1945 and, in dramatic fashion, announcing that she was "very important" to Brecht. She then demanded royalty payments for the book version of *Master Race,* which Brecht had asked her to pick up. Luise Rainer, who called her "loony," remembers Berlau's coming to her apartment in New York with a version of *Galileo* and ordering her to get out her recording machine so she could read it aloud for her. In her determination to record Brecht's works for posterity, Berlau also took a three-month photography course from Joseph Breitenbach in the spring of 1944, specifically to learn how to make microfilm copies.[14] After 1947 this skill enabled her to photograph and to produce "model books" showing exemplary scenes from his plays as he staged them himself. Her abrasiveness, however, did not please Brecht, nor did her use of his name in money matters. In promoting his affairs, she felt entitled to use people. She never paid Breitenbach for his instruction, and she generally avoided settling debts by explaining that she and Brecht did not have the money.

For years Weigel had tolerated Brecht's female collaborators and even entertained them in her home. During Brecht's American exile, she explained her forbearance by stoically telling a friend that when one is married to a genius, one tolerates things one would not in a normal marriage.[15] She knew Brecht needed women for his writing, and normally she endured it silently. But she could not abide Berlau. All his life Brecht paid inordinate attention to the opinions of his female alter egos. In the United States, Berlau's role was magnified because he was in a strange land struggling for success, and at the outset she was the lone surviving member of his coterie of ego reinforcers. Friends close to both of them maintain that she was very important to him at this time and that, in contrast to other relationships, their closeness virtually made her Brecht's second wife.[16] Weigel reacted strongly against her because she recognized this unusual intimacy. In her opinion, Berlau's near worship of Brecht was a destructive influence on him.

Berlau's notorious indiscretion angered Weigel. To fellow employees of the OWI in New York, she trumpeted that she was the "whore of a classical writer"; in Santa Monica after her breakdown, she broadcast that she was "Brecht's backstreet wife."[17] Berlau's intimidating aggressiveness in promoting him soured friendships, and more than once Brecht felt obliged to defend her bizarre actions to his own detriment. In dealing with Brecht's translators in New York, this Danish woman, who commanded neither English nor German well, condemned nearly every translation of Brecht into English in which he did not personally have a hand. Overly protective of his works, she was excessively critical of Kreymborg's *Schweyk* translations, of the Stern and Auden *Chalk Circle*, and of lesser translations. Repeatedly Brecht's letters to her rebut her criticisms, gracefully reject bad advice, and generally try to mollify her. In them, one of the few times in his life, he was usually defensive.

In spite of an overbearing manner and a demanding nature, Berlau was blindly devoted to Brecht. She claimed, for example, that she dressed in the puritanical fashion he dictated, which included wearing dark, solid colors and long dresses. Because she had once been an actress at the Danish Royal theater and an aspiring writer herself, in American exile Berlau felt increasingly frustrated at having accomplished nothing of note. Brecht demanded that all his collaborators produce their own works, and he usually assisted them unselfishly. In Denmark he had helped Berlau write several pieces, but in America this almost stopped. She could not or would not write, and this intensified a sense of inadequacy that she compensated for by her work for and with Brecht. In a series of vignettes about his feelings for her which he wrote during his Scandinavian and American exile and appended to the *Me-Ti/Book of Changes*, Brecht characterizes her importance to him in terms that he intends as complimentary. One passage demonstrates how completely she lived for him. Using the mask "Lai-tu" for her, he writes: "Lai-tu has a low regard for herself because she had not produced any great work. . . . Neither as an actress nor as a writer has she accomplished anything special. . . . Me-ti [Brecht] said to her: it is true that you have not delivered any goods, but that does not mean you have not accomplished anything. Your kindness has been noticed and appreciated by its being used. Thus an apple achieves fame by being eaten."[18]

Weigel's analysis of Berlau's baleful influence on Brecht may or may not have been correct, but, if Brecht's letters are credible, his devotion to Berlau was undisputable. There the mode of speech is always "we," not "you" or "I." Repeatedly he speaks of wanting her to return to Santa Monica as soon as he can support her. When she returned to New York in 1945, she extracted a promise of complete fidelity from him and agreed on a code phrase that appeared in many subsequent letters reassuring her that he was faithful to her. The phrase was: "Everything is all right." She was apparently the first to violate this promise when she had an affair with a Danish acquaintance shortly before her breakdown. Her infidelity clearly hurt Brecht. In reaction to it he wrote a poem entitled "The Writer Feels Himself Betrayed by a Friend," an unusual expression of personal vulnerability on Brecht's part. Speaking obliquely of his reaction as though it were someone else's experience ("the writer") and being intentionally vague about what is felt, this poem about a faithless beloved uses the title to make six simple comparisons lacking commentary:

> What a child feels when its mother goes away with a strange man.
> What a carpenter feels when overcome by dizziness, a sign of aging.
> What a painter feels when his model does not return and the picture is not finished.
> What a physicist feels when he discovers the error at the beginning of his series of experiments.
> What a flier feels when the oil pressure drops while over the mountains.
> What an airplane, if it could feel, feels when its pilot is drunk.
>
> (GW, 10:938)

Berlau reproached herself when Brecht disapproved of her behavior. To a puzzled roommate she quoted a statement she heard him use many times: "Call a dog a bitch, and it turns into a bitch." She appended to it, "Call a woman a whore, and she becomes a whore. I am now a whore."[19]

Berlau's hysterical, sometimes maniacal behavior in the years following her breakdown and convalescence became one of the heaviest burdens that Brecht bore in the last decade of his life. It also stretched Weigel to the limit of her endurance. Rhoda Riker, a friend of the family, remembers receiving a phone call from Weigel in the spring of 1946, saying her husband had just phoned from New York. If she did not take in Berlau, he said, he would not come home. With her usual sense of realism, Weigel accepted necessity and arranged for Berlau to stay with Anna Harrington in her "Uplifters" apartment in Santa Monica. Her only condition was that Berlau be kept out of her sight.

Helene ("Helli") Weigel

Helene Weigel shared at least one trait with her husband — each put his career ahead of personal feelings. Unusually devoted to him, and as convinced of his genius as he was, her life in American exile displayed the same single-mindedness in promoting Brecht's career that marked his own actions. When she told a friend that Berlau's affection for Brecht inflated his ego in a way harmful to his creativity,[20] she was speaking less from jealousy than from the conviction that emotional pampering was not good for him. She seems to have understood his emotional makeup and, if possible, she was more tough-minded than he was in protecting him against excessive passion, especially if it were for a demanding and difficult woman. Knowing his need to be surrounded by stimulating friends and collaborators, she put on weekly socials for him. Many European and American friends report attending her Sunday night "kindergarten," as it came to be called by some.

On the surface their marriage manifested what appeared to be a de-personalization of feeling by two artists who respected and promoted each other. Brecht, for example, never spoke of her by her first name, but only as "Weigel"; she in turn never referred to him in the presence of close friends or in letters as "my husband" or "Bertolt," but always as "Brecht." Yet beneath this exterior existed genuine admiration and concern for the other. But, in the Brecht household, private affairs were seldom discussed, to say nothing of emotions. Their relationship apparently minimized the emotional or private side of life. As Brecht's dramas prove, concealing them this way can sometimes be the most effective means of expressing them. Elsa Lanchester recalls that "she was loyal to him; they understood each other."[21] Moreover, they learned from each other. Bentley believes that Weigel, along with one or two other actors and actresses who were close to Brecht over the years, did more to shape his conception of acting than all abstract considerations of theatrical theory. A number of his characters and much of his theory of unemotive "epic" acting can be traced directly to this woman who excelled at this type of portrayal.

That is not to say that Weigel lacked emotions. She possessed great sensitivity and deep feelings. She was enormously generous, whether in supporting Salka Viertel financially for a period of five to six months during 1946 when Mrs. Viertel was without funds,[22] or in turning her home after the war into a relief center that dispatched countless packages to relatives and to acquaintances in Europe. Friends and neighbors recount dozens of anecdotes about her thoughtfulness and compassion. Brecht's long absences in 1946 (he spent nearly six months of that year on the East Coast) also moved her to something unusual—this normally very private woman expressed her frustration to a friend.[23] But this was uncharacteristic. She was a lady all her life, albeit a Marxist lady in proletarian garb, and she seldom lost control or surrendered her natural graciousness.

[Morton] Wurtele recalls overhearing a conversation in their home which illustrates her toughness of mind. Weigel had maintained that women have more physical fortitude than men and had cited menstruation, child-bearing, etc., as evidence. Brecht, who was noted for an ever-present two-day growth of beard, lamely retorted, "Men shave," to which Weigel fired back, "How do you know?" Weigel appears to have been one of the few persons, especially among those closest to Brecht, who could hold her own with him. Tenacity and devotion; unshaken conviction of her husband's greatness; total commitment to a common political ideology; stoic forbearance, charm, and a splendid sense of humor—these made her equal to the difficult demands of consorting with this complex man. She learned English better than Brecht and probably adjusted to daily life in America more readily than he. In refusing to be frustrated by the circumstances of exile, she established surprisingly stable conditions for him and for his writing. It is impossible to estimate how much her sheer presence helped to keep alive his dramatic gifts during a period when he had no stage to write for. As a genius of theater *praxis* who also happened to be a dramatist, Brecht needed contact with actors and actresses in order to write. Throughout his exile, the actress Weigel represented the only uninterrupted connection he had with someone whose ideas on the performability of his works were accompanied by credibility as his kind of performer. In America, Weigel had no chance to display her ability anywhere except in conversations with Brecht.

Speaking of Weigel's lot in American exile, Salka Viertel claims she went through hell for Brecht: "I can't imagine another woman taking all that." Nor did she mean only Brecht's peccadillos. Flight from Germany in 1933 had abruptly ended Weigel's flourishing career as an actress and had cast her in the unaccustomed role of housewife, mother, business manager and support troops for the exiled dramatist. American theater people often expressed disbelief when they learned that this frugal, hard-working German *hausfrau*, whose bobbed hair and plain features made her resemble a Käthe Kollwitz drawing, had been a prominent European actress. They saw only how she furnished their home from junk shops and Good Will, cooked, scrubbed, painted, gardened, sewed, and baked excellent Viennese apple strudel for her Sunday night socials. In addition to housework, she nursed dying trees and a tubercular daughter; exchanged recipes, fruits, and baked goods with her neighbors; and tried to surround Brecht with the stimulating friends he needed for his writing.

Those who had known Weigel as an actress in Europe generally pitied her, and there is no question that she felt frustrated by lack of opportunity.

Salka Viertel states that "It is not easy to be a domestic slavey, but Helli never complained."[24] Oskar Homolka called her a "kitchen slave" who did not participate in conversations and who always withdrew voluntarily when Brecht's male friends gathered. Elsa Lanchester claims that Brecht "did not want her—he would not allow her—to appear in Hollywood films in small character parts. Because, of course, she would have had a German accent. . . . And so she was a rather unhappy woman."[25]

Most of these perceptions are not accurate, especially the remark that Brecht did not want Weigel to appear in Hollywood films. His vain attempts to secure roles for her is a token of the admiration he felt. He explicitly wrote what he thought would be a role for her in *Hangmen Also Die* and extracted a promise from [director Fritz] Lang to let her play it. A copy of the script at one point shows her name on a tentative cast list for the role of Mrs. Dvorak, the vegetable woman,[26] and Brecht's journal claims that Lang gave her a brief screen test for the role.[27] Lang denies having made such a promise or having given her a screen test,[28] and she did not get the role. In 1944, through the help of refugee friends, Weigel did play a 30-second silent part in the film *The Seventh Cross* starring Spencer Tracy. Weigel later told friends that this represented the highest paid part per second in her acting career.[29] It was her only professional appearance in more than six years of American exile, a dormant period that left her uncertain about her ability as an actress. As a consequence, the first drama in which she appeared after returning to Europe had to be in a small provincial theater in Chur, Switzerland, since she lacked the confidence to make her debut in a major city.

Claims have been made that Weigel gave acting instruction to aspiring actresses in Hollywood,[30] but reality was less glamorous. Sometime during 1941–1942 she met a Hungarian-born, German-speaking actress who had been studying at Max Reinhardt's Hollywood dramatic school. After hearing her complain of her lack of success, Weigel gave her acting lessons (in English) in their living room.[31] Generally her activities were restricted to this type of behind-the-scenes work to promote someone else's career.

Salka Viertel remembers hearing Brecht say how it upset him that Weigel was not given more parts in Hollywood films. He was as concerned about her career as he was about his own, for he considered her a first-rate actress. In September 1946, after watching Elisabeth Bergner open on Broadway in *The Duchess of Malfi*, Brecht sent a telegram to Weigel succinctly comparing her to this internationally known stage and film star: "As for Bergner, I see what an actress you are."[32] This expression of admiration, referring to her professional rather than personal qualities, is typical of Brecht's tendency to structure even the most intimate human relationships with as much detachment as possible.

Weigel was a silent but significant figure in Brecht's American exile. His journal and reports of friends prove that she was present at far more discussions about the theater and about his works than one might expect of a "kitchen slave," for Brecht esteemed her practical judgment on the theater as highly as he did her political commitment. During preparations for the Hollywood *Galileo* production in 1947, she was also a dominant behind-the-scenes presence, sewing costumes, rehearsing actors and actresses, and helping with hundreds of details. In the American exile she dedicated her great gifts to promoting the works and image of Bertolt Brecht at a time when she had no chance to use her own talent.

When Brecht left Santa Monica for Washington and New York in October 1947 on the way to Europe, Weigel closed up the house, sold their goods, and followed a few days later. In New York for the first time, preparing to embark for Europe and a renewed stage career, she and her daughter Barbara did what they never could do in Santa Monica — went to Broadway musicals. Among others, they saw *Finian's Rainbow* and *Oklahoma!* But it was Ethel Merman in a performance of *Annie Get Your Gun* who proved that the actress in Weigel was still alive and learning. At one point, Merman responded to seeing the man she loved by standing with her mouth agape. Less than three years later, Weigel borrowed the same gesture for her smash success in *Mother Courage* at the point when Courage met her former love, the cook.[33] With one exception, this minor addition to her acting career and the wide circle of friends she gained were the only positive results of her years in America. That exception was to help to keep alive Bertolt Brecht's dramatic talent in American exile.

Notes

1. Interview, Salka Viertel. Viertel declined to identify the actress.

2. Guy Flatley, "Remembrances of Joseph Losey's Past." [*Los Angeles Times*, 9 March 1975.]

3. [Bertolt Brecht,] *Arbeitsjournal*, [2 vols., ed. Werner Hecht (Frankfurt am Main: Suhrkamp, 1973)], 2 Dec. 1945, [2:766. Hereafter cited as *AJ*.]

4. Letter dated 11 Jan. 1946, Ida Bachmann to Brecht.

5. Fritz Sternberg, *Der Dichter und die Ratio. Erinnerungen an Bertolt Brecht* (Göttingen: Sachse & Pohl, 1963), pp. 53–54.

6. Letter dated January, 1946, Brecht to Reyher.

7. Interview, Ruth Berlau.

8. Gisela Bahr, unpublished paper, "Brecht's Fellow Exile in America: Ruth Berlau," p. 3, delivered at the International Brecht Symposium College Park, Maryland, 29 March 1979. Bahr is citing a statement by Brecht from a [then] unpublished biography of Ruth Berlau. [Ed. note: see Ruth Berlau, *Brechts Lai-tu. Erinnerungen und Notate*, ed. Hans Bunge (Darmstadt: Luchterhand, 1985), 250). See also the review by Gisela E. Bahr, in *Theatre Journal* 39 (1987):524–28.]

9. According to Bahr, *ibid.*, p. 1, Berlau by her own account donated to the East German Academy of Arts a total of 1007 letters which Brecht wrote to her.

10. Letter dated 23 June 1943, Brecht to Berlau. [Ed. note: see Bertolt Brecht, *Briefe 1913–1956*, ed. Günter Glaeser (Frankfurt am Main: Suhrkamp, 1981), 463.]

11. Letter dated 2 May 1943, Brecht to Berlau.

12. Bertolt-Brecht-Archiv 1185/35.

13. Quoted from an unpublished agent's report in Brecht's FBI files.

14. Interview, Joseph Breitenbach.

15. Interview, Rhoda Riker Pecker.

16. Interviews with Rhoda Riker Pecker; Anna Hagen Harrington; and Salka Viertel.

17. Interview, Anna Hagen Harrington.

18. [Ed. note: Bertolt Brecht, "Me-ti/Buch der Wendungen," *Gesammelte Werke in 20 Bänden* (Frankfurt am Main: Suhrkamp, 1967), 12:585. Subsequently cited as *GW*.]

19. Letter dated 11 Jan. 1946, Ida Bachmann to Brecht.

20. Interview, Rhoda Riker Pecker.

21. Elsa Lanchester, "Brecht in Hollywood," [*Annual Annual* (Berkeley, Calif.: Pacifica Foundation, 1965),] p. 7.

22. Interview, Salka Viertel.

23. Interview, Rhoda Riker Pecker.

24. [Salka Viertel,] *The Kindness of Strangers* [(New York: Holt, Rinehart and Winston, 1969)], p. 285.

25. "Brecht in Hollywood," p. 7.

26. Unpublished screenplay of *Hangmen Also Die*, University of Wisconsin Library.

27. *AJ*, 24 Nov. 1942 [2:547.]

28. Letter dated 23 Aug. 1971, Lang to this author.

29. Interview, Morton Wurtele.

30. See her "biography" in *Helene Weigel zu Ehren*, eds. Werner Hecht and Siegfried Unseld (Frankfurt am Main: Suhrkamp, 1970), p. 132.

31. Interviews, Barbara Brecht and Günther Anders.

32. Interview, Morton Wurtele.

33. According to interview with Barbara Brecht, who accompanied her mother.

Brecht and Discourse: A Contribution to the Study of Discursivity

Roland Barthes*

The Third Discourse[1]

Poor B. B.: this is the title of a poem by Bertolt Brecht, written in 1921 (Brecht is twenty-three).[2] These are not the initials of fame; this is the person reduced to two markers; these two letters (and repetitive ones at that) frame a void, and this void is the apocalypse of Weimar Germany; out of this void will rise (around 1928–30) Brechtian Marxism. Hence, there are two discourses in Brecht's oeuvre: first, an apocalyptic (anarchizing) discourse concerned to express and to produce destruction without

*Excerpted from *The Rustle of Language* by Roland Barthes. Translation © 1986 by Farrar, Straus & Giroux, Inc. Reprinted by permission of Hill & Wang, a division of Farrar, Straus & Giroux.

trying to see what comes "*afterwards*," for "*afterwards*" is just as undesirable; this discourse generates Brecht's first plays (*Baal, Drums in the Night, In the Jungle of Cities*): then, an eschatological discourse: a critique constructed *with a view to* ending the fatality of social alienation (or the belief in this fatality): what does not go well with the world (war, exploitation) is *remediable:* a time of cure is conceivable; this second discourse generates all of Brecht's oeuvre after *The Threepenny Opera.*[3]

A third discourse is missing: an apologetic discourse. There is no Marxist catechism in Brecht: no stereotype, no recourse to the vulgate. Doubtless, the theatrical form shielded him from this danger, since in the theater, as in any text, the origin of the speech-act cannot be located: impossible the — Sadean — collusion of subject and signified (this collusion produces a fanatic discourse), or the — hoaxing — collusion of sign and referent (which produces a dogmatic discourse); but even in his essays — I refer here to the French anthology *Ecrits sur la politique et la société,*[4] published in 1970, a crucial work which has gone virtually unnoticed, as far as I know — Brecht never allows himself the facility of *signing* the origin of his discourse, of imprinting upon it the official stamp of the Marxist imperium: his language is not a coinage. In Marxism itself, Brecht is a permanent inventor; he reinvents quotations, accedes to the inter-text: "He thought in other heads; and in his own, others besides himself thought. This is true thinking." True thinking is more important than the (idealist) thought of truth. In other words, in the Marxist field, Brecht's discourse is never a priestly discourse.

The Shock

All that we read and hear covers us like a layer, surrounds and envelops us like a medium: the logosphere. This logosphere is given to us by our period, our class, our métier: it is a "datum" of our subject. Now, to displace what is given can only be the result of a shock; we must shake up the balanced mass of words, pierce the layer, disturb the linked order of the sentences, break the structures of the language (every structure is an edifice of levels). Brecht's work seeks to elaborate a shock-practice (not a subversion: the shock is much more "realistic" than subversion); his critical art is one which opens a crisis: which lacerates, which crackles the smooth surface, which fissures the crust of languages, loosens and dissolves the stickiness of the logosphere; it is an *epic* art: one which discontinues the textures of words, distances representation without annulling it.

And what is this distancing, this discontinuity which provokes the Brechtian shock? It is merely a reading which detaches the sign from its effect. Have you ever seen a Japanese pin? It is a dressmaker's pin whose head is a tiny bell, so that you cannot forget it once the garment has been finished. Brecht remakes the logosphere by leaving the bell-headed pins in it, the signs furbished with their tiny jingle: thus, when we hear a certain language, we never forget where it comes from, how it was made: the shock is a *reproduction:* not an imitation, but a production that has been disconnected, displaced: *which makes noise.*

Hence, better than a semiology, what Brecht leaves us with is a seismology. Structurally, what is a shock? A moment difficult to sustain (and therefore antipathetic to the very notion of "structure"); Brecht does not want us to fall under the spell of another smooth surface, another language-"nature": no positive hero (the positive hero is always sticky), no hysterical practice of the shock: the shock is distinct, discrete *(and* discreet), swift, repeated if need be, but never *established* (this is not a theater of subversion: no great contestatory apparatus). For instance, if there is a field buried under the smooth layer of the quotidian logosphere, it is certainly that of class relations; now, Brecht does not subvert this field (this is not the role he assigns to his dramaturgy; moreover, how would a *discourse* subvert these relations?), he imprints a shock upon it, sticks in a bell-headed pin: for example, it is Puntila's drunkenness, a temporary and recurrent laceration, imposed upon the sociolect of the big landowner;[5] contrary to so many scenes of bourgeois theater and cinema, Brecht never deals with drunkenness as such (the sticky tedium of boozer's scenes): drunkenness is never anything but the agent which modifies a relation, and consequently *offers it to be read* (a relation can be read only *retrospectively* when somewhere, at some point, however remote or tenuous, this relation has altered). Alongside so exact a treatment (exact because kept to its strictest economy), how absurd seem most films about "narcotics"! Using the alibi of the *underground,* it is drugs "as such" which are always represented, their evil effects, their ecstasies, their style, in short their "attributes," not their functions: does this representation permit a critical reading of some supposedly "natural" configuration of human relations? Where is the reading-shock?

Rehearse Softly

In his political texts, Brecht gives us a reading exercise: he reads us a Nazi speech (by Hess) and suggests the rules for a proper reading of this kind of text.[6]

Thus, Brecht joins the group of Exercise-Givers, of "Regulators"; those who give not regulations but regulated means for achieving a goal; in the same way, Sade gave rules for pleasure (it is a veritable exercise that Juliette imposes upon the lovely Countess de Donis), Fourier those for happiness, Loyola those for communication with the Divine. The rules taught by Brecht aim at reestablishing the truth of a text: not its metaphysical (or philological) truth, but its historical truth: the truth of a governmental script in a fascist country: an action-truth, a truth *produced* and not asserted.

The exercise consists in saturating the mendacious text by intercalating between its sentences the critical complement which demystifies each one of them: "Legitimately proud of the spirit of sacrifice . . . " Hess pompously began, in the name of "Germany"; and Brecht softly completes: "Proud of the generosity of those possessors who have sacrificed a little of what the non-possessors had sacrificed to them . . ." — and so forth. Each sentence is reversed because it is supplemented: the critique does not diminish, does not suppress, it adds.

In order to produce the proper supplement, Brecht recommends *rehearsing* the text, the exercise, *softly*. The critique is first produced in a kind of clandestinity: what is read is the text *for oneself*, not *in itself*; the low voice is *the one that concerns me*: a reflexive (and sometimes erotic) voice, producing what is intelligible, the original voice of reading. To repeat the exercise (to read the text several times) is gradually to liberate its "supplements"; thus, the haiku compensates for its conspicuous brevity by repetition: the tiny poem is murmured three times, in echoes; this practice is so well coded that the amplitude of the supplements (the "length of the resonance") bears a name: *hibiki;* as for the infinity of links liberated by repetition, this is called *utsuri*.

What is astonishing, at the endurable limit of the paradox, is that this refined practice, closely linked to an erotics of the text, is applied by Brecht to the reading of a hateful text. The destruction of monstrous discourse is here conducted according to an erotic technique; it mobilizes not the reductive weapons of demystification but rather the caresses, the amplifications, the ancestral subtleties of a literary mandarinate, as if there were not, on one side, the vengeful rigor of Marxist science (the science which knows the reality of fascist speeches) and, on the other, the complacencies of the man of letters; but rather as if it were natural *to take pleasure in the truth*, as if one had the simple right, the *immoral* right to submit the bourgeois text to a critique itself formed by the reading techniques of a certain bourgeois past; and indeed where would the critique of bourgeois discourse come from if not from that discourse itself? Discursivity is, till now, without alternative.

Concatenation

Because they are concatenated, Brecht says, errors produce an illusion of truth; Hess's speech may seem true, insofar as it is *successive*. Brecht questions concatenation, questions successive discourse; all the pseudo-logic of the discourse — links, transitions, the patina of elocution, in short the continuity of speech — releases a kind of force, engenders an illusion of assurance: concatenated discourse is indestructible, triumphant. The first attack is therefore to make it discontinuous — to discontinue it: literally to dismember the erroneous text is a polemical act. "To unveil" is not so much to draw back the veil as to cut it to pieces; in the veil, one ordinarily comments upon only the image of that which conceals, but the other meaning of the image is also important: the *smooth*, the *sustained*, the *successive;* to attack the mendacious text is to separate the fabric, to tear apart the folds of the veil.

The critique of the *continuum* (here applied to discourse) is a constant one in Brecht. One of his first plays, *In the Jungle of Cities,* still seems enigmatic to many critics because in it two partners take part in a duel incomprehensible not on the level of each of its peripeties but on the level of the whole, i.e., according to a continuous reading: Brecht's theater is henceforth a series (not a consequence) of cut-up fragments deprived of what in music is called the Zeigarnik effect (when the final resolution of a musical sequence retroactively gives it its meaning). Discontinuity of discourse keeps the final meaning from "taking": critical production does not wait — it will be instantaneous and repeated: this is the very definition of epic theater according to Brecht. Epic is what cuts (shears) the veil, disaggregates the stickiness of mystification (see the preface to *Maha-gonny*).[7]

The Maxim

Brecht's praise of the fragment (of the scene presented "for its own sake") is not that of the maxim. The maxim is not a fragment; first of all, because the maxim is generally the point of departure of an implicit reasoning, the outset of a continuity surreptitiously developing in the docile inter-text which inhabits the reader; then, because the Brechtian fragment never generalizes — it is not "concise," it does not "assemble"; it can be loose, relaxed, fed on contingencies, specifications, dialectical *données;* whereas the maxim is a statement minus History: it remains a bluff of "Nature."

Hence, Brecht's unceasing supervision of the maxim. The Hero is doomed, one might say, because the maxim is his "natural" language ("Wherever you find great virtues, you can be sure that something is going wrong"); the same applies to widespread Custom, for it is based on gnomic truths: "He who takes the first step must also take the second": who says this, and in this form? The cultural code, whose false logic is abusive, for he who takes the first step does not necessarily have to take the second. To break the custom is, first of all, to break the maxim, the stereotype: under the rule, discover the abuse; under the maxim, discover the concatenation; under Nature, discover History.

Metonymy

In his speech, Hess constantly speaks of Germany. But Germany, here, is only the German "possessors." The Whole is given, abusively, for the part. Synecdoche is totalitarian: it is an act of force. "The whole for the part" — this definition of metonymy means: one part *against* another part, the German possessors *against* the rest of Germany. The predicate ("German") becomes the subject ("the Germans"): there occurs a kind of local *Putsch:* metonymy becomes a class weapon.

How to combat metonymy? How, *on the level of discourse,* to restore the sum to its parts, how to undo the abusive Name? This is a very Brechtian problem. In the theater, the undoing of the Name is easy enough, for it is inevitably only bodies that are represented there. If we must speak of the "People" on the stage (for this word itself can be metonymic, can engender abuses), we must divide up the concept: in *The Trial of Lucullus,* the "People" is the meeting of a peasant, a slave, a schoolmaster, a fishmonger, a baker, a prostitute. Brecht says somewhere that Reason is never what the totality of reasonable people think: the (invariably abusive?) concept is reduced to a summation of historical bodies.

However, de-nomination — or ex-nomination — because *infinitely subversive,* is difficult to sustain. It is tempting to exculpate a Cause, to excuse the errors and stupidities of its partisans, separating the excellence of the Name from the imbecilities of its subjects. Berdyaev once wrote a brochure entitled *On the Dignity of Christianity and the Indignity of Christians . . .* Ah, if we could similarly purify Marxist discourse of the dogmatism of Marxists, the Revolution of the hysteria of revolutionaries, and in a general way the Idea from the neurosis of its supporters! But in vain: political discourse is fundamentally metonymic, for it can only be established by the power of language, and this power is metonymy itself. Thus, there recurs in discourse the major religious figure, that of Contagion, of Fault, of Terror, i.e., in all these cases, the subjection by violence of the part to the whole, of the body to the Name; religious discourse is indeed the model of all political discourse: no theology could acknowledge that Faith is merely the entirety of those who believe. Now, from the viewpoint of Marxist "custom," Brecht is very heretical: he resists all metonymies; there is a kind of Brechtian individualism: the "People" is a collection of individuals assembled on the stage; the "Bourgeoisie" is here a landlord, there a rich man, etc. The theater compels undoing the Name. I can readily imagine some theoretician, ultimately disgusted with Names yet reluctant to abandon all language — I can imagine this Brechtian epigone renouncing his past speeches and resolving henceforth to write only novels.

The Sign

Yes, Brecht's theater is a theater of the Sign. But if we want to understand how and whereby this semiology can be, more profoundly, a seismology, we must always remember that the originality of the Brechtian sign is that it is *to be read twice over:* what Brecht gives us to read is, by a kind of disengagement, the reader's gaze, not directly the object of his reading; for this object reaches us only by the act of intellection (an alienated act) of a first reader who is already on the stage. The best example of this "turn," paradoxically, I should borrow not from Brecht but from my personal experience (a copy is readily more exemplary than the original; "Brecht-like" can be more Brechtian than "Brecht").

Here then is a "street scene"[8] of which I was a witness. The public beach of Tangier, in summer, is carefully supervised; one is not permitted to undress there—not out of modesty, no doubt, but rather to compel bathers to rent the cabanas which line the promenade—i.e., to keep the "poor" (this category exists in Morocco) off the beach, thereby reserved for the bourgeois and the tourists. On the promenade, an adolescent boy, solitary, sad, and poverty-stricken (signs *for me*, I confess, deriving from a *simple* reading, which is not yet Brechtian), is walking along; a policeman (almost as filthy as the boy) passes him and looks him up and down, I *see* his scrutiny, I see it reach and linger over the *shoes;* then the cop orders the boy off the beach.

This scene invites two commentaries. The first will accommodate our indignation provoked by the barricading of the beach, the grim subjection of the boy, the arbitrary action of the police, the segregation of money, the Moroccan regime; now, this commentary would not be Brecht's (though this would certainly be his "reaction"). The second commentary will establish the mirror action of the signs; it will note first of all that there is a feature in the boy's garments which is the major sign of poverty: the shoe, it is here that the social sign explodes in all its violence (there used to be, not so long ago, in the days when we had "the poor," a mythology of the cast-off shoe: if the intellectual rots from his head down, like fish, the poor man rots from the feet up—which is why Fourier, seeking to invert the civilized order, imagines a corps of flamboyant cobblers); and, in the realm of the shoe, the extreme point of poverty is the old slipper, without laces, the upper flattened beneath the heel, precisely in the fashion exhibited by the boy. But what this second commentary would especially note is that this sign is read by the cop himself: it is when his gaze, descending the body's length, perceives the wretched shoe, that the policeman, with a single impulse, by a veritable paradigmatic leap, classifies the boy among those to be expelled: we understand that he has understood—and why he has understood. The action may not stop here: the cop himself is almost as ragged as his victim: except, precisely, for his shoes! Round, shiny, solid, old-fashioned, like all policemen's shoes. Whence we can read *two alienations confronting one another* (a situation sketched in a scene from a neglected play by Sartre, *Nékrassov*). Our exteriority is not simple: it establishes a dialectical (and not a Manichaeist) critique. "Truth-as-action" would be to awaken the boy, but also to awaken the cop.

Pleasure

The theater must give pleasure, Brecht has said a thousand times: the great critical tasks (liquidation, theoretization, problematization) do not exclude pleasure.

Brechtian pleasure is chiefly a sensualism; there is nothing orgiastic about it, it is more oral than erotic, it is "good-to-be-alive" (rather than "good-living"), it is "eating-well," not in the French sense, but in the rural, woodsman, Bavarian sense. In most of Brecht's plays, food is served (let us note that food is at the intersection of Need and Desire; hence it is, alternatively, a realistic theme and a utopian theme); the most complex Brechtian hero (hence no "hero" at all), Galileo, is a sensual man: having abdicated everything, alone upstage, he eats his goose and lentils, while down front, apart from him, his books are feverishly packed up—they will cross frontiers and spread the anti-theological scientific spirit.[9]

Brechtian sensualism does not stand in opposition to intellectualism; there is a kind of circulation from one to the other: "For a vigorous thought, I would give any woman, almost any. There are many fewer thoughts than women. Politics is good only when there are enough thoughts (here, too, the blanks are boring!) . . ." The dialectic is a kind of delight. It is therefore possible to conceive, *revolutionarily*, a culture of pleasure; apprenticeship to "taste" is "progressive"; Paul Vlassov, the Mother's militant son [in *The Mother*], differs from his father in this (according to his mother): he reads books and he is picky about his soup. In the 1954 *Propositions on Peace*, Brecht outlines the program for a School of Aesthetics,[10] ordinary objects (utensils) must be the sites of beauty, it is licit to recuperate old styles (no "progressive" reward for "modern" furnishing). In other words, aesthetics is absorbed into an art of living: "All the arts contribute to the greatest of all: the art of living"; hence, it is less a matter of making pictures than furniture, clothes, tablecloths, which will have distilled all the juice of the "fine" arts; the socialist future of art will therefore not be the work (except as a productive game) but the object of use, the site of an *ambiguous* flowering (half functional, half ludic) of the signifier. The cigar is a capitalist emblem, so be it; but *if it gives pleasure?* Are we no longer to smoke cigars, to enter into the metonymy of the social Fault, to refuse to compromise ourselves in the Sign? It would be hardly dialectical to think so: it would be to throw out the baby with the bathwater. One of the tasks of a critical age is precisely to pluralize the object, to separate pleasure from the sign; we must de-semanticize the object (which does not mean de-symbolize it), give the sign a shock: let the sign *fall*, like a shed skin. This shock is the very fruit of dialectical freedom: the freedom which judges everything in terms of reality, and takes signs conjointly for operators of analysis and for games, never for laws.

Notes

1. [Ed. note: first published in *L'Autre Scène*, 1975.]

2. [Ed. note: Bertolt Brecht, "Of Poor B. B.," *Poems 1913–1956*, ed. John Willett and Ralph Manheim with the co-operation of Erich Fried (New York: Methuen, 1976), 107–8.]

3. [Ed. note: see Ulrich Weisstein, "Brecht's Victorian Version of Gay: Imitation and Originality in the *Dreigroschenoper*," in this volume.]

4. [Ed. note: see Bertolt Brecht, *Schriften zur Politik und Gesellschaft*, vol. 20 of *Gesammelte Werke in 20 Bänden* (Frankfurt am Main: Suhrkamp, 1967). Subsequently cited as *GW*.]

5. [Ed. note: see Klaus Völker, "*Herr Puntila and His Servant Matti*," in this volume.]

6. [Ed. note: Bertolt Brecht, "Weihnachtsbotschaft des Stellvertreters des Führers ([Rudolf] Hess) im Jahre 1934," *GW* 20:195–98.]

7. [Ed. note: see Bertolt Brecht, "Notes on the Opera *Rise and Fall of the City of Mahagonny*," *Collected Plays*, ed. Ralph Manheim and John Willett (New York: Vintage Books, 1971–), 2:279–83.]

8. [Ed. note: see Bertolt Brecht, "The Street Scene. A Basic Model for an Epic Theater," *Brecht on Theatre*, trans. and ed. John Willett (New York: Hill and Wang, 1964), 121–29. (*GW* 16:546–58).]

9. [Ed. note: see M. A. Cohen, "History and Moral in Brecht's *The Life of Galileo*," in this volume.]

10. [Ed. note: see Bertolt Brecht, "Schule der Ästhetik," *GW* 20:333.]

Brecht and "Inoperative Thinking"

David Pike*

Brecht's life and work pose many riddles; perhaps the most bewildering is his attitude toward the Soviet Union and international communism. Yet answers to this riddle have an immeasurable worth because they open the door to dimensions of Brecht's political philosophy and to his art that otherwise remains shut. Nevertheless, locating the hidden paths of his "dialectical thinking" usually proves frustrating for literary scholars baffled by the ideological intricacies of Marxism-Leninism-Stalinism. The reasons for such frustration are numerous, but a particularly common one is that Brecht's recurrent apologetic assessments of Stalinism often come across as systemic criticism. One of the best examples is Brecht's off-the-cuff remark to Sidney Hook in late 1935. In response to Hook's mention of the wave of arrests that followed the assassination of Kirov, Brecht quipped, "the more innocent they are, the more they deserve to die."[1] This remark has been the cause of much speculation; some commentators use it

---

*This essay was written specifically for this volume and is published here for the first time by permission of the author.

to indict Brecht for his cynicism, others to dismiss all charges of Stalinism by lauding the keen insight into totalitarianism that they infer from his remark. Somewhat surprisingly, one of the most influential interpretations remains Hannah Arendt's; she reads it as a clever way for Brecht to say that those wrongly charged with conspiring to assassinate Stalin deserved to die precisely for failing to do so.[2] Still others, usually reacting to interpretations damaging to Brecht's reputation, suggest that the remark is entirely out of character for Brecht and that Hook must have made it up.

But neither Arendt's interpretation nor those of others who consider it a reflection of his essential anti-Stalinism have much validity; Arendt's, for instance, wilts under closer scrutiny if only because she dates Brecht's remark to the time of the Moscow show trials, whereas he made the comment months before the first of the trials and long before he was at all alert to the pattern of Stalinist atrocities. Indeed, unlike during later years, in 1935 he scarcely perceived the latent potential for purposeless terror; the genocidal proclivities of Stalinism were still in their infancy in 1935, though growing; besides, there is nothing in Brecht's later public or private assessments of the Soviet Union during the more advanced stages of Stalinism to suggest a belief that the USSR would be best rid of Stalin — the premise of Arendt's interpretation. I allude to these reactions here only because such views shed light on a pair of problems, both of which help to explain the long-standing scarcity of studies devoted to Brecht's attitude toward Stalin and the Soviet Union. The first is one of ignorance; many critics have lacked the capacity for or interest in ferreting out hard facts and have therefore tried to compensate for this absence of reliable information with inadequate interpretations of a few statements made by or attributed to Brecht that appear to fit certain prior assumptions. The second problem points toward the impulse to shield Brecht from the defamation usually presumed to be the ulterior motive behind much criticism. Indeed, the urge to shelter Brecht from scathing indictments of his attitude toward Stalin's Russia has been a recurrent theme in Brecht scholarship, though this impulse has often resulted less in an open defense of Brecht than in the denial that an important issue exists at all. Too many of Brecht's advocates habitually presume that harsh criticism amounts to little more than provocations engaged in by ideologues with dubious ulterior motives.

To be sure, pointing out this tendency on the part of Brecht's defenders to gloss over the issue of Brecht and Stalinism is not the same as denying that Brecht's Marxism made him the center of controversy after World War II. But things were somewhat different then in the sense that much of the vilification of Brecht dating back to the fifties, along with the passionate attempts to vindicate him, fall more into the category of cheap polemics; both prosecution and defense vied with each other in an erratic blend of astonishing ignorance and purposeful distortion. Later, as the cold war subsided and Brecht's plays gained wider acceptance, the number of ill-informed and unvarnished attacks declined. Ideological controversies by no means died out, but the arena changed with the passage of time; serious scholars began reflecting upon Brecht's political positions and their artistic implications, though even then his admirers often retained their previous reflex. They still shied away from dealing with the range of moral issues raised by a brand of politics borne of Stalinism and subjected critics who impugned the quality of Brecht's political thought to harsh invective, even when these critics praised his artistry.

Nevertheless, these rituals nowadays seem confined more to mainstream East German scholarship and the fringe of criticism in the West. For instance, Martin Esslin's *Brecht: A Choice of Evils* (1959) is one of the earliest full-scale treatments of Brecht and can be considered pioneering without denying the flaws that such a study may have. But for years the criticism of Esslin has shown how politically committed Brecht scholarship responds to a discussion of Brecht that is unencumbered by his own ideological presuppositions. Few studies of Brecht published in East Germany (and residual ones in the West) fail to lash out at Esslin, often reducing his arguments to a few vulgarities that are all the easier to refute. One discussion of Brecht's theory of fascism, for instance, objects to Esslin's remark that his "Communist convictions" not only failed to help Brecht understand the essence of national socialism but actually hindered him; they caused Brecht to overlook the nihilistic and revolutionary side of German fascism.[3] Such an assessment must be challenged in East Germany because it questions the wisdom of Brecht's theory of fascism and strongly suggests that the obverse of his antifascism was a brand of Marxism-Leninism tightly interwoven with Stalinism.

The point is that critics in both the East and the West who embrace the view that economics answers most if not all questions related to national socialism will see in Brecht's position a perfect articulation of the problem, praise his dialectical thinking, and move on to more important matters. But it seems worth considering whether all the problems raised by German fascism can really be reduced to phrases such as "fascism can only be combated as capitalism, as the most naked, most insolent, most oppressive, and most deceitful brand of capitalism," or "wanting to fight fascism while maintaining capitalism is impossible," or "the most dangerous, the only genuine enemy of fascism, is communism, as fascism itself knows."[4] The quality missing in such categorical assessments is the very one that Brecht's Herr Keuner complained about: "I've noticed . . . that we scare many people away from our message [*Lehre*] because we know the answer to everything. In the interests of propaganda, could we not prepare a list of questions that strike us as being entirely unresolved?" (*GW*, 12:382).

But the East Germans often ignore Herr Keuner's advice, for they embrace Brecht's assessment of national socialism without reservation.

Some Western critics, and not only the Marxists among them, occasionally do likewise. For instance, consider the reaction to my suggestion that Brecht's "analysis of some sides of fascism and features of life in a fascist state . . . remained in the realm of partial truths, and however accurate some of them may have been, they never added up to a broad perspective of the whole."[5] Evidently, the act of criticizing someone victimized by fascism for a brand of ideological thinking that produced simplistic perceptions of his persecutors strikes some of Brecht's advocates as an illogical proposition. One in particular, Dwight Steward, took something akin to Brecht's own line and linked insight and persecution: because fascism knew best that communism was its most lethal enemy, it was perfectly understandable that the fascists longed to get their hands on Brecht. To presume otherwise "suggests that, being marked for imprisonment and/or death by the Nazis, specifically because of . . . convincing political insights," Brecht failed to see "the bigger picture."[6] Such an argument, attributed to this writer, is difficult to follow because of the twisted grammar and logic; but Steward's bone of contention seems to hinge on Brecht's own argument that fascism best recognized its own worst enemy — communism. The Nazis' hatred of Brecht thus embossed his theory of fascism with the stamp of inspired truth. The trouble with such a premise is that, among other things, it cheapens any opposition to Hitler not grounded in Marxism-Leninism, and Steward might as well conclude that the head of the German Communist party, Ernst Thälmann, was similarly marked for "imprisonment and/or death by the Nazis" because of his insights into the nature of fascism, presumably including the Stalinist reduction of social democracy to "social fascism" and Weimar democracy to an essentially or latently fascist "bourgeois dictatorship."

My point here is twofold. First, when dealing with Brecht one may not extoll various aspects of his political thought — in this instance Brecht's theory of fascism — without accepting the obligation of taking full account of its implications. Like it or not, these include the Stalinist ones. Selective applause is intellectually inconsistent, and it does not work well to ignore the problem by insisting that Brecht be handled first and foremost as an artistic genius. Taking that route runs the risk of bypassing or underestimating the entire issue of Brecht and Stalinism as an irrelevance, largely extrinsic to a fuller understanding of his art. Those who do so anyway forfeit the opportunity to uncover key dimensions of Brecht's artistry. In addition, this approach makes it impossible to hold Brecht to the same standards that he applied to other artists and *Tuis*, contemptible intellectuals, with respect to their perceptions of contemporary events. Indeed, this may be one of the few contexts in which measuring Brecht against some of his own standards yields valuable insights rather than hiding them. Certainly politics may be irrelevant to the artistry of writers who dabble in them; Hannah Arendt, for instance, is right to lash out at the second-, third-, and fourth-class literati who used Brecht's politics to deny him any artistic qualities.[7] But politics are hardly immaterial or even secondary to a writer who claims a central artistic and intellectual exclusivity because inspired historical truth guides his political and creative insights; and politics are most certainly not beside the point as long as many critics continue to mistake Brecht's political verdicts for serious historical statements on fascism. For those who do so accept not only his undeniable artistic genius but go beyond that to declare Brecht to be a political prophet of vast significance.

My second point is that many of Brecht's defenders indeed have a habit of judging him according to many of his own ideological preferences and prejudices. Some commentators actually mimic his thinking along lines that try to "explain" and "understand" the crimes committed by Stalin. For my treatment of Brecht's Stalinist political positions during the thirties, for instance, I was accused of having a "strong pro-Western bias"; that is, I was insufficiently appreciative of the fact that "Stalin's acts" sprang from what must have been honorable motives—apparently from his unhappiness with "intolerable circumstances and the determination to change them," in the course of which there occurred certain "excesses."[8] But if the term "excesses" in reference to mass murder has any meaning at all, especially combined with talk of the need for a "tragic sense of history," it can only connote a basic acceptance of Stalinist practices that regrettably but understandably derived from certain intractabilities inherent to the historical process; and this essential agreement is apparently tempered only by some reservations regarding the lengths to which Stalin went in trying to improve a world craving for such change. In other words, my "obvious revulsion" for Stalin's acts ought to be mitigated by some understanding of the historical stakes involved. But this argument really boils down to another defense of Brecht couched in his own dialectics, something of a restatement of his attitude voiced privately following the twentieth congress of the Soviet Communist party in 1956, when he said that the barbaric features of life under Stalin needed to be seen and judged, even vindicated, from the vantage point of the greater historical good. Thus, Stalin's intemperate conduct must presumably be accepted as the opposite side of the process of prevailing over the barbarity caused by the capitalist bondage of the past—an answer to Lenin's "terrible question" *What is to be Done?*[9] This line of reasoning is easy to spot as an unattributed rendition of Brecht's comment that "breaking out of the barbarity of capitalism can itself reveal barbaric traits" (*GW*, 20: 325).

The level of discourse that persists in Brecht scholarship to this day thus continues to suffer from a compulsive urge to protect Brecht from critics who are presumed to be out to ruin his reputation for ideological reasons. For instance, R. G. Davis recently wondered why a genius like Brecht "had so little influence on American culture and Leftist thinking and creativity" and suggested that Eric Bentley had played the role of an "underminer" by using "the least politically aggressive language" in mistranslating Brecht's plays. Acting with something like malice afore-thought, Bentley blunted or eliminated the revolutionary thrust of key passages; after all, Davis asks, "if you're not a Marxist, how can you translate [Brecht's] plays?" Besides, much more than "syntax is at work here," Davis suggests and accuses Bentley of having made "half his career (and possibly half his income) on the back of a man's work he so disreputably under-mined." How and why? In order to de-politicize Brecht and eliminate any chance that the songs sung by Bentley in his public performances might "activate" the consciousness of the audience, Bentley sang the most political ones last and in German. That way most of Brecht's fans in the audience "couldn't understand them."[10] So it seems that Bentley actually had two motives, one ideological, the other pecu-niary.

Davis's is one of the more deplorable instances of an outlook that still exists in Brecht criticism, but like the more sophisticated examples it derives from the same impulse to shield Brecht from attacks viewed as unprincipled, though still ideological conspiracies — anticommunism at best, something far more invidious at worst, but always motivated by opposition to his commitment to Marxism. What must be understood, however, is that Brecht's "Marxism" is not really the issue. That is, twentieth-century Marxism never existed in a theoretical vacuum; rather, many intellectuals, and certainly Brecht, considered it self-evident that Marxism had been largely realized in the Soviet Union by the thirties, regardless of its lingering "dark" side and ephemeral imperfections. This is the real problem because Brecht's allegiance to international communism molded his attitude toward Stalin and that aggregate of policies and practices subsumed under the rubric of the -ism named after him. The question of Brecht and Stalinism thus hits at the very heart of Brecht's political philosophy and raises a welter of specific issues, his understanding of Stalin's show trials, for instance, or the matter of the blood purges. This problem also involves other matters such as Brecht's assessment of national socialism, his attitude toward the Western democracies, and his concept of real democracy generally. Into this latter category, for instance, falls Brecht's plan for his *Tui* novel: "The book's main twist is that the original application of democracy results in its elimination; for the liberated people to dictate, they must be ruled" (*GW*, 12:590). Questions about Brecht's manner of dealing with information damaging to many of his basic premises and about the "dialectical" means by which he filtered and fitted this information to his own doctrinal assumptions simply must be ad-dressed.

None of these problems can be dealt with exhaustively in a single article, but it may suffice to raise some of the general issues related to the "dialectical" or "operative" (*eingreifendes*) thinking that Brecht took to be the source of insights denied the uninitiated. One of the major problems that used to stand in the way of any re- and subsequent *de*construction of Brecht's political positions during Stalin's time, the paucity of reliable information, has been at least partially eliminated. The manuscript of *Me-ti*, for instance, came out almost a decade after Brecht's death, in 1965 (ten years later in East Germany); Walter Benjamin's report of conversations with Brecht in *Versuche über Brecht* followed a year later; the important essays and statements on politics and society in his collected works (*GW*, 19 and 20) appeared in 1967, the *Arbeitsjournal* became available by 1973, and Brecht's letters went into print in 1981 (1983 in East Germany). Finally, various poems and drafts of poems, including those about Stalin that Brecht wrote for his desk drawer after the twentieth party congress, came out in 1982.[11]

These materials, combined with many others, indeed "permit a fairly precise reconstruction of Brecht's attitude toward contemporary communism," to quote Iring Fetscher.[12] But some of the same habits of mind referred to above hurt Fetscher's handling of these documents. As he indicates, caution is called for when dealing with these materials, though certainly not just because "Brecht avoids . . . definitive judgments." As a matter of fact, Brecht's very reluctance to draw certain conclusions already reached by others at the time, some specific instances of which are discussed below, reveals much about his "dialectical thinking"; besides, even if Brecht approached "reality," including the "reality of social systems," as a "learner" modest enough to know that he did not understand these systems completely, as Fetscher contends, it remains unclear why such "modesty" should suffice to provide his misjudgments with a positive twist and give Brecht and his dialectical thinking a considerable benefit of the doubt not normally accorded other intellectuals. Moreover, to suggest that Brecht preferred to reserve "final" judgment on critical developments is the same as contending that his thoughts on key ideological or political issues concerning not just the Soviet Union but German fascism and Western democracy as well remained flexible and never congealed into anything resembling a rigid dogma.

Granted, Brecht made statements about developments in the Soviet Union that appear skeptical; perhaps his most famous is the remark in 1938 to the effect that some suspicion regarding events there was warranted. "Should it be confirmed someday, then one would have to fight the regime — and do it publicly. But 'unfortunately, or thank God, however you want,' this suspicion is not yet a certainty today." There is no denying the importance of this comment, but it should not be cited as proof of Brecht's blanket opposition to Stalinism. It followed a clear reference to "Stalin's tremendous accomplishments" that discloses the same dialectical side to Brecht's criticism evident in another remark passed on by Benjamin; in it Brecht drew the seemingly devastating conclusion that "in Russia there rules a dictatorship *over* the proletariat." These comments illustrate Brecht's determination not to detach himself from the dictatorship as long as it continues to do "practical work for the proletariat." So outside of the necessary historical context, what Benjamin called a Brechtian maxim, "Don't begin with what's good about the old, but with the bad in the new,"[13] can range in meaning anywhere from a trite banality to a brilliant aperçu; but read in relation to the years of mature Stalinism it is plainly borne of an attitude that automatically vindicates Stalinism.

It might be another matter if Brecht had ever ceased this kind of historical justification in the face of overwhelming evidence of systematic, perhaps even systemic criminality; that is, had Brecht ever concluded that the "suspicion" to which he referred was indeed warranted. But unlike Trotsky, to whom he alludes, Brecht never decided that the system needed to be overthrown, not even during the worst years of Stalinism; to derive a program such as Trotsky's from suspicions about Stalin, Brecht said, was unjustified.[14] If one wishes to take Brecht's remark about justified suspicions concerning developments in the Soviet Union seriously, it seems perfectly legitimate to ask when these might have been "confirmed" and what dimensions the terror needed to reach before Brecht would have contemplated a public break with the Soviet Union.

To use Fetscher's phrase, Brecht remained a "learner" to the end of his life, but only in the sense that he continued his close observations without ever perceiving a compelling need to draw the final conclusion mentioned in conversation with Benjamin. As late as 1956 Brecht was still crafting dialectical witticisms to capture the essence of a historical period, witticisms that ultimately only veil his reluctance to conclude anything definitive, or definitively negative, about Stalin. The phrase, "without knowledge of dialectics such transitions as those from Stalin as motor to Stalin as brake are incomprehensible" (*GW*, 20:326), jotted down in 1956, leaves the impression that Brecht understood these transitions, though little exists in his writings that would explain his understanding any further. If Brecht only realized after the twentieth party congress that Stalin had become a hindrance, did this belated insight ever cause him to question the premises responsible for the slow working of his mind? Or did his willingness to suspend final judgment still strike Brecht as a virtue rather than a vice? One of Brecht's insights referred to earlier, the idea that the act of "breaking out of the barbarity of capitalism can itself reveal instances of barbarity" (*GW*, 20:325), may be a partial answer, but it merely updates Brecht's injunction to begin not with *"das gute Alte"* but *"das schlechte Neue."* It remains a conclusion almost mechanically justificatory of Stalinism, only with a slightly new twist—capitalism, not Marxism or Leninism, is ultimately responsible for Stalinism because decades of capitalist barbarity made it impossible to overcome that legacy other than through barbarity. Thus, as Brecht put it, "the revolution unleash[ed] wonderful virtues and anachronistic vices" (*GW*, 20:325); he concluded that overcoming the latter required more time than the mere act of initial revolution, but he failed to indicate in this or any other context that such "vices," even the worst of Stalin's terror, tipped the scales against postulated virtues.

Related thinking can be found in yet another of Brecht's private utterances following the twentieth party congress in early 1956: "The historical assessment of Stalin is of no interest at present and cannot be undertaken due to the absence of facts. But his authority must be liquidated in order to eliminate the harm caused by his example."[15] This conclusion captures the essence of Brecht's conversion to an anti-Stalinist in 1956, but the transformation failed to alter a pattern of thought that had remained relatively set since the late thirties. For then as well as in 1956 Brecht concluded that the only "definitive judgment" called for by the earlier "suspicions" and Krushchev's later revelations was that no final judgment was yet possible. Even though Brecht readily concluded in 1956 that Stalin was an (un)common killer, coining the bitter phrase "distinguished murderer of the people" (GW, Supplement 437), his call for a delay in assessing Stalin's overall record must be taken to mean that history, and thus Brecht, still needed to reserve final judgment. For facts might later emerge and prompt future generations to conclude that the predominant color of the final ledger was black, regardless of the blood shed by Stalin. Even in 1956 Brecht concluded in one of his "Stalin poems" that the weights on the scale were heavy, but they weighed heavily on both sides; on the one pan, presumably, were the machines of industrialization and the trophies won in victory over fascism, the latter in Brecht's opinion surely resulting from the former; weighing down the other pan, however, were such considerations as the "child without bread" and the unheard cry of "bleeding comrades" (GW, Supplement 438). Evidently, the historical scales had not yet settled reliably, leaving wide open the question of ultimate balance; in 1956 Brecht seemed prepared to go no further than to advocate the liquidation of Stalin's "authority" only because the damage in need of immediate repair could not be undertaken without challenging the lingering effects of Stalin's imposing personality. As for the rest, let history judge.

Even though Krushchev's disclosures seemed to confirm Brecht's worst "suspicions" of twenty years earlier, then, according to Fetscher he continued to "judge the 'construction of the grand order' in the Soviet Union positively without denying the dark sides of development necessarily encumbered with shortcomings and mistakes."[16] This is one of those assessments that are partially true but that, by judging Brecht within his own political frame of reference, lead to confusing results. The observation that mistakes accompany progress is innocent enough; the harm comes when the borders are obscured between genocide on the one hand and "mistakes," "excesses," even "shortcomings" on the other — euphemisms predicated on the assumption of historical necessities. But potentially beneficial measures whose implementation caused the regrettable deaths of countless millions, deaths that were ultimately necessary because acts of barbarism accompany the process of breaking the grip of the barbaric past, are not the question; the real issue is the occurrence of unadulterated terror — economically purposeless and extraordinarily injurious to the aims of the revolution itself.

For example, Fetscher cites a remark from *Me-ti* intended to characterize the concomitants of historical progress: "The bread is hurled at the people with such ferocity that many are slain by it" (*GW*, 12:524). What Brecht appears to find lamentable, however, is merely the "ferocity" with which the bread was thrown; it apparently never entered his mind that something other than bread, or measures ostensibly designed to provide the grain for baking it, killed millions of people during collectivization. Equally inconceivable to him apparently was the idea that economic "necessity," much less necessity in a Marxist-Leninist context, might have had precious little to do with Stalinist policy in the Ukraine, for instance. Instead Brecht wrote of this earlier period of collectivization that agriculture itself had to be transformed into an industry; this was "violent business," and he argued for the need to repress those peasant masses resisting the construction of a "powerful industry" because such repression was a prerequisite for the establishment of conditions capable of rendering dictatorships "superfluous" (*GW*, 20:103). Nor did Brecht later alter his underlying attitude regarding dictatorships that exist only to tear themselves out by the roots. "When the helper appeared, he was / leprous. But the leper / helped, after all" (*GW*, Supplement 436), Brecht wrote in 1956, blending his own lingering cult of Stalin's personality with his much older theory of Stalin's "usefulness." For Stalin's policies undeniably aided historical progress, regardless of other considerations. Under those historical circumstances, for Marxist theoreticians and sympathetic intellectuals to withhold their support for the Soviet Union merely because of an absence of freedom there and until the country ridded itself of Stalin was tantamount to facilitating "the preparation of war" against the USSR (*GW*, 20:103). This general theory of "usefulness," from which Brecht derived the need to back the Stalinist status quo, runs through many of Brecht's later "Stalin poems." But considering the full implications of this theory it seems entirely appropriate to ask whether Brecht's attempt to discern the "dialectical" side of mass terror could ever accomplish more than rationalize it. After all, "Those who distanced themselves from the people / Called their opponents enemies of the people. But / They were not liars about everything" (*GW*, Supplement 436).

Among Brecht's comments on the subject of the Soviet Union, the following from *Me-ti* probably best captures the essence of his dialectical thinking:

> The new system, the most progressive in the history of the world, continues to function very poorly, hardly at all organically, and requires such an effort and exercise of violence that individual freedom is

severely curtailed. Because [the system] is being forced into existence by small numbers of people, there is coercion everywhere and no meaningful rule by the people. Freedom of opinion, of assembly, lip-service, the acts of violence practiced by the judiciary — all these go to show that by no means all of the basic elements of the Great Order are realized and in the process of being developed. (*GW*, 12:535)

At first glance this enumeration of the various blemishes disfiguring the new system appears to qualify Brecht's approval of it; yet read "dialectically" it is apparent that the opening apposition alters the thrust of everything following it and predetermines the justificatory thrust of the entire assessment. For if one has concluded that a regime is inherently progressive, none of its shortcomings may be considered unquestionably systemic; even when the system is seen as the immediate cause of problems, they remain transitory in the sense of "childhood diseases." After all, Brecht was admittedly not prepared to conclude that "freedom reigns in the workers' state of Russia"; but he was content to conclude that the process of "liberation rules there" (*GW*, 20:103). Another facet of this argument may help clarify Brecht's reasoning. In a letter to Lion Feuchtwanger dated August 1937 Brecht praised the former's *Moscow 1937*. This booklet contained similar criticism of surface problems combined with a strong defense of the Soviet Union under Stalin and included Feuchtwanger's account of the show trials. It was clear as daylight, he said of Stalin, that "this modest, impersonal man cannot possibly have committed the colossal indiscretion of producing with the assistance of countless performers so coarse a comedy, merely for the purposes of holding a sort of festival of revenge with Bengal lights to celebrate the humiliation of his opponents."[17] Brecht applauded the book not because he was unmindful of the excrescences on the Stalinist body politic but because he regarded the day-to-day implementation of truth as the necessary domain of enlightened, if imperfect human beings. That being so, success in transforming "reason" into a system of state governance hinged on experimentation. If reason itself was something so "practical and human," he went on, "something with its own morality and immorality," it acquired an experimental nature capable of benefitting humanity only if left to continue experimenting; to impose any system of "rigid morality" upon that experimentation would rule it out because experimentation was by nature of a "somewhat doubtful morality."[18] The full implications of what Brecht considered dialectical reasoning here are clear, considering that the price in lives lost during "experimentation" becomes one worth paying as long as the need to experiment continues.

The examples of Brecht's dialectical thinking just given suffice to challenge Fetscher's contention that Brecht's concurrently "distanced and engaged stance" with regard to the Communist movement might be criticized as inconsistent but that it "provided for a degree of lucidity (though by no means infallibility) attained by precious few Marxists during those years." Fetscher grants that Brecht's "information was not always accurate, or even adequate, and for that very reason his conclusions occasionally missed the mark." But the need for Brecht to alter "his method never arose because [this method] was never affected by dogmatic accents."[19] Actually, the attribute "dogmatic" fits Brecht and his brand of "dialectical thinking" quite well. He believed fervently in the singularity of the Soviet Union and thus regarded certain kinds of sociopolitical and ideological insights as unequivocally valid when directed toward the USSR, though just as categorically invalid when applied to the Western democracies; the former was automatically "progressive," the latter were just as mechanically "regressive" because they amounted to bourgeois dictatorships. Thus, the political and social vices of a Stalinist dictatorship, commonly referred to as a socialist (or proletarian) democracy, constitute unavoidable but ephemeral blights that normally and naturally tag along with historical progress; whereas the "weaknesses and mistakes," or rather crimes and brutality, of bourgeois dictatorships that fancied themselves democracies are all perceived to be systemically engendered; not symptomatic of a passing malaise or curable indisposition at all, they were clear signs of terminal illness.

But Fetscher's notion of Brecht's "lucidity" raises another issue. Brecht may indeed have understood more about the Soviet Union and thus developed more critical views, at least privately, than run-of-the-mill Stalinists or even, as Fetscher puts it, "Marxists," but how much do Brecht and his political insights into the dynamics of a single-person dictatorship gain for being superior to the public opinions of mainstream Marxist-Leninist-Stalinists? Relatively little, it seems; furthermore, the implication that Brecht consistently saw things more clearly than other "Marxists" who had broken with official communism is not necessarily true. Besides, comparing Brecht's political insights only with "Marxists" of whatever specific persuasion derives from a familiar double standard; for one, it precludes the process of assessing Brecht's insights outside the context of his own ideological premises, and, for another, it tends to presuppose that the full truth about the USSR and its putative antithesis, German fascism, resided within the parameters of Marxism or Marxism-Leninism. Moreover, Fetscher's assessment of Brecht's dialectical thinking requires a closer look. Is it indeed the case that Brecht was disadvantaged with respect to the information available to him and that this lack of knowledge helps explain his distorted perceptions? Quite the opposite is true; on many issues Brecht was exceptionally well informed, though his knowledge of certain sad occurrences had no effect upon his general approval of the Soviet Union. Perhaps the best example concerns his awareness of the disappearance of many close friends—for instance, Ernst Ottwalt. By the time Bernard von Brentano wrote him about Ottwalt's arrest, Brecht had already heard about it, but he explained to Brentano in early February 1937 that the source of the news, "bourgeois newspapers," was hardly reliable. Even if the story should turn out to be correct, Brecht wrote, "I continue to regard the Bolshevist party as being deeply rooted in the Russian proletariat and consider the Russian economy to be caught up in a profound revolutionary process." That being so, the Paris *Temps* and London *Times* struck Brecht as an inappropriate forum for discussing differences of opinion "with the Bolshevist party" (*B*, 1:287).

For somewhat different reasons Brecht's reaction to the arrest of Carola Neher is even more revealing; on the one hand, Brecht tended to believe that an honest mistake had been committed. The arrests occurred generally as part of "justified actions" taken against "Goebbels's organizations" in the USSR; that is, the various waves of terror were dragnets designed to catch fascist spies, with the webbing perhaps having been sewn together a bit too tightly. But on the other hand, Brecht declined to rule out the possibility that Neher had indeed been involved in "treasonous activity," and either way he was anxious to prevent his concern about Neher from becoming public; it might then be suggested that he was causing "mistrust of the praxis of the [Soviet] Union" (*B*, 1:309). It is especially noteworthy that Brecht was so inclined to accept the notion of Neher's guilt, for it appeared logical to him that an arrest followed by a conviction and sentencing could scarcely have occurred in the absence of "abundant material" against her. In that event Brecht's only objection in November 1937 was that "over there" the harshness of punishment did not always fit the crime, but then the overriding and presumably understandable consideration was that "they wish solely to protect the Soviet state" (*B*, 1:328–29).

Neither indiscriminate terror nor trumped-up charges, followed by confessions extracted by torture, ever occurred to Brecht as the best explanation for the disappearance of Neher or anyone else. His poem written in response to the news of Tretjakov's arrest, unpublished at the time, is a suitable example of Brecht's confusion: "Out of 50 condemned / One may be innocent" (*GW*, 9:743). Brecht apparently never dreamt that turning the proportions around would have yielded at least a marginally more realistic appraisal. If this all seems naive, Brecht's guilelessness carried over into his response to the disappearance of other friends. Upon hearing the news of Michail Koltsov's arrest, Brecht remarked in late 1938 or early 1939 that he could not imagine what Koltsov could have done (*B*, 1:362); that is, Brecht's imagination seemed insufficiently vivid to allow for the possibility of Koltsov's complete innocence. Because the simplest explanation escaped Brecht, he searched instead for one located within an appropriately dialectical context, as in the following passage from *Me-ti*:

> Numerous arrests had taken place because the organization [the party] sensed that enemies were at work internally. Me-ti emphasized with praise that hardly anyone regarded people as guilty just because they had been arrested. On the other hand, many approved the arrest of those merely under suspicion. It was seen as an error that the authorities

were not in a position to single out the guilty; but it met with approval that, incapable of being certain, they at least made a crude attempt to deal with the evil. The good surgeon separates the cancer from the healthy flesh, the bad ones cut out healthy flesh along with the cancerous portion, it was said. (*GW*, 12:546)

Perhaps the supreme irony inherent in Brecht's attitude toward the Soviet Union, however, lies less in the realm of his political philosophy than in the pattern of abuse to which Brecht was subjected over the years by those representatives of Stalinist literary policies who believed that his writing violated established norms. As for Brecht, he certainly knew that something was profoundly wrong with Soviet culture; he concluded in January 1939, for instance, that literature and art were "shitty" and that "the theoretical line thwarted everything he had worked for over the last two decades."[20] But he had difficulty understanding why the political system in which he so fervently believed spawned attitudes toward literature and the stage that directly contravened his positions. As a result he had a hard time accounting for the discrepancy between inherently sound political, but inept cultural policies. One of Brecht's few attempts at an overarching explanation of all such conflicts took place in a diary entry of 16 October 1943: "To begin with, about all one can say is that the Bolsheviks simply did not know how to develop a literature. There is no need even to assert that their methods failed in this area; it perhaps suffices to say that the methods applied by them in this area failed. The situation was surely disadvantageous. The proletariat's takeover of power took literature by surprise" (*AJ*, 2:636).

This is another of Brecht's verdicts that are so difficult to comprehend, though it is entirely possible that such instances of convoluted logic mirrored the state of Brecht's own mind and that the remark amounts to a "dialectical" way of saying very little at all. Brecht's dilemma was this: he needed to account for the incongruity that the Bolshevist party—comprised of people responsible, in Brecht's opinion, for a revolution that had now reached an advanced stage of maturity—produced miserable results in literature and art. Why exactly did those persons influential in cultural and literary matters habitually behave like apparatchiki, as "enemies of [literary] production" fearful of unsupervised art and bent upon controlling things?[21] At some point Brecht may have pondered whether "Bolshevist methods" used in the takeover of political power and applied to social change were, by their very nature, inappropriate to the realm of art; if they were, then there was nothing surprising about its deplorable state. But Brecht may also have consoled himself by arguing later that it had nevertheless been necessary to try out these Bolshevist methods on art as the only way of discovering their inappropriateness. Although hindsight now made it clear that their failure was inevitable, there was no way of foreseeing this breakdown without trying first. That Brecht may have thought along these lines seems at least plausible because of a certain conceptual parallelism. Having embraced the notion of "immoral" social and political experimentation, which created the human misery that he considered unavoidable, perhaps Brecht was also prepared to allow for a similar kind of havoc wrought by trial and error in the cultural sphere — or he took the disastrous results to be the regrettable consequence of the search for artistic solutions appropriate to socialism. Of course Brecht himself advocated "experimentation" in art, but only the kind he chose to engage in, not cultural-political experimentation he deemed detrimental to his own writing. There is certainly no evidence that Brecht was ever willing to sacrifice his art for the good of the cause. Then again, he may have concluded that the Bolsheviks indeed applied different, "non-Bolshevist" methods to culture, but if so, what was the exact nature of Bolshevism in art?

There were various riddles here, even "suspicions," that apparently perplexed Brecht. The problem was that he could not resort to the same webwork of dialectical contrivances used to account for the failed political policies of the thirties to excuse what he perceived to be blundering in art. In the case of internal Soviet sociopolitical policies Brecht's rationalizations usually produced a dialectic involving necessity, but this could not help him understand the need, for instance, to shut down Meyerhold's theater. The answers to the riddles posed by the modalities of cultural affairs under Stalin were simply rarer; the result was that the reasons for practices that struck Brecht as gratuitous mystified him. Unwilling to concede that the political and economic dislocation was the outgrowth of a dictatorship that had no intention of tearing itself out by the roots, Brecht must have found it all the more difficult to conclude that cultural affairs suffered from the same malaise. There were similarities only to the extent that both sets of problems converged in Brecht's assumption that political and cultural difficulties alike would eventually iron themselves out.

But can Brecht's difficulties with the party's mainstream cultural functionaries and politicians ever be taken back to a single general cause? This is not the place to provide a detailed history of Brecht's disputes with the party over literary theoretical issues but only to sum up certain constants in the problems that dogged him during the last years of the Weimar Republic, during his exile, and following his return to East Germany in 1948. On 17 October 1943 Brecht noted in his journal that "realistic art is art that confronts the ideologies with reality and that allows for realistic feeling, thinking, and behaving" (*AJ*, 2:637). Did Brecht's writing contrast reality with that semblance of it fashioned by ideologies as a means of stressing the singularity of a particular socioeconomic status quo? Certainly in his stage depictions of capitalist societies Brecht sought to do this and did it well, avoiding the oversimplifications of an "imperalism-as-the-highest-stage-of-capitalism" message, or, when certain of these were present, avoiding the schematic effect of staging ideological premises through the sheer genius of his art. Brecht's "First comes food, then morality" as a substitute for "Being determines consciousness" is an illustration. But perhaps Brecht misgauged the potential for his work to turn against the very source of its inspiration. For the ideology behind Brecht's work, Marxism-Leninism, never regarded itself as an ideology at all but as inspired truth. According to Brecht's characterization of realistic art, writing realistically must therefore produce an almost automatically truthful, dialectical depiction of social reality — a concept, ironically, that also existed in the original Soviet definitions of socialist realism.

Yet such assumptions about socialist realism were an obvious hoax because the politicians defined the nature of dialectical truth, invented much of the reality through which absolute truth manifested itself, and mandated the artistic methods to be used in rendering both; whereas Brecht reserved the right to make his own judgments in all three areas — the paramount source of his conflicts with the party. Present in all of his confrontations with the party's designated spokesmen was the fact that he did not move in their circles and was not subject to their control; indeed, Brecht never joined the party, an unthinkable affront to those who either believed in the cause or profited in some way by pretending that they did. But Brecht's very independence, combined with the geographic circumstances of his exile, limited the degree of influence that the party could exert over him. Years later Georg Lukács was right to point out the political inconsistency of that position, probably acutely envious because of his own awareness that Brecht's relative autonomy guaranteed him a measure of artistic integrity unavailable to a Marxist such as Lukács, who by his own admission felt compelled to make intellectual compromises. Shortly before he died Lukács noted that "Brecht always wanted, in the most fantastic way, . . . to reserve a secure and kosher place for himself within the party, on the one hand, and maintain complete freedom on the other hand."[22]

My point is this: even if Brecht adopted essentially Stalinist positions on political issues, he did so with a mind much less fettered by the constraints governing the public posture of mainstream party intellectuals; regardless of his periodic identification with such positions, Brecht's thinking was not captive in the same way and only influenced to the degree that he voluntarily shared many of the theoretical or ideological premises. In this sense Brecht was correct to indicate in the early fifties in response to the suggestion that his ideas were not his own because he lived in East Germany, "I have not formed my opinions because I live here, but rather I live here because of my opinions" (GW, 19:499). Because Brecht had a considerable reservoir of intellectual integrity (though he by no means drew upon an inexhaustible supply), there was a constant danger that he might some day see suspicions confirmed, deviate from the party, and do so publicly. Certainly deviations of an unintentional kind had often occurred, for instance in *The Measures Taken*, where Brecht divulged truths and realities that the party preferred to conceal. As Hannah Arendt put it, "in this case a poet loyal to the party disrupted the party's line."[23] But it is important to remember that this potential for deviations did not result from divergent ideological premises; rather, the problems that Brecht caused the party sprang from a natural urge to develop his own aesthetic correlates to ideological assumptions, put these correlates on stage, and resist the further fictionalization of realities already fictionalized by the party. Brecht insisted upon arriving at his own political conclusions, even if these coincided with those of the party; but the art resulting from an ideological stance that often differed little from that assigned to other writers produced aesthetic or dramaturgical results unacceptable to the orthodox. Indeed, during his years of exile Brecht's aesthetic principles squared generally with the ones marked for eradication in the Soviet Union during the confluence of indiscriminate terror and the articulation of socialist realism. This convergence criminalized two different sets of "counter-revolutionary" aesthetics by merging them into one; the indictment always listed formalism and decadence, and the party's spokesmen found Brecht guilty on both counts.

Brecht's development of an experimental stage theory designed to advance the cause of the revolution by constraining the audience to "feel, think, and act realistically" simply clashed with the modalities of a utilitarian art created to fulfill the new needs of a revolution gone astray. Whereas Brecht remained a somewhat out-of-touch blend of ideologue and idealist, as the revolution degenerated many of its original artists and cultural politicians disappeared altogether or turned into Stalinist *Tuis*, apologists of the status quo; they desired "revolutionary" art only in the abstract sense of art offering unqualified support for a Stalinist establishment that legitimized itself ideologically as the direct outgrowth of the revolution. In this sense they perceived Brecht's writing to be counter-revolutionary and were probably right to do so. The result was that his and other kinds of unrestricted experimentation, regardless of the ideological commitment, were essentially outlawed; the artistic experiment was equated with formalism because, by its very definition, formalism was apolitical in its emphasis of form over content and thus, as Lukács argued, emblematic of "ideological decay" or decadence in the age of imperialism.

Brecht had few illusions about the original source of the problems caused by art; "you never know what will come out of it,"[24] and the apparatchikis' urge to control art through "planning" derived from that uncertainty. Not that Brecht himself opposed planning; for example, he considered a planned economy to be the ultimate expression of intellect and reason; as a matter of fact he once defined "operative thinking" (*eingreifendes Denken*) not only as thinking that "intervened" in the economy but as "thinking operative above all in the sense that thought develops with economics constantly in mind" (*GW*, 20:158). There was also a sort of reverse parallelism here; the main reason for "inoperative thinking" (*nichteingreifendes Denken*) on the part of ordinary intellectuals, the *Tuis*, was "inoperative democracy" (*GW*, 12:590) — the kind that never "intervened" in the economy. Brecht's point is that real democracy involves control over the economy through planning, but how does that general principle apply to its cultural equivalent? By 1950 Brecht was doubtless mindful of the dangers; he noted that "you have to proceed very carefully when you start planning in the area of the arts," for it was "not easy to get sovereign works from cowed people." Brecht also knew that the party succumbed to a natural impulse to attack the artists whenever it failed to understand them, and he cautioned against it; "as in sexual intercourse, seductive urges exist in the area of art, but as in intercourse harsh words ought not to be uttered" (*GW*, 2:926).

But if the urge to domineer writers through intimidation is suggestive of rape, were there nevertheless circumstances under which Brecht would have agreed that the state must still force its ideological affections upon writers who resisted its doctrinal advances by exercising their prerogative to render reality as they saw fit? Brecht clearly held apolitical *Tuis* generally and writers who, as he put it, chose to decorate the walls of a sinking ship with still lifes in utter contempt (*GW*, 18:225). But in a future socialist society might Brecht have been capable of stepping over the line from contempt to advocating the use of administrative solutions in dealing with such writers because of the harm caused by their "untruthful" renditions of reality? True, in 1951 Brecht called for the "complete freedom" of art, contingent upon single limitation: "No freedom for writings and works of art that glorify war or depict it as unavoidable" (*GW*, 19:495–96). But this is hard to square with Brecht's own ideology. For one, unless he was also alluding to the censorship of Stalinist literature, Brecht refuses to consider that the unavoidability of war was an idea firmly rooted in Marxism-Leninism-Stalinism and not disavowed until Khrushchev renounced it in 1956. For another, a glance at Brecht's many cold-war utterances concerning the peace-loving intentions of the East and the war-mongering of the West often contain all the logic needed to label unmanageable writers as objective advocates of war.

True, Brecht objected to certain assaults on art, such as when he ridiculed the "Office of Literature" or the "Art Commission" after the uprising in 1953. Equally well known is Brecht's sarcastic remark to the effect that the people had forfeited the confidence of the government and that the government ought to dissolve *"das Volk"* before voting another into office (*GW*, 10:1007–9). But what might he have regarded in later years as an appropriate response to writers whose integrity led to the creation of art that was indeed antagonistic toward political and economic goals with which Brecht identified? My question is whether Brecht ever demonstrated a readiness to respect the integrity — political or aesthetic — of other writers or whether such integrity remained irrelevant whenever it clashed with his notion of the objective imperatives of historical progress? It is worth wondering, for instance, how Brecht would have responded to antiestablishmentarian thinking in East Germany during the latter half of 1956 if only because Hans Mayer engaged in just such speculation. Mayer believes that Brecht could not have done much to stop the crackdown in late 1956 but that "there would not have been a trial of Harich and Janka during Brecht's lifetime. Ulbricht would have held back out of respect for the political power of the playwright."[25] But two of those jailed, Gustav Just, the editor of the review *Sonntag*, and Walter Janka, the head of the Aufbau Verlag and Brecht's East German publisher, knew Brecht well enough to have an informed opinion and suffer from no illusions on that score; neither thinks that Brecht would have threatened to close his theater and leave the country unless Ulbricht released the two of them along with Wolfgang Harich, though just such an ultimatum was the only kind of protest with any chance of success.[26] Naturally such speculation remains just that; but I see nothing wrong with using Brecht's earlier habit of denouncing a broad spectrum of intellectuals and their "wrong (pernicious or useless)" "*Tui*-thinking," as well as his talk of the need to "overcome and eliminate" them (*GW*, 12:590-91), to call attention to an attitude with worrisome implications.

In any case it remains paradoxical that Brecht shared any number of basic doctrinal presuppositions with established Stalinism but that this orthodoxy yielded aesthetic ideas contrary to socialist realism — creating the potential in both areas for conflict with the party. With respect to politics one might wish to ponder Arendt's view that Brecht "would never have stood up to the onslaught of Russian reality, even as he failed to withstand the much less frightening assault of reality in Ulbricht's East Germany."[27] Of course it is impossible to know whether the clash between a firsthand experience with daily Soviet reality and the nature of postulated reality, ideology, would have served to confirm Brecht's "suspicions" about the Soviet Union; others faced with the contradictions proved remarkably adept at filtering reality until it matched the ideal. But there is every reason to believe that many of those people in the party who themselves lived with the conflict in Soviet exile worried about Brecht because he was not really one of them. When he "toed" the political line, he did so differently, not out of fear and intimidation but usually out of conviction, and I would venture to say that his detractors spent long hours brooding over the possibility that Brecht's art might someday begin contrasting reality and ideology in countries other than those run by capitalists.

It is thus apparent that those in the party who oversaw culture had a visceral sense of the potential threat posed by Brecht; some of them, it seems, hated him precisely because of his unwillingness to make the kinds of compromises that they had made, and they knew perfectly well that Brecht's brand of political commitment was, from their point of view, unreliable. It suffered from too much of an idealistic or, rather, genuinely ideological slant and was therefore less susceptible to the kind of manipulation that made intellectual positions and artistic postures politically serviceable. The party clearly benefitted most, at least during Stalin's lifetime, from intellectuals who could not only change their minds and their opinions upon demand, but be able to provide as persuasive a theoretical rationale as possible for new circumstances and perhaps produce a fictional or dramatic representation of it. Brecht did not fit into this category because there were limits to his pliability; his artistic integrity remained intact and so did his political principles, though saying so is different from inquiring into the intrinsic value of either. As interesting as the relationship between the two sets of problems is, the answers to such inquiries, as this article suggests, will probably differ.

But all of these questions come back to Brecht's notion of exclusive truth, his perception of reality, and his definition of the role played by intellectuals and artists. For Brecht clearly disdained those intellectuals who failed to pursue truth using the dialectical methods of thought that Brecht regarded as singularly appropriate; they were all *Tuis* (which in German sounds as much like an expectoration as a mutation of the pejorative "intellectual"); such people were egg-heads, *Kopfarbeiter*, primarily paid to construct counter-realities or rival ideologies passed off as the essential social truth of the ruling class; through their unrealistic art they impeded realistic "thinking, feeling, and acting." Yet for Brecht there was only "one truth," not two truths or as many as there were special interest groups (*GW*, 20:189); to the extent that intellectuals had social consciences at all, their very inconsistency and inability to determine truth rendered their positions useless with respect to changing the status quo. Some of them, said Brecht, went on to conclude that thinking indeed needed to serve a purpose; but without embracing materialist dialectics they could find no way of doing so "operatively" (*eingreifend*), resigned themselves to the powerlessness of the intellect, and eventually took the next logical step. They renounced serious thinking altogether (*GW*, 20:158).

Thus it was that such intellectuals became supreme "apologists"; they condoned the status quo precisely because of their inability to practice what Brecht called *eingreifendes Denken*, operative or activist thinking that intervened in politics and the economy. "When someone starts talking about necessity," Brecht wrote, "insisting that the very beginning of human activity and its range of possibilities are preestablished by insurmountable historical tendencies, contradict him: for his feet are firmly planted on the soil of facts, he is a eulogist of things as they are inasmuch as he supplies the reasons as proof of what he considers necessity." Because everything necessarily occurred as it occurred, such a person was an "apologist" (*GW*, 20:68). But Brecht had something in common with such *Tuis*; if he defined "operative thinking" and realistic art as the debunking of ideologies and all deceptive semblances of realities, the underlying pattern of Brecht's dialectical thinking was in many respects similarly idealistic and thus equally apologetic. For in certain historical and social contexts Brecht's operative thinking quickly became nonintervening (*nichteingreifend*):

> There is a crowd of head workers who have a definite sense that the world (their world) is beset by incongruities, but they fail to react accordingly. If one eliminates those who simply use their imaginations to construct a world that is incongruent unto itself (and exists precisely due to its incongruity), one has to do with people who, more or less mindful of the incongruity, nevertheless conduct themselves as if the world were congruent. Consequently the world intervenes only inadequately into the thinking of such people; it comes as no surprise, then, when their thinking fails to intervene in the affairs of the world. (*GW*, 20:175)

One probably ought to ask whether Brecht did not himself respond to a world full of "incongruities," or one-sixth of it, by treating the USSR as ideally congruent; it is certainly legitimate to suggest that the world of Stalinism never "intruded" into Brecht's thinking in the sense that those abhorrent realities caused him to revise his own "working hypotheses," and, no less surprisingly, Brecht's thinking "intervened" into this particular world only inadequately. Indeed, using his own language one might term Brecht's thinking "defeatist" because such a pattern of thought denied itself the possibility of exerting influence (cf. *GW*, 20:159). That is, if operative thinking works to "change the economy," Brecht's thinking became automatically nonoperative as soon as he concluded that the Soviet economy was indeed "caught up in a profound revolutionary change." Analytical to a point, his reasoning remained defeatist regardless of his suspicions and carried over into other areas, both personal and artistic. "I can do nothing for you" (*GW*, 9:607), Brecht said in a poem about Carola Neher, and his private inquiries about her whereabouts had no chance of winning her release. Or, to take another example with artistic implications, upon learning of Tretjakov's arrest Brecht asked, "Is it best to keep silent?" (*GW*, 9:743). He concluded that it was, despite the following words: "But people will not say: those were dark times / Rather: why were their poets silent?" (*GW*, 9:587).

Though he appears not to have taken his admonition personally, in his own defense Brecht would likely have answered that silence is abject, servile, and indefensible in the one instance (more contemptible still are manifestations of *Tuism* when the silence is broken only in a doctrinally inarticulate, inoperative way). But silence is entirely warranted in a different instance for the sake of an ideal whose inherent presence is posited in some other, only temporarily imperfect social formation; indeed, the dialectical obverse of operative thinking is its very readiness to be inoperative, and the ability to know when not to "intervene" stands for qualities contrary to *Tuism*. Shorn of its dialectical underpinnings, however, Brecht's logic really comes down to faith in an ideal that seems quintessentially idealistic in a way not incomparable to the idealism of common *Tuis:* "*Tuism* reaches its pinnacle in the Third Reich. Idealism, having fallen to its lowest level, celebrates its most gigantic triumphs. Put philosophically and thus most adequately, consciousness sets out to confront social existence with its demands most imperiously at the very time in which it finds itself most hopelessly enslaved. The 'idea' is nothing more than a reflex, and this reflex rises up against reality in an especially peremptory and terroristic manner" (*AJ,* 1:213).

Even where one most hopes to find it, in Brecht's "Stalin poems" of 1956, a fleeting look suffices to show that he never arrived at a definitive verdict on the meaning of the heinous crimes of Stalinism. Still, this very unwillingness to render even a tentative historical judgment must be regarded as Brecht's "last word" on the subject, and by no means only in a limited sense, as James K. Lyon suggests—because "everything was temporary" for him, and he may have changed his opinions had he lived longer.[28] Brecht went to his grave trying desperately to reconcile two views of the dead dictator; Stalin had been enormously "useful" to the revolution, but it was now impossible to overlook the sad fact that he had also distinguished himself as a "meritorious murderer of the people." So ever the learner and unable to say which would weigh more heavily on the scales of history, Brecht's private deliberations ended in a hung jury. He failed to announce a verdict at all and died silent.

Notes

1. See Sidney Hook, "A Recollection of Bertold [*sic*] Brecht." *New Leader* 10 (October 1960):22–23.

2. Cf. Hannah Arendt, *Walter Benjamin. Bertolt Brecht. Zwei Essays* (Munich: R. Piper, 1971), 83–84.

3. See Rolf Tauscher, *Brechts Faschismuskritik in Prosaarbeiten und Gedichten der ersten Exiljahre* (Berlin: Brecht-Zentrum der DDR, 1981), 11.

4. Bertolt Brecht, "Fünf Schwierigkeiten beim Schreiben der Wahrheit," *Gesammelte Werke in 20 Bänden* (Frankfurt am Main: Suhrkamp Verlag, 1967), 18:226–27 (hereafter cited as *GW*), and "Plattform für die linken Intellektuellen," *GW* 20:239–40. Translations from the German are my own.

5. David Pike, *Lukács and Brecht* (Chapel Hill: University of North Carolina Press, 1985), xi–xii.

6. See Dwight Steward, review of *Lukács and Brecht, CLIO* 2 (1986):224.

7. Arendt, *Brecht,* 64.

8. See Patricia Hoffmann, review of *Lukács and Brecht, Gestus* 2, no. 3–4 (June 1986):145–46.

9. Hoffmann, review, 145–46.

10. See R. G. Davis, "Eric Bentley," *Communications from the International Brecht Society* 16, no. 1 (November 1986):24–28, and *Communications* 16, no. 2 (April 1987):6–7.

11. See the notes below for complete bibliographical information.

12. Iring Fetscher, "Brecht und der Kommunismus" *Merkur* 21, no. 9 (September 1973):872.

13. This and the above comments are from Walter Benjamin, *Versuche über Brecht* (Frankfurt am Main: Suhrkamp Verlag, 1971), 131 and 135. The latter quotation reads, "Nicht an das gute Alte anknüpfen, sondern an das schlechte Neue."

14. See Benjamin, *Versuche*, 131–32.

15. Bertolt Brecht, *GW*. Supplementband IV: *Gedichte aus dem Nachlaß* 2 (Frankfurt am Main: Suhrkamp Verlag, 1982), 438. Hereafter cited as Supplement.

16. Fetscher, "Brecht und der Kommunismus," 875.

17. Lion Feuchtwanger, *Moscow 1937* (New York: Viking Press, 1937), 138–39.

18. Bertolt Brecht, *Briefe 1913–1956*, 2 vols, ed. Günter Glaeser (Berlin: Aufbau Verlag, 1983), 1:316. Subsequently cited as *B*.

19. Fetscher, "Brecht und der Kommunismus," 873.

20. See Bertolt Brecht, *Arbeitsjournal*, 2 vols., ed. Werner Hecht (Frankfurt am Main: Suhrkamp Verlag, 1973), 1:36. Hereafter cited as *AJ*. Klaus Völker, *Brecht-Chronik: Daten zu Leben und Werk* (Munich: Hanser Verlag, 1971), 72–73.

21. See Benjamin, *Versuche*, 132.

22. Georg Lukács, *Gelebtes Denken: Eine Autobiographie im Dialog* (Frankfurt am Main: Suhrkamp Verlag, 1981), 151.

23. Arendt, *Brecht*, 99. [Ed. note: see also A[lfred] Kurella, "What Was He Killed For? Criticism of the Play *Strong Measures* by Brecht, Dudov and Eisler," in this volume.]

24. Benjamin, *Versuche*, 132.

25. Hans Mayer, *Ein Deutscher auf Widerruf. Erinnerungen* (Frankfurt am Main: Suhrkamp Verlag, 1984), 156.

26. Just and Janka voiced their opinions in conversations with me.

27. Arendt, *Brecht*, 72; Arendt's main hypothesis is that Brecht lost his poetic powers after his return to East Germany in 1949.

28. See James K. Lyon, "Brecht und Stalin — des Dichters 'letztes Wort,' " *Exilforschung: Ein internationales Jahrbuch* 1 (1983):128.

BIBLIOGRAPHY

Primary Works

In German

Arbeitsjournal. 2 vols. Edited by Werner Hecht. Frankfurt am Main: Suhrkamp, 1973. Includes commentary.

Briefe. Edited by Günter Glaeser. Frankfurt am Main: Suhrkamp, 1981. Includes commentary.

Gesammelte Werke in 20 Bänden. Frankfurt am Main: Suhrkamp, 1967. Supplementbände III–IV: *Gedichte aus dem Nachlaß.* Edited by Herta Ramthun. Frankfurt am Main: Suhrkamp, 1982.

Tagebücher 1920–1922: Autobiographische Aufzeichnungen. Edited by Herta Ramthun. Frankfurt am Main: Suhrkamp, 1975.

Werke: Große kommentierte Berliner und Frankfurter Ausgabe. 30 vols. Edited by Werner Hecht, Jan Knopf, Werner Mittenzwei, and Klaus-Detlef Müller. Frankfurt am Main: Suhrkamp, 1988–1991.

In English

Brecht on Theatre: The Development of an Aesthetic. Edited and translated by John Willett. New York: Hill & Wang, 1964.

Collected Plays. 9 vols. Edited by Ralph Manheim and John Willett. New York: Vintage Books, 1971– .

Diaries 1920–1922. Edited by Herta Ramthun. Translated by John Willett. New York: St. Martin's Press, 1979.

Threepenny Novel. Translated by Desmond Vesey and Christopher Isherwood. New York: Grove Press, 1956 (reissue of the 1937 trans.).

The Messingkauf Dialogues. Translated by John Willett. London: Methuen, 1965.

Poems 1913–1956. Edited by John Willett and Ralph Manheim with the cooperation of Erich Fried. New York: Methuen, 1976.

Seven Plays. Edited and introduced by Eric Bentley. New York: Grove Press, 1961.

Short Stories 1921–1946. Edited by John Willett and Ralph Manheim. London: Methuen, 1983.

Works of Bertolt Brecht. Grove Press Edition (of plays in paperbacks). General Editor: Eric Bentley.

Secondary Works

Biography
Cook, Bruce. *Brecht in Exile.* New York: Holt, Rinehart & Winston, 1983.

Esslin, Martin. *Brecht: A Choice of Evils. A Critical Study of the Man, His Work and His Opinions*. 4th rev. ed. London: Methuen, 1984.

Ewen, Frederic. *Bertolt Brecht: His Life, His Art and His Times*. New York: Citadel Press, 1967.

Hayman, Ronald. *Brecht: A Biography*. New York: Oxford University Press, 1983.

Lyon, James K. *Bertolt Brecht in America*. Princeton, N. J.: Princeton University Press, 1980.

Völker, Klaus. *Brecht: A Biography*. Translated by John Nowell. New York: Seabury/Continuum, 1978.

Critical Studies

Bentley, Eric. *The Brecht Commentaries 1943–1980*. New York: Grove Press, 1981.

Dickson, Keith. *Towards Utopia: A Study of Brecht*. Oxford: Clarendon Press, 1978.

Fuegi, John, *Bertolt Brecht: Chaos, According to Plan*. Cambridge: Cambridge University Press, 1987.

Hill, Claude. *Bertolt Brecht*. Boston: Twayne, 1975.

Parmalee, Patty. *Brecht's America*. Columbus: Ohio State University Press, 1981.

Pike, David. *Lukács and Brecht*. Chapel Hill: University of North Carolina Press, 1985.

Speirs, Ronald. *Brecht's Early Plays*. Atlantic Highlands, N. J.: Humanities Press, 1982.

Suvin, Darko. *To Brecht and Beyond: Soundings in Modern Dramaturgy*. Totowa, N. J.: Barnes & Noble, 1984.

Tatlow, Antony. *The Mask of Evil: Brecht's Response to the Poetry, Theatre, and Thought of China and Japan*. Berne: Peter Lang, 1977.

Whitaker, Peter. *Brecht's Poetry: A Critical Study*. Oxford: Clarendon Press, 1985.

White, Alfred D. *Bertolt Brecht's Great Plays*. New York: Barnes & Noble, 1978.

Willett, John. *Brecht in Context: Comparative Approaches*. London: Methuen, 1984.

Willett, John. *The Theatre of Bertolt Brecht: A Study from Eight Aspects*. 3rd, rev. ed. New York: New Directions, 1968.

Collections of Essays

Bartram, Graham, and Anthony Waine, eds. *Brecht in Perspective*. London: Longman, 1982.

Demetz, Peter, ed. *Brecht*. Englewood Cliffs, N. J.: Prentice-Hall, 1962.

Mews, Siegfried, and Herbert Knust, eds. *Essays on Brecht: Theater and Politics*. Chapel Hill: University of North Carolina Press, 1974; New York: AMS Press, 1979.

Munk, Erika, ed. *Brecht*. New York: Bantam, 1972.

INDEX